Mathematics Education Library

VOLUME 16

The titles published in this series are listed at the end of this volume.

MATHEMATICS FOR TOMORROW'S YOUNG CHILDREN

Edited by

HELEN MANSFIELD

Curriculum Research & Development Group,
University of Hawaii, U.S.A.

NEIL A. PATEMAN

Department of Curriculum & Instruction,
University of Hawaii, U.S.A.

and

NADINE BEDNARZ

CIRADE, Université du Québec à Montréal, Canada

KLUWER ACADEMIC PUBLISHERS

DORDRECHT / BOSTON / LONDON

Library of Congress Cataloging-in-Publication Data

```
Mathematics for tomorrow's young children : international perspectives
  on curriculum / edited by Helen Mansfield and Neil A. Pateman and
  Nadine Bednarz.
      p.   cm. -- (Mathematics education library ; v. 16)
  Papers from meetings of a working group at the 7th International
Congress on Mathematical Education, held in Québec, Canada, in 1992.
  Includes bibliographical references.
  ISBN 0-7923-3998-3 (hardcover : alk. paper)
  1. Mathematics--Study and teaching (Elementary)--Congresses.
I. Mansfield, Helen (Helen M.)  II. Pateman, Neil A.  III. Bednarz,
Nadine.  IV. International Congress on Mathematical Education (7th :
1992 : Québec, Québec)  V. Series.
QA135.5.M36924   1996
372.7--dc20                                          96-10933
ISBN 0-7923-3998-3
```

Published by Kluwer Academic Publishers,
P.O. Box 17, 3300 AA Dordrecht, The Netherlands.

Kluwer Academic Publishers incorporates
the publishing programmes of
D. Reidel, Martinus Nijhoff, Dr W. Junk and MTP Press.

Sold and distributed in the U.S.A. and Canada
by Kluwer Academic Publishers,
101 Philip Drive, Norwell, MA 02061, U.S.A.

In all other countries, sold and distributed
by Kluwer Academic Publishers Group,
P.O. Box 322, 3300 AH Dordrecht, The Netherlands.

Printed on acid-free paper

Printed in the Netherlands

TABLE OF CONTENTS

PART ONE

PART TWO

PART THREE

PART FIVE

H. M. MANSFIELD

YOUNG CHILDREN'S MATHEMATICAL LEARNING:
COMPLEXITIES AND SUBTLETIES

The papers in this book originated in the meetings of a Working Group at the seventh International Congress on Mathematical Education held in Québec, Canada, in 1992. The title of the Working Group was *Formation of elementary mathematical concepts at the primary level,* a title determined by the International Committee for the congress. We interpreted the title as calling for an examination and discussion of the factors that interact with children's development of mathematical concepts.

A broad view of curriculum was adopted, because teachers' decisions about the program of work they develop for their classes reflect how they determine which concepts are "appropriate" to which children and how it is possible to know whether concepts have been formed by their pupils. In this way, the topic opens up the problematic nature of content. Teachers' decisions about teaching strategies and their view of learning as implemented in the classroom also help to determine the mathematics curriculum implemented in their classrooms and set the context within which concepts are constructed by children. Thus papers were invited to address different aspects of the factors that contribute to young children's development of mathematical concepts and were expected to explore our themes in their impact on children.

1.THE THEORETICAL CONTEXT

Over the last few years, mathematics educators have been re-examining their views of the nature of mathematics learning and of mathematics itself. People working within such theoretical frameworks as neo-behaviorism, constructivism/socio-constructivism, Vygotskian, and cognitive science/information processing have different views of the nature of mathematical concepts, how they are formed by young children, and what factors affect the formation of mathematical concepts by young children.

Constructivist views of learning, while not new as discussed by Pateman (this volume), have achieved recent prominence in the wider mathematics education community, driven in part by the accumulation of research that has examined closely students' conceptions of mathematics, with many studies exploring students' ideas as they develop over extended periods of time, and many studies showing that students often develop ideas in mathematics that differ in significant ways from the ideas the teacher is trying to teach.

In tandem with the increased acceptance of constructivist views of learning, there has been a burgeoning of interest in identifying and documenting the complex interactions that have an impact on any classroom situation. The increasing complex-

1

H. Mansfield et al. (eds.), Mathematics for Tomorrow's Young Children, 1–8.
© 1996 *Kluwer Academic Publishers. Printed in the Netherlands.*

ity of research in mathematics education over the last twenty or so years is presented graphically by Koehler and Grouws (1992, pp. 115-126), but their level 4 research model can be extended by considering the wider social and systemic contexts within which classrooms operate.

It is instructive to consider the nature of educational research regarded as desirable, not only in mathematics education but in other fields as well. In earlier decades, quantitative research seemed most valuable and often the most valid, but its main thrusts were based on a view of education that took educational settings as given and not very different from one another. Changes were implemented with quantifiable outcomes serving as the measures of the success or otherwise of the experimental intervention. This view of educational research seemed to be posited on a view of the classroom as a location in which something was done to the setting or the pupils and measurable change occurred directly attributable to the intervention.

More recently, various qualitative forms of educational research have become fashionable, and of particular importance perhaps in mathematics education has been case study research. In this form of research, the emphasis is on the identification and exploration of interactions between all the factors that operate in individual educational settings each with its own classroom practitioner working within his or her individual framework with children of unique backgrounds and experiences, beliefs and abilities. The nuances with which such factors interact with the educational endeavour and each other may clearly be idiosyncratic, and so there is not immediate generalizability to other classrooms. It is also clear that the identification of factors to be examined in such research depends on the sensitivities and the philosophical lenses of the researcher or researcher/practitioner involved. It seems that only the accumulation of many such studies can lead to the recognition of common threads and implications for classroom practice.

Constructivism is of course a set of beliefs about how students learn; it is not a set of beliefs about how teachers should teach. Yet if educators hold constructivist views of learning, they will explore different classroom teaching strategies and different ways of organising the classroom, and make decisions about the curriculum that will enhance students' opportunities to construct meaningful and useful mathematical ideas. For this reason, a number of different aspects of constructivism have attracted close examination. In particular, the role of social interaction in students' construction of mathematical ideas has been particularly singled out as suggesting approaches to teaching that many classroom practitioners find appealing. Yet there remains much work to be done to identify how social interactions best work for individual pupils with all their varying experiences, attitudes and beliefs engaging in particular kinds of mathematics tasks. Classroom practitioners will want to explore ways to make social discourse in their classrooms inclusive of all pupils, supportive of exploration of ways of thinking deeply about mathematical situations. They will also want to question how the nature of what passes for mathematics and mathematics learning in the classroom is changed by the implementation of opportunities for social interaction in the construction of mathematical ideas.

Social constructivism is just one view of learning that places emphasis on the social aspects of learning. Other theoretical positions, such as activity theory, also emphasise the importance of social interactions. Along with social constructivism, Vygotsky's writings on children's learning have recently also undergone close scrutiny and researchers are attempting a synthesis of aspects of Vygotskian theory and social constructivism. This re-examination of Vygotsky's work is taking place in many other subject fields besides mathematics, such as language learning by young children. It is interesting to speculate why Vygotsky's writings have appealed to so many researchers in different cultures and decades later than his own times.

Given the recent increased emphasis on the social nature of learning and on the interactions between student, teacher and context factors, a finer grained analysis of the nature of different theories of learning now seems to be critical, and it was considered that different views of students' learning of mathematics needed to be acknowledged in the discussions of the Working Group.

Since so many perspectives are possible on the formation of concepts, speakers were sought who could provide an analysis of the latest views on the nature of mathematics concepts, how they are formed by children, and what factors affect the formation of mathematical concepts by young children. It is a perennial question raised about mathematics curriculum to ask what mathematics is important for children to learn and who should decide this. Curriculum decisions for young children are made within a broad social and political context. Secondary teachers and university teachers may have input into curriculum for young children. They may approach this task through a perspective of ensuring that children entering secondary schools have already achieved the skills that are deemed to be important for success at that level. Secondary schools in turn operate within systems that require the acquisition of particular skills and concepts deemed necessary by universities or employers. Top-down approaches to curriculum development can make at best coarse-grained decisions about the selection and sequencing of topics in the curriculum for young children. Since the final outcomes are required to be met in a particular time-frame, the penalties for individual children who do not reach those outcomes at the scheduled time may be severe. It is not possible in such a system for teachers working with young children to be comfortable in negotiating individual learning agendas for the young children in their classrooms.

Teachers of young children have traditionally been concerned with the individual learning of the children in their classrooms. A New Zealand publication in my archive collection describes a key principle of teaching number in the infant school (first two years of formal schooling) in the following terms:

As arithmetic is pre-eminently a subject in which a child should proceed at his natural pace full account should be taken of individual differences in native ability, attitude and temperament, and general experience of life. This calls for diagnosis of "readiness" for number work, frequent checks on progress made, efficient and flexible grouping of children, and remedial work.
(School Publications Branch, New Zealand Education Department, 1944; p. 7)

For teachers steeped in teaching cultures which value the learning of individual children and see cooperative group activities as important in each child's mathematical learning, the tenets of social constructivism or activity theory hold no fears and may be welcomed as validating traditional classroom practices that are taken for granted.

New questions about curriculum content have arisen in recent years as Pateman (this volume) stresses. For example, what impact do new technologies have on the curriculum? Who decides what technologies are to be provided? How is access to be made equitable? How have new technologies changed the nature of the mathematics to be included in the curriculum? Perhaps more importantly, what types of activities might children be involved in as they interact with new technologies?

An examination of the latest thinking on context both within classrooms and within the broader social setting seemed to be critical to the discussions of the Working Group. Within the social environments of the school setting, young children interact with other children and the teacher. The acts of assimilation of individual children depend on the kinds of reality presented by others and by the particular conceptual operations used by the individual child in assimilating those realities. Paper writers were asked to consider questions such as the effects of social interactions within school and out-of-school settings on the development of mathematics concepts in young children and how knowledge and reasoning take form and are differentiated in different social and cultural contexts.

The role of language is critical in the mathematical development of young children because it mediates social contexts of learning. Symbolism and language contribute not only to the communication of concepts but also to their elaboration. Important aspects are the role that natural language plays in the formation of elementary concepts; the place of symbolism; and how conceptual development can be articulated with symbolism developed by children. A fairly traditional view of the role of language would hold that a rich vocabulary of qualitative and quantitative terms in common use in the social experiences of the young child should be introduced through the medium of a wide range of activities, such as song, games, puzzles, handicrafts, the manipulation of concrete materials and so on. The child's grasp and use of the language of mathematics should precede his or her knowledge of more formal written symbols. Perhaps, though, the development of natural and more formal symbolic mathematical language is best achieved symbiotically, a question for researchers. Of importance is the role language plays in the interactions of young children with other children as they attempt to articulate their own mathematical realities and as they interpret the mathematical realities being articulated by other children and the teacher. How teachers can initiate, encourage, and use these interactions is of crucial importance.

All of these factors impinge on classroom practice and teacher decision-making in classrooms for young children. Teachers must be concerned not only with the content they are to teach but also have a repertoire of teaching strategies they can use to enhance the learning of individual children. Teachers of young children need to be sensitive to the evolving needs, beliefs, and cognitive repertoires of individuals within the large group setting of the classroom. Teachers with a strong set of beliefs about how children learn will structure lessons in ways that make strong demands on children to act in specific ways in the common discourse about mathematics that occurs in their classrooms.

2. THE THEMES

Four major themes were used to provide the framework for the program of the Working Group based on our own perspective of the topic. Each of these themes provided two sub-themes for small group discussions. The themes and sub-themes were as follows:

1.   What concepts are and how concepts are formed.

     1(1). What are the mechanisms that intervene in conceptual development, for example conceptions, implicit models, spontaneous reasoning, already developed by children?

     1(2). What are the mechanisms that can contribute to conceptual change?

2.   The influences of social and cultural environments on the formation of elementary concepts at the primary level.

     2(1). Within the social environments of the school setting, how do the interactions between children contribute to the learning of individual children?

     2(2). How do knowledge and reasoning take form and become differentiated in different cultural contexts?

3.   Language and the formation of elementary concepts by young children.

     3(1). What are the roles of natural language and of symbolism in the formation of elementary concepts; how can conceptual development be articulated with symbolism developed by children?

     3(2). What is the role played by language in the interactions of young children with other young children as they attempt to articulate their own mathematical realities and as they interpret the mathematical realities being articulated by other children and the teacher?

4.   The mathematics curriculum for young children: Deciding content and developing classroom strategies for optimal formation of mathematical concepts in young children.

     4(1). How are decisions made about what the content should be in a class room for young children and how do these decisions reflect the teacher's (or curriculum writer's) beliefs about how concepts are formed by young children?

4(2). How can classroom strategies be developed that may lead to the best possible formation of mathematics concepts by young children and how do these strategies reflect the teacher's beliefs about how concepts are formed by young children?

3. THE CONFERENCE

The Working Group had four sessions in which to meet. The first session was organised as a plenary session with all participants meeting together. Three speakers were invited to present papers, and these presentations formed the basis of chapters 2 to 4 in this volume. Acknowledging that there are multiple perspectives on the nature of concepts, how they are formed by young children, and what factors affect the formation of mathematical concepts by young children, these speakers were asked to reflect on these fundamental issues, thus setting the context for the discussions in the following three sessions.

In the second session, participants elected to join one of four theme groups, each focusing on one of the themes given above, namely concept formation, social and cultural factors, language and the curriculum. In this session, two people were invited to present papers addressing the theme and to lead a discussion of issues arising from their papers.

One key objective in the organisation of the program was to provide as much opportunity as possible for participation in discussion. Another objective was to ensure as far as possible that people from a variety of national backgrounds were able to make a contribution as a paper writer. In session 3 and the first half of session 4, participants chose to attend one of eight small discussion groups. Each discussion group had as its topic one of the sub-themes given above. In order to ensure the viability of each discussion group and to meet the objectives of participation and internationalism, several people for each sub-theme were invited to prepare discussion papers that were distributed in the second session. The authors of the discussion papers initiated and encouraged dialogue between the participants.

Finally, in the second half of session 4, the four larger theme groups re-convened to enable the discussion groups to report on the key ideas that emerged in their discussion and to identify issues and new directions that research might take.

Participants at the congress chose which theme and discussion groups they wished to attend. Many more chose to participate in the concept formation and curriculum groups than in the context and language groups. In fact, it was difficult to locate before the congress people who could address some of the substantive issues in context and language that it was anticipated would be important to the participants. There may be several possible reasons for this. Researchers have only comparatively recently begun to tease out the complex contextual factors operating inside classrooms and the impact of the wider social contexts within which classrooms function. Such research must build up a critical mass before the impact of context on the development of mathematical concepts by young children is generally recognised and addressed [included as a matter of course] in research. Since fundamental questions related to how children develop mathematical ideas have been explored so extensively over the last few years, many participants may have regarded the more theoretical topics of the first theme to be important. By contrast, participants who work extensively in classrooms may have regarded the fourth theme as more directly relevant to classroom practice. It may also be true that themes other these might have had more appeal to some participants. Nevertheless, all of the discussion groups attracted participants who were keen to discuss issues with others and who contributed to the lively debates that took place.

Many people contributed to the success of the Working Group. The three keynote speakers in the first session and the speakers in the theme groups of the second session provided stimulating analyses of their topics and set the theoretical foundations for the discussions. The discussion paper writers submitted their papers to us in advance of the congress and ensured that participants in their discussion groups received copies; they helped ensure the liveliness of the debate in the discussion groups. The chairpersons of the theme groups and discussion groups had the key roles of ensuring that the debate was focused and that all participants were able to contribute to the discussion in an equitable way. Since both English and French were official languages for the congress, one English-speaking person and one French-speaking person acted as reporters for each of the eight discussion groups. The role of the reporters was to keep a record of the discussion during sessions 3 and 4 and to collaborate in writing a report after the congress based on the relevant aspects of the papers presented in the first two sessions, on the invited discussion papers, and on the actual discussions of their discussion group. Above all, the participants who attended the sessions ensured the success of the Working Group by their keen interest in the topics they chose and their willingness to contribute to discussions and learn from others interested in the same topic but perhaps coming from different theoretical perspectives and from different national backgrounds.

4. USING THIS VOLUME

This volume is organised around the keynote papers and discussion papers of the Working Group. The three chapters in part 2 discuss, from the different theoretical points of view of their authors, what concepts are, how concepts are formed by young children, and what factors affect the formation of concepts. Parts 3 to 6 address the four themes that were used to structure the meetings of the Working Group. In each of these parts, there are two papers based on the presentations in the theme groups. There are also two papers addressing the related subthemes that were the focus of the discussion groups at the congress. Each of these discussion group papers was included because it provided an interesting discussion of aspects of the theme and in order to represent a range of international perspectives. The reports prepared after the congress by the reporters and the remaining discussion papers will be published elsewhere. The final section of the book identifies the key issues that arose in the Working Group and identifies future directions for research into the factors that help set the mathematics curriculum for young children.

It is envisaged that the theoretical papers will provide points of departure for people examining their own views of the nature of mathematics and of mathematics learning. They allow insight into how different theoretical points of view can address these fundamental questions. The other papers provide fascinating insights into the research and practical classroom concerns of people working in a variety of settings. They carry the message that mathematics educators in all settings have the same commitment to ensuring the best possible mathematics education for young children but they also show that there are many different ways of meeting that commitment.

REFERENCES

Koehler, M. S., & Grouws, D. A. (1992). Mathematics teaching practices and their effects. In D. A. Grouws (Ed.), *Handbook of research on mathematics teaching and learning* (pp. 115-126). New York, NY: Macmillan.

School Publications Branch, New Zealand Education Department (1944). *Number work in the infant room*. Wellington, NZ: Government Printer.

Helen Mansfield
University of Hawaii
United States of America

CONTRIBUTIONS TO PART TWO

The second section of the book contains the three principal chapters, first the chapter by Cobb et al, then the chapter by Renshaw (replacing Davydov) and finally the commentary chapter by Steffé. Originally the three writers were to be Cobb, Davydov, and Steffé who were invited to write emphasizing their personal views. Cobb and Davydov were to critique each other's perspective through their own lenses, while Steffé as commentator was to critique both of the others' perspectives and to further develop his own theoretical framework from his own well-known perspective. We thought this would provide maximum possibilities for lively debate of the theoretical issues and their relationship with mathematics teaching.

The first chapter was written with the understanding by Paul Cobb that Davydov would be attending the conference as one of the keynote speakers for our group. The chapter was written to bring to the forefront the major differences between Cobb's and Davydov's positions from Cobb's perspective with the anticipation that Davydov would similarly analyze Cobb's position and bring out differences from his side of the argument. When it became apparent rather late in the day that Davydov would not be attending, Peter Renshaw, a well-respected cognitive psychologist with a distinct Vygotskian bent, agreed to take on a similar role arguing from a Davydovian perspective. Les Steffé then had the advantage of having read both papers as he prepared his commentary on each. Davydov's non-attendance was unfortunate; clearly Cobb wrote with the intention drawing the lines strongly in anticipation of a personal debate. However we feel that Peter Renshaw did an admirable job under the circumstances, both in establishing the Davydovian position and in his personal presentation at the ICME 7 conference.

The Editors.

CONSTRUCTIVISM AND ACTIVITY THEORY: A CONSIDERATION OF THEIR SIMILARITIES AND DIFFERENCES AS THEY RELATE TO MATHEMATICS EDUCATION[1, 2]

The primary purpose of this chapter is to clarify the basic tenets of activity theory and constructivism, and to compare and contrast instructional approaches developed within these global theoretical perspectives. This issue is worthy of discussion in that research and development programs derived from these two perspectives are both vigorous. For example, the work of sociocultural theorists conducted within the activity theory tradition has become increasingly influential in the United States in recent years. One paradigmatic group of studies conducted by Lave (1988), Newman, Griffin, and Cole (1989), and Scribner (1984) has related arithmetical computation to more encompassing social activities such as shopping in a supermarket, packing crates in a dairy, and completing worksheets in school. Taken together, these analyses demonstrate powerfully the need to consider broader social and cultural processes when accounting for children's development of mathematical competence.

In the first part of the chapter, we focus on activity theory as it has evolved in the former Soviet Union, and differentiate between two general positions, those which draw primarily on Vygotsky's writings and those which take the work of Leont'ev and his colleagues in the Kharkov group as their primary point of reference. We then focus on the second of these two positions and take Davydov's (1982, 1988b, 1990) arithmetic program as an example of an instructional approach compatible with this perspective. In the course of the discussion, we trace the rationale of Davydov's program to the works of seminal Soviet theoreticians and thus further clarify underlying theoretical assumptions. This analysis is then used as a backdrop in the second section of the chapter when we explicate the assumptions of constructivism and compare them with basic tenets of activity theory. An instructional approach to arithmetic developed within the constructivist perspective is described to facilitate the delineation of both pragmatic and theoretical differences. In the third part of the chapter, we discuss possible rapprochements between activity

[1] The research reported in this chapter was supported by the National Science Foundation under grant No. MDR 885-0560 and by the Spencer Foundation. The opinions expressed do not necessarily reflect the views of these foundations.

[2] Several notions central to this chapter were elaborated in the course of discussions with Heinrich Bauersfeld, Gotz Krummheuer, and Jorg Voigt at the University of Bielefeld, Germany, and with Koeno Gravemeijer at the Freudenthal Institute, State University of Utrecht, Netherlands. The authors are also grateful to Bert van Oers, King Beach and Jack Smith for numerous helpful comments on a previous draft.

H. Mansfield et al. (eds.), Mathematics for Tomorrow's Young Children, 10–58.
© 1996 *Kluwer Academic Publishers. Printed in the Netherlands.*

theory and constructivism, and consider the relevance of each to issues of reform in mathematics education.

1. ACTIVITY THEORY

Activity theory encompasses a variety of positions that each emphasize the important role played by social and cultural processes in psychological development. The current diversity within the activity theory community is indicated by a bifurcation that occurred at the First International Conference on Sociocultural Research held in 1993 (Beach, personal communication). Some of the participants followed Vygotsky in emphasizing the importance of social interaction and semiotics, whereas others took positions more compatible with Leont'ev's work and tended to emphasize practical activity. This diversity of views is also apparent in the debate that is currently being conducted in the former Soviet Union between followers of two of the founders of activity theory, Rubinstein and Leont'ev (van Oers, personal communication). This debate centers on the precise role of the subjective in learning and development, and reflects the differing emphases that Rubinstein and Leont'ev gave to personality, the problem-solving activity of individual students, and subjectivity. In general, the different positions within the activity theory community can be related to different readings of Vygotsky. Below, we outline Vygotsky's account of development and consider the modifications that Leont'ev made when developing his own position. We then consider how Vygotsky's work was subsequently rehabilitated by Leont'ev's followers.

1.1 Vygotsky and Leont'ev

Vygotsky's cultural-historical theory of development stresses the importance of both social interaction and the use of cultural tools. The role that Vygotsky attributed to social interaction is captured in a frequently cited passage in which he argued that

any higher mental function was external and social before it was internal. It was once a social relationship between two people...We can formulate the general genetic law of cultural development in the following way. Any function in the child's cultural development appears twice or on two planes. . .It appears first between people as an intermental category, and then within the child as an intramental category (1960, pp. 197-198).

As this passage indicates, Vygotsky assumed that an asymmetrical relationship between the child and the social environment is the normative case. He was in fact concerned about situations in which a peer group is left to cooperate without adult supervision (van der Veer & Valsiner, 1991). In Vygotsky's view, it is the adult's responsibility to help the child perform actions that are beyond his or her individual competence. As the child interacts with the adult, he or she gradually takes over and internalizes these intermental or socially distributed actions. The significance that Vygotsky attributed to cultural tools can be clarified by taking account of the sociohistorical setting in which he developed his theory. As van der Veer and Valsiner (1991) observe, Marx (1890) had defined man as a toolmaking animal. Vygotsky drew on Engel's (1925) elaboration of this view to argue that human history is the history of artifacts which make possible the mastery of nature. Given this orientation, it was reasonable for Vygotsky to focus on the technology-like aspects of culture that support the control of the environment (e.g., language, counting systems, and writing), and to ignore a variety of other aspects (e.g., systems of law, moral thinking, art, and religion) (van der Veer & Valsiner, 1991). Further, Vygotsky restricted his focus to cultural procedures that can be treated both as sign systems and as tools.

A convincing demonstration of the similarity between tools and the uniquely human feature of speech would [therefore] be yet another marvelous proof of the validity of Marxist thought (van der Veer & Valsiner, 1991, p. 217).

Vygotsky fleshed out this analogy between physical tools and sign systems by contending that child development is to a considerable extent equivalent to mastering these cultural tools. Further, he took an explicitly developmental perspective and argued that the cultural tools become psychological tools for thinking. In his view,

people do not only possess mental tools, they are also possessed by them. Cultural means—speech in particular—are not external to our minds, but grow into them, thereby creating a "second nature." ... [M]astering cultural means will transform our minds: a child who has mastered the cultural tool of language will never be the same child again (van der Veer & Valsiner, 1991, p. 225).

In accounting for this process of qualitative change in thought, Vygotsky combined an emphasis on the socially-organized environment with a focus on the active role of the developing child in the domain of semiotic activity.

Kozulin (1986, 1990), and van der Veer and Valsiner (1991) both argue that there is a significant discontinuity between Vygotsky's work and Leont'ev's psychological theory in that Leont'ev downplayed social and semiotic mediation in favor of physical activity or labor. Further, Kozulin, and van der Veer and Valsiner account for this discontinuity by focusing on the sociopolitical setting within which Vygotsky and Leont'ev worked. Thus, they observe that from 1931

the Party culture, with its fear of dissenting opinions and its demand for a strictly uniform world-view, was being imposed on scientific debates. More and more frequently, researchers were forced to demonstrate their loyalty to the latest ideological point of view (van der Veer & Valsiner, 1991, p. 375).

In this intellectual climate, Vygotsky had to cope with a series of systematically organized attacks that commenced in 1932 and continued until his death in 1934. For example, one of his critics argued that

Everywhere where it would have been necessary from our point of view to speak about the class, [and] production environment of the child, about the influence of the school, the Pioneer vanguard, and the Komosmol movement as bearers of the influence of the Party and proletariat on the children...Vygotsky...simply speaks about the influence of the collective, without deciphering about which collective he is speaking and what he means by "collective" (Razmyslov, 1934, p. 81; as quoted in van der Veer & Valsiner, 1991).

Attacks also focused on the pivotal role that he attributed to cultural tools because this deviated from the official ideology which dictated that material production or labor should take precedence over semiotic mediation. Vygotsky, for his part, consistently refused to give labor or physical activity a more prominent role in his analysis of psychological development.

It was against this background that Leont'ev developed

a theory of psychological activity based on the paradigm of material production as it is interpreted in traditional Marxism. In Leont'ev's psychological theory, human motives and objects of activity are determined by the division of labor of society, while more concrete actions are related to practical goals... Leont'ev and his followers also seem to have been determined to show that human interpersonal relations and communication are derivatives of the activity of material production (Kozulin, 1990, p. 121).

Accounts of psychological development formulated from this perspective therefore emphasize the child's activity as it relates to objective reality rather than his or her interpersonal and semiotic interactions. Kozulin and van der Veer and Valsiner both note that in advancing this thesis, Leont'ev aligned himself with the official ideology.

Zinchenko, one of Leont'ev's collaborators, succinctly summarized the fundamental difference between Vygotsky's and Leont'ev's positions when he claimed that

Vygotsky's fundamental error is contained in this thesis [of semiotic mediation], in which he misconstrued the Marxist conception of the historical and social determination of the human mind...The conditioning of the human mind by social and historical factors was reduced to the influence of human culture on the individual (Zinchenko, 1983, pp. 66-67; as quoted in Kozulin, 1990).

This same difference appears to divide the activity theory community today. Our focus throughout this chapter will be on the branch of activity theory developed by Leont'ev and his followers. Unless otherwise noted, we will refer exclusively to work conducted in this tradition when we speak of activity theory.

1.2 The rehabilitation of Vygotsky

Vygotsky's writings were banned in the Soviet Union shortly after his death in 1934, and Leont'ev became their de facto official interpreter when they became available after a lapse of 20 years. In line with the prevailing ideology, it was essential to argue that Vygotsky had in fact assumed that labor activity was the primary determinant of psychological development. Davydov and Radzikhovskii's (1985) analysis illustrates the main points of such an interpretation.

Davydov and Radzikhovskii focus on Vygotsky's claim that signs come to fulfill the role of psychological tools. They note that,

according to Vygotsky, all the "tools" that are developed artificially by humanity are the elements of culture. This was not a simple assertion, but a concrete proposal for the scientific analysis of the sociohistorical determination of mind. Initially, "psychological tools" were directed "externally," towards a partner. Subsequently they turn in "on themselves," that is, they become the means of controlling one's own mental processes. Furthermore, they become internal (i.e., they "go underground") (Davydov & Radzikhovskii, 1985, p. 54).

Davydov and Radzikhovskii then claim that the relationship that Vygotsky proposed between physical and cultural tools is not merely an analogy. Thus, they contend that

the introduction into psychology of psychological tools as *nothing more than an analogy with the process of labor* can represent only a fortuitous step that is completely incompatible with Vygotsky's fundamental methodological search for an explanatory principle in his theory (p. 56; italics in original).

Instead,

in the analysis of the determination of the mind through practical activity, Vygotsky relied on a Marxist idea. He singled out the presence of tool mediation as the structurally and genetically central feature of labor activity. He proposed the possibility of an analog to this in the structure and genesis of mental functions (p. 56).

Consequently, "the very idea of *sign meaning,* as an important concept in psychological theory, *does not contradict* the idea of activity as a general explanatory principle" (p. 57; italics in original). This is because

if one accepts as a basis of psychological theory the concept of historically evolving object-practical activity (carried out by humankind), and assumes that this activity determines the genesis, structure, and contents of the human mind, then communicative sign systems that emerge as a product of this activity can reasonably be considered as a specific form of this type of determination (p. 57).

Although Davydov and Radzikhovskii legitimize analyses of psychological development in which sign systems "function as the vehicle of determination that mediates mental functions" (p. 57), they say little about social interaction. This issue is, however, addressed by Lektorsky (1984), one of the best-informed theoreticians on activity theory in the former Soviet Union (Bauersfeld, personal communication). Like Davydov and Radzikhovskii, Lektorsky necessarily had to indicate his allegiance to the official ideology:

Marxist analysis of the problem of the cognitive relation starts with a recognition of the basic fact that cognition is reflection of the objective reality existing independently of consciousness, that the cognizing and cognizant subject himself is a natural being included in the objective reality, and that cognition ... presupposes the action of external objects on man's sense organs. These propositions are shared by all materialist conceptions, and Marxist-Leninist philosophy as the highest form of materialism includes them in its theory (Lektorsky, 1984, p. 116).

In this scheme, it is practical activity or labor that mediates between the individual and objective reality. Lektorsky first hints at the social aspect of cognition when he suggests that thought is based on definite standards and objective norms that are formed in practical activity with material objects. He then argues that these cognitive norms cannot be accounted for unless practical activity is conceived of as a joint or collective activity that involves the use of cultural tools. This, in turn, enables him to argue that there is a continuity between Vygotsky's work and that of Leont'ev and his followers:

The outstanding Soviet psychologist L. S. Vygotsky, who relied on the fundamental propositions of Marxist philosophy, expressed an idea that later became the basis of numerous theoretical and practical developments and was, in particular, realized in the studies of A. N. Leontyev, A. R Luriya, P. Ya. Galperin, A. V. Zaporozhets, V. V. Davydov, V. P. Zinchenko, and others: the idea that internal psychical processes are a result of "interiorization," that is, "growing in" or transposition onto the inner plane of those actions of the subject which are originally performed externally and directed at external objects (Lektorsky, 1984, pp. 144-145).

In this interpretation, the intermental actions to which Vygotsky attributed such importance are equated with practical activity or labor. Internalization from the interpsychological to intrapsychological plane then becomes a key step in the process by which practical activity determines psychological development.

It is readily apparent that the interpretations of Vygotsky's theory developed in the former Soviet Union after his death downplay the active role of the child. The emphasis is instead on teaching the child to use cultural tools appropriately. Thus, Lektorsky argued that the child should be

included in the living communicative connection with other persons existing at present, with adults teaching him [or her] the human modes of using man-made objects and thereby developing his [or her] cultural attitudes and norms, including the standards of cognitive activity (p. 151).

It is in this way that

psychical processes and functions are modeled or created in the process of joint-but-separate activity of child and adults, an activity in which the social experience of using man-made objects is transmitted to the child (p. 151).

In the next section, we outline Davydov's arithmetic program to illustrate the possible implications of this emphasis on practical activity involving cultural tools for mathematics education.

1.3 Davydov's arithmetic program

Davydov was a student of Elkonin, himself a student of Vygotsky who attempted to defend the latter's views shortly after his death. For the past three decades, Davydov has been the most prominent Russian psychologist to address mathematics education issues in a systematic way. The ideological constraints under which he had to work for most of his career have been such that it is sometimes difficult to discern his own views from his writings. This is particularly the case in those instances where he found it necessary to demonstrate that his instructional approach is consistent with the basic tenets of Marxist-Leninist materialist philosophy. Significantly, even these acknowledgments of the official ideology were not sufficient, and he came under fire from critics in the early 1980s, eventually losing his position as the director of the Moscow Institute of Psychology. It is only with glasnost that he has returned to favor and has been appointed vice-president of the Academy of Pedagogical Sciences.

Almost all of Davydov's texts available in English were produced in the pre-glasnost era and do not reflect the modifications he has made to his publicly expressed views in the last few years. These texts are, however, still highly relevant given the influence that Soviet activity theory currently enjoys in the West. An examination of the public statements of the main proponent of this theory for mathematics education is therefore of interest in its own right. We again stress that the analysis presented in the following pages focuses on Davydov as a representative of the Soviet activity theory community and makes no claims about his own personal views.

In presenting his program, Davydov (1982) argues that although traditional instruction in arithmetic is very proficient at teaching computational skills in a mechanical manner, it does not lead to an intrinsic understanding of these skills. In his view, students will not develop this crucial understanding unless they come to appreciate how numbers and arithmetical operations arose. This claim appears to be based on the assumption that there is a certain logic to any history of the development of a mathematical concept and that students will not develop a full understanding of the concept unless they participate in classroom activities that acquaint them with the functional aspects of this logic (Beach, personal communication). It is also important to understand that in talking of number, Davydov does not restrict himself to the natural numbers, but also includes the integers, rationals, and reals. He clarifies the origin of numbers and numerical operations in this broad sense by drawing on the mathematical analyses of Lebeque, Kolmogorov, and Bourbaki and emphasizes that numbers can be treated as quantities represented by the formula $Q = a.L$, where L is a unit of measurement and a a positive real number (Davydov, 1982, p. 229). Thus, it would seem that when Davydov speaks of the origin of number concepts, he is referring to their development in a formal mathematical exposition. This leads him to conclude that an understanding of the general properties of quantity is a prerequisite for the development of number concepts. For example, he contends that

acquainting small children with the properties of quantity fulfills exactly the function of introducing them to the process of how the concept of number came about. Only when there is such an introduction can children begin to understand the concept of number (Davydov, 1982, p. 230).

Davydov builds on this recommendation by basing his arithmetic program on the fundamental practical action of comparing. In the first phase of the program, students are taught to identify the equality or inequality of, say, the length of physical objects, and to symbolize these relationships by writing formulas such as $A = B$ and $A > B$. The specific instructional activities are designed to move children away from direct observation and to encourage them to study the general properties of equalities and inequalities. In the second phase of the program, which occurs during the second half of their first year in elementary school students are taught the addition and subtraction of inequalities. Here, they compare properties of objects by considering their differences and express these comparisons by writing equations of the form $A - B = C$. Davydov clarifies this phase of the program by giving "a description of actions by which a child may isolate and master properties of quantity" (1982, p. 230). The first of these actions is that of identifying increments and decrements when the teacher manipulates an attribute of some object (e.g., the amount of water in a flask). The next action is that of describing the change, and here "the teacher helps the children write down the equation $A + K = C$ and explains the meaning of the symbol = and the letter K" (1982, p. 222). Both in this instance and elsewhere, literal symbols are introduced near the beginning of an instructional sequence because, Davydov argues, this permits children to study mathematical relationships in their "pure guise" (1988b, p. 68;1990, p. 371). The third action in the sequence is that of using visual aids such as paper strips to show transformations that correspond to pairs of expressions such as $B = D$ and $B < D$. As the sequence of lessons continues, "it becomes less and less necessary for the children to use direct aids. Tasks can now be carried out primarily on the basis of verbalizing possible relationships" (1982, p. 222). It is then possible to teach children that "x"

stands for the unknown quantity that can be used to transform an inequality into an equality. If $A < B$ then $A = B - x$ and $A + x = B$. Children, as a rule, quickly understand the meaning of this symbol (1982, p. 233).

On this basis, children soon learn to solve equations involving the addition and subtraction of quantities by using visual aids. In addition, they are taught to symbolize their solutions as sequences of literal expressions such as the following:

$A < B$	(the initial condition)
$A + x = B$	(the planned transformation)
$x = B - A$	(determining the difference)
$A + (B - A) = B$	(the actual difference) (1982, p. 233).

Next, the students' use of visual aids is gradually reduced and graphical representations such as line segments are introduced. According to Davydov, this ensures that the acts of transforming literal expressions will take on particular significance for children. As a consequence,

children begin to determine x without the help of any concrete objects or their graphic analogs, using instead a theoretical examination of the relationships of the parts of an inequality (1982, p. 234).

This ability to solve equations symbolically forms the basis for the final instructional activities in the sequence on the addition and subtraction of quantities. Here, tasks of the following type are posed:

$A = B$	$A > C$	$E < B$
$\underline{K > M}$	$\underline{N = D}$	$\underline{M < G}$
$A - K \_\_\_ B - M$	$A \pm N \_\_\_ C + D$	$E + M \_\_\_ B + G$

It is at this point that children also solve tasks that involve the substitution of two, three, or more addends for the value of a quantity:

In a series of special exercises, children "expand" or "contract" literal expressions on the basis of given conditions (for example, they rewrite the inequality $A > B$, given the fact that $A = K + M + N$). All of this provides children with a good preparation for the commutative and associative, properties of addition (1982, p. 235).

As Davydov makes clear, the entire instructional sequence aims at "the shaping in them [children] of the abstract concept of mathematical quantity" (1988b, p. 68). This sequence and the associated actions that children are taught to perform is a prerequisite for arithmetical computation in that it focuses on what he calls the structural relations that regulate numerical calculation.

Davydov takes this sequence on the addition and subtraction of quantities to be exemplary and uses it to discuss the essential characteristics of an elementary mathematics course. In doing so, he argues that the child should initially be introduced

into the world of concrete objects, which serve as the source of the appropriate concepts. . . While solving these problems children learn to isolate the specific relationships of objects being transformed into a quantity. These actions are the starting points for the child's understanding of the meaning of the operations of addition and subtraction and for the mastery of their basic properties (1982, p. 237).

However, this exploration of relationships between physical objects should not be unduly extensive because "one must make extensive use, even at the elementary school level, of [mathematical] generalizations shaped on the basis of a minimum number of appropriately organized observations" (1988b, p. 39). This can be achieved by ensuring that the actions children perform on physical objects are those that "permit an object or situation to be transformed in such a way that a person can immediately single out in them the relationship that was a *universal* character" (1990, p. 346; italics in original). Further, it is important that intermediate methods for representing the results of concrete actions be introduced once children learn to isolate these relationships.

Our successful work in the experimental program is due in large measure to the fact that we were able to find and introduce such intermediate means, for example graphic representations of objects and abstract drawings used in isolating and depicting the relationships of the compared objects (1982, p. 237).

Gradually, the use of these intermediate means or models is reduced and the emphasis given to symbolic models such as symbolic formulas is increased.

These instructional tenets are further illustrated by the next phase of his arithmetic program. Here, the extensive work with the addition and subtraction of quantities provides a basis for developing the theoretical concept of number.

In our course, the teacher, relying on the knowledge previously acquired by the children, introduces number as a particular case of the representation of a *general relationship* of quantities... A number is obtained by the general formula $F(A,N) = C$ where N is any number, A any object represented as a quantity, and C is any [unit of] measure (1990, pp. 361-2; italics in original).

To this end, children are taught to compare objects by considering ratios and then to express their comparisons by writing equations of the form $F(A,N) = C$. In the initial problems, the two objects cannot be compared directly and the children are encouraged to use a mediator object as a measure and thus establish the relationship between the quantities involved. For example, the child might use a short stick C to measure two sticks A and B. The discussion focuses on the multiplicative relations $F(A,C)$ and $F(B,C)$ and eventually the children are taught to express the results of the comparison as, say, $F(A,C) = 4$. Kozulin (1990) notes that "this is a 'genetic' definition because it provides a method for generating numbers, and it is universal because any whole number can be generated in this way" (p. 260).

In the final phase of the sequence, the children explore what happens when the value of the measure C is changed while A remains the same (e.g., F(A,C) = K and B < C, then F(A,B) > K). This leads to

the understanding of two important characteristics of numbers. First, an object as a quantity in itself is not determined numerically. It gains a numerical determinacy when a person chooses another quantity as a unit of measurement. Second, one and the same object can be measured with different units and thus be designated with various numbers. If a child in particular [practical] problems can freely change the units of measurement of some quantity, designating with various numbers, then...the child has mastered the concept [of number] proper (1982, pp. 237-8).

To further clarify his argument, Davydov lists four sample practical tasks including the following:

Require a child to determine how many large glasses of water are contained in a series of three large glasses and four small glasses if a small glass is equal to one-half of a large one. Here, the child must count two small glasses as one large one and obtain the result five (1982, p. 226).

Davydov's central contention is that, in this and other practical tasks, children will only realize that the unit of measure is arbitrary and can be exchanged for another if they have a clear understanding of the abstract properties of quantity. Only then can children quantify objects numerically in a variety of different ways in particular practical situations.

This contention illustrates Davydov's more general argument that the development of formal, abstract understanding should precede the use of that understanding in pragmatic problem solving: Children "have to be trained to assimilate a general mode of task resolution" (1988b, p. 27). In this approach, it is the universal relationships of the subject matter under study that serve as the basis for general solution processes.

The effectual nature of this mode [or general solution process] is verified during the resolution of discrete particular [practical] tasks, when school children approach those tasks as variants of the initial learning task and immediately—"on the spot," as it were—identify the general relationships in each of them.(1988b, p. 32).

In the case of arithmetic, this means that elementary equations are introduced in first grade, and then students solve word problems for the following four years by setting up equations (1990, p. 355).

In his empirical work, Davydov has attempted to show that his instructional approach makes it possible for students to develop particular conceptions at a far earlier age than would be predicted by traditional developmental theories, including that of Piaget. Further, he has attempted to demonstrate that students' developmental potentials are not absolute, but are instead profoundly influenced by the general type of instruction they receive (van Oers, personal communication). These investigations were designed to both clarify and add credence to Vygotsky's claim that education in school precipitates rather than follows psychological development. Davydov emphasizes this presumed relationship between school instruction and development by calling his general instructional approach developmental education.

1.4 Scientific and empirical concepts

Davydov notes that his instructional proposals involve an "ascent from the abstract to the concrete" (1988b, p. 20). He contrasts this approach with the inductiveness of what he calls traditional empirical programs and argues that "the ability to solve practical problems does not necessarily imply children's knowledge or understanding of deeper [mathematical] principles" (1982, p. 225). In making this comparison between instructional approaches, Davydov draws on the distinction that Vygotsky made between spontaneous, everyday concepts and scientific concepts. Vygotsky defined everyday concepts as those acquired without explicit instruction on the basis of unsystematic individual experience. In contrast, he defined scientific concepts as those that are explicitly introduced by the teacher in school. Davydov accepted the distinction between the two types of concepts, but argued that the definitions should be revised because spontaneous concepts can display a certain degree of systematicity, and because much of what is typically taught in elementary school does not go beyond what he terms non-scientific, empirical generalizations. He therefore proposed that

the central discriminating factor between "scientific" and spontaneous concepts should be their content, which is theoretical for the first group, and empirical for the second. Such a dichotomy, however, cannot be formulated within a psychological theory, and requires an appropriate epistemological study, which, according to Davydov, was neglected by Vygotsky as well as other specialists in learning processes (Kozulin, 1990, p. 256).

This revised view of scientific and empirical concepts finds expression in Davydov's arithmetic program in his contrast between the theoretical concept of number and the practical uses of numbers. Further, it is on the basis of this distinction between the theoretical and the practical that he rejects so-called empiricist approaches, arguing that they obscure the difference between the two types of concepts. In his view, the overriding task of education is to develop in students a scientific world view, and this requires that they be taught theoretical concepts from the very beginning of classroom instruction. Davydov also draws on the distinction between scientific and everyday concepts when he discusses the process of development. For example, he and Markova (1983) define one of Vygotsky's central constructs, that of the zone of proximal development, as the distance between the cultural knowledge and scientific concepts made accessible through explicit instruction and the everyday experience of individuals (cf. Lave & Wenger, 1991, p. 48). To account for the development of the two types of concepts, he proposes that everyday concepts are acquired via an inductive process of empirical generalization which involves identifying similar features of concrete objects and observable phenomena. In contrast, theoretical generalization reproduces the essence of an object on the mental plane as an ideal form that can be used in thought experiments. The epistemological study to which Davydov referred involves clarifying the nature of these ideal mental forms.

1.5 Ideal forms and mathematical structure

Davydov's emphasis on the ascent from the abstract to the concrete appears to be in direct conflict with the emphasis that American interpreters of Soviet activity theory typically give to the situated, context-specific nature of cognition. It should therefore be noted that Davydov takes considerable care to relate his instructional approach to the basic tenets of Soviet activity theory. For example, he observes that his approach to quantity exemplifies Leont'ev's general account of conceptual development. Thus, his program is designed to support the

passage from [concrete or material] actions detailed outside to actions on a verbal level and finally gradual internalization of the latter, as a result of which they take on the character of curtailed mental operations, intellectual acts (Leont'ev 1965, p. 283; quoted by Davydov, 1990, p. 346).

More specifically,

in doing certain object-related operations [i.e., physical actions] as indicated by the instructor, the pupils detect and establish essential features of objects...These operations are initially performed in a material or materialized form, and then are converted *step by step* into mental operations that are done with symbolic substitutes for the material objects. (Davydov, 1990, p. 349; italics in original).

Thus, in line with Leont'ev's theory, ideal mental activity is derived from physical activity or labor. In the case of the arithmetic program, the initial material actions for quantity are those of comparing various attributes of physical objects. It can also be noted that the introduction of symbols as substitutes for physical objects is consistent with the claim that, historically, sign systems emerged as a product of labor activity. In the arithmetic program, the mental operations done with symbols are those of writing formulas that involve literal symbols. The critical role that students' use of these symbols plays in the internalization process illustrates the claim that signs and communicative systems serve as vehicles of determination in psychological development. We can both clarify the developmental role that Davydov attributes to symbols and delineate some of the basic epistemological assumptions of Soviet activity theory by considering the central construct of the ideal object.

The notion of the ideal object is generally attributed to Ilyenkov. Davydov (1988a), who collaborated with Ilyenkov, reports that Ilyenkov considered himself to be one of Vygotsky's followers. Further, he suggests that some of the theoretical difficulties that Vygotsky encountered become understandable when it is noted that Soviet philosophers, especially Ilyenkov, did not reconstruct dialectical materialism until the 1960s (Davydov & Radzikhovskii, 1985). By way of corroboration, Bakhurst (1988) says that Ilyenkov "was adopted by the psychologists of the Vygotsky school as their philosophical mentor" (p. 31). The primary problem that Ilyenkov sought to resolve was that of explaining how an object with only physical properties can be the kind of thing that interacts with a mind. In addressing this issue, he challenged the standard Cartesian view that we come to know a pre-given external world by constructing internal representations that correspond to it. Thus, he observed that as soon as one argues that the mind is only indirectly aware of external objects in virtue of its direct awareness of internal objects (ideas), one cannot avoid a catastrophic form of skepticism (Bakhurst, 1988, p. 36).

Ilyenkov attempted to avoid this calamity by reasoning that we can only experience or think about an object if the object has meaning. The crucial theoretical move he made was to argue that material objects can objectively possess the ideal properties of meaning and value that make them directly accessible to the human mind. These properties, which are not material in nature, are acquired by objects when they are incorporated in social practices.

"Ideality" is rather like a stamp impressed on the substance of nature by human social life activity; it is the form of the functioning of a physical thing in the process of social human life activity. Therefore, all things which are included in the social process acquire a new "form of existence" which is in no way part of their physical nature (from which it differs completely); an ideal form (Ilyenkov, 1977, p. 86; quoted by Bakhurst, 1988, p. 37).

To illustrate this claim, Bakhurst (1988) discusses the example of a pen. He notes that any purely physical description of it as a lump of material stuff fails to capture its existence as an artifact that is endowed with social significance and meaning.

It is this significance which constitutes the object's "ideal form." Where does it get this significance? In the case of a pen the answer seems clear: the fact that is has been created for specific purposes and ends and that, having been so created, it is put to a certain use... One might say, with Ilyenkov, that social forms of activity have become objectified in the form of a thing (Bakhurst, 1988, p. 37).

The distinction Bakhurst draws is that between an object as a piece of physical matter and as a cultural artifact or tool. The key point of Ilyenkov's argument is that the meanings that acculturated members of a community give to an object when they use it in a social practice transform it into a cultural tool endowed with ideal properties. These properties are objective in the sense that they become accessible to the minds of children when they participate in those same social practices. As a consequence, objects-in-practice, as cultural tools, can serve as carriers of meaning (cf. Bauersfeld, 1990). Thus far, our discussion of Ilyenkov's epistemology has considered only physical objects. It is therefore important to note that when he speaks of objects, he also intends to include signs such as formal mathematical symbols. This aspect of Ilyenkov's philosophy is apparent in Lektorsky's (1984) contention that man-made mediator objects carry the reified sociohistorical experiences of practical and cognitive activity. Lektorsky is careful to clarify that these cognitive norms and standards are carried by symbols-in-practice, not by symbols per se. Thus, he says that in learning to use a mediator object, a child singles out the features of external objects that are essential for activity that involves the use of the mediator. This notion that mediators-in-practice are carriers of meaning is also stressed by Minick (1989a) in his recent discussion of Soviet activity theory. As he puts it, psychological development involves "mastering psychological characteristics of the human species that are consolidated in the system of objects and activities that constitute social and cultural systems" (p. 90). Similarly, Davydov (1990) argued that, in the course of his or her upbringing and education, every individual *appropriates to himself*, converts into forms of *his our* activity, the means and methods of thought that have been created by society at that historical epoch. The more completely and profoundly a person has appropriated the universal categories of thought, the more complete and logical is his mental activity...[V]arious means of idealization, such as assorted sign models, are created and exist in this activity. The ways of mastering these means *individually* and consequently the process of the emergence and formation of idealization as capacities of the individual are the major objects of *psychological* investigations (p. 311; italics in original).

This view implies that children in Davydov's arithmetic program are studying the properties of equality and inequality relationships in their "pure guise" when they manipulate literal symbols appropriately. Thus, the process of mastering these symbols is synonymous with that of isolating ideal mathematical forms. Davydov's decision to stress the use of literal symbols rather than, say, the manipulation of numerals also follows from Ilyenkov's analysis. For Ilyenkov, ideal properties are objective. Consequently, "mathematical, physical, and other relations of things really exist" (Davydov, 1990, p. 315). These objective mathematical relations are impressed on things by the routine actions of mathematicians and therefore find their reflection in what Davydov terms the collective "social consciousness" of the mathematics community (1988b, p. 49). By this, he means the specialized practices that define mathematics as discipline. A key practice that differentiates mathematics from other fields of study is that of setting up and solving equations within a formal system. Consequently, the ideal mathematical forms that school children are to isolate correspond to the structural relations of these abstract systems. In Davydov's words,

if school wishes to introduce students to scientific knowledge, it not only should not conceal the generalized and abstract character of it—it is obliged to specify these abstractions and generalizations at a wholly contemporary level (1990, p. 341).

It is important to note that in focusing on the solving of equations within a formal system, Davydov tends to characterize mathematical thought in terms of its products rather than in terms of its dynamics (van Oers, personal communication).

Thus, for him, theoretical "concepts are those universal semiotic models that serve as hypothesized formulas of collective experience" (Kozulin, 1990, p. 256). The instructional approach that he develops on the basis of Ilyenkov's analysis therefore

seems to be rather similar to the proposals of the "structure of knowledge" advocates of the sixties. In these initiatives, the assumption was made that in a discipline there are fundamental, essential, universal properties of major theoretical significance that could be used to structure and reproduce any of the particular phenomena (Confrey, 1991, p. 31).

Davydov acknowledges this parallel and refers favorably to Bruner's (1962) views concerning the primacy of the basic structures of the subject matter. Thus, he says that Bruner has "a proper grasp of the fact that the transition from the general to the particular is the modem method of presenting a science" (1990, p. 331). This method is one in which the content of "courses is subordinated to the *logic of the subject* (with the laws of mastery assured taken into account)" (1990, p. 350; italics in original).

1.6 Exposition and Investigation

Davydov offers a further perspective on his "structure of knowledge" approach by observing that it involves exposition rather than investigation. In making this distinction, he describes investigation as a process that moves from "sensory-concrete diversity" to a discovery of universal or ideal mathematical forms. In contrast, exposition begins with the ideal mathematical form and logically derives particular concrete manifestations of it. Number, for example, is a particular manifestation of the abstract form of quantity. He argues that instruction need not be based on investigation because children are in a very different position to the original discoverers of ideal forms:

By virtue of scientific work that has already been done before, they [children] have before this a complete and accomplished exposition of the "real movement" of the material [from the ideal to the concrete]. And they can begin to learn the knowledge on the basis of such an exposition (Davydov, 1990, p. 345).

As a consequence,

the thinking that a school child does in the process of learning activity shares a certain amount of common ground with the thinking of scientists expounding the results of their research by means of substantive abstractions, generalizations, and theoretical concepts, which come into play in the process of ascent from abstract to concrete (1988b, pp. 20-21).

Davydov's views can be further clarified by considering Wilensky's (1991) elaboration of the view that "the actual process of knowledge development moves from the abstract to the concrete" (p. 201). Wilensky suggests that,

metaphorically, the abstract object is high above, as opposed to concrete objects, which are down and hence reachable, "graspable."...Objects of thought which are given solely by definition, and operations given only by simple rules, are abstract in this sense. Like the word learned only by dictionary definition, it is accessible through the narrowest of channels and tenuously apprehended (p. 199).

In contrast,

the more connections we make between an object and other objects, the more concrete it becomes for us. The richer the set of representations of the object, the more ways we have of interacting with it, the more concrete it is for us. Concreteness, then, is that property which measures the degree of our relatedness to the object, (the richness of our representations, interactions, connections with the object), how close we are to it (p. 198).

In many respects, this contrast between the abstract and the concrete corresponds to that which Skemp (1976) makes between instrumental and relational understandings.

It also echoes the distinction that Vygotsky made between scientific and everyday concepts. In Vygotsky's view,

"scientific" concepts run the risk of remaining empty verbal formulas applicable to a rather narrow range of topics learned in school. School practice is full of situations in which a child becomes helpless when required to apply the concepts learned in the classroom to phenomena outside the school curriculum. Everyday concepts, in contrast, are rich in experiential connotations, but they lack a system and are bound by concrete life contexts (Kozulin, 1990, p. 169).

Wilensky also refers to classroom instruction to illustrate the movement from the abstract to the concrete.

In the school setting, rather than moving from the concrete to the formal, we often begin our understanding of new concepts (just as we often do with new people) by having a formal introduction. Gradually, as the relationship develops, it becomes more intimate and concrete (Wilensky, 1991, p. 201).

For example,

most of us who have participated in mathematics classes have had the experience of myriad definitions and theorems swirling about you, in the air, out of reach, any attempt to grab hold of one sends the others speeding away... If you were one of the fortunate ones, at some point in the class something clicked and it all came together... I argue here that this sudden click of understanding, this dawn of early light, is nothing other than our old friend the concretizing process (p. 201).

Davydov's expositional approach appears to be consistent with this discussion of learning from instruction that involves a formal introduction. The originality of his approach stems from his attempt to ensure that something clicks for all students. Thus it is clear that although he advocates exposition, he is also deeply concerned with the development of meaning. In this regard, it can be noted that the "structure of knowledge" approach of the 60s was motivated by a similar concern.

Davydov also indicates his desire to foster meaning by stressing that although ideal mathematical forms should be introduced as early as possible, this should not be done until they are accessible to students. Here, he draws on Leont'ev's and Galperin's learning theory to argue that visual aids and models can play a crucial role in making these ideal forms accessible. In his view, these manipulatives and models will not be effective unless they reflect ideal mathematical connections and relationships in a sensory-visual form.

The label "learning model" cannot be attached to any random representation but only to a representation that specifically registers the universal [ideal] relationship in an integral object and allows it to be analyzed further (1988b, p. 31).

Thus, there appears to be a further parallel with the "structure of knowledge" approach in that manipulatives and models are designed to embody abstract mathematical relationships. Both this parallel and Davydov's preference for an expositional approach reflects his characterization of mathematical thought in terms of its products—universal semiotic models. There is, however, one aspect of Davydov's instructional approach that differentiates it from the structuralism of the 1960s. This concerns his focus on the way that students use manipulatives and models while performing social actions. It is to this issue that we now turn.

1.7 The "activity" in activity theory

In outlining his instructional program, Davydov says little about the role that social interaction might play in development. This is, of course, consistent with Leont'ev's contention that practical activity or labor constitutes the source of intellectual functions. As has already been noted, Leont'ev's followers characterize practical activity as a collective activity that involves the use of cultural tools. It is therefore possible to distinguish between two senses in which an individual's action are social. The first reflects Vygotsky's views and the second those of Leont'ev:

1. An individual's actions are often cooperative actions in that they involve face-to-face interactions with others;
2. An individual's actions are elements of a broader sociocultural system.

This second sense of social is more encompassing than the first because it implies that every individual action is necessarily social in nature. Here, the individual is viewed as participating in a cultural practice even when he or she acts in isolation from others (Axcl, 1992; Scribner, 1990). For example, a child completing a mathematics worksheet during individual seatwork is participating in the social practice of doing mathematics in school. The identification of an overall goal or motive such as learning mathematics for its own sake serves to differentiate this social practice from others in which mathematical activity is carried out for a pragmatic purpose such as making a price comparison while shopping for groceries (cf. Lave, 1988). We can note in passing that this distinction underpins the recent spate of studies which compare mathematical activity in school with that in out-of-school situations. In these investigations, mathematics is treated as a social activity in the strong sense of the term.

According to Minick (1989a), the distinction between the two senses of social implies that psychological analyses based on activity theory must focus on the individual's inclusion in new forms of social activity as well as in new forms of face-to-face interaction. Consequently,

the key to understanding Soviet activity theory and its implications for concrete research is to recognize that within this framework psychological characteristics are conceptualized not as characteristics of the individual but as characteristics of the individual-in-[social]-action (Minick, 1989a, pp. 8-9).

This admonition is consistent with Ilyenkov's philosophical analysis in that social activity is assumed to relate the individual to objective reality:

social action is that which brings the individual into a relationship with the object world in such a way that he [or she] forms an adequate conception of that world as a world of human objects (Minick, 1989, p. 93).

This world of human objects is Ilyenkov's realm of ideal forms impressed on objects by social activity. People who perform these actions therefore come into contact with

the world of spiritual [i.e., intellectual] culture which people have created collectively—the world of historically evolved and socially fixed universal impressions of the actual, material world, which is contraposed to the individual mind and to which individual consciousness is subject (Davydov, 1988a, p. 40).

This account of the relationship between social action and the individual mind underpins Davydov's attempt to elaborate Leont'ev's theory of psychological development. In addition, Davydov accepted Leont'ev's contention that each age has its own form of leading activity within which specific intellectual skills can be developed. For example,

the period from three to six years was believed to be dominated by *play* activity, which facilitates the development of imagination and symbolic functions, the generalization of experience, and the orientation into the world of human relations and actions. The next period (six to ten years) is dominated by *learning* activity, which engenders theoretical reasoning, analysis, conscious planning of actions, and mental reflection (Kozulin, 1990, pp. 256-257).

In Davydov's view, this periodization of development "corresponds to the characteristics of the development of Soviet children under the conditions of education and upbringing prevalent in socialist societies" (Kozulin, 1990, p. 257). His research program can therefore be viewed as an attempt to elaborate specific learning activities that generate theoretical reasoning, and to differentiate this from the empirical reasoning developed during the preceding period of play activity. It should also be noted that the specific learning activities he sought to identify are such that students who perform them "execute mental actions commensurate with actions whereby those products of spiritual [i.e., intellectual] culture have been historically elicited" (Davydov, 1988a, p. 21). Thus, learning activities are social activities in the strong sense of the term, and students' participation in them leads them to identify ideal mathematical forms. Given this emphasis on social action, it seems reasonable to differentiate Davydov's instructional approach from the structuralism of the 1960s by calling it *structuralism-in-social-action*. Davydov's assumption that social action drives individual thought is central to activity theory. Thus, Leont'ev claimed that

it has been proved that concepts, as they develop in the head of the child, are the result of an acquisition of "ready" historically elaborated meanings (Leont'ev, 1975; quoted in Bauersfeld, 1993).

Similarly, for Ilyenkov, to orient oneself to an ideal environment is "to mould one's movements to the dictates of the norms which constitute man's spiritual [i.e., intellectual] culture" (Bakhurst, 1988, p. 17). Lektorsky (1984) argues that these cognitive norms are reified in cultural tools, and that in using them "man looks at the world through the eyes of society" (p. 145). Davydov, for his part, observes that "according to Galperin's general position, all of man's mind is specified for him from without; he appropriates it" (Davydov, 1990, p. 314). Davydov clarifies the implications of this view for instructional development by noting that

only particular object-related actions permit an object or situation to be transformed in such a way that a person can immediately single out in them the relationship that was a *universal* character (Davydov, 1990, p. 345; italics in original).

This means that

at times it is necessary to conduct a lengthy psychological investigation in order to find these "particular actions" that reveal the content of the abstractions, generalizations, and concepts (1990, p. 346).

Once psychological research has identified the particular actions; that reveal the ideal relationships, the instructional developer attempts to devise tasks that require students to perform these actions. Here it is assumed

that the concrete characteristics of the object that enter the subject's consciousness are a function of the task that relates the subject and the object, that is, on the assumption that what the object is for the subject is a function of his or her [social] activity with it (Minick, 1989a, p. 6).

We therefore have a sequence that leads from psychological research, to the identification of social actions, to the development of instructional tasks, to the determination of the way in which the child interprets an object such as an equation involving literal symbols. The teacher's role in this process is to forge the last link in the chain by ensuring that children execute the specified social actions that make it possible for them to isolate ideal mathematical forms.

1.8 The mind-in-social-action

Leont'ev's three-part scheme of subject, object, and social action can be viewed as an attempt to transcend the two-part scheme of behaviorism (Davydov & Radzikhovskii, 1985). The notion that social actions relate the developing child to the world of ideal objects is derived from Marx's analysis of the labor process. In his analysis, Marx linked the development of

"commodities" with the emergence of a market oriented system of exchange, and the development of "workers," "owners," and "labor" with the development of capitalism (Minick, 1989a, p. 121).

Thus, in Marx's view, the concept of a commodity did not originate in the mind. Instead, its source is to be found in a particular type of social activity, that of engaging in a new form of economic exchange. For individuals who participate in this social practice, the product of their work is transformed from a material object into an ideal object—a commodity. As Davydov notes, this ideal object in turn determines the actions of individual workers.

In the labor process a person foresees and envisages what the labor is to produce. This foresight takes the shape of constructing an ideal representation, which, as a conscious goal, precedes the output of the product. This goal determines, as would a law, the mode and character of the actions of the person who subordinates his will to that goal (Davydov, 1988a, p. 34).

Here, the ideal representation which precedes production is that of a commodity. Analogously, in Davydov's arithmetic program the ideal representation of quantity that children are assumed to develop when they engage in the social activity of using literal symbols determines the mode and character of their individual mathematical actions.

This view that concepts originate in social practice rather than in the mind implies that "thought (cognition) must not be reduced to a subjectively psychological process" (Davydov, 1988a, p. 16). Thus, "school children do not create concepts, images, values, and norms of social morality, but appropriate them in the process of learning activity" (Davydov, 1988b, p. 21). In making these claims, Davydov echoes Ilyenkov's contention that thought should not be viewed

as an event in a private, inner world of consciousness, but as something essentially "on the surface," as something located...on the borderline between the organism and the outside world. For thought, on Ilyenkov's picture, has a life only in an environment of socially constituted meanings (Bakhurst, 1988, p. 38).

This borderline between the individual and the external world consists of the social practices that link the two. Consequently, to locate thought on the borderline is to locate it in the appropriate performance of social activities that involve the use of cultural tools. This performance *is* the mind of the user of the cultural tools. Thus, the line of argument that we have traced from Marx, through Leont'ev and Ilyenkov, to Davydov leads to a conclusion that has been expressed forcefully by several American interpreters of activity theory: "Thought is literally 'not in the head'" (Bakhurst, 1988, p. 38).

1.9 Glasnost

As we noted at the outset, all of Davydov's writings that are available in English were produced in the pre-glasnost era. Although Davydov continues to promulgate the core tenets of activity theory, he has gradually modified certain aspects of his publicly-stated position in the last few years (Davydov, 1993). On the one hand, he continues to argue that there is a continuity between Vygotsky's and Leont'ev's work, and that Leont'ev was simply trying to elaborate some of Vygotsky's ideas. Further, he still views the ideal as the determinant of individual consciousness, thus elevating social and cultural processes above individual cognitive process. In addition, his pedagogical recommendations continue to emphasize theoretical thought and the ascent from the abstract to the concrete. On the other hand, he appears to be much more sensitive to the diversity of personal meanings and to social interaction, collaboration, and dialogue (van Oers, personal communication). For example, he previously seemed to imply in his writings that teaching is an impositional process in which the teacher ensures that students perform the specific social actions identified by psychological research. In contrast, he proposes in his more recent work that teaching should be conceptualized as a collaboration between the adult and the child in which the teacher directs and guides the child's activity, but does not dictate it (Davydov, 1993). With regard to the issue of personal meanings, he previously argued that individual variations in mental activity should be treated as "different degrees of approximation to universal generic thought" (Davydov, 1990, p. 311). In this formulation, ideal, universal thought is used as the standard against which to assess individual activity. In contrast, he has recently argued that the child brings a personal perspective to his or her collaboration with the teacher, and that this should constitute the basis of the educational process. The teacher's skill therefore resides both in his or her ability to interest the child in an activity for which he or she is ready, and in the ways in which he or she regulates that activity. Thus, although the teacher pursues a pedagogical agenda when collaborating with the child, he or she should always attend to the child's interests and concerns (Davydov, 1993).

Analogous changes can be detected in Davydov's characterization of psychological development. He previously proposed that it involves "a transition from the subjective idea (the concept) by way of [social] practice to the creation of an objective picture of the world" (Davydov, 1988a, p. 19). With regard to his arithmetic program, for example, the appropriate performance of specified actions with physical objects was presumed to "reveal the essential relationship of things" (Davydov, 1990, p. 316). In contrast to this apparent lack of concern for the child's activity and interests, he now suggests that psychological development involves the assimilation of historical values via personal activity in collaboration with others (Davydov, 1993). This in turn implies that the teacher should start with practical problems that are recognizable and of interest to the child, and that he or she should attend to both problem-solving activity and discussion in the classroom.

Despite the significant changes that Davydov has made in his publicly-stated views, his new position gives rise to a difficulty. In particular, there appears to be a tension between his recent emphasis on the child's activity and interests, and his continued characterization of learning almost exclusively in terms of acculturation. This tension is implicit in the contention that the sole purpose of the teacher's and child's collaboration is to master human values and culture (Davydov, 1993). We have seen that, in the case of Mathematics, culture corresponds to mathematical ideals that determine the child's developing psyche. Further, we have noted that Davydov locates mathematical ideals in social actions such as those of solving equations involving literal symbols. Thus, he has recently argued that signs and symbols created in the history of the culture function as transmitters from the objective ideal to the individual. Consequently, although Davydov recommends starting with practical problems that are of interest to the child, he also expects that the child will soon use the semiotic formulas of the discipline and thus think theoretically. It would therefore appear that, at a certain point in the instructional sequence, Davydov's teacher attempts to impose theoretical thought on the child. This remaining aspect of imposition and the associated characterization of learning exclusively in terms of acculturation differentiate approaches compatible with Soviet activity theory from those compatible with both constructivism and certain interpretations of Vygotsky's work (cf. van Oers, 1990, in press).

2. CONSTRUCTIVISM

Constructivism, like activity theory, rejects the representational view of mind, and the underlying Cartesian dualism between knowledge and a pre-given world that exists independently of human activity. Both theories view mathematics as an adaptive, functional activity and emphasize the role of social interaction in mathematical learning (Bauersfeld, 1990). In addition, both attempt to explain how, in Saxe's (1991a) terms, mathematics as cultural knowledge becomes interwoven with individual cognitive processes in the course of development. Nevertheless, a detailed examination "reveals certain contradictions, in particular when extrapolations for the orientation of education and innovation are drawn" (Bauersfeld, 1990, p. 1).

2.1 Basic assumptions

The antecedents of constructivism can be traced to Piaget's genetic epistemology (1970,1980), to ethnomethodology (Mehan & Wood, 1975), and to symbolic interactionism (Blumer, 1969). As this set of references indicates, it is possible to distinguish between what might be called psychological and interactionist variants of constructivism. von Glasersfeld's (1989a) development of the epistemological basis of the psychological variant incorporates both the Piagetian notions of assimilation and accommodation, and the cybernetic concept of viability. von Glasersfeld uses the term "knowledge" in "Piaget's *adaptational* sense to refer to those sensory-motor and conceptual operations that have proved viable in the knower's experience" (1992, p. 380). Further, he dispenses with traditional correspondence theories of truth and instead proposes an account that relates truth to the effective or viable organization of activity: "Truths are replaced by viable models—and viability is always relative to a chosen goal" (1992, p. 384). In this model, perturbations that the cognizing subject generates relative to a purpose or goal are posited as the driving force of development. As a consequence, learning is characterized as a process of self-organization in which the subject reorganizes his or her activity in order to eliminate perturbations (von Glasersfeld, 1989b). As von Glasersfeld notes, his instrumentalist approach to knowledge is generally consistent with the views of contemporary neo-pragmatist philosophers such as Bernstein (1983), Putnam (1987), and Rorty (1978).

Although von Glasersfeld defines learning as self-organization, he acknowledges that this constructive activity occurs as the cognizing individual interacts with other members of a community. Thus, he elaborates that "knowledge" refers to "conceptual structures that epistemic agents, given the range of present experience within their tradition of thought and language, consider *viable*" (1992, p. 381). Further, he contends that "the most frequent source of perturbations for the developing cognitive subject is interaction with others" (1989b, p. 136). The interactionist perspective developed by Bauersfeld and his colleagues (Bauersfeld, 1980; Bauersfeld et al., 1988) complements von Glasersfeld's cognitive focus by viewing communication as a process of mutual adaptation wherein individuals negotiate meanings by continually modifying their interpretations. However, whereas von Glasersfeld tends to focus on individuals'

construction of their ways of knowing, Bauersfeld emphasizes that the descriptive means and the models used in these subjective constructions are not arbitrary or retrievable from unlimited sources, as demonstrated through the unifying bonds of culture and language, through the intersubjectivity of socially shared knowledge among the members of social groups, and through the regulations of their related interactions (1988, p. 39).

Further, he contends that "learning is characterized by the subjective reconstruction of societal means and models through negotiation of meaning in social interaction"

(1988, p. 39). In accounting for this process of subjective reconstruction, Bauersfeld focuses on the teacher's and students' interactive constitution of the classroom microculture. Thus, he argues that

participating in the processes of a mathematics classroom is participating in a culture of mathematizing. The many skills, which an observer can identify and will take as the main performance of the culture, form the procedural surface only. These are the bricks of the building, but the design of the house of mathematizing is processed on another level. As it is with culture, the core of what is learned through participation is when to do what and how to do it... The core part of school mathematics enculturation comes into effect on the meta-level and is "learned" indirectly (1993, p. 24).

Bauersfeld's discussion of indirect learning clarifies that the occurrence of perturbations is not limited to those occasions when participants in an interaction believe that communication has broken down and explicitly negotiate meanings. Instead, for Bauersfeld, communication is a process of often implicit negotiations in which subtle shifts and slides of meaning frequently occur outside the participants' awareness. Newman et al. (1989), speaking within the activity theory tradition, make a similar point when they say that in an exchange between a teacher and a student, "the interactive process of change depends on...the fact that there are two different interpretations of the context and the fact that the utterances themselves serve to change the interpretations" (p 13). However, it should be noted that Newman et al. use Leont'ev's (1981) sociohistorical metaphor of appropriation to define negotiation as a process of mutual appropriation in which the teacher and students continually coopt or use each other's contributions.

In contrast, Bauersfeld uses an interactionist metaphor when he characterizes negotiation as a process of mutual adaptation in the course of which the participants interactively constitute obligations for their activity (Voigt, 1985). It can also be noted that in Newman et al.'s account, the teacher is said to appropriate students' actions into the wider system of mathematical practices that he or she understands. Bauersfeld, however, takes the local classroom microculture rather than the mathematical practices institutionalized by wider society as his primary point of reference. This focus reflects his concern with the process by which the teacher and students constitute the classroom microculture in the course of their interactions. Further, whereas activity theory gives priority to social and cultural processes, analyses conducted from the interactionist perspective propose that individual students' mathematical activity and the classroom microculture are reflexively related (Cobb, 1989; Voigt, 1992). In this view, individual students are seen as actively contributing to the development of the classroom microculture that both enables and constrains their individual mathematical activities. This reflexive relationship implies not merely that individual and collective mathematical actions are interdependent, but that one literally does not exist without the other. From this point of view, it is essential to coordinate psychological analyses of individual children's activity with interactional analyses of taken-as-shared classroom practices when accounting for development.

2.2 An approach to arithmetical computation compatible with constructivism

We outline a sample instructional sequence to both provide an anchor for the subsequent discussion and illustrate the relationship between the psychological and interactional aspects of constructivism. The sequence, which is called "The Candy Factory," is designed to support children's construction of increasingly sophisticated conceptions of place-value numeration and increasingly efficient paper-and-pencil algorithms for adding three- and four-digit numbers. It was developed in the course of a third-grade teaching experiment conducted in collaboration with Koeno Gravemeijer (Cobb, Yackel, & Wood, 1992). As background to this experiment, we assumed that the third graders (eight years old) in the experimental class could interpret a bar of ten unifix cubes as a unit of ten as a consequence of their instructional experiences in experimental second-grade classrooms.

To introduce the scenario, the teacher with whom we collaborated first described a candy factory in which candies are packed into rolls, rolls into boxes, and boxes into cases. Classroom observations indicated that this scenario was experientially real for the children and that the compatibility between their and the teacher's interpretations constituted an initial basis for communication. The first issue posed by the teacher in the whole-class setting was to decide how many candies to put in a roll, how many rolls to put in a box, and so on, with the constraint that the people in the factory wanted to figure out easily how many candies were in the factory storeroom. The children seemed to consider that this constraint was reasonable, and they made several suggestions including that of repeatedly packing by tens. The teacher acknowledged that the various proposals were plausible and told the children that the people in the factory decided to pack the candies in tens.

The teacher next gave pairs of children bags of unifix cubes and asked them to pretend that they worked in the factory. Their task was to pack the "candies." In this situation, the individual cubes and the bars the children made served a dual role. On the one hand, they signified candies and rolls in the experientially-real scenario of the candy factory. On the other hand, they signified units of one and of ten for the children as a consequence of their mathematical experiences in second grade. With the teacher's guidance, the children next pooled their "candies" to make boxes and cases. This then gave the teacher the opportunity to raise a variety of issues such as the number of candies in a box, the number of rolls in a case, etc. These questions led to genuine mathematical problems for many children, and their explanations reflected significant differences in the conceptual sophistication of their interpretations. For example, some gave purely numerical explanations that indicated they could conceptually coordinate arithmetical units of different ranks. Others gave explanations which indicated that they had to re-present the packing activity in order to coordinate arithmetical units. Still others were yet to internalize their activity in this way and actually had to pack or unpack candies in order to find, say, the number of rolls in a case. The teacher for her part built on children's contributions by describing purely numerical explanations in terms of packing activity and vice versa as guided by her knowledge of individual children's conceptual understandings. This intervention can be viewed as an attempt to both facilitate their individual conceptual development and guide the classroom community's establishment of increasingly sophisticated taken-as-shared interpretations.

Our intent in developing the instructional activities described thus far was to support the establishment of situations in which children's actions would provide a basis from which they could subsequently abstract and construct increasingly sophisticated arithmetical conceptions and algorithms. This is not to say that we viewed either ourselves or the teacher as presenting the situations ready-made to the children. Instead, we analyzed how the children contributed to the constitution of the situations in which they learned as they explained and justified their thinking. With regard to the instructional activities, we attempted to capitalize on their prior acculturation into particular social practices when we devised a scenario that might be experientially real for the children. Clearly, none of the children had visited a factory similar to the one discussed in the classroom, and it is doubtful if one actually exists. However, we did assume that the children were familiar with the social activity of packing and unpacking. This would then make it possible for them to each construct viable interpretations of the scenario.

In addition, we attempted to ensure that the initial instructional activities make sense when the mathematical meanings and practices institutionalized by wider society are taken as a point of reference. It was this concern for the potential endpoints of the learning sequence that led to the decision to introduce packing by tens as a convention. Given our initial observations of the children's mathematical activity and inferences about their differing interpretations, the issue that we then had to address was that of supporting their transition from situated, pragmatic problem solving to more formal mathematical activity. The development and use of models and symbols proved to be valuable in supporting this process of conceptual reorganization.

As an example, in one activity, the children were given an array of small circles that signified the candies in the factory storeroom and were asked to make a drawing to show how they would pack the candies. In this activity, which was routine for the children, the act of creating a collection of candies signified the conceptual act of creating a unit of ten or one hundred. Once these solutions had been discussed, the teacher explained that a shop had ordered a certain number of candies and asked the children to show how they would repack the candies in the storeroom so that the factory could fill the order. The array and the number of candies to be sent had been chosen so that the children would have to develop a way of symbolizing the act of unpacking candies (or of decomposing units). This activity was genuinely problematic for many children, and the teacher again redescribed explanations that reflected differing conceptual understandings in the ensuing whole class discussion.

In subsequent instructional activities, the teacher and children developed a taken-as-shared way of making freehand drawings to symbolize transactions in which candies were moved into the storeroom or sent out to a shop. It should be stressed that the children were not explicitly taught to make drawings as an end in itself. Instead, they could decide whether or not to make drawings as they completed particular instructional activities. Making drawings therefore served as a possible way in which they could both make sense of events in the factory and communicate their thinking. Later, an inventory form was introduced by the teacher as the means by which the factory manager decided to record transactions in the storeroom. This form consisted of four columns that were headed from left to right, "Cases," "Boxes," "Rolls," "Candies." Conventions for using numerals to symbolize these transactions and the composition or decomposition of numerical units were explicitly negotiated, and the children eventually constructed and used a variety of efficient non-standard addition and subtraction algorithms. As a final step in the instructional sequence, the inventory form was dropped, and addition and subtraction tasks were presented in standard vertical, column format.

Both our classroom observations and interviews conducted individually with the children indicated that they gave their overt acts of manipulating conventional symbols on the inventory form a variety of different meanings. This implies that their interpretations of their own and others' mathematical activity did not necessarily correspond or match. Instead, their individual interpretations were compatible for the purposes at hand in that they could coordinate their mathematical activities and communicate effectively (von Glasersfeld, 1984,1990). It is for this reason that we say the classroom community's evolving basis for mathematical communication was taken-as-shared rather than shared. For example, some children's symbol-manipulation acts signified purely numerical transformations, indicating that they had completely interiorized the acts of creating numerical units by packing or unpacking candies. It seemed that other children had to re-present packing and unpacking activity in order to give meaning to their manipulation of numerals. In Piaget's (1970) terms, these children appeared to have internalized but not interiorized the acts of creating experientially-real units as they participated in the classroom community's establishment of increasingly sophisticated mathematical practices. As a consequence, another scenario that involves modeling and symbolizing was developed and coordinated with the candy factory sequence to further support the children's conceptual development.

In the account we have given of the candy factory sequence, the children are characterized as actively contributing to the mathematical practice established by the classroom community. For example, we noted that they contributed to the establishment of drawing as a taken-as-shared practice by giving explanations that the teacher could capitalize on as she pursued her pedagogical agenda. These and other communal mathematical actions were therefore constrained by and did not exist apart from the teacher's and children's individual activities. The description we have given of the candy factory sequence also suggests that this relation holds in the opposite direction: Individual children's mathematical activity and learning are both enabled and constrained by the mathematical practices institutionalized in the classroom. On the one hand, making drawings was enabling in that it appeared to play an important role in supporting children's internalization and interiorization of their activity. On the other hand, it was constraining in that it delimited the various ways in which the children interpreted and solved tasks (Gidden, 1984). It is in this sense that individual children's mathematical activity and classroom mathematical practices can be viewed as reflexively related.

2.3 The concrete and the abstract

One striking difference between Davydov's instructional approach and that illustrated by the candy factory sequence concerns the relationship between practical, real world problem solving and more formal mathematical activity. As we have seen, Davydov's program involves what he calls an ascent from the abstract to the concrete in which children are taught to isolate the formal, abstract properties of quantity as rapidly as is feasible. They are then expected to solve practical arithmetical problems by using general solution methods that are based on their knowledge of the ideal form of quantity. In contrast, the candy factory sequence begins with a prolonged phase of informal, pragmatic mathematical problem solving. Subsequent instructional activities are designed to support children's transition to more formal mathematical activity. Ideally, at the culmination of the sequence, children have constructed efficient, personally-meaningful computational algorithms that reflect relatively sophisticated understandings of place-value numeration and involve the manipulation of conventional written mathematical symbols. Davydov might argue that this latter approach to arithmetical computation is merely a variant of instructional programs that begin with tasks close to the experience of children and treat learning as an inductive process. In arguing that this is not the case, we contrast the role of models and symbols in the two programs by drawing heavily on the work of Treffers (1987,1991).

Treffers (1987) distinguishes between three general approaches to instructional development that he terms structuralist, empiricist, and realist. In this regard, we have noted that Davydov's program is reminiscent of the "structure of knowledge" approach of the sixties.

Structuralists emphasize the insightful building-up and shaping of knowledge and abilities within the system of the subject matter area. To develop instruction they start from the structure of the teaching matter (Treffers, 1991, p. 345).

This characterization is consistent with Davydov's concern for meaning and with his identification of mathematical thought with the product of mathematicians' activity. Treffers also observes that structuralists typically develop instructional materials that embody the structure of the subject matter. Similarly, in Davydov's view, a crucial feature of a learning model is that it "specifically registers the universal [ideal] relationship in an integral object and allows it to be analyzed further" (1988b, p. 31). Davydov's primary contribution to the structuralist tradition in mathematics education is to introduce social actions into the development process. Thus, whereas structuralists typically attempt to embody the structures and relationships to be acquired in a readily apprehensible form, Davydov stresses that children can only isolate ideal mathematical forms by performing specific social actions that have been identified by research. It is in fact for this reason that we have characterized his approach as structuralism-in-social-action.

In contrast to structuralist approaches,

the empirical trend does choose as its starting point for mathematical activities the *neighborhood of* the child's everyday experience... This innovation is characterized by its didactical approach rather than by a strict methodological structure or a mathematical source of inspiration. In practice this leads to an enrichment of arithmetical instruction but sometimes also to a badly organized collection of activities originating in 'environmental situations' (Treffers, 1987, p. 10).

Treffers' characterization of empirical approaches brings to mind incidental learning programs in which children select projects almost exclusively on the basis of their personal interests. In such programs, the mathematical problems that children solve arise incidentally as they pursue their investigations, and attempts are rarely made to systematically support their transition to more formal yet personally-meaningful mathematical activity. In our view, Davydov's critique of approaches that treat mathematical learning as an inductive process is particularly applicable to programs of this type. In his writings, Davydov seems to imply that any approach which does not involve an ascent from the abstract to the concrete must necessarily be empiricist. However, Treffers identifies a third distinct approach to instructional development, that of realistic mathematics education.

The realistic approach draws on the observation that, historically, pragmatic, informal mathematical activity constituted the basis from which formal, codified, academic mathematics evolved (Ekeland, 1988; Tymoczko, 1986). As a consequence, this approach strives to avoid what Freudenthal called the anti-didactic inversion wherein applications follow an attempt to teach formal mathematical structures (Gravemeijer, 1990). From this point of view, the first phase of an instructional sequence should involve extensive exploration in a range of situations that are experientially real for children (Freudenthal, 1981). In contrasting this and the structuralist approach, Treffers (1987) argues that

a vast phenomenological exploration is not a luxury one can dispense with but, on the contrary, is a sheer necessity. This necessity is shunned by the formal, logical approach...leading to a kind of mathematics detached from and isolated from reality (p. 257).

Here, the reality to which Treffers refers is children's phenomenological or experiential reality. Treffers goes on to explicate other features that distinguish the realist and structuralist approaches:

"embeddedness" versus "embodiment"; the naturally organizable versus the artificially organized matter; eliciting structuring activity in everyday life in physical or imagined reality versus debasing mathematical structures and forcing them into an artificially created environment (1987, p. 275).

In our terminology, the contrast between the two approaches is that between helping children isolate the pre-given products of mathematicians' activity, and supporting both their individual conceptual self organization and the evolution of the classroom community's mathematical practices. One of the primary ways of giving such support is to guide the development of ways of modeling and symbolizing (Treffers, 1987). In the candy factory sequence, for example, the teacher attempted to overcome the inductiveness to which Davydov refers by guiding the development of modeling activity that involved making drawings and, later, using the inventory form to record transactions in the factory. As has been noted, these ways of modeling were specifically designed to fit with the children's problem-solving activity (Gravemeijer, 1991) and were introduced as ways that they might decide to express their mathematical thinking when completing instructional activities. The observation that the children spontaneously engaged in modeling and symbolizing activity when they were not obliged to do so indicates that this fit was achieved. Opportunities for the children to progressively reorganize their activity then arose because they created records of their mathematical activity, and these served to support their reflection on and representation of that activity (cf. Steinbring, 1989; Treffers, 1987). In addition, the negotiation of taken-as-shared ways of modeling and symbolizing facilitated mathematical communication. For example, the children manipulated physical materials, made drawings, and used conventional arithmetical symbols to explain and justify their interpretations and solutions.

From what has been said thus far, it should be clear that we do not view models and symbols as pre-given cultural tools whose use enables children to isolate ideal mathematical forms. We instead treat modeling and symbolizing as social practices established by the classroom community with the teacher's guidance. It is as children actively participate in the establishment of these classroom practices that opportunities arise for them to progressively reorganize their initially informal problem-solving activity. Consequently, in such an approach, what is experientially real or concrete for children becomes increasingly abstract. This characterization can, of course, be contrasted with Davydov's (and Wilensky's) ascent from the abstract to the concrete. The use of the term "concrete" is similar in the two approaches in that, from the realistic perspective, it denotes whatever is phenomenologically real for children in the world of their experience. However, differences become apparent when we consider the term "abstract". For Davydov and Wilensky, it signifies an instrumental understanding based, perhaps, on little more than a formal definition. In contrast, within the realistic perspective, it refers to the developmental sophistication of particular conceptions. From this point of view, instruction that gives rise to an abstract conception in Davydov's and Wilensky's sense is considered to be inadequate because it starts out at too high a level (Gravemeijer, 1991). Instructional sequences are instead designed to support children's development of increasingly formal mathematical activity while ensuring that they experience this activity as concrete. The notion that instructional activities are a means of bringing students into contact with ideal mathematical forms is therefore displaced by a view in which teachers initiate and guide emerging systems of mathematical meanings and practices in their classrooms.

2.4 The teacher's role

We have seen that Soviet activity theory characterizes educational goals primarily in terms of acculturation wherein children acquire their intellectual inheritance. In contrast, the assumption that children actively create their own ways of knowing is one of the basic tenets of constructivist theory. This does not of course imply that learning is an isolated, solo activity in which the child follows the "epistemological Adventures of Robinson Crusoe" (Mamardashvili, 1968; as quoted by Davydov, 1990, p. 323). As we have argued, children's cognitive constructions occur as they contribute to the classroom community's establishment of taken-as-shared mathematical meanings and practices. Thus, whereas an activity theorist might see children appropriating the objective mathematical knowledge of the culture, a constructivist sees them participating in the classroom community's constitution of a mathematical reality. This difference in theoretical perspectives has immediate implications for the teacher's role.

For Davydov, one of the teacher's primary obligations is to ensure that students perform specified social actions and use cultural tools such as literal symbols appropriately. From the constructivist perspective, it is to initiate and guide the development of both individual children's mathematical ways of knowing and the classroom community's taken-as-shared mathematical meanings and practices so that they become increasingly compatible with those of wider society. A crucial type of guidance of this type was exemplified during the discussion of the candy factory sequence when we described how the teacher introduced drawings as a way of modeling transactions in the factory. We noted that the teacher did not demonstrate the appropriate way to make drawings and then have the children practice this use of a cultural tool until they had mastered it. Instead, she made drawings in a whole-class discussion to clarify solutions that children presented verbally. Some of the children then began to make drawings as they completed subsequent instructional activities even though they were not obliged to do so. An activity theorist might simply describe this as an instance of appropriation. However, we would also want to stress that making drawings was both personally meaningful and relevant to the children as they attempted to make sense of events in the candy factory. It was only because these criteria of meaningfulness and relevance were satisfied that some students made drawings when they solved problems and explained their reasoning in subsequent whole-class discussions. This in turn made it possible for the teacher to initiate a discussion of drawings both in terms of transactions in the factory and in terms of the composition and decomposition of arithmetical units. Once the teacher capitalized on the children's contributions in this way, other children began to make drawings and, in the process, the teacher and children together established it as a classroom mathematical practice.

The manner in which the teacher introduced the making of drawings illustrates how she guided children's constructive efforts by redescribing their interpretations and solutions in ways that fit with her pedagogical agenda and yet might make sense to them. This process occurred in all phases of the instructional sequence. For example, at the beginning of the candy factory sequence, the children used unifix cubes to simulate the packing of candies. When the teacher asked the children questions such as how many rolls make a case, she built on their responses by redescribing explanations that focused on packing and unpacking activity in terms of the composition and decomposition of arithmetical units. In doing so, she in effect provided a commentary from the perspective of one who could judge which aspects of the children's mathematical activity might be significant for their future learning and acculturation. The children for their part had to actively make sense of the teacher's descriptions. In the process, some appeared to make personally-novel mathematical interpretations that would not otherwise have arisen. Thus, in these exchanges, the children actively constructed their own mathematical ways of knowing. It therefore seems reasonable to say that they participated in their own acculturation into the mathematical practices of wider society.

The account we have given of children's learning in the classroom appears to clash with activity theory's contention that children's minds are specified for them from without. Further, whereas we characterize the teacher's role as that of guiding the negotiation of mathematical meanings, Davydov emphasizes that the teacher should teach children to perform social actions and ensure that they use cultural tools appropriately. In his post-glasnost work, he is clearly more sensitive to children's personal activity and interests. However, even here, it appears that the teacher is expected to impose theoretical thought on children at some point by teaching them to use the semiotic formulas of the discipline. It seems reasonable to speculate that when the children's use of symbols is inappropriate, the teacher has to become increasingly explicit and, as a last resort, spell out precisely what he or she expects them to do (Voigt, 1985). From the perspective of Soviet activity theory, interventions of this type might be viewed as necessary to support children's mathematical acculturation. However, from the constructivist perspective, there is the danger that instruction designed to help children isolate ideal forms will in practice become a social guessing game in which children try to figure out how the teacher wants them to behave (Bauersfeld, 1980). In general, situations in which the teacher becomes increasingly explicit about what it is that students are to learn can lead to the excessive proceduralization of mathematics and the disappearance of conceptual meaning (Steinbring, 1989). Brousseau (1984) makes this point succinctly when he states that

the more explicit I am about the behavior I wish my students to display, the more likely it is that they will display that behavior without recourse to the understanding which the behavior is meant to indicate; that is, the more likely they will take the form for the substance (quoted by Mason, 1989, p. 7).

Similarly, Lave and Wenger (1991) observe that

when directive teaching in the form of prescriptions about proper practice generates one circumscribed form of participation (in school)...the goal of complying with the requirements specified by teaching engenders a practice different from that intended (pp. 96-97).

In view of these considerations, it seems reasonable to question whether teaching children to manipulate conventional symbols necessarily leads them to isolate ideal mathematical forms.

The distinction we have made between guiding the negotiation of meanings and ensuring children perform specified social actions might seem to imply that the teacher is an authority in Davydov's program but not in approaches compatible with constructivism. In our view, the teacher is an authority in the classroom in both cases. The issue that differentiates the two approaches is instead the manner in which the teacher expresses that authority in action (Bishop, 1985). In Davydov's program, it appears that the teacher sometimes has to impose his or her view of what counts as appropriate mathematical activity. In contrast, in approaches compatible with constructivism, the teacher pursues his or her pedagogical agenda by attempting to build on children's mathematical activity. In the process, the teacher guides both their individual mathematical development and the classroom community's establishment of taken-as-shared mathematical practices. Mathematical argumentation in which children are expected to explain and justify their thinking is therefore placed at the heart of the educational process. As we will see, this has important implications for instructional development.

2.5 Instructional development

In Davydov's approach to instructional development, the researcher identifies the ideal forms that children are to appropriate and specifies social actions that might lead children to isolate them. This analysis in turn guides the development of instructional tasks. The effectiveness of these tasks and thus of the specified social actions is then investigated by conducting teaching experiments. The way that the problem of instructional development is formulated from the constructivist perspective differs markedly from this approach. We have already noted that it is essential to both take account of possible developmental end points and to devise starting points that might be experientially real for children. In addition, the discussion of the teacher's role indicates that the instructional activities should enable teachers to achieve their pedagogical agendas by capitalizing on children's solutions. Thus, the instructional activities should be such that mathematically significant issues arise in a way that is experienced as natural when children's interpretations and solutions are discussed (Gravemeijer, 1992). In the case of the candy factory sequence, for example, the composition and decomposition of units of ten and one hundred arose in a reasonably natural way when the teacher guided the discussion of children's packing activity with unifix cubes. Similarly, issues concerning the modeling and symbolizing of these composing and decomposing actions grew out of the children's solutions to the instructional activities. As a consequence, the teacher did not have to funnel children to the response she considered appropriate by giving a series of increasingly explicit cues.

In general, instructional development as it is formulated from the constructivist perspective brings together issues concerning children's mathematical activity and learning, the teacher's activity, and the nature of classroom social interactions. The approach of attempting to anticipate how instructional activities might be realized in the classroom in the course of mathematical argumentation can be further clarified by considering an example taken from a third-grade classroom teaching experiment. In this case, the intent was to support the development of instructional situations in which a mathematically significant issue, the equivalence of different fractional partitionings, might emerge naturally as a focus of activity and as a topic of conversation. To this end, we developed a sequence of instructional activities by making only minor modifications to those proposed by Streefland (1991). A situation that was experientially-real to the children, that of dividing pizzas fairly, served as the starting point for the sequence. In one of the initial tasks, the children worked in pairs to share two pizzas between four people. The task statement was accompanied by a picture of two circles, and the children were encouraged to draw lines to document how they would divide the pizzas. During the subsequent whole class discussion of their solutions, some children explained that they had divided each pizza in half whereas others said that they had divided each into fourths. The teacher wrote "1/2" and "1/4 + 1/4" to symbolize the portion that one person would receive in each case. One child then commented on the second solution as follows:

Richard: Yeah, but instead, in this one [the drawing of two pizzas divided into fourths], you'd get two
            pieces, or you'd get a big half.
Teacher: Well, do they still get the same amount?
Richard
and Dawn: Yeah.
Richard: Yeah, they still get the same amount. Both of those equal a half.
Teacher: What could you find out here? Do you know?
Richard: They're both the same, but just done differently.
Teacher: So two-fourths is the same, or equal to, one-half, right? (writes " 1/4 + 1/4 = 1/2")

Here, the issue of the equivalence of different partitionings emerged naturally in the sense that the question of whether a person would receive the same amount of pizza in each case appeared to be both relevant and personally meaningful to the children. It can also be noted that the teacher redescribed Richard's response by talking of two-fourths as being equal to one-half and by introducing conventional written symbols. In doing so, she was attempting to guide both individual children's reorganization of their informal, situated activity and the classroom community's establishment of increasingly sophisticated mathematical practices.

    In a subsequent task, the children shared four pizzas between eight people. Their various solutions involved dividing the pizzas into either two, four, or eight pieces. Referring to these solutions, the teacher asked, "Do you get more pizza one way than another?"

Jenna: It wouldn't make a difference
John: Well, in a way they're the same, and in a way they're different.
Teacher: How are they the same?
John: They're the same because if you put four-eighths together, it equals a half.

He subsequently elaborated:

John: I know a way you can tell. Four plus four equals eight, and one plus one equals two.
Teacher: Four plus four equals eight. Now how does that help us?
John: It tells us that it's just half.
Teacher: So, in other words, you're saying that if we add four-eighths and four-eighths (writes
            "4/8 + 4/8 = 8/8"), that would equal eight-eighths would be the whole thing.
Jenna: What could we do with the [solution that involved dividing pizzas into] fourths?

Jenna's final question indicates that the task for her was now not simply to partition pizzas fairly, but also involved demonstrating the equivalence of different partitionings. This goal, which became increasingly taken-as-shared, was not given to the children by either the instructional developers or by the teacher. Instead, it grew out of children's mathematical activity with the teacher's guidance.

It is also apparent that this shift in taken-as-shared goals was accompanied by a change in classroom mathematical practices. Initially, these practices had involved partitioning and comparing amounts of pizza per se. me above exchange indicates that drawings of pizzas now seemed to signify fractional parts of a numerical whole. Thus, neither John nor Jenna referred to amounts of pizza but instead spoke of fourths and eighths. What these terms might have meant for the children is, of course, an open question. We can, however, note that there were significant qualitative differences in the ways that individual children reorganized their partitioning activity. For example, during a subsequent discussion, one child explained that 3/6 was equal to 1/2 by dividing a circle in half and then partitioning one of the halves into three equal pieces called "sixths". However, another child explained, "I do it backwards."

Six-sixths. . .Half of six-sixths is three-sixths and so that would be. . . Since six-sixths is a whole, then three-sixths is one-half.

It would seem that this child had internalized partitioning activity to a considerable degree and could conceptually compose and decompose fractional units of some type. These qualitative differences in the children's mathematical interpretations subsequently made it possible for the process of establishing the equivalence of partitionings to emerge as a natural topic of conversation.

These instructional activities are just the first in an elaborate sequence that Streefland (1991) developed by conducting a series of teaching experiments. In later activities, ways of modeling and symbolizing are introduced to support children's progressive reorganization of their informal problem-solving activities. Our primary purpose in presenting the sample episodes is to illustrate that the constructivist developer needs to have a detailed understanding of the various ways that individual children might interpret and solve particular tasks if he or she is to succeed in developing activities that make it possible for the teacher to capitalize on children's contributions. The developer draws on these understandings when proposing specific instructional activities in which mathematically significant issues might arise naturally in the course of classroom interactions. Thus, it was not merely a matter of luck that differences in the explanations the children gave in the sample episode constituted a resource that the teacher could draw on. The approach Streefland used to develop the instructional activities involved analyzing individual children's solutions in some detail, and this enabled him to anticipate the range of solutions that might arise in any classroom including the one in which we worked.

Streefland's concern for individual children's mathematical activity can be contrasted with Davydov's pre-glasnost characterization of individual variations as different degrees of approximation to universal generic thought. For Streefland, individual children's solutions and explanations are of interest in themselves and need to be explained by inferring the quality of the children's thinking. In contrast, the personal meanings that children give to their sometimes idiosyncratic activity are not necessarily of immediate relevance to Davydov (cf. Confrey, 1991). Even in his postglasnost work, Davydov treats mathematical learning almost exclusively as a process of acculturation and stresses that conventional signs and symbols serve as transmitters from the ideal to the individual. His primary concern when these signs and symbols are introduced appears to be on the extent to which children's activity approximates the desired social actions. Thus, at this point in an instructional sequence, his focus on children's personal activity and interests appears to fade into the background. It would therefore seem that whereas Streefland's goal is to guide children's (re)construction of the mathematical ways of knowing institutionalized by the wider community, Davydov's goal is to help children isolate the objective mathematical ideals of the culture This difference in perspective is reflected in the types of teaching experiments that activity theorists and constructivists conduct to develop instructional activities. For activity theorists, the intent of the experiment appears to be to investigate whether instructional materials work in the sense that children eventually perform the desired social actions. The findings are then used to revise the materials before another teaching experiment is conducted. For constructivists, the overall goal is to analyze both the development of individual children's thinking and the evolution of the taken-as-shared mathematical practices established by the classroom community. The results of these ongoing analyses are then used to modify both the instructional activities and the instructional strategies while the experiment is in progress. These general differences in purpose reflect differences in the role that symbols and signs are considered to play in learning, and in the way that mathematical thought is characterized.

2.6 Cultural tools and mathematical symbolizing

The notion that cultural tools such as conventional mathematical signs and symbols are carriers of meaning is a core assumption of activity theory. It is on this basis that Davydov assumes that children who engage in the practice of manipulating equations involving literal symbols will develop theoretical conceptions of quantity. We would agree that equations involving literal symbols are experienced by mathematicians as carrying abstract mathematical meanings. However, we would also contend that, within a mathematics research community, writing relations of this sort is synonymous with elaborating relations in and communicating one's understanding about an experientially-real world of abstract mathematical objects. This implies that the activity of manipulating literal symbols is intelligible for mathematicians against a background of largely unarticulated meanings, suppositions, and assumptions. Putnam, Lampert, and Peterson (1990) make a similar point noting that

within communities of working mathematicians, as within all such working communities, there are a host of agreed-upon assumptions: Assumptions whose legitimacy is taken for granted so that they can get on with the conversation. Working mathematicians may not stop to convince themselves or anyone else that these assumptions are legitimate: Being a member of the discourse community simply implies being willing to play by the same rules by which everyone else is playing (p. 121).

Part of the mathematician's acculturation into his or her research community involves learning to construe situations in accord with these implicit assumptions. It is only when he or she can make these taken-as-shared interpretations that equations involving literal symbols come to be experienced as having objective meanings and as serving as a reliable way to convey one's thoughts to others.

In constructivist terms, Davydov's contention that mathematics instruction should involve an ascent from the abstract to the concrete rests on the assumption that children who are taught to manipulate literal symbols will, like the mathematician, elaborate relations in a world of taken-as-shared mathematical objects. This can only occur if an observable activity such as writing equations carries with it the consensual suppositions, assumptions, and construals that give it meaning and significance within an established microculture. However, as Putnam et al. (1990) observe, "mathematical arguments cannot be imported whole into settings where the participants do not already understand something of what they are about" (p. 122). The contention that activities involving cultural tools can carry background assumptions from a mathematics research community to the classroom community therefore appears implausible.

As an alternative to the view that cultural tools are carriers of meaning, we have argued that social practices do not exist apart from the activities of the community members who participate in their establishment. From this perspective, the activity of writing equations in a mathematics research community and in the classroom are two different social practices. Thus, as Lave and Wenger (1991) have put it,

the didactical use of language, not itself the discourse of practice, creates a new linguistic practice, which has an existence of its own. Legitimate peripheral participation in such a linguistic practice is a form of learning, but does not imply that newcomers learn the actual practice the language is supposed to be about (p. 108).

The crucial question when accounting for children's mathematical learning then becomes to understand what the activity of writing equations comes to mean in the classroom. An investigation of this issue would involve analyzing individual children's active contributions to the development of this classroom practice, and identifying the ways in which it enables and constrains their individual activity and learning. Such an analysis would explicitly compare and contrast the taken-as-shared meanings established for literal symbols by the classroom community and by the mathematics research community. In the process, an issue that does not arise if one assumes that cultural tools are carriers of meaning becomes the object of empirical investigation. In general, empirical analyses conducted from the perspective of activity theory focus on the extent to which children develop the concepts of the adult community when they learn to use pre-given cultural tools appropriately. In contrast, analyses conducted from the constructivist perspective focus on the ways in which children reorganize their activity as they contribute to the development of the taken-as-shared ways of symbolizing established by the classroom community. Bauersfeld (1990) succinctly expressed a basic tenet of this latter perspective when he observed that "everything in social interaction can be loaded with meaning and thus develop into a socially taken-as-shared 'mediator'" (p. 5). This in turn implies that pictures, graphical presentations, and other mediator objects typically used in instruction are by no means self-explanatory or self-speaking terms. There is no simple "reading" of meaning, which the objects "carry" to the potential reader. They are means the use of which students have learned across many typical situations in the mathematics classroom. And the actual construction of meaning is clearly bound to the subject's actual definition of the situation (p. 13).

This viewpoint was exemplified during our discussion of the candy factory sequence. There, we described how drawings became socially taken-as-shared mediators in the classroom, and emphasized that children's contributions to this process were bound to their actual definitions of the situation. The discussion of the candy factory also illustrated a general feature of instructional approaches developed within the constructivist perspective. The taken-as-shared ways of symbolizing that emerged with the teacher's guidance are designed to both fit with the children's informal activity and to support their construction of more sophisticated conceptions and strategies. This approach can be contrasted with that in which cultural tools are taken from established communities of practice and imported into the classroom. Here, both the tools that children are to use and the ways in which they are to use them are largely dictated by the cultural practices of the wider community. Gravemeijer (1993) calls this a top-down approach and contrasts it with the bottom-up approach compatible with constructivism.

2.7 Theoretical concepts and conceptual actions

We have seen that Davydov equates theoretical thought with the product of mathematicians' activity. Further, even in his post-glasnost work, he treats mathematical signs and symbols as cultural transmitters. We have also documented that the instructional recommendations that Davydov develops within this framework bear a striking resemblance to the structure-of-knowledge approaches of the 1960s. Interestingly, Davydov's claims concerning the ascent from the abstract to the concrete also appear to have much in common with mainstream American psychology. This becomes apparent when we consider Lave's (1988) critique of this mainstream view.

Lave clarifies her view that mathematics is a socially-situated activity by critiquing the notion of transfer. For her, the mainstream perspective assumes

that children can be taught general cognitive skills (e.g., reading, writing, mathematics, logic, critical thinking) *if* these "skills" are disembedded from the routine contexts of their use. Extraction of knowledge from the particulars of experience, of activity from its context, is the condition for making knowledge available for *general* use (p. 8; italics in original).

This implication is similar to Davydov's contention that children should be taught the formal properties of quantity as early as possible so that they can solve practical problems by applying a general method of solution. Lave also notes that, in the mainstream view, there is "a binary opposition between 'abstract, decontextualized' knowledge and immediate, 'concrete, intuitive' experience" (p. 41). This is because the "operationalization of cognitive processes in the laboratory consists of building tasks to reflect norms of 'scientific thought'" (p. 79). Davydov, for his part, emphasizes that instructional materials should register what Lave calls "idealized 'rational science'" (p. 70). Lave goes on to observe that these "normative models for correct solution are used to evaluate subjects' performances" (p. 23). This makes "it difficult to seriously acknowledge, much less analyze, the variety of levels of structural relations generated by subjects" (p. 70).

We have seen that Davydov is more sensitive to children's activity and interests in his post-glasnost work. However, even here, a point is reached in instructional sequences when children are taught to use the semiotic formulas of the discipline appropriately. At this point in the sequence, it appears that the child's activity is interpreted in terms of its approximation to normative models for correct solution. When this occurs, the task for both mainstream psychologists and Davydov "becomes to get the subject to match the experimenter's expectations" (Lave, 1988, p. 37). Thus, whereas mainstream psychology involves experimentation by imposition, Davydov's arithmetic program involves phases of teaching by imposition. In both cases, it is assumed that "society and culture shape the particularities of cognition and give it content" (p. 87). To account for this process, each "posits a functioning social order in equilibrium, and individuals molded and shaped though socialization into performers of normatively governed social roles and practices" (p. 87).

Lave continues her critique by observing that "the common remedy cognitivists have proposed for 'cognitive deficiencies' has been to increase the conscious, verbally explicit strategies available to problem solvers" (p. 182). Similarly, in Soviet activity theory, "direct instruction, very detailed and precise in presentation, using powerful mediator objects, and the explication of reflexive [i.e., conscious] strategies are in high favor" (Bauersfeld, 1990, p. 13). Lave concludes her argument at this point and does not attempt to develop the implications of her research for mathematics education in any detail. However, it appears that the implications that other contemporary American sociocultural theorists have drawn for educational practice are more consistent with recommendations derived from constructivism than from Soviet activity theory. To illustrate this point, we consider the recommendations of a second researcher whose work focuses on the differences between mathematics in school and mathematics in out-of-school situations.

Saxe (1991a) analyzes in detail the mathematical practices developed by the Oksapmin people of Papua New Guinea and by young candy sellers working in the streets of Recife, Brazil. In discussing the implications of his findings for school mathematics instruction, Saxe (1991b) argues that it is important "to engage children in a classroom practice that has the properties of the daily practices involving mathematics in which children show sustained engagement" (p. 22). To illustrate such an approach, Saxe describes a treasure hunt game in which personally-meaningful and relevant mathematical problems arise for children in a natural way. Presumably, the game is effective because making trades and developing strategies to acquire treasure are experientially-real activities for children. It would therefore seem that, for Saxe, informal, practice-linked mathematics should serve as the starting point in the learning-teaching process. Thus, like the candy factory sequence and the pizza activities, Saxe's approach avoids the anti-didactic inversion inherent in Davydov's ascent from the abstract to the concrete.

In general, recent American research on the social and cultural aspects of mathematical activity appears to be both theoretically and pragmatically more compatible with constructivism than with Soviet activity theory. Further, it would seem that, ironically, activity theory has more in common with traditional American cognitive psychology than it does with either constructivism or recent American sociocultural research. In this regard, it can be noted that mainstream American psychology and Soviet activity theory both emerged as reactions to the behaviorist stimulus-response scheme. In mainstream psychology, cognitive processes mediate between stimulus and response, whereas, in Leont'ev's activity theory, social action links subject and object. Psychological constructivism has, however, evolved within a different tradition, one that draws on Piaget's genetic epistemology and treats mathematics as a conceptual activity. Within this tradition, the goal of a psychological analysis is to infer the nature of students' mathematical realities, and to specify the interpretive acts that make possible those experienced realities. Thus, whereas analyses conducted within the mainstream American tradition attempt to delineate students' knowledge of pre-given mathematical structures and relations, those conducted within the constructivist tradition are concerned with the ways of knowing wherein they enact mathematics. Further, whereas Davydov identifies mathematical thought with its culturally-given products, constructivist analyses focus on its dynamics. In addition, whereas Davydov treats mathematical learning as a process of identifying ideal mathematical forms, constructivist analyses portray it as a process of conceptual self-organization.

This notion of learning as self-organization was illustrated during the discussion of the candy factory sequence. There, we saw that some children had internalized their physical packing and unpacking activity by creating figural imagery whereas others had interiorized and did not need to rely on situation-specific imagery. The discussion of the candy factory sequence also illustrated that this self-organization does not occur in a social vacuum but instead arises as children participate in the mathematical practices established by the classroom community. For example, it is apparent that the goals the children attempted to achieve emerged in the course of their participation in these practices (cf. Saxe, 1991a). Further, what counted as a problem, a solution, and an explanation were highly normative (Yackel & Cobb, 1993; Solomon, 1989). Thus, both the process of individual construction and its products, increasingly sophisticated mathematical ways of knowing, were social through and through. Conversely, it can be argued that classroom mathematical practices were cognitive through and through in that they emerged as the teacher and students coordinated their individual constructive activities. This is, of course, but another way of saying that individual students' mathematical activity and the classroom microculture were reflexively related.

3. THE INDIVIDUAL AND THE SOCIAL

In the course of the discussion, we have identified several basic differences between constructivist and Soviet activity theory perspectives on development. Constructivists locate the mind in the head, whereas activity theorists locate it in the individual-in-social-action. Further, activity theorists give primacy to social and cultural processes, whereas constructivists typically argue that these and individual psychological processes are reflexively related, with neither having primacy over the other. In addition, the two groups of theorists differ on the role that cultural tools such as mathematical symbols play in cultural development. Constructivists argue that the meanings of these symbols are negotiated by the classroom community, whereas activity theorists contend that they serve as carriers of mathematical meanings from one generation to the next. In general, activity theorists seek to explain how participation in pre-established social and cultural practices influences the development of individual activity, whereas constructivists seek to explain how individuals reorganize their activity as they participate in the constitution of the social and cultural practices of the local community.

We gain a deeper appreciation for the two perspectives when we consider the problems and concerns that motivate them. Vygotsky, for his part, was concerned with the problems of cultural diversity and change from the outset, and it was within this setting that he framed psychological issues. In particular, he seems to have been committed to the notion of "the new socialist man" and viewed education as a primary means of bringing about this change in Soviet society (van der Veer & Valsiner, 1991). Further, much of his research focused on differences in the activity of members of different cultural groups in the Soviet Union. The vantage point from which he analyzed psychological development therefore appears to be that of an observer located outside the cultural group. From this point of view, thought and activity within a cultural group appear to be relatively homogeneous when compared with the differences across groups. Additionally, intellectual culture appears to be pre-given from this perspective. This in turn makes it reasonable to account for development in terms of children's inclusion in established social practices.

Although Leont'ev modified Vygotsky's theory in several significant respects, both he and Davydov followed Vygotsky in attempting to account for development from an outside observer's perspective. In contrast, constructivists approach psychological development from the vantage point of an observer located inside the cultural group. From this perspective, the emphasis is on the heterogeneity of thought and activity within the group. Further, culture is considered to be dynamic, and is treated as an activity that people participate in, rather than something that they appropriate. In addition, the notion that children are included in pre-existing cultural practices is displaced by the contention that they actively contribute to the establishment of the social practices that constitute their social realities. This in turn makes it reasonable to account for psychological development in terms of individual self-organization that occurs while participating in the practices of a local community.

In the remaining pages of this chapter, we will take a pragmatic approach and consider what the two general perspectives might have to offer with respect to problems and issues in mathematics education. As the reader has doubtless already discerned, we contend that the insider's perspective offered by constructivism is more useful when accounting for learning and teaching at the classroom level. In addition, we suggest that instructional approaches developed within the constructivist perspective are more compatible with recent reform recommendations. Nonetheless, we also believe that some of the central notions of activity theory might also be relevant in an era of reform that is both concerned with the restructuring of the school and takes the issue of diversity seriously. Below, we consider each of these issues in turn.

3.1 Individual construction and social acculturation

Activity theory's emphasis on social processes implies that social action drives individual thought, and that children who engage in these actions are pursuing objective goals and construing objects and events in specific ways. Kozulin (1990) observes that these assumptions lead to three difficulties. First, Leont'ev and other activity theorists have not been able to explain what Kozulin terms the phenomenon of individualization (i.e., the process by which individuals develop their own at least partly idiosyncratic concepts). Second, the results of empirical investigations make it "clear that a subject's performance of the relevant activity does not guarantee his or her conscious control over the dependent cognitive processes" (Kozulin, 1990, p. 250). This, of course, calls into question one of the basic tenets of Soviet activity theory. Third,

by rejecting semiotic mediation and by insisting on the dominant role of practical actions Leont'ev forced himself to elaborate the connection between the Marxist categories of production and objectivation, and the psychological category of action. This task was not an easy one by any standard. Even the most sophisticated of Western Marxists...were remarkably unsuccessful in depicting the positive creative aspects of human action as conditioned by a social system (Kozulin, 1990, pp. 251-252).

This lack of success is particularly significant given that most mathematics educators value creativity and consider it a highly desirable feature of children's mathematical activity in school.

In contrast to activity theorists' emphasis on social action, constructivists stress both individual and social processes, and argue that neither should be given priority over the other. From this perspective, the educational task is not that of leading children to isolate their pre-given mathematical inheritance. Instead, it is to guide both the development of individual children's thinking and the evolution of classroom mathematical practices so that they become increasingly compatible with those of wider society. Further, mathematics is considered to be dynamic and to have the characteristics of a forum. This in turn implies that

education, if it is to prepare the young for life as lived, should also partake of the spirit of a forum, of negotiation, of recreating of meaning. But this conclusion runs counter to traditions of pedagogy that drive for another time, another interpretation of culture, another conception of authority— one that looked at the process of education as a *transmission* of knowledge and values by those who knew more *to* those who knew less and knew it less expertly (Bruner, 1986, p. 123; italics in original).

Thus, in contrast to an emphasis on acquiring the "accumulative experience of mankind" that stands apart from the child, the classroom has to be organized like a living culture, providing chance and challenge for active participation, in order [for the child] to become a knowing and responsible member. Thus the accentuation shifts from truth to self-organization, from building the "ideal" to the processes of relative improvement and related self-control from authority to viability, and from conscious activity to active participation in a culture (Bauersfeld, 1990, p. 14).

An activity theorist might object that in focusing on the emerging systems of meaning in the classroom, constructivists ignore the established practices of wider society. However, as Gravemeijer (1993) notes, the cultural tools metaphor used by sociocultural theorists implies a top-down approach in which signs and symbols are treated as pre-given tools that can be imported into the classroom. In contrast, the notion of symbolizing advanced in this chapter implies a bottom-up approach in which taken-as-shared ways of using symbols grow out of children's activity with the teacher's guidance. Here, mathematical learning is viewed as both a process of active individual construction and a process of acculturation. We note that this characterization of learning is consistent with a tension many mathematics teachers experience in the course of their classroom practice. Lampert (1985) expresses this tension succinctly when she says that teaching

is an argument between opposing tendencies within oneself in which neither side can come out the winner. From this perspective, my job would involve the tension between...pushing students to achieve and providing a comfortable learning environment, between covering the curriculum and attending to individual understanding (p. 183).

We conclude that a constructivist perspective is generally of greater relevance to teachers than one based on activity theory when they attempt to cope with their competing and often conflicting agendas.

3.2 School mathematics and inquiry mathematics

Throughout our discussion of constructivism, we have spoken of the goal of acculturating children into the mathematical practices of wider society. However, this is not strictly correct even when we restrict ourselves to the central topics of elementary school mathematics. To see why this is the case, we again refer to Lave's (1988) investigation of mathematical activity in different social situations. Lave's analysis of adult shoppers' activity in a supermarket indicates that they used informal methods to make price comparisons between two or more similar products. In doing so, they identified the product that was the best buy 97% of the time. Lave also asked the shoppers to solve similar problems in a simulated school-worksheet situation. Here, the shoppers attempted to use the formal school-taught algorithms and arrived at the correct answer only about 60% of the time. When Lave questioned the shoppers about their various methods, they were actually apologetic about the informal methods they had used to solve problems in the supermarket. It became apparent they believed they were being objective and fully rational only when they used the universally-applicable school-taught algorithms. Lave labels these beliefs the "folk beliefs" about mathematics. She concludes that these beliefs are generally taken-as-shared in wider society, and argues that school mathematics instruction in the United States serves to induct successive generations of students into this interpretive stance.

Analyses that we have conducted of social interactions in traditional American classrooms support Lave's conclusions (Cobb, Wood, Yackel, & McNeal, 1992). Further, there appear to be profound differences between the classroom microcultures established in these traditional classrooms, and in classrooms that are compatible with recent American reform recommendations (e.g., National Council of Teachers of Mathematics, 1989,1991). We have previously followed Richards' (1991) example, and called the microcultures established in these two types of classrooms the school mathematics tradition and the classroom mathematics tradition respectively. Current reform proposals which recommend that teachers guide the development of inquiry mathematics traditions in their classrooms are, in effect, asking them to challenge folk beliefs about mathematics that are deeply ingrained both in the school as a social institution, and in wider society. Thus, in contrast to their traditional role of supporting students' acculturation into the mathematical practices institutionalized by wider society, teachers are being asked to help revolutionize those practices. The challenge that faces them is therefore that of acculturating children into the mathematical practices of wider society as we would like them to be, rather than into the practices as they currently are. Seen in this light, recent recommendations for mathematics education reform in the United States are indeed radical. The distinction that we have made between the school mathematics and the inquiry mathematics traditions also enables us to further clarify instructional approaches developed within Soviet activity theory. Davydov contrasts exposition and investigation, and argues in favor of an instructional approach that involves mathematical exposition and the ascent from the abstract to the concrete. Richards (1991) makes a distinction analogous to that between investigation and exposition when he explains what it means by the terms "research mathematics" and "journal mathematics":

Research Math—the spoken mathematics of the professional mathematician and scientist...The mathematical research community discourse is structured according to a "logic of discovery" stressing the actions of making conjectures and refutations. The characteristics that distinguish mathematicians from other research communities is their subtle reliance on notions regarding the nature of proof (p. 15);

Journal Math—the language of mathematical publications and papers. The emphasis is on formal communication, at a distance or across time, where there is no opportunity to clarify ambiguities. This language is very different from the spoken language of the community, that is, it is very different from the logic of discovery. Papers and publications are based on a "reconstructed logic" (p. 15-16).

Exposition, as Davydov defines it, seems to correspond to Richards' journal math, and investigation to research math. Thus, reformers, in emphasizing inquiry, and Davydov, in emphasizing exposition, are focusing on different aspects of the mathematician's activity. In this regard, Richards notes that

journal articles, with their dependence on "reconstructed logic," are designed to transfer information to a community that has already accepted many propositions and constructed a great deal of mathematics. This is useless for students who are faced with the need to make these presuppositions and to construct mathematics for themselves (p. 16).

These presuppositions and prior constructions are what we previously called background understandings. From the constructivist perspective, this expositional approach of traditional school mathematics is inappropriate because children are not already members of a community that communicates by a means analogous to journal mathematics.

It will be recalled that in arguing for an expositional approach, Davydov takes mathematicians to be the custodians of the intellectual culture that children are to appropriate. In this regard, we note that in the view of two practicing mathematicians, Davis and Hersh, "mathematicians know they are studying an objective reality. To an outsider, they seemed to be engaged in an esoteric communication with themselves and a small group of friends" (pp. 43-44). As we have seen, Davydov focuses on this esoteric communication and attaches particular significance to the results of mathematicians' creative activity as stated in journals in the form of equations, literal symbols, and so forth. In contrast, the teacher and children in an inquiry mathematics classroom elaborate a taken-as-shared mathematical reality—they know they are studying an objective reality. It would therefore seem that constructivism has more to offer than activity theory if we want students' mathematical activity in school to bear some resemblance to mathematical activity as mathematicians themselves understand it.

3.2 Reform in mathematics education

Reform in mathematics education can be conceptualized both in terms of changes in instructional practices at the classroom level, and in terms of cultural changes at the broader societal level. In the previous section, we argued that a constructivist perspective is generally more useful when we deal with problems and issues at the classroom level. However, perspectives derived from activity theory appear to have greater utility when we consider the broader sociopolitical setting of reform. In this regard, it can be recalled that Vygotsky's analysis of psychological development was motivated at least in part by an interest in the issues of cultural diversity and change. This outsider's perspective on cultural activity is also inherent in Leont'ev's contention that individual actions are elements of a broader social action system. Thus, in Leont'ev's view, the teachers' and students' actions in the classroom are elements of the social action system of formal schooling at the school district and societal levels. An analysis of teachers' and students' actions conducted along these lines therefore serves to locate them within a socially and institutionally defined setting (Wertsch, 1985).

We can best illustrate the pragmatic relevance of this broader perspective by briefly recounting a sequence of events that occurred in the course of our own work with approximately thirty teachers in one school district. It appears that, for the most part, these teachers significantly modified their teaching practices in the course of their induction into our project. Further, our analyses indicate that their interactions with their students in their classrooms were the primary situations in which they learned (Cobb, Wood, & Yackel, 1990). Thus, change initially began at the classroom level. However, as Dillon (1993) has documented, some members of the governing school board of the school district objected to these changes in mathematics instruction. They seemed to assume without question that it was their right to decide both what mathematics should be taught and which instructional strategies should be used when doing so. The school board's assumption was reasonable in that, in the past, teachers had rarely challenged its pronouncements openly. However, as a consequence of their learning in the classroom, the teachers had become able to justify both their new view of mathematical activity in school and their new instructional practices in terms of the quality of children's learning (Simon, 1993). They therefore believed that they were now more qualified than the school board members to make instructional decisions that directly affected the learning and teaching of mathematics at the classroom level.

During the next two years, there was an ongoing debate between the teachers and the school board as to whose interpretation of the situation was most appropriate. The teachers organized themselves into a support group and set about gathering data and developing arguments to justify their position. Eventually, their interpretations won out in that the school board voted unanimously to allow them to decide how they should teach mathematics.

In this sequence of events, changes that initially occurred at the classroom level within existing institutional arrangements eventually precipitated a reorganization of those arrangements. The teachers, for their part, appeared to modify their conceptions of their own and others' roles in the school and in the school district when they participated in this debate and attempted to explain and justify their classroom practices. Thus, the teachers' participation in the process of change at the school district level precipitated further change at the classroom level. Their classroom practices and the social action system at the school-district and wider-community level therefore appeared to be reflexively related (cf. Lave, 1988a).

It is self-evident that reform in mathematics education will occur only to the extent that teachers individually and collectively modify their instructional practices. It is equally apparent that modifications in institutional arrangements can greatly enhance teachers' efforts to reorganize their pedagogical activity. Such changes might include revising testing and assessment procedures, developing new instructional activities designed to support teaching through inquiry, giving teachers more time to plan, prepare, and reflect on lessons, and creating databases that document children's diverse conceptions and strategies. One can in fact argue with considerable justification that institutional changes of this type are essential if large-scale, self-sustaining reform in mathematics education is to occur. This implies that "the links between dyadic or small-group interactions and the broader socio-cultural system must be recognized and explored" (Minick, 1989a, p. 93). Thus, both individual classroom communities and pedagogical communities established by groups of teachers must be seen as situated within a broader socio-political setting. It is here that the relevance of an activity theory perspective comes to the fore.

4. A CHALLENGE FOR THE FUTURE

In light of the above comments, activity theorists could argue with considerable justification that constructivists have tended to ignore the wider sociopolitical setting of reform in mathematics education. However, from the constructivist perspective, the resolution is not simply to adopt an activity theory perspective intact when conducting analyses beyond the level of the classroom. This is because the relationship between macrosociological phenomena at the level of wider society and microsociological phenomena at the level of small communities is primarily one-way in Leont'ev's theory, with the former dominating the latter. In other words, Leont'ev emphasized the influence of the activity systems that constitute society on both individual actions and the interactions of members of local communities. However, our discussion of the events in the school system in which we worked indicate that it can be productive to view this as a two-way, reflexive relationship. The challenge is therefore to develop a level of discourse that extends beyond the classroom community by finding a rapprochement between constructivism and activity theory. A theoretical advance of this kind would not, of course, provide a recipe or procedure to be followed when attempting to reform mathematics instruction. Instead, an elaboration of the reflexive relationship between macrosociological and microsociological phenomena in an empirically-grounded way would offer a way of looking at and reflecting on specific opportunities for reform. To the extent that such a view becomes taken-as-shared, it would constitute a basis for individual and collective judgment in the ongoing reform process.

REFERENCES

Axel, E. (1992). One developmental line in European Activity Theories. *Quarterly Newsletter of the Laboratory of Comparative Human Cognition, 14*(1), 8-17.
Bakhurst, D. (1988). Activity, consciousness, and communication. *Quarterly Newsletter of the Laboratory of Comparative Human Cognition, 0*, 31-39.
Bauersfeld, H. (1980). Hidden dimensions in the so-called reality of a mathematics classroom. *Educational Studies in Mathematics, 11*, 23-41.
Bauersfeld, H. (1988). Interaction, construction, and knowledge: Alternative perspectives for mathematics education. In T. Cooney & D. Grouws (Eds.), *Effective mathematics teaching* (pp. 29-46). Reston, VA: National Council of Teachers of Mathematics and Lawrence Erlbaum Associates.
Bauersfeld, H. (1990). *Activity theory and radical constructivism—What do they have in common and how do they differ?* Bielefeld, Germany: University of Bielefeld, Institut für Didaktik der Mathematik, Occasional Paper 121.
Bauersfeld, H. (1993). *"Language Games" in the mathematics classroom—Their function and their effects.* Unpublished manuscript, University of Bielefeld, Germany, Institut für Didaktik der Mathematik.
Bernstein, R. J. (1983). *Beyond objectivism and relativism: Science hermeneutics and praxis.* Philadelphia, PA: University of Pennsylvania Press.
Bishop, A. (1985). The social construction of meaning—a significant development for mathematics education? *For the Learning of Mathematics,5*(1), 24-28.
Blumer, H. (1969). *Symbolic interactionism: Perspectives and method.* Englewood Cliffs, NJ: Prentice-Hall.
Brousseau, G. (1985). The crucial role of the didactical contract in the analysis and construction of situations in teaching and learning mathematics. In H. G. Steiner (Ed.), *Theory of mathematics education* (pp. 110-119). Occasional paper 54. Bielefeld, Germany: Institut für Didaktik der Mathematik.
Bruner, J. (1962). *The process of education.* Cambridge, MA: Harvard University Press.

Bruner, J. (1986). *Actual minds, possible worlds.* Cambridge, MA: Harvard University Press.

Cobb, P. (1989). Experiential, cognitive and anthropological perspectives in mathematics education. *For the Learning of Mathematics, 2*(2), 32-42.

Cobb, P., Wood, T., & Yackel, E., (1990). Classrooms as learning environments for teachers and researchers. In R. B. Davis, C. A. Maher, & N. Noddings (Eds.), *Constructivist views on the teaching and learning of mathematics.* Journal for Research in Mathematics Education Monograph No. 4 (pp. 125-146). Reston, VA: National Council of Teachers of Mathematics.

Cobb, P., Wood, T., & Yackel, E. (in press). Discourse, mathematical thinking, and classroom practice. In N. Minick, E. Forman, & A. Stone (Eds.), *Education and mind: Institutional, social and developmental processes.* Oxford: New York University Press.

Cobb, P., Wood, T., Yackel, E., & McNeal, G. (1992). Characteristics of classroom mathematics traditions: An interactional analysis. *American Educational Research Journal, 29,* 573-604.

Cobb, P., Yackel, E., & Wood, T. (1992). A constructivist alternative to the representational view of mind in mathematics education. *Journal for Research in Mathematics Education, 23 ,* 2-33.

Confrey, J. (1991). Steering a course between Vygotsky and Piaget. *Educational Researcher, 20*(8), 28-32.

Davis, P. J., & Hersh, R. (1981). *The mathematical experience.* Boston, MA: Houghton Mifflin.

Davydov, V. V. (1982). The psychological characteristics of the formation of elementary mathematical operations in children. In T. P. Carpenter, J. M. Moser, & T. A. Romberg (Eds.), *Addition and subtraction: A cognitive perspective* (pp. 224-238). Hillsdale, NJ: Lawrence Erlbaum Associates.

Davydov, V. V. (1988a). Problems of developmental teaching (Part I). *Soviet Education, 30*(8), 6-97.

Davydov, V. V. (1988b). Problems of developmental teaching (Part II). *Soviet Education 30*(9), 3-83.

Davydov, V. V. (1990). *Types of generalization in instruction.* Reston, VA: National Council of Teachers of Mathematics.

Davydov, V. V. (1993, April). *The influence of L. S. Vygotsky on educational theory research and practice.* Paper presented at the annual meeting of the American Educational Research Association, Atlanta, GA.

Davydov, V. V., & Markova, A. (1983). A concept of educational activity for school children. *Soviet Psychology, 11*(2), 50-76.

Davydov, V. V., & Radzikhovskii, L. A. (1985). Vygotsky's theory and the activity-oriented approach in psychology. In J. V. Wertsch (Ed.), *Culture communication and cognition: Vygotskian perspectives* (pp. 35-65). New York, NY: Cambridge University Press.

Dillon, D. R. (1993). The wider social context of innovation in mathematics education. In T. Wood, P. Cobb, E. Yackel, & D. Dillon (Eds.), *Rethinking elementary mathematics: Insights and issues* (pp. 71-96). Journal for Research in Mathematics Education Monograph No. 6. Reston, VA: National Council of Teachers of Mathematics.

Ekeland, I. (1988). *Mathematics and the unexpected.* Chicago, IL: University of Chicago Press.

Engels, F. (1925). *Dialektik der Natur.* Berlin, Germany: Dietz Verlag.

Freudenthal, H. (1981). Major problems of mathematics education. *Educational Studies in Mathematics, 12,* 133-150.

Gidden, A. (1984). *The constitution of society.* Berkeley, CA: University of California Press.

Gravemeijer, K. (1990). Context problems and realistic mathematics instruction. In K. Gravemeijer, M. van den Heuvel, & L. Streefland (Eds.), *Contexts. free productions tests and geometry in realistic mathematics education* (pp. 10-32). Utrecht, Netherlands: OW & OC Research Group.

Gravemeijer, K. (1992). *Educational development and developmental research in mathematics education.* Unpublished paper, State University of Utrecht, Freudenthal Institute.

Gravemeijer, K. (1993). *Educational development as a research programme.* Unpublished manuscript, Freudenthal Institute, State University of Utrecht.

Ilyenkov, E. V. (1977). The concept of the ideal. In *Philosophy in the USSR: Problems of dialectal materialism.* Moscow: Progress.

Kozulin, A. (1986). The concept of activity in Soviet psychology: Vygotsky, his disciples and critics. *American Psychologist, 41,* 264-274.

Lampert, M. L. (1985). How do teachers manage to teach? Perspectives on the problems of practice. *Harvard Educational Review, 55,*178-194.

Lave, J. (1988). *Cognition in practice: Mind mathematics and culture in everyday life.* Cambridge, MA: Cambridge University Press.

Lave, J., & Wenger, E. (1991). *Situated learning: Legitimate peripheral participation.* Cambridge, MA: Cambridge University Press.

Lektorsky, V. A. (1984). *Subject object cognition.* Moscow: Progress Publishers.

Leont'ev, A. N. (1965). *Problemy razvitiya psikhiki* [Problems in the development of the mind] (2nd ed.) Moscow: "Mysl."

Leont'ev, A. N. (1978). *Activity. consciousness. and personality.* Englewood Cliffs, NJ: Prentice-Hall.

Leont'ev, A. N. (1981). The problem of activity in psychology. In J. V. Wertsch (Ed.), *The concept of activity in Soviet psychology*. Armonk, NY: Sharpe.

Mamardashvili, M. K (1968). *Formai soderzhanie myshleniya* [Form and content of thought]. Moscow: Vysshaya Shkola.

Marx, K.(1890/1981). *Das Kapital.* Berlin, Germany: Dietz Verlag.

Mason, J. (1989). Mathematical abstraction as the result of a delicate shift of attention. *For the Learning of Mathematics, 2*(2), 2-8.

Mehan, H., & Wood, H. (1975). *The reality of ethnomethodology.* New York, NY: John Wiley.

Minick, N. (1987). The development of Vygotsky's thought; An introduction. In R W. Reiber & A. S. Carton (Eds.), *The collected works of Vygotsky L. S. (vol. 1; Problems of general psychology* (pp. 17-38). New York, NY: Plenum.

Minick, N. (1989a). *L. S. Vygotsky and Soviet activity theory: Perspectives on the relationship between mind and society.* Literacies Institute, Special Monograph Series No. 1. Newton, MA: Educational Development Center, Inc.

Minick, N. (1989b). Mind and activity in Vygotsky's work: An expanded frame of reference. *Cultural Dynamics, 2,* 162-187.

National Council of Teachers of Mathematics (1989). *Curriculum and evaluation standards for school mathematics.* Reston, VA: National Council of Teachers of Mathematics.

National Council of Teachers of Mathematics (1991). *Professional standards for teaching mathematics.* Reston, VA: National Council of Teachers of Mathematics.

Newman, D., Griffin, P., & Cole, M. (1989). *The construction zone: Working for cognitive change in school.* Cambridge, MA: Cambridge University Press.

Piaget, J. (1970). *Genetic epistemology.* New York, NY: Columbia University Press.

Piaget, J. (1980). *Adaptation and intelligence: Organic selection and phenocopy.* Chicago, IL: University of Chicago Press.

Putnam, H. (1987). *The many faces of realism.* LaSalle, IL: Open Court.

Putnam, R. T., Lampert, M., & Peterson, P. L. (1990). Alternative perspectives on knowing mathematics in elementary schools. In C. B. Cazden (Ed.), *Review of research in education* (vol. 16, pp. 57-149). Washington, DC: American Educational Research Association.

Razmyslov, P. (1934). O "Kul'turno-istoricheskoj teorii psikhologii" Vygotskogo i Lurija. *Kniga i Proletarskaja Revoljucija, 4,* 78-86.

Richards, J. (1991). Mathematical discussions. In E. von Glasersfeld (Ed.), *Radical constructivism in mathematics education* (pp. 13-52). Dordrecht, Netherlands: Kluwer.

Rogoff, B. (1990). *Apprenticeship in thinking: Cognitive development in social context.* Oxford, UK: Oxford University Press.

Rorty, R (1978). *Philosophy and the mirror of nature.* Princeton, NJ: Princeton University Press.

Saxe, G. B. (l991a). *Culture and cognitive development: Studies in mathematical understanding.* Hillsdale, NJ: Lawrence Erlbaum Associates.

Saxe, G. B. (l991b, April). *From the field to the classroom: Studies in mathematical understanding.* Paper presented at the annual meeting of the National Council of Teachers of Mathematics, Research Presession, New Orleans, LA.

Scribner, S. (1984). Studying working intelligence. In B. Rogoff & J. Lave (Eds.), *Everyday cognition: Its development in social context* (pp. 9-40). Cambridge, MA: Harvard University Press.

Scribner, S. (1990). Reflections on a model. *Quarterly Newsletter of the Laboratory of Comparative Human Cognition, 12,* 90-94.

Simon, M. (1993). Context for change: Themes related to mathematics education reform. In T. Wood, P. Cobb, E. Yackel, & D. Dillon (Eds.), *Rethinking elementary school mathematics: Insights and issues* (pp. 109-114). Journal for Research in Mathematics Education Monograph No. 6. Reston, VA: National Council of Teachers of Mathematics.

Skemp, R. R. (1976). Relational understanding and instrumental understanding. *Mathematical Teaching, 77,* 1-7.

Solomon, Y. (1989). *The practice of mathematics.* London: Routledge.

Steinbring, H. (1989). Routine and meaning in the mathematics classroom. *For the Learning of Mathematics, 2*(1), 24-33.

Streefland, L. (1991). *Fractions in realistic mathematics education. A paradigm of developmental research.* Dordrecht, Netherlands: Kluwer.

Treffers, A. (1987). *Three dimensions: A model of goal and theory description in mathematics instruc-tion—The Wiskobas Project.* Dordrecht, Netherlands: Reidel.

Treffers, A. (1991). Meeting innumeracy at primary school. *Educational Studies in Mathematics 22,* 333-352.

Tymoczko, T. (Ed.) (1986). *New directions in the philosophy of mathematics.* Boston, MA: Birkhauser.

van der Veer, R., & Valsiner, J. (1991). *Understanding Vygotsky: A quest for synthesis.* Cambridge, MA: Blackwell.

van Oers, B. (1990). The development of mathematical thinking in school: A comparison of the action-psychological and the information-processing approach. *International Journal of Educational Re-search, 14,* 51-66.

van Oers, B. (in press). Learning mathematics as meaningful activity. In P. Nesher, L. Steffe, P. Cobb, G. Goldin, & B. Greer (Eds.), *Theories of mathematical learning.* Hillsdale, NJ: Lawrence Erlbaum Associates.

Voigt, J. (1985). Patterns and routines in classroom interaction. *Recherches en Didactique des Mathematiques, 6,* 69-118.

Voigt, J. (1992, August). *Negotiation of mathematical meaning in classroom processes.* Paper presented at the International Congress on Mathematics Education, Québec City, Canada.

von Glasersfeld, E. (1984). An introduction to radical constructivism. In P. Watzlawick (Ed.), *The in-vented reality* (pp. 17-40). New York, NY: Norton.

von Glasersfeld, E. (1989a). Constructivism. In T. Husen & T. N. Postlethwaite (Eds.), *The Interna-tional Encyclopedia of Education* (1st ed., supplement vol. 1, pp. 162-163). Oxford, UK: Pergamon.

von Glasersfeld, E. (1989b). Cognition, construction of knowledge, and teaching. *Synthèse, 80,* 121-140.

von Glasersfeld, E. (1990). Environment and communication. In L. P. Steffe & T. Wood (Eds.), *Trans-forming children's mathematics education: International perspectives* (pp. 30-38). Hillsdale, NJ: Lawrence Erlbaum Associates.

von Glasersfeld, E. (1992). Constructivism reconstructed: A reply to Suchting. *Science and Education, 1,* 379-384.

Vygotsky, L. S. (1960). *Razvitie vysshikh psikhicheskikh funktsii* [The development of the higher mental functions]. Moscow: Akad. Ped. Nauk. RSFSR.

Vygotsky, L. S. (1979). Consciousness as a problem in the psychology of behavior. *Soviet Psychology, 17*(4), 3-35.

Vygotsky, L. S. (1984). Problema vozrasta [The problem of age]. In D. B. El'konin (Ed.), *L. S. Vygotskii. Sobranie sochinenie: Detskaia psikhologiia (Tom 4)* [L. S. Vygotsky, Collected works: Child psy-chology (Vol. 4)] (pp. 244-268). Moscow: Pedagogika.

Walkerdine, V. (1988). *The mastery of reason.* London, UK: Routledge.

Wertsch, J. V. (1985). *Vygotsky and the social formation of mind.* Cambridge, MA: Harvard University Press.

Wilensky, U. (1991). Abstract meditations on the concrete and concrete implications for mathematics education. In J. Harel & S. Papert (Eds.), *Constructionism* (pp. 193-204). Norwood, NJ: Ablex.

Yackel, E., & Cobb, P. (1993, April). *Sociomath norms argumentation and autonomy in mathematics.* Paper presented at the annual meeting of the American Educational Research Association, Atlanta, GA.

Zinchenko, P. (1983). The problem of involuntary memory. *Soviet Psychology, 22*(2), 34-86.

Paul Cobb
Vanderbilt University

Marcela Perlwitz & Diana Underwood
Purdue University

United States of America

P. RENSHAW

A SOCIOCULTURAL VIEW OF THE MATHEMATICS EDUCATION
OF YOUNG CHILDREN

1. INTRODUCTION

The social origins and inherently social nature of thought has been examined by a number of sociocultural theorists throughout this century (Baldwin, 1899; Dewey, 1899; Vygotsky, 1987). This chapter provides an overview of Vygotsky's writing on conceptual development in young children, and presents and evaluates Davydov's interpretation and application of Vygotsky's theory to the mathematics curriculum for young children. Davydov's (1975b) teaching experiments (designed to show that the abstract representation of the relations of quantity [<, >, =] could be the basis of the early number curriculum), were conducted in the early 1960s, and have been available in English since the mid 1970s. Recent interest in these experiments in the West has been spurred by the view that sociocultural theory offers an innovative framework for the reform and renewal of teaching and learning in schools (Moll, 1990; Tharp & Gallimore, 1989; Forman, 1993). My purpose in presenting an account of Davydov's work is to clarify with reference to the mathematics curriculum some central sociocultural concepts such as: the pseudoconcept as the vehicle for instructional dialogue; appropriation; connecting spontaneous and scientific concepts; and teaching the general before the specific. Some limitations in Davydov's approach are discussed, and the importance of providing various social contexts (teacher directed, collaborative peer interaction, and self-regulated activity) for connecting everyday and scientific concepts is highlighted.

In concluding the chapter, I examine recent attempts to consider the individual as enmeshed in ongoing cultural practices, rather than as a detached repository of knowledge. Specifically, Wertsch's (1991) analysis of Bakhtin's notion of voice suggests that learning involves a process of acquiring voices that are simultaneously personal and social. Wertsch argues that meaning is established in the ongoing dialogue of the community, and retains a dual quality of being both personal and social. The individual must appropriate words from the community in order to be understood, but in giving voice to particular ideas the individual invests the words with traces of personal experience and perspective. I examine teaching episodes from Davydov's teaching experiments, and from Walkerdine (1988) to show how children learn to engage in dialogue with adults using the mathematical voice. To give personal voice to the mathematical perspective, a child will rely initially on the guidance of more expert practitioners in order to flexibly and adaptively participate in classroom discourse. The concept of voices provides a way of considering the interconnections between face-to-face interactions in the classroom and the broader cultural and historical context of education.

H. Mansfield et al. (eds.), Mathematics for Tomorrow's Young Children, 59–78.

2. CONCEPTUAL DEVELOPMENT: VYGOTSKY'S VIEW

Development, examined from the sociocultural perspective, is a process of acquiring cultural tools (various ways of acting, speaking, gesturing, conceptualizing, representing and so on) during joint activities with adults and peers who act as guides and partners in an on-going cultural apprenticeship (Rogoff 1990). Children do more than simply learn from others during social exchanges-the actual tools that allow social interaction to occur such as speech and gesture are internalized by children to form the means for thinking, problem-solving, remembering, and so on (Wertsch 1985).

Vygotsky's examination of the relationship between speaking and thinking provides a compelling illustration of the process of development. As Wertsch (1985) noted, the title of Vygotsky's book, *Thought and Language*, is translated more accurately as *Thinking and Speaking* which captures the notion that thinking arises from engagement with others in activities. In Vygotsky's analysis, the changing functional relationship between speaking and thinking exemplifies the general developmental process where social tools, such as speech and gesture that initially serve social and communicative functions, are transformed into internal tools of thinking and problem solving. The movement from the social plane of functioning to the internal plane of functioning, however, requires active engagement by children in social interaction with peers and supportive adults. During social exchanges, children and their partners employ speech and gesture to regulate joint attention, to conceptualize objects, to integrate experiences, to recall and recast events, to devise plans, and offer explanations. It is the socially situated and functional use of speech during activities that enables children to transform their thinking. As Levina noted, Vygotsky did not claim that speech has some magical power to create intellectual functioning. It acquires this capacity only when it is used in a socially-situated and instrumental capacity (Levina, 1981). The opportunity to use speech, therefore, in collaborative activities with others is central to conceptual development from the sociocultural viewpoint.

2.1 The underlying form of children's concepts

In *Thinking and Speaking* Vygotsky analyzed conceptual development in two separate chapters-five and six (see Minick, 1987, for an account of the evolution of Vygotsky's theorizing). The research reported in chapter five was an effort to unravel the natural, spontaneous line of development from the cultural line[1]. That is, conceptual development was examined using an experimental methodology de-

---

[1] Vygotsky distinguished between two lines of development-the natural line of development and the cultural line of development. This duality is similar to others that he explored such as spontaneous concepts and scientific concepts, or rudimentary mental functions and higher mental functions. These dualities were proposed and examined by Vygotsky to demonstrate that progress in thinking involved the transformation and interpenetration of more natural, spontaneous and elementary processes by the cultural, abstract, and organized processes.

signed specifically to reveal the form of children's concepts when studied in isolation from the influence of adult speech and actions. Vygotsky argued that in everyday activities, children's concepts are impossible to examine independently of the determining cultural influence of the speech and actions of others. In summarizing the nature of children's concepts as revealed in the experimental situation, Vygotsky described three forms: a syncretic form where concepts are based on subjective and shifting criteria of spatial and temporal contingencies; a complexive form where concepts are based on observable and concrete features of objects rather than subjective associations, but nonetheless, complexes are limited in abstraction and generalization and remain inseparable from the specific group of objects to which they are applied; and a mature form where concepts are characterized by the functional use of words in order to isolate and abstract features of objects, as well as synthesize and generalize abstracted features across contexts. Although these three forms of concepts increase in abstraction and generalization, Vygotsky did not endorse a stage-sequential theory of conceptual development. The use of concepts by children occurs within everyday activities, where with the assistance of more capable partners, children may apply concepts in quite abstract and general ways prior to gaining conscious awareness or control of concepts. Thus, at a particular point in time, children may engage in various forms of conceptual thinking depending on the effectiveness of the guidance provided by the people with whom the child is communicating.

In chapter five of *Thinking and Speaking* Vygotsky was careful to avoid equating the spoken word with the meaning of a concept. He argued that the underlying meaning of the spoken word varies for individuals depending on their developmental level, experience, and so on. As children speak with adults in the context of ongoing interaction it may appear that they have similar meanings for the words that they employ, however, Vygotsky maintained that the underlying form of thought remains different. Nonetheless, children's thinking is not immune to the influence of the adults' words. Just as an infant's direct physical action of reaching for an object is transformed gradually into the signifying and social action of pointing by the interpretation and response of nearby adults ("Look, she wants the rattle. Is this what you want? Were you pointing at this?), so too children's understanding of the words used in interaction with adults is influenced by the interpretation and significance read into the words by the adults. During on-going dialogues with children, adults will reinterpret, elaborate, and provide broader contexts for children's ideas. In this way, speech, employed as a means of coordinating attention and interaction during activities with more capable members of the culture, gradually transforms the concepts of children

2.2 The pseudoconcept: A vehicle for instructional dialogue

An important form of concept discussed by Vygotsky in chapter five is the pseudoconcept which he saw as characterizing the thinking of pre-school and elementary school children. The pseudoconcept stands between complexive concepts and the mature form of concepts, and in this intermediate position it creates the

possibility of an on-going dialogue between children and adults, where paradoxi-
cally, misunderstanding can be productive of conceptual change. To explore the
paradox further-during interaction with adults, children begin to use words in a
manner that appears to overlap with adult usage, but in fact, adults understand the
words in a more abstract and general manner than children. Nonetheless, the appearance of a substantially overlapping set of meanings enables the adult and child
to maintain joint attention and collaborate in activities. Vygotsky wrote in this regard,

> The paths through which word meanings are extended or transferred are determined by the people
> around the child in their verbal interaction with him. However, the child cannot immediately learn adult
> modes of thinking. The product he receives is similar to that of the adult. However, it is obtained through
> entirely different intellectual operations. This is what we call a psuedoconcept. In its external form, it
> appears to correspond for all practical purposes with adult word meanings. However, it is profoundly
> different from these word meanings in its internal nature (Vygotsky, 1987, p. 143).

While the pseudoconcept appears to be a mature form of thinking, the underlying
meaning is less abstract and remains bound to specific contexts. Dialogues between adults and children reveal some of the characteristics of the more mature
concepts. This creates tension in children's thinking, and the social conditions con-
ducive for development. That is, the apparent similarity of the pseudoconcept and
the mature concept enables adults to act toward children as if they were further
advanced in understanding a concept than actually is the case. Such misunderstanding
is productive because it reveals to children the underlying structure of their thinking and creates conditions for a more deliberate and reflective application of concepts.

In their recent interpretation and extension of Vygotsky's sociocultural theory,
Newman, Griffin and Cole (1989) applied the idea of productive misunderstanding
to the zone of proximal development. They argued that creating conditions for conceptual change necessarily requires a divergence in understandings. They elaborated their case on the basis of the pervasive indeterminacy of the meaning of speech.
Any word or utterance has a number of meanings, depending not only on the relative levels of development of the communicative partners (as discussed above), but
also on differences in personal experiences, or interpretations of the present situation. To coordinate their actions and regulate joint attention, the child and adult
necessarily speak and act in ways that are responsive to the words and actions of
the other. In such dialogues adults will expand the contributions of children, para-
phrase, reinterpret, and substitute more general concepts for the children's everyday forms of speaking and acting. In this manner, collaborative interaction with
adults enables children to enter into new more abstract and general ways of speaking about, and acting towards objects-that is, it opens up a zone of proximal development. To encapsulate their view of such interaction, Newman Griffin and Cole
(1989) describe the partners as entering into "a strategic fiction"—a space of productive misunderstanding where children are assisted to transform their
pseudoconcepts by the words and actions of more advanced participants.

2.3 Spontaneous and scientific concepts

In chapter six of *Thinking and Speaking*, Vygotsky moved beyond the experimental study of the relationship between the word and the concept, to consider how organized systems of concepts (mathematics, science, literature, and so on) constructed over generations, transform children's everyday concepts. As in chapter five, Vygotsky described conceptual development as an interaction between natural, spontaneous concepts and the organized systems of concepts referred to as "scientific" concepts. He argued that scientific concepts do not simply replace spontaneous concepts during the process of development but in fact build on the existing fabric of children's spontaneous thought. He used the metaphor of growth to describe the reciprocal influence of concepts-scientific concepts growing downward through spontaneous concepts, while spontaneous concepts grow upward through scientific concepts. The two conceptual forms are seen as weaving together, intertwining to produce a form of thinking that is both personal and social-personal in the sense that the abstract concepts are bound into networks of experiences and perceptions that are unique to each person, and social in the sense that individuals are able to understand their own experiences in more general, transcendent, and abstract terms.

The interaction between spontaneous and scientific concepts provides a window through which to view the relationship between education and the conceptual development of children. Vygotsky argued that spontaneous concepts provide the necessary but not sufficient conditions for progress toward more powerful forms of thinking. He saw culture, in this case the systems of abstract concepts incorporated in school curriculum, as being the driving force in development. However, scientific concepts presented to children in general and abstract terms without connection to their concrete, empirical and personal experience must remain empty formalism. On the other hand, spontaneous concepts remain limited in their application and generality without being connected to more systematized concepts. Thus, the education of children requires the creation of social contexts in which there is an optimal mix of scientific and spontaneous concepts. It involves creating contexts of collaborative thinking where everyday concepts are intermeshed with the scientific concepts (Kozulin, 1990). Scientific concepts cannot be appropriated by children in a direct manner, as implied in a transmission model of teaching. A particular social process—effective teaching in the zone of proximal development—is required to weave together a child's everyday concepts with the more abstract scientific concepts.

2.4 The institutional context of conceptual development

The institutional focus in chapter six of *Thinking and Speaking*, (though only sketched by Vygotsky) provides a way of locating children's conceptual development within local communities of face to face interaction-their families, their peer group, and their classrooms. The classroom, as distinct from the other settings, is organized purposefully to promote conceptual development within specific domains of knowledge. In the optimal case, the classroom is an activity setting where patterns of speech, conventions for representing concepts, forms of argumentation, procedures for gathering and sifting evidence, and so on, provide the immediate context in which children learn how to participate in the cultural practices of the wider community of mathematicians, scientists, writers, etc. Teachers are placed in a powerful mediating role, therefore, between children and the wider community of practitioners. The conceptual development of children will depend in large measure on teachers' level of knowledge of the domain, their understanding of children's everyday patterns of thinking, and their capacity to create dialogues with children in which everyday forms of speaking and acting are woven together with those of the wider community of practitioners.

2.5 Relevance of Vygotsky's theory to Davydov's early mathematics curriculum

Two ideas explored above, the pseudoconcept, and weaving together of spontaneous and scientific concepts, are particularly relevant when examining and evaluating Davydov's application of sociocultural theory to the mathematics curriculum for young children. First, the pseudoconcept is positioned between immature and mature concepts-a position which is crucial in creating the possibility of productive instructional dialogues. As shown below, Davydov's teaching experiments included episodes where pseudoconcepts mediated teacher student dialogues. That is, particular ways of representing mathematical relationships were devised that could be interpreted either in concrete or more abstract terms, and this ambiguity enabled teachers to assist children to move toward a more abstract understanding of mathematical relations. Second, weaving together spontaneous and scientific concepts is crucial for ensuring that concepts acquired in classrooms are not simply abstract formalisms. Vygotsky emphasized the necessity for building mathematical concepts on the fabric of the children's existing forms of speaking, representing, and conceptualizing. Davydov designed the teaching experiments to begin with children's existing concepts but his major goal was to demonstrate that even young children could work with quite abstract representations of quantitative relationships. A rapid progression in the level of abstraction and generalization was required of children over the course of Davydov's teaching experiments, so that eventually under the guidance of their teachers, children were working with algebraic formulas. We must ask, therefore, whether the children maintained a secure understanding of the quantitative relationships as they began working with the abstract representations-in short, whether the optimal mix of spontaneous and scientific concepts was maintained.

3. DAVYDOV'S INTERPRETATION OF SOCIOCULTURAL THEORY

Davydov (1975a, 1975b) developed an educational program based on his interpretation of sociocultural theory, an interpretation influenced by Leont'ev, El'konin and Gal'perin, in addition to the seminal writings of Vygotsky (see El'konin & Davydov, 1975). Davydov emphasized in particular the central role of the content of the curriculum in determining the child's intellectual development. His concern with curriculum content, (which reflects the influence of chapter six of Vygotsky's *Thinking and Speaking*) arose as part of a research endeavor during the 1960s to reform the elementary mathematics curriculum in the Soviet Union. There were parallel movements in the West, with Bruner's claim, that the fundamental concepts of academic subjects could be taught in some authentic manner to even very young children, being positively though not fully endorsed by Davydov (1975a).

For Davydov, the setting-up of a curriculum in elementary mathematics, required three types of analysis-logical, psychological, and pedagogical. Logical analysis was carried out to identify the fundamental mathematics concepts that could provide the basis for elaborating in a systematic manner a variety of mathematical concepts. He argued, however, that logical analysis should not be carried out independently of psychological and pedagogical considerations because mathematical concepts have to be made amenable to interpretation within the children's existing concepts, and teaching materials and procedures have to be devised to actually link the mathematical concepts with the children's existing concepts.

3.1 Number and the relations of quantity

The teaching experiments conducted by Davydov (1975b) explored how a mathematics curriculum could be established on the central concept of the relations of quantity (less than <, greater than >, and equal to =). This is in line with Vygotsky's view that instruction should begin with the natural arithmetical endowment of the child. Vygotsky wrote

The first stage in the child's arithmetic ability is formed by the natural arithmetical endowment of the child, that is, his operation of quantities before he knows how to count. We include here the immediate conception of quantity, the comparison of greater and smaller groups, the distribution into single objects where it is necessary to divide, etc. (Vygotsky, 1929, p. 428).

Davydov maintained, however, that progress in mathematical thinking involved building a more abstract understanding of quantitative relations, and representing these relations in algebraic form, since such an abstract and general form of representation enabled a smooth transition to be made to the operations of addition and subtraction even before children applied their knowledge of counting to such operations. That is, children could be made aware of the inverse nature of addition and subtraction by considering how quantities can be made equal, as in the following example where equality can be achieved by either adding or subtracting a specific amount-d.

$$c > b$$
$$c = b + d$$
$$b = c - d$$

Furthermore, work by Minskaya (1975) demonstrated that an understanding of the relations of quantity could be used to introduce both whole numbers and fractions to children. The notion of number (n) was represented as a quantity (K) divided by a unit of measure (a) -

$$n \quad = \quad \frac{K}{a} \quad = \quad \frac{\text{Some Quantity}}{\text{Unit of Measure}}$$

This conceptualization of number facilitates the use of concrete materials to demonstrate that number varies according to the unit of measurement that is employed, and that at times some portion of the unit of measurement will be left over when a quantity is measured with that unit-that is, children work from the beginning with whole numbers and fractions.

3.2 Teaching the general before the specific

Teaching was viewed as a predominantly top-down process-the general and abstract concepts enable the learner to reassess their empirical and concrete experiences. Davydov wrote in this regard,

Succeeding in making the particular visible through the general is a characteristic feature of the kind of academic subject which awakens and develops the child's ability to think theoretically... (Davydov, 1975b, p. 204).

This reversal of the common-sense assumption that higher-order thinking must be built by mastering lower-order procedures, is reflected also in the work of Newman Griffin and Cole (1989). In working with children on division and multiplication problems, they found that those who experienced most difficulty with division seemed to lack an understanding of the functional significance of the multiplication facts. For some children, confronting the division algorithm organized the multiplication facts for the first time, according to Newman et al, giving them a clear functional significance. They suggested a re-ordering of curriculum content where higher level actions (concepts) are taught prior to lower level operations (Newman, Griffin & Cole, 1989, p.155).

Davydov's logical analysis to identify the fundamental quantitative nature of number has not received universal endorsement. What is important to highlight, however, is not his conclusion but his general approach to the issue. He sought to build the curriculum from a few central abstract concepts that could be appropriated by children in a form that connected to their "natural arithmetical endowment." Davydov emphasized that appropriation was not "in place" of development nor simply "alongside" development. Appropriation was seen as the process of development, but only when it involved the grasp of general concepts. Davydov's preoccupation with identifying the fundamental concepts in mathematics was based on his conviction that development cannot occur by the appropriation of any set of cultural tools-only by the appropriation of general and systematized concepts, he argued, could new opportunities for conceptual growth be created.

4. THE TEACHING EXPERIMENTS OF DAVYDOV

Davydov's (1975b) teaching experiments involved working closely with teachers and groups of children to devise materials, activities and collaborative tasks that would assist children to form an abstract understanding of the notion of number. Children began by making simple quantitative judgments of features of concrete objects and progressed to more general and abstract representations of quantitative relations. In examining the transcripts of the teaching episodes and the general design of the programme, a number of characteristics can be discerned that are consistent with a sociocultural approach to teaching.

4.1 Connecting spontaneous and mathematical concepts

Appropriation of mathematical concepts cannot occur automatically-a teaching process that builds connections between the everyday and scientific concepts is required. The teaching programme of Davydov engaged children in a series of activities that required comparison of quantities, or the construction of quantitative relations of equality and inequality with regard to common objects. These activities were within the children's capabilities, and they could use familiar comparative terms such as shorter, thicker or heavier to describe the relations that they had constructed. Teachers opened up a zone of growth (ZPD) for these children by showing that all their various comparisons involving different features of the common objects could be represented by drawings of increasing abstraction and ultimately by the symbols ">" "<" or "=." Attempts were made throughout the teaching experiments to ensure that the symbols were imbued with personal meaning, by gradually increasing the level of abstraction required of the children both in terms of their language and the drawings they used to represent quantitative relations. The actual procedures used in the teaching programme to connect the everyday and the mathematical concepts are described below.

4.2 Teaching strategies used to connect everyday and mathematical concepts

Children were guided by leading questions to use speech to conceptualize their experiences in more abstract and precise terms. The teachers often asked children to expand and clarify their thoughts -

What might you say? How can you express that more precisely? What does that mean-heavier? That the black weight weighs less than the white one? The white weight is lighter-how else might you say that?" (Davydov, 1975, pp. 150-151).

The use of leading questions enabled the children to use somewhat more abstract terms to describe their comparisons. Children preferred the comparatives (thicker, larger, heavier, or the same) to the more abstract "less than in width," or "more than in length," "equal in weight." The children's use of comparatives was derived from their everyday conversations, whereas the teacher's purpose was to prepare them to participate in speaking about and representing mathematical ideas. In later episodes, the children have begun to adopt the more abstract speech, as illustrated in the dialogue below.

The pupils raise their hands. The class is animated.

Teacher We won't help him for the time being! Now think.
Misha V (after a short pause) The letters tell me about the length of the pencils - this one and this one.
Teacher Is that all? If the letters tell about the length, then I'll take a pencil of this length-this is A, and one of this length-this is B: What I get is that A is less than B.
Pupils   You can't take those - then you have a different formula.
Misha V We have an equality-there is an equal sign there. We have to take pencils of equal length and then it's right.
Teacher Then what tells about the equality itself?
Pupils   The symbol between the letters - the whole formula.
Teacher Now I'm changing the symbol in my formula to read A is less than B. Can you find objects to show what this means?

The teacher began with the words that the children brought with them into the classroom, and she assisted them by leading questions to employ other words, more precise, more abstract and more general, that could be used in place of their everyday words.

A second strategy used by teachers was staging mistakes. For example, in guiding children to represent unequal weights by drawing lines of different length, a teacher remarked:

Teacher I'll make them the same length, since one of the weights weighs less than the other.
Pupils   (Many of them raise their hands immediately; there is a buzz of astonishment) Not that way. They shouldn't be equal.
Teacher Then what should I do? Can I use lines to show what the weights are like, or not?

The teacher invited the children to take over the decision-making in the lesson, so that to a limited extent they became "the teacher of the teacher." At other times, children compared their representations of equality or inequality, or their choices of objects based on a particular representation, and were required to justify their choices. While less confident children may be inhibited in such public debates, the deliberate staging of mistakes by the teacher prepared the children to accept different answers as a productive part of teaching and learning, and to view each other as collaborators in the activity.

A third strategy was termed clashing. Children were encouraged to compare their representations of quantitative relations. The clashes between the children occurred when they drew lines according to different scales to represent a particular quantitative comparison. For example, equality of weight might be represented

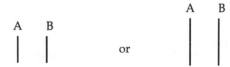

The clashes were managed by the teacher who challenged children to judge which was correct. The discussion revealed to children that each representation was correct since the crucial feature was not the actual length of the line (an empirical and concrete element) but the underlying meaning-that is, the comparative length of the lines which represented quantitative relations. The use of clashing is an example of the way subjective representations are raised to be more objective through social interaction. Each child could draw lines of any length or thickness depending on their preferences for short or long lines, or indeed other visual means of representation. The underlying meaning of the representation, however, remained general and abstract because the crucial feature was the comparative length, not the actual length of the lines.

A fourth strategy was the integration of spoken and visual representation of mathematical concepts. Connecting everyday concepts and mathematical concepts was accomplished in the context of classroom activities where objects were manipulated, selected, grouped, and drawn. In carrying out these overt actions, children were assisted to talk in mathematical ways about their actions and the visual representations of various quantitative relations. Thus, everyday forms of speaking and drawing were incorporated in the teaching-learning activity. The terms used by children to describe quantities were extended to be more precise and general. In addition, children's understanding of visual representation built-up in everyday activities of painting, drawing, cutting out, and so on, was applied to the representation of mathematical concepts. The talk of the children made sense only in the context of the objects and drawings to which they referred. The whole story is told neither by their words alone, nor by their drawings-it is meaningful only by co-referencing the words and the visual representations. Thus, the mathematical talk of the children (guided by the teachers) differed from everyday dialogue-it was not addressed to the other participants in the activity, but rather was directed at the objects and representations. In this sense it has some properties that are similar to private speech, and like such speech it functioned to organize and direct intellectual activity. One could assume also, that just as private speech has been found to decline in the presence of an audience perceived as unwilling to give assistance (Wertsch, 1985), so too mathematical talk requires the maintenance of a supportive classroom community. The children's words and drawings also served the social purpose of conveying to the teacher and to the other children the thinking behind overt actions and thereby provided the social context in which individual concepts could be changed.

4.3 Intermediate means of representing relations of quantity

Davydov's teaching experiments demonstrated also the importance of forms of representation that stand midway between the concrete objects and the abstract relations of quantity. At first the children were encouraged to draw the actual objects being compared, but in such a manner that the feature being compared (such as the height, width, or volume) was emphasized. Later, comparisons of various objects

based on different features, were represented more abstractly using equal or unequal lines to convey the relations of eqality or inequality. The lines are intermediate between concrete and abstract (algebraic) methods of representing quantities
and can be interpreted as equivalent to pseudoconcepts. Visual forms such as the
following were used.

Simple Line Drawing   Geometric Shapes   Everyday Objects

These visual representations are abstract and have a form equivalent to the algebraic representation A < B. At the same time they retain a concrete and empirical
character because the symbols (lines) themselves differ in size. A child may appear
to understand the abstract nature of the representation but remain centered on the
concrete and empirical features of the representation. Such intermediate representations are analogous to pseudoconcepts. For example, at a particular time a child
and teacher may co-ordinate their interactions and productively engage in a teaching-learning episode on the assumption that they have a similar understanding of
the representation. In fact, the teacher may see the intermediate representation in
abstract algebraic terms, while the child is focused on the empirical visual features
of the lines. To encapsulate the notion, one could say that the child is looking back
while the teacher is looking forward in conceptual development.

In Davydov's account of the teaching experiments, he provides evidence that
supports the interpretation that I described above. He noted that one other odd matter should be mentioned. At first some children (as a rule, several in each class)
would record the results of comparisons using letters of different sizes; that is, they
would carry over the principle of using models of the objects as symbols [A > b; c
< D; E = E]*. The teacher would show that this is unnecessary in a formula since
the relationship is indicated by the symbol for inequality (Davydov, 1975b, p.170;
*examples added to the original).

The children's records revealed that their representations of the relations of quantity
retained earlier traces of concreteness, yet it had not prevented them from engaging
productively in teaching episodes, and moving toward a more general and abstract
understanding of the concept. The misunderstandings that surfaced along the way
were windows of opportunity to extend the children's concepts. Teachers acted as if
children's symbolic representations of quantities were equivalent to general algebraic formulae, whereas the children were still tied to some extent to a more concrete understanding of the representations. Nonetheless, within the context of the
instructional dialogue, the teacher was able to move the children progressively toward greater abstraction and generality. It was not the creation of high fidelity or
noiseless communication channels that produced effective teaching and learning
but the intersection of differing perspectives. As Newman et al (1989) note, dialogue in the zone of proximal development is a dialogue not with the past but with
the child's future.

5. REFLECTING ON THE TEACHING EXPERIMENTS

5.1 Encouraging the movement to self-regulation

The teaching strategies identified in Davydov's research included leading questions, staging mistakes, clashing (comparing differences in representations), and integrating spoken and visual representations. In each case the teacher maintained an active guiding role, while the children constructed various representations and joined the teacher in discussing differences in their representations. As children's competence increased we would expect the teachers to loosen their control of the classroom activities and to encourage children to self-regulate and begin to guide the speech and actions of their peers (Tharp & Gallimore, 1988; Rogoff, 1990; Renshaw, 1992b). It is not clear from Davydov's account of the teaching experiments, however, how the movement to self- and peer-regulation was promoted by teachers, nor the classroom procedures that were employed to encourage children to engage in self-directed problem finding and problem solving. In other writing, Davydov has argued that promoting children's self-initiated activity, and ensuring their voluntary participation in social practices, is the goal of effective teaching (Davydov & Markova, 1983). Voluntary engagement and self-regulation in social practices implies that children have imbued the activity with personal meaning. Davydov wrote in this regard,

It is necessary to ascertain and create conditions that will enable activity to acquire personal meaning, to become a source of the person's self-development, and comprehensive development of his personality, and a condition for his entry into social practice (Davydov & Markova, 1983, p. 57).

To enable children to build the personal meaning that Davydov endorses in the quotation above, children should engage in a variety of teacher-directed, peer-directed and self-directed activities at school. Each type of activity creates particular demands and opportunities for conceptual development.

In teacher-directed activities, children are guided to speak about and represent objects in a manner that is more abstract and general than they could achieve alone. As their competence and confidence grows children can be expected to anticipate and play a more active role in such teacher-directed activities. However, if children's engagement in abstract conceptual thinking occurs only when initiated and guided by the teacher, then it has limited scope, application and transformative potential in their lives.

A variety of social partnerships and settings must be provided in schools where mathematical talk and representation are sanctioned (Forman, 1993). To echo Levina's (1981) comment about the instrumental function of speech, mathematical concepts do not have a magical power to transform children's everyday concepts. A variety of situations have to be created where children in collaboration with peers and the teacher can work back and forth between their everyday and their emerging mathematical concepts in proposing solutions to problems. The relevance and application of mathematical concepts to various tasks and settings is not established simply by scaffolding such concepts in teacher-directed classroom activities. The mathematical concepts have to be intermeshed with the children's existing forms of speaking and acting in a variety of activities.

5.2 Peer interaction and self-regulation

In activities with peers in the classroom, children collaborate with (comparative) equals as they employ everyday and mathematical concepts to solve problems. While peer interaction does not demand of children the increased levels of generality and abstraction characteristic of teacher-directed activities, it does provide children with the opportunity to weave together the everyday and the mathematical concepts to create a richer tapestry of personal meaning. In dialogue with teachers the abstract and general are privileged over the experiential and concrete, whereas in interaction with peers, children are more likely to employ everyday terms and examples, to appeal to personal experiences; in short, to operate more confidently and frequently with their spontaneous concepts rather than scientific concepts. Their activity will be influenced by the scientific concepts, however, as children begin gradually and tentatively to incorporate the ways of speaking and representations previously scaffolded by the teacher.

With peers, the goal or direction of on-going interaction is not predetermined by the guiding speech and actions of the teacher. The peer context, therefore, presents new challenges to children-no longer can they rely on teachers to propose plans of action. Children themselves have to assume greater responsibility for monitoring and evaluating the speech and actions of their partners, suggesting alternative courses of action, and justifying their suggestions. In short, they have to assume at times the role of the teacher by employing speech and action to regulate the behaviour of their partners. These episodes place children in new roles in classroom activities that involve the use of speech to regulate their own and their partners' actions. As children consider the appropriateness of their partners' actions according to criteria that are formulated explicitly (for example, "You need to have two equal lines because the weight is the same") they are made more aware of their own thinking processes and more able to reflect on and control those processes.

5.3 Avoiding empty formalism

In this chapter everyday concepts and scientific concepts have been described in terms of opposites-the concrete versus the abstract, the empirical versus the general, the unsystematic and uncoordinated versus the systematic and integrated. Such stark contrasts imply a sudden qualitative shift in conceptual thinking as the former are transformed into the latter under the guidance of the teacher. Such an implication is reinforced by the design of Davydov's teaching experiments, where children were expected to move rapidly from their everyday quantitative judgments expressed in familiar speech and drawings, to the algebraic representation of quantitative relationships. This carries the risk that the mathematical concepts became detached from children's everyday concepts, and as a consequence developed into empty formalisms. Rather than a sudden shift, however, Vygotsky's image of the reciprocal growth of the conceptual forms implies a gradual transformation that occurs during on-going teaching and interaction.

Lampert's (1990) work on connecting classroom mathematical discourse with the discourse of the wider community of mathematicians provides, in my view, an example of educational practice that captures the essence of reciprocal growth. In Lampert's classroom, the teacher's role is to model a mathematical way of knowing rather than to provide answers or demonstrate correct procedures. Children devise solutions to problems posed by the teacher and defend their solutions by appealing to proofs that seem reasonable in the light of previously established classroom practices. Lampert notes that the notion of proof is likely to be quite concrete for elementary-school children:

According to my current pedagogical thinking, what matters is that the seat of authority is not the teacher or the "answer book," but some argument that makes sense to the participants. Often their arguments refer to concrete instantiations of operations to prove that an answer is reasonable, or that a procedure is appropriate (Lampert, 1990, p. 257).

The children in Lampert's class are engaging in mathematical discourse (illustrated by the objective form of their arguments, their appeal to criteria accepted by the group etc.) but their dependence on relatively concrete and empirical examples demonstrates the persistence of everyday forms of conceptualization. This is to be applauded rather than resisted by the teacher because the mix of concrete examples within an abstract form of argumentation seems to provide optimal conditions for personal understanding to develop.

As children reported proofs to their classmates, Lampert intervened at times to re-present their ideas in mathematical notation on the blackboard, and would also offer them conventional mathematical vocabulary to express more succinctly their reasoning. By employing these strategies she translated the children's speech into more abstract and more widely shared forms of "doing mathematics." She also recalled arguments and specific forms of representation previously devised by the class while working on similar problems. These are powerful strategies for gradually establishing a link between children's established concepts (ways of talking about and representing their solutions) and more abstract mathematical concepts, and thereby avoiding the pitfall of teaching empty formalisms

6. CONCLUSION

6.1 Learning to employ the mathematical voice

In extending Vygotsky's analysis of conceptual development, Wertsch (1991) turned to Bakhtin and to the central theoretical concept of voices. Bakhtin's theory of language emphasizes the dialogical, active, situated, and functional nature of language as it is employed by various communities within a particular society. In order to be understood, he maintained, speakers must be able to employ a variety of genres and social languages that are characteristic of particular culturally and historically situated communities of language-users. When one enters into a dialogue, personal voice is given to words that belong to the wider community of users. A person's utterances draw on words from the community of users, so a number of voices can be heard in any utterance- the personal voice of the individual but also traces of the voices of other community members who had previously employed those words to convey their own meanings. It should be noted that the term "words" is used throughout this section to refer to all the communicative means employed by the speakers including verbal and non-verbal means, as well as written, visual and other symbolic forms of communicating.

Wertsch (1991) introduced the insightful metaphor of *renting meaning*. Renting conveys the notion that meaning, rather than being fixed or static, depends on the way speakers employ words in particular settings. Each speaker rents meaning in the sense that they take and give back words to the community of users. Each speaker gives voice not only to his or her own meanings but to meanings that have been implicated in the words by the other voices that have rented those same words. Meaning cannot be fixed, therefore, because it is established in the on-going dialogue between the voices, present and past, that have uttered the same words.

The episodes of teaching reported by Davydov (1976b) illustrate how teachers induct children into employing the voice of mathematics at school. Children commence school with a variety of speech genres that they might call on in order to participate in classroom activities. What the teachers did was to demonstrate a particular way of talking, and encourage children to "ventriloquate" (speaking with) her voice. This can be seen in the following episode:

Pupils	They can be compared by weight (they point to the scales), by height, or by their bottom (they mean the size or area of the base).
Teacher	What might you say?
Pupils	They are unequal (in weight or height).
Teacher	How can you express this more precisely?
Pupils	The black weight is heavier, higher, bigger, thicker than the white one.
Teacher	What does that mean-heavier? That the black weight weighs less than the white one?
Pupils	(They laugh). No, not less, but heavier...It weighs more !
Teacher	The white weight is lighter-how else might you say that?
Pupils	(About half the class raise their hands). The white weight is less, lighter in weight than the black one.

The children initially used comparative terms that were familiar to them, but the teacher's purpose was to prepare them to participate in speaking about and representing mathematical ideas, so she used leading questions (What might you say?) and hints (What does that mean-heavier? That the black weight weighs less than the white one?) to induct children into using the "mathematical voice." In later episodes, the children ventriloquate the teacher as they discuss "having an equality" or choosing pencils "equal in length." The teacher began with the words that the children brought with them, and she assisted the children to begin using a form of speech that was more abstract, analytical and precise.

Walkerdine (1988) provides an analysis of conversations between pre-school children and their mothers in which the mothers can be seen scaffolding the mathematical voice of children. The following transcript of one such conversation shows a mother and her daughter cooperating in choosing cakes for members of the family. The child's participation in the dialogue is guided by both words and other mediational means such as holding up fingers to count out the correct number of cakes. What is interesting in the transcript is the way the mother momentarily adopts the child's voice—ventriloquates the child—in order to direct the child back to the mathematics of the situation. Initially in the dialogue, the child resisted the mathematical voice and seemed momentarily to focus on her desire to eat the cakes ("I'll have them") but the mother reasserts the mathematical voice in a subtle way by using the child's own words ("Well how many's them"):

Mother   Kerry can have two, how many I'm gonna have?
Child   Same as me. I'm gonna have one, two and you're gonna have two.
Mother   Two and Daddy can have three, that right?
Child   I'll have them.
Mother   Well how many's them?
Child   Three.
Mother   Three? Well if you're gonna have two (mother holds up first two fingers) and
          Daddy's gonna have two, (then another two fingers) how many's that?

The mother conveyed to the child that the privileged voice in this activity involved mathematical considerations of counting and adding. The goal of delivering cakes to the family did not require the introduction of the mathematical voice into the dialogue. However, by asking the child how many cakes were needed, the mother transformed the activity. The mediational means privileged by the mother's question is the mathematical voice, that is, it required of the child a particular form of words (one two etc.) and corresponding actions (raising fingers). The concept of privileging is defined by Wertsch (1991) as addressing the organization of mediational means in a hierarchy of status. The hierarchy is not a static structure-it changes across settings, and even in the one setting, it is possible for the participants to introduce extraneous voices, and to move back and forth between voices, as illustrated above.

These dialogues illustrate how the notion of voice might be used to analyze teaching-learning activities. From this perspective, teaching consists of inducting children into particular communities that have shared ways of acting, speaking, and representing objects and experiences. A researcher employing the notion of voices asks questions about: (i) the variety of ways that participants in a classroom can represent their actions and experiences (heterogeneity of voices); (ii) why a particular voice is used in this context (appropriateness); and (iii) the hierarchical organization of voices, or why one voice is preferred over others (value or privilege). Conceptual development from this perspective consists not only of learning to speak with new voices, but learning also to move flexibly between voices in order to maintain communication, and being able to adopt the privileged voice as a means of influencing one's partners.

The notion of voices has promise, also, in helping to explicate the central sociocultural concept of appropriation. Appropriation implies a process of acquiring and storing away various cultural tools in a mental tool kit. Appropriation can be misunderstood, therefore, as endorsing a static, reproductive, and transmissive model of learning that ignores the constructive and creative activity of individuals. When the concept of appropriation is interpreted within Bakhtin's theory, however, it can be seen to be an unfinished and on-going dialogical process. As children are inducted into the communicative practices of a particular classroom, for example the mathematics classroom of Lampert described above, we could describe the event as the children appropriating the words and practices of the teacher and their peers. Yet the children do not have a full grasp of the teacher's meaning, nor an understanding of the words and practices that completely overlaps with that of other practitioners. Rather, appropriation (speaking with the voice of another) enables the student to participate actively as a member of an on-going dialogue that will, over time and contexts, reveal and add to the range of possible meanings of the words and practices of the community. Appropriation, therefore, is never complete. It provides access to the on-going social processes of knowledge production. It enables participants to continue their conversation rather than being an acquisition or end state.

6.2 Synthesizing the individual and the social

Sociocultural theory locates all human activity in particular historical, cultural and institutional contexts. Human endeavor cannot be understood by focusing on the individual in isolation, nor by considering the individual only in face to face interactions with social agents such as parents or teachers. Episodes of teaching and learning need to be analyzed as they articulate with more encompassing social, cultural, and historical factors (Leontiev, 1981; Wertsch, 1985; Renshaw, 1992a). The episodes of teaching that were analyzed in this paper occurred in the context of an educational system that was designed for a specific purpose. In Leontiev's terms, this purpose can be described as the motive-the overriding sociocultural purpose that gives meaning to diverse institutional structures and practices. With regard to schools, it might be assumed that the motive system that gives purpose to classroom activities is "learning for the sake of learning" (Wertsch, Minick, & Arns, 1984). If such a motive system were taken-for-granted, assumed by all participants in a given society, one would predict that institutional resources would be directed at supporting children's learning regardless of their gender, cultural background, or any other characteristic. The motive system of education as it is instantiated in modern societies, however, is a complex and contested notion. In addition to promoting "learning for the sake of learning," schools operate to sort children into categories that influence further education and employment opportunities. Schools also sustain and reproduce social and political privileges that have been structured by social class, ethnicity, gender and so on.

These diverse and conflicting features of the education motive will influence pedagogical practices in all classrooms, to some extent. When teachers scaffold children's mathematical talk and visual representation (voice), they not only extend children's conceptual reasoning, but also induct the children into membership of particular groups in society, and thereby offer new personal identities for the children to accept or reject. To use Wertsch's term of voices, children may hear not only the mathematical voice when the teacher talks, but traces of other voices that, in this particular society and historical period, are associated with that voice. The traces of other voices may indicate that to enter the mathematical conversation one must be male rather than female, or from a high status social or cultural group, or aspire to a particular role in society. To resist or appropriate the mathematics voice, therefore, is not simply a matter of conceptual development, but involves decisions regarding personal identity.

To conclude, what sociocultural theory assists us to achieve, I believe, is some sense of the articulation between the personal and the social, between the individual and the community, between the micro-level processes of face to face interaction in schools and the macro-level practices of the culture. For this reason it is worth further exploration and application.

REFERENCES

Baldwin, J. M. (1899). *Social and ethnical interpretation in mental development: A study in social psychology.* New York: Macmillan.

Davydov, V. V. (1975a). Logical and psychological problems of elementary mathematics as an academic subject. *Soviet Studies in the Psychology of Learning and Teaching Mathematics, 7,* 55-108.

Davydov, V. V. (1975b). The psychological characteristics of the prenumerical period of mathematics instruction. *Soviet Studies in the Psychology of Learning and Teaching Mathematics, 7,* 109-206.

Davydov, V. V. and Markova, A. A. (1983). A concept of educational activity for school children. *Soviet Psychology, 2*(2), 50-76.

Dewey, J. (1899). *School and society.* Chicago, IL: Chicago University Press

El'konin, D. B. & Davydov, V. V. (1975). Learning capacity and age level: Introduction. *Soviet Studies in the Psychology of Learning and Teaching Mathematics, 7,* 1-11.

Forman, E. A. (1993). Forms of participation in classroom practice: Implications for learning mathematics. In E. A. Forman, N. Minick, & C. A. Stone (Eds.), *Contexts for learning: Sociocultural dynamics in children's development.* New York, NY: Oxford University Press

Kozulin, A. (1990). *Vygotsky's psychology: A biography of ideas.* Cambridge, MA: Harvard University Press.

Lampert, M. (1990). Connecting inventions with conventions. In L. P. Steffe & T. Wood (Eds.), *Transforming children's mathematics education: International perspectives,* (pp. 253-265). Hillsdale, NJ: Lawrence Erlbaum Associates.

Leontiev, A. N. (1981). The problem of activity in psychology. In J. V. Wertsch (Ed.), *The concept of activity in Soviet psychology.* Armonk, NY: M. E. Sharpe.

Levina, R. E. (1981). L.S. Vygotsky's ideas about the planning function of speech in children. In J. V. Wertsch (Ed.), *The concept of activity in Soviet psychology.* Armonk, NY: M. E. Sharpe.

Minick, N. (1987). The development of Vygotsky's thought: An introduction. In R. W. Rieber & A. S. Carton (Eds.), *The collected works of L. S. Vygotsky, Volume 1: Problems of general psychology,* (pp. 17-36). New York: Plenum Press.

Minskaya G. I. (1975). Developing the concept of number by means of the relationship of quantities. *Soviet Studies in the Psychology of Learning and Teaching Mathematics 7,* 207-261.

Moll, L. C. (1990). *Vygotsky and education: Instructional implications and applications of sociohistorical psychology.* New York, NY: Cambridge University Press.

Newman, D., Griffin, P., & Cole, M. (1989). *The construction zone: Working for cognitive change in school.* Cambridge, MA: Cambridge University Press.

Renshaw, P. D (1992a). Reflecting on the experimental context: Parents' interpretations of the education motive during teaching episodes. In L. T. Winegar & J. Valsiner (Eds.), *Children development within social contexts: Metatheoretical theoretical and methodological issues.* Hillsdale, NJ: Elbaum.

Renshaw, P. D. (1992b). The reading apprenticeship of preschool children In J. Cullen & J. Williamson (Eds.), *The early years: Policy research, and practice.* Perth, Australia: Meerilinga Young Children's Foundation.

Rogoff, B. (1990). *Apprenticeship in thinking: Cognitive development in social context.* New York, NY: Oxford University Press.

Tharp, R. G., & Gallimore, R. (1988). *Rousing minds to life.* Cambridge, MA: Cambridge University Press.

Vygotsky, L. S. (1929). The problem of the cultural development of the child. *Journal of Genetic Psychology, 36,*, 415-434.

Vygotsky, L. S. (1987). *The collected works of L. S. Vygotsky, Volume 1: Problems of general psychology.* New York, NY: Plenum Press

Walkerdine, V. (1988). *The mastery of reason: Cognitive development and the production of rationality.* London, UK: Routledge.

Wertsch, J. V. (1985). *Vygotsky and the social formation of mind.* Cambridge, MA: Harvard University Press.

Wertsch, J. V. (1991). *Voices of the mind: A sociocultural approach to mediated action.* Cambridge, MA: Harvard University Press.

Wertsch, J. V., Minick, N., & Arns, F. J. (1984). The creation of context in joint problem solving: A cross-cultural study. In B. Rogoff & J. Lave (Eds.), *Everyday cognition.* Cambridge, MA: Harvard University Press.

Peter Renshaw
University of Queensland
Australia

L . P. STEFFE

SOCIAL-CULTURAL APPROACHES IN EARLY CHILDHOOD MATHEMATICS EDUCATION: A DISCUSSION[1]

*Knowledge implies interactions, and we cannot step out of
our domain of interactions, which is closed. We live,
therefore, in a domain of subject-dependent knowledge and
subject-dependent reality (Maturana, 1978, p. 60).*

The caption that I have chosen for my discussion of the papers by Peter Renshaw and Paul Cobb is particularly relevant because it encapsulates much of what I want to say. Both authors emphasize that socio-cultural theory, whatever its form, has come to the fore in early childhood mathematics education. Renshaw provides an excellent overview of Vygotsky's socio-cultural theory and how it has influenced mathematics education at the Academy of Pedagogical Sciences in Moscow, and Cobb provides an equally insightful comparison and contrast of Soviet Activity Theory and social constructivism. Rather than attempt to carry on with comparing and contrasting the two theories, my goal is to bring Piaget's genetic epistemology squarely into sociocultural theory and to explore the consequences of doing so. Piaget based his genetic epistemology on interaction as a hard core principle, so in my view it is unnecessary to keep genetic epistemology and sociocultural theory separate as we create our visions of what early childhood mathematics might be like. In fact, I believe that including Piaget's genetic epistemology in sociocultural theory is especially important in the context of early childhood mathematics education.

1. INTERACTION AS A HARD-CORE PRINCIPLE

My claim that Piaget based his genetic epistemology on interaction already has been made by Piattelli-Palmarini in the Introduction to *Language and Learning: The Debate between Jean Piaget and Noam Chomsky*. In boiling Piaget's genetic epistemology down to its most fundamental hard core statement, he commented that:

These presuppositions lead to a core hypothesis, out of which the entire program of genetic epistemology has been developed. We read the following, italicized in the original text: "Cognitive processes seem, then, to be at one and the same time the outcome of organic autoregulation, reflecting its essential mechanisms, and the most highly differentiated organs of this regulation at the core of interactions with the environment." This I take to be the "hard core" of the Piagetian program, around which a protective belt of strictly psychogenetic hypotheses has been fastened (p. 4).

---

[1] This is a revision of a paper presented in the Plenary Session of ICME-7 Working Group No. 1, Formation of Elementary Mathematical Concepts at the Primary Level.

H. Mansfield et al. (eds.), Mathematics for Tomorrow's Young Children, 79–99.
© 1996 *Kluwer Academic Publishers. Printed in the Netherlands.*

Cobb interprets the influence of Piaget's genetic epistemology as psychological rather than as interactional. In Cobb's (this volume) terms, "...it is possible to distinguish between what might be called psychological and interactionist variants of constructivism" (p. 31), and traces a psychosocial emphasis to the influence of the work of Piaget. This is certainly appropriate, but to acknowledge that Piaget's influence has been mainly psychological does not mean that Piaget did not include interaction as a basic hard core principle in his genetic epistemology. Without interaction, Piaget's theory would be incomprehensible.

1.1 An interpretation of constructivist learning

In an interpretation of constructivist learning, Renshaw (1992) commented that:

In promulgating an active, constructive and creative view of learning, however, the constructivists painted the learner in close-up as a solo player, a lone scientist, a solitary observer, a meaning-maker in a vacuum (p. 91).

In this interpretation, constructivist learning includes interaction, but not social interaction with other human beings. I see at least three possible reasons why constructivist learning is interpreted in this univocal way. The first is that mathematics may be viewed as being innate, a view similar to Chomsky's (1980) view of language as being innate. Among the neo-Vygotskians like Renshaw, however, this assumption would be in conflict with Vygotsky's general genetic law of cultural development. So, it is unlikely that Renshaw would provide an innatist interpretation of constructivist learning.

A second, more plausible reason is the constructivists' view of human beings as self-organizing, self-reproducing, living systems. This second reason, when coupled with the principle of subject-dependent knowledge and reality, may very well lead neo-Vygotskians to interpret constructivist learning as a univocal process. A third reason for the belief that constructivists omit social interaction in their accounts of learning may be a belief that Piaget did not regard social interaction as being essential in genetic epistemology. However, Piaget's work can be legitimately understood as a socio-cultural approach although those who concentrate specifically on social interaction interpret Piaget as taking an almost exclusive biological approach to genetic epistemology (Shotter, 1995).

It has never been clear to me how such an interpretation can survive without being modified to include the social factors that Piaget (1964) regarded as contributing to development.

It seems to me that there are four main factors: first of all, maturation, in the sense of Gessell, since this development is a continuation of the embryogenesis; second, the role of experience, of the effects of the physical environment on the structures of intelligence; third, social transmission in the broad sense (linguistic transmission, education, etc.), and fourth, a factor which is too often neglected but one which seems to me fundamental and even the principal factor. I shall call this the factor of equilibrium or if you prefer it, of self-regulation (p. 10).

Piaget regarded each of these four factors that contribute to development as being by themselves insufficient to explain development. In particular, what he said of the third factor follows.

The third factor is social transmission[2]—linguistic transmission or educational transmission. This factor, once again, is fundamental. I do not deny the role of any one of these factors; they all play a part (p. 13).

It always seems strange to me to read interpretations of the constructing individual that omit social interaction if for no other reason than the early interdisciplinary work that Ernst von Glasersfeld, John Richards, and I engaged in along with Patrick Thompson and Paul Cobb (Steffe, von Glasersfeld, Richards, and Cobb, 1983) was based in part on the results of interactive mathematical communication with children in teaching experiments (Steffe, 1983). My reason for pointing this out is not to somehow defend our early work against Renshaw's implied criticism, nor is it to critique Renshaw's current emphasis on social interaction. Rather, it is to emphasize and to re-establish our view of the constructing individual as a socially interactive being as well as a self-organizing and maturing being. To me, it is crucial that all four factors of development that Piaget identified be included in our model of the learner. But how we include them is just as important as including them in the first place.

1.2 Interaction in genetic epistemology

In a Vygotskian framework, Renshaw (this volume) focuses on interaction in a broad sense of the term: "Vygotsky described conceptual development as an interaction between natural, spontaneous concepts and the organized systems of concepts referred to as 'scientific' concepts (p. 62)." Interaction in this Vygotskian sense is compatible with interaction in Piaget's system. There are important differences, however, that Cobb (this volume, p. 29) has pointed to in quoting Bakhurst's notion of an "outside world." In the case of Davydov's (1975) notion of quantity, we also see a paradigmatic reference to an objective mathematical reality.

mathematical relationships are an objective reality, relationships among things that really exist. The activity of the mind just discovers them, and to the degree that it discovers their content, it itself develops (p. 90).

In Piaget's theory, the individual has access to nothing but its own construction of the object. "External objects" means that the objects are external to the individual's present cycle of operations, but not external to the possible experiential worlds of the individual (von Glasersfeld, 1991).

Interactions of an individual with its environment[3] are in the province of empirical abstraction. It is empirical because its "information is drawn directly from ex-

---

[2] I do not interpret "social transmission", to mean transmission from an impersonal, objective social reality to the individual. Such an interpretation would countermand Piaget's hard core principle of interaction.

[3] By "environment", I refer to the social and cultural environment of an individual as well as to the physical environment.

ternal objects" (Piaget, 1980, p. 89). But whatever is "out there" must be assimilated by the individual.

In order to derive information from an object ... the use of an assimilatory apparatus is indispensable (Piaget, 1980, p. 90).

An assimilatory apparatus for Piaget was endogenic.

We understand by "endogenous" only those structures which are developed by means of the regulations and operations of the subject.... By serving as an assimilatory framework, then, these structures are added to the properties of the external object, but without being extracted from it (p. 80).

In constructivism, then, there are two forms of interaction. The way von Glasersfeld (personal communication) puts it, one is the basic sequence of action and perturbation, and the second is the interaction of constructs in the course of re-presentation or other operations that involve previously constructed items. The first type of interaction can be translated into "individual-environment" interaction, with the proviso that "perturbation" not be understood as the transferal of information from an environment outside of the experiential world of the individual to the individual.

Piaget's notion that assimilatory structures are added to the properties of the external object without being extracted it from might be regarded as standing in contrast to Davydov's notion of an objective mathematical reality that can be discovered. It would be in contrast if the mathematical concepts and operations of one person were thought to be knowable by another person without regard to the assimilatory process of that other person. However, there is a possibility for rapprochement because of Vygotsky's understanding of Piaget's early work and Davydov's functional use of Piaget's work on quantity.

2. TWO VIEWS OF LEARNING

2.1 Learning from a Vygotskian perspective

Renshaw (this volume, p. 60) emphasizes learning as a dynamic cultural apprenticeship, which he further elaborated as a dynamic process of internalization of shared social behavior. Internalization is regarded as more than the social transmission of preformed cultural knowledge. It is to involve the building of bridges, with the assistance of other members of the culture, from personal concepts to cultural concepts. In this perspective, there are top-down and bottom up processes. He discusses Vygotsky's view of the interaction between spontaneous and scientific concepts.

Scientific [non-spontaneous] concepts grow downward through spontaneous concepts; spontaneous concepts grow upward through scientific concepts (Vygotsky, 1986, p. 194).

This view of learning is much more useful than the view of learning as an association between a stimulus and a response as explained by Guthrie (1942). But in Davydov's (1975) work on quantity, there is no account of the quantitative concepts and operations of the child provided except for his interpretation of Piaget's work on children's construction of quantitative concepts and operations. Interestingly enough, Davydov takes Piaget's work as constituting the personal knowledge of children and his formal account of quantity as what the children are to discover.

If we assume that the child's actual mathematical thought develops within the very process which Piaget designates as the formation of operative structures, then these curricula can be introduced much earlier ..., as the child begins to perform concrete operations with a high level of reversibility (p. 91).

This is a beautiful fit with the idea of scientific concepts growing downward through personal concepts and personal concepts growing upward through scientific concepts. It also offers a rather close alliance between the Vygotskian sociocultural approach to mathematics education and a social constructivist approach. A basic difference is in Davydov's assumption that "mathematical relations are an objective reality, relationships among things that really exist."

To illustrate my point more concretely, I appeal to Renshaw's (this volume) discussion of the teaching strategies used by Davydov (1975) in his teaching experiment. One main strategy was to begin with the comparative words that children brought with them into the classroom and then ask leading questions in an attempt to encourage the children to use more precise, more abstract, and more general mathematical words and written terms. In this way, the teacher could access the children's everyday, spontaneous concepts through the use of their natural language. This can be a powerful teaching strategy, and one which I use in my current teaching experiment[4]. Without a model of the children's quantitative concepts, however, the strategy can lead a teacher to stressing relationships among things that "really exist" independently of the children's knowledge.

When a child like Misha V. (Renshaw, This volume, p. 67) says, "The letters tell me about the length of the pencils—this one and this one," it is essential to know, for example, if Misha V. can make indirect length comparisons using an intermediate measuring tool. It is possible for children to use letters A and B to stand for two different pencils and to even write an algebraic form "$A < B$ " to express a direct comparison between them, but not be able to reason transitively. Writing algebraic forms to express length relationships can be a powerful symbolizing process for those children who independently engage in relational reasoning. But for those children who cannot do so, such algebraic forms can not possibly attain the status of *symbols*.

I made essentially the same points in 1975 in an introduction to *Children's Capacity for Learning Mathematics* (Steffe, 1975, p. xv). There, I also suggested that because the authors assumed Piaget's concrete operations, they took quantitative relational reasoning of children as a given and proceeded to unproblematically teach children to express their relational reasoning using more precise mathematical language and algebraic forms. Other than the possibility that some children may not be able to engage in abstract relational reasoning, I find the approach to be like walking over an essentially unexplored terrain under the light of a full moon.

---

4 NSF Project 89-54678 Children's Construction of the Rational Numbers of Arithmetic.

If the children in Davydov's teaching experiment had indeed constructed relational reasoning and what Piaget called extensive quantity, they would be capable of inserting units into re-presentations of the physical objects they regarded as having length (Steffe, 1991). In this case, the children could do more than simply let a letter stand for the unsegmented length of the physical object. The children could also segment a re-presentation of a physical object into smaller but equal sized units and symbolize the unknown numerosity of these equal sized units using a letter. This would be a first step in exploring what essentially remains an unexplored terrain in Davydov's (1975) teaching experiment—the mathematical constructions of the children. A second step would be to realize that the first step is simply a starting point in the constructive itineraries of children. The light of an excellent logical mathematical analysis of quantity served as the beacon of Davydov's work. But this light apparently was not used by Davydov to illuminate the children's constructive possibilities in quantitative reasoning[5].

Davydov's use of Piagetian theory to support his curriculum on quantity to me reveals a very serious issue within sociocultural approaches to education, where learning is viewed as a dynamic cultural apprenticeship. In my readings, rarely have I found an account of the mathematics of the individuals who are doing the learning. If there is a theory of the mathematical concepts and operations of the learner, and I find this to be rather rare; it is borrowed from a closely allied research program in a way that is similar to Davydov's use of Piaget's theory of the quantitative concepts and operations of children. I say this in all due respect for the sociocultural theoreticians and the rather daunting task that they have set for themselves.

Nevertheless, in my view, regarding learning as a dynamic cultural apprenticeship suppresses the personal concepts of the children in favor of the cultural concepts. The children appear as what Maturana (1978) calls *instructable systems* rather than as *self-organizing* systems.

If the state a system adopts as a result of an interaction were specified by the properties of the entity with which it interacts, then the interaction would be an instructive interaction.... all instructable systems would adopt the same state under the same perturbations and would necessarily be indistinguishable to a standard observer (p. 34).

Viewing learning as a dynamic cultural apprenticeship essentially leaves out Piaget's fourth factor contributing to development—autoregulation or equilibration—is equivalent to viewing the learner as an instructable rather than as a self-organizing system.

2.2 Learning in social constructivism

Cobb's (this volume) view of learning is apparently different from Vygotsky's.

Mathematical learning is viewed as both a process of active individual construction and a process of acculturation (p. 61).

---

[5] Of course, it could be said that Davydov did investigate children's possibilities in quantitative reasoning. But he did not explore children's modifications of their spontaneous quantitative reasoning.

This view of learning can be regarded in a way that retains an emphasis on Piaget's genetic epistemology. The most obvious contact is with the idea of conceptual construction, which is at the heart of the basic problem of genetic epistemology as expressed by Piaget (1971).

We can formulate our problem in the following terms: by what means does the human mind go from a state of less sufficient knowledge to a state of higher knowledge? . . . Our problem, from the point of view of psychology and from the point of view of genetic epistemology, is to explain how the transition is made from a lower level of knowledge to a level that is judged to be higher (pp. 12-13).

Any model of knowing that has as its basic problem the explanation of how the transition is made from a lower level of knowledge to a level that is judged to be higher seems to be particularly relevant in mathematics education. Individual-environment interactions as explained above are at the core of such transitions, but they cannot be regarded as *explaining* the transitions. Explanation must reside in a theory of construction.

In addition to the above view of mathematical learning, Cobb (1990, p. 209) also has commented that learning is interactive as well as constructive. His comment leaves open the question of the relations among learning, interaction, and construction. Here, I focus only on the question of the possibility of noninteractive constructions. My argument is that this phrase has no meaning.

Noninteractive constructions might be possible in a view of constructivist learning as painted by Renshaw (1992). However, my claim is that "noninteractive" is an observer's concept. The individual may appear to be not interacting with any observable thing or item, but this is one thing that is meant by the second case of interaction in constructivism—the interaction of constructs in the course of re-presentation or other operations that involve previously constructed items. That is, it is only from an observer's point of view that the constructing individual may not be involved in some form of interaction.

A construction that occurs in the case of "subject-environment" interaction does, of course, involve interaction. So, for me a construction always involves interaction of some type, and this is how I interpret Cobb's comment that learning is interactive as well as constructive (Steffe, 1995).

2.21 Learning as accommodation. In my opinion, we should focus on accommodation as a way of understanding constructivist learning in the context of social interaction and as a way of understanding the concept of construction more generally[6] (Steffe, 1995, 1990; von Glasersfeld, 1980, 1990). The concept of accommodation is powerful enough to explain the modifications that might occur in children's mathematical knowledge as they interact in their environments. It can be used to explain such notions as negotiated and shared meanings, and it can be used to account for the reorganizations that are involved when an individual solves a prob-

---

[6] Not all constructions can be said to constitute learning. I regard the products of an assimilation as a construction, and in so far as the conceptual structures involved in an assimilation are not modified, no learning is involved.

lem. But it is even more inclusive than problem solving, because it accounts for qualitative changes in mental and physical actions, operations, images, and schemes. In fact, it can be used to account for the production of concepts and operations of all kinds. In particular, Cobb (this volume) indicates how it might be useful in understanding communication (p. 31).

Insofar as the processes of accommodation are set in motion through interaction of some type, they are brought forth through the interactions and modify the interactions. The relationship between the two types of interaction in constructivism is clarified by Maturana's (1978) idea of nonintersecting phenomenal domains.

A scientist must distinguish two phenomenal domains when observing a composite unity (a) the phenomenal domain proper to the components of the unity, which is the domain in which all the interactions of the components take place; and (b) the phenomenal domain proper to the unity, which is the domain specified by the interactions of the composite unity as a simple unity (p. 37).

In the case of human interaction, I interpret the first of Maturana's phenomenal domains as compatible with the interaction of constructs in re-presentation or other operations involving previously constructed items and the second as compatible with the basic sequence of action and perturbation. In this, I find a way to interpret Cobb's (this volume) assertion that "This is, of course, but another way of saying that individual students' mathematical activity and the classroom microculture were reflexively related (p. 48)."

2.22 Interaction and construction. If the mathematical concepts and schemes of an individual are regarded as a composite unity, then as an individual interacts in his or her environment, interactions among components of the composite unity may be brought forth and perhaps sustained. In other words, the first form of interaction in constructivism may engender interaction of the second form, which in turn may engender modifications of the interacting components.

Interaction of the second form in constructivism may transpire in the absence of interaction of the first form in immediate experience, but that assumes that there has been a history of the latter type of interaction. In any case, interaction of the second form may yield modifications of the interacting constructs or relations among them, which in turn might modify subsequent interactions of the first form. I am now in a position to discuss Cobb's (this volume) view that:

Individual students are seen as actively contributing to the development of the classroom microculture that both enables and constrains their individual mathematical activities. This reflexive relationship implies not merely that individual and collective mathematical actions are interdependent, but that one literally does not exist without the other (p. 32).

Cobb's view implies that each of Maturana's two nonintersecting phenomenal domains do not exist without the other. In my discussion of these two phenomenal domains, I have already indicated my agreement with this implication of Cobb's view. However, there is a possible divergence in the realization that interactions in the second of Maturana's two phenomenal domains are not causally connected to interactions in the first nor are they causally connected to any particular construction in either domain.

There are two cases of interaction in the second of Maturana's two phenomenal domains of interaction (the sociological) that I now consider, both of which contribute noncausally to children's construction of mathematical operations and schemes. Piaget (1980) regarded the basic mental operations involved in mathematics learning as products of spontaneous development.

Within the space of a few years he (the child) spontaneously reconstructs operations and basic structures of a logico-mathematical nature, without which he would understand nothing of what he will be taught in school... He reinvents for himself, around his seventh year, the concepts of reversibility, transitivity, recursion, reciprocity of relations, class inclusion, conservation of numerical sets, measurements, organization of spatial references (Piaget, 1980, p. 26).

Children certainly do not intend to construct operations and basic structures of a logical mathematical nature. The intentionality of other human beings with regard to children's constructions is not as certain. But I believe that only rarely do other human beings with whom children interact intend for the children to construct operations and structures of a logical mathematical nature. We simply do not know *which* child-adult or child-child interactions are critical in the spontaneous constructive process Piaget identified. That children must interact with others is not at issue, but my opinion is that a majority of those interactions would be classified as "nonmathematical" by most mathematics educators (Sinclair, 1990).

In an epistemology where mathematics is viewed as a product of the functioning of mind, we should not ignore Piaget's third factor contributing to spontaneous development; that is, that human beings construct concepts and operations through their interactions in their physical environments. This realization forms a context for understanding mathematics as being "added to the properties of the external object, but without being extracted from it" (Piaget, 1980, p. 80). For example, to claim that the origins of representational or operative space (Piaget & Inhelder, 1963) can be found in the interactions of children with others has always been incomprehensible to me. Although children do interact with their parents, their siblings, their friends, and others, and these interactions do contribute to their representational or operative space, in my view it is possible for human beings to construct a representational or operative space quite independently of their interactions with others. I would make the same claim for the construction of units and pluralities (von Glasersfeld, 1981). In this, I stress that children construct representational or operative space as well as units and pluralities as a product of their interactions, but in a noncausal way.

I certainly agree with Cobb that the mathematical learning with which we in mathematics education are concerned does transpire in the context of classrooms. In that context, I also agree that individual and collective mathematical actions are interdependent. But, in this, the connections between the two forms of interaction in constructivism seem no more causal to me than in the case of spontaneous development. It is in this noncausal sense that I interpret Cobb's assertion that individual and collective mathematical actions each do not exist without the other. In this view, mathematical teaching and mathematical learning are both problematic.

2.23 Learning as a process of acculturation. So far, I have mainly discussed Cobb's view of learning as a process of active individual construction. In his view of learning as a process of acculturation[7], I believe he is acting as a second-order observer, which is:

the observer's ability through second-order consensuality to operate as external to the situation in which he or she is, and thus be observer of his or her circumstances as an observer (Maturana, 1978, p. 61).

The frames of reference of two or more interacting individuals must be considered in a process of acculturation if Bauersfeld's and Cobb's vision of a classroom culture is to be maintained.

Applying the social constructivist perspective can lead towards an understanding of the classroom process as a kind of "culture," as Bruner has already pointed out. Culture only exists through living interaction among human beings. What is done in the classroom, both by teachers and by students, in its totality constitutes ... the specific culture of this classroom (Bauersfeld, 1995, pp. 156-157).

I interpret the idea of the culture of a classroom as a consensual domain and consider the dynamic relation between the knowledge of children and the knowledge of the teacher. Ackermann (1995) has called this relation the "teacher's dilemma."

How can a teacher give reason to a student (Duckworth, 1987) by appreciating the uniqueness and consistency of her thinking, while, at the same time, giving right to the expert whose views coincide with more advanced ideas in a field (p. 341)?

Without engaging in what Ackermann (1995) called "indirect teaching", the role of the teacher would be limited to regarding children from the point of view of conventional adult knowledge.

As a teacher learns to appreciate her students' views for their own sake, and to understand the deeply organic nature of cognitive development, she can no longer impose outside standards to cover "wrong" answers. She comes to realize that her teaching is not "heard" the way she had anticipated, and that the children's views of the world are more robust than she thought (p. 342).

The four teaching strategies identified by Renshaw (this volume) could be used in indirect teaching, but there would need to be an emphasis on the teacher as a first-order observer. As a first-order observer, the teacher tries to assume the point of view of the learner.

It is not excessive to say that, from a learner's point of view, there are no such things as misconceptions. There are only discrepancies, either between points of view or between a person's activity and some unexpected effects of this activity (Ackermann, 1995, p. 342).

This last quotation from Ackermann may be interpreted as a retreat to Maturana's first phenomenal domain of interaction and to a view of children as lonely voyagers devoid of human interaction. But this interpretation would completely ignore the interactions in Maturana's second phenomenal domain from the point of view of

---

[7] Cobb (personal communication) defines acculturation as the process by which the developing child grows into and becomes increasingly able to participate in the practices of the culture.

the teacher. It is the teacher who decides that, from the learner's point of view, there are no such things as misconceptions.

Because of the noncausality of the actions of a teacher, she is forced to assume a certain ambivalence regarding the interactions in the two domains. For example, regardless of my best attempts to interactively communicate with children, I could never establish interactions that I would consider as sufficient or even necessary for the children with whom I worked to construct one hundred as a unit of ten units of ten. I could never explain whatever successes may have occurred solely on the basis of the experiential interactive communication and always found it necessary to appeal to the children's actions and operations that I could bring forth as their teacher to gain any insight at all into their mathematical education.

However, without establishing rich consensual domains of interactive mathematical communication with children, we adults cannot possibly understand children's mathematics as a dynamic and living subject nor could we understand how to bring it forth.

We literally create the world in which we live by living it. If a distinction is not performed, the entity that this distinction would specify does not exist (Maturana, 1978, p. 61).

Just as children must contribute mathematics to experiential situations to establish them as mathematical situations, we adults must contribute our mathematical concepts and operations to what we observe children do to transform our experience of the children's actions and operations into mathematical actions and operations. I certainly agree with Renshaw (this volume) that, "In everyday activities, children's concepts are impossible to examine independently of the determining cultural influence of the speech and actions of others (p. 60)." Interpreting our experiences of children's actions and operations is a very tricky business, because the adult must create mathematical concepts and operations that she may not attribute to her own mathematical reality.

So, children's mathematical activity forms experiential realities of observers, and what the observers make of these realities is the single most important aspect of education. It is also the single most ignored aspect, which I consider to be unfortunate because what teachers make from children's mathematical activity is precisely where education in mathematics is failing worldwide.

Regarding an observer's constructions of the observed as a result of interacting in both of Maturana's phenomenal domains in part clarifies the crucial role of the teacher's knowledge in children's mathematical constructions. But it does not complete it unless the teacher assumes the role of a second-order observer and makes a distinction between her own mathematical knowledge and her mathematical knowledge of the children whom she is teaching and establishes relations between the two.

The notion of a teacher as a second-order observer, however, involves more than clarifying the relation between adult and child knowledge. It also involves the teacher becoming aware of how she interacts and of the consequences of interacting in a particular way as opposed to some other way. It involves being aware of her own interactional routines, the roles she and the children play in contributing to the constitution of the pattern of interaction, and of the interpretations each makes of the other's contributions to the interaction. In essence, the teacher as a second-order observer is aware of her own activity in interaction, and of the influence this might have on the children's activity.

In this, learning as acculturation takes some perhaps unexpected twists. I agree with Cobb, and presumably with Renshaw because of his emphasis on multiple voices, that as a teacher interacts with her students and as the students interact with one another, a microculture or a culture of the classroom is produced by the recursive interactions. But, I believe that such a microculture is a construction of a second-order observer who abstracts a composite unity that could be referred to as "the culture of the classroom." This abstraction is a very high level of achievement and essentially lies outside of the awareness of the participants in the interactions who retain their status as actors or first-order observers.

Learning as a process of acculturation, then, refers to what the teacher learns as she interacts with children. Defining learning as involving two processes as does Cobb is but an expression of the principle of relativity in radical constructivism, a principle which rejects an hypothesis when it does not hold for two instances together although it may hold for each instance separately (von Foerster, 1984, p. 59). Not only does this principle of relativity take into account the frame of reference of two interacting self-organizing systems, it takes into account the frame of reference of an observer of the interactions, which may be one of the interacting systems observing the occasions of its own observations (a second-order observer).

I find learning as a process of acculturation as I have defined it to be compatible with the idea of learning as a dynamic process of internalization[8] of shared social behavior as emphasized by Renshaw. The point of compatibility resides in my interpretation of internalization in Soviet Activity Theory as being a second-order observer's concept. As pointed out by Confrey (1995, p. 189), Vygotsky argued that it is necessary that everything internal in higher forms was once external; that is, for others it was what it now is for oneself. This statement is that of a second-order observer.

There is a point of incompatibility that seems removable if the neo-Vygotskians would accept the principle of relativity. In an activity theory where action is regarded as an attempt to change some material or mental object from its initial into another form and learning is regarded as a dynamic cultural apprenticeship, or a dynamic process of internalization of shared social behavior, the necessity to include the contextual experience of the theoretician, not in simply applying the theory, but in building living models of the theory, would seem to come to the fore. As it is, the sociocultural theory of Vygotsky and the social constructivism of Bauersfeld and Cobb are incompatible on this point. Social constructivism, as part of Bauersfeld's or Cobb's notion of culture, exists only through the products of living

---

[8] In my view, Cobb's definition is made from the point of view of a second-order observer, because the process he refers to involves both types of interaction in constructivism. For me, it is crucial that acculturation be a part of subject-dependent knowledge and subject-dependent reality.

interaction among human beings and its use is instrumental. Another way to pose the idea is to ask: "If learning is regarded as a process of enculturation, is such an enculturation process involved in learning a living model of sociocultural theory?"

It is critical how this question is answered in mathematics education, because we want to learn what may count as culture in mathematics classrooms, which is how I interpret the work of Bauersfeld and Cobb. Investigators must be actors, first-order observers, and second-order observers to learn what might be possible, because the very process of the creation of classroom cultures stands to radically transform whatever those involved in their production might have originally envisioned. In this, I see the social constructivism of Bauersfeld and Cobb as an open and living model of knowing that is enriched, transformed, and enlarged by the contextual experiences of the theoreticians. It does not simply borrow principles from radical constructivism. Rather, it is constitutively a radical constructivism (von Glasersfeld, 1989).

3. MATHEMATICAL REALITIES OF CHILDREN

My reformulation of learning in social constructivism as being those accommodations that follow on from interacting and of acculturation as what a second-order observer learns, has consequences for sociocultural theory in mathematics education. Its most immediate consequence is in how I understand "the mathematical practice established by the classroom community (Cobb, This volume, p. 35)." In Cobb's view of acculturation, these practices are those into which children are being acculturated and are constantly changing. For me, these dynamic and fluid practices are constructions emerging from children by means of social interaction. To adequately understand them involves distinguishing between first and second order models.

3.1 First and second order models

The distinctions that have been made between first and second order models are based on the principle of relativity as explained by von Foerster (1984). A first order model refers to the subject's knowledge—i.e., the models the observed subject constructs to order, comprehend, and control his or her experience. This level of knowing is fundamentally involved in making second order models—i.e., the models observers may construct of the subject's knowledge in order to explain their observations (their experience) of the observed subject's states and activities (Steffe, von Glasersfeld, Richards, & Cobb, 1983, p. xvi). It is the second order models that involve the principle of relativity because they by necessity involve the frames of reference of both the observer and the observed. They are necessarily constructed through social interaction and are the models of primary concern in mathematics education. One can legitimately say that they are co-constructed by the observer and the observed.

3.2 The Candy Factory

These two types of models help me to understand Cobb's (this volume) discussion of a sample instructional sequence he calls "The Candy Factory." The Candy Factory is:

designed to support children's construction of increasingly sophisticated conceptions of place-value numeration and increasingly efficient paper-and-pencil algorithms for adding three- and four-digit numbers (p. 33).

"Place-value numeration" and "paper-and-pencil algorithms" are certainly conceptions of the designers of The Candy Factory and presumably of the teachers who taught the sequence. But, I assume that the conceptions were not part of the knowledge of the children prior to "instruction" and so consider the conceptions to be part of conventional adult knowledge—first order models. There is indication that the designers of The Candy Factory also included a second order model in its design:

the third graders (eight years old) in the experimental class could interpret a bar of ten unifix cubes as a unit of ten as a consequence of their instructional experiences in experimental second-grade classrooms (p. 33).

Yet, there is no indication of what type of unit of ten was involved. Apparently, the unit types must have varied quite extensively across the children because:

These questions led to genuine mathematical problems for many children, and their explanations reflected significant differences in the conceptual sophistication of their interpretations. For example, some gave purely numerical explanations that indicated they could conceptually coordinate arithmetical units of different ranks. Others gave explanations which indicated that they had to re-present packing activity in order to coordinate arithmetical units. Still others were yet to internalize their activity in this way and actually had to pack or unpack candies in order to find, say, the number of rolls in a case (p. 33).

These distinctions can be called "individual differences" with respect to packing candies in packages of ten. They indicate much more, however, because they point to different operative schemes of the children involving composite units (Steffe, 1992). Regardless of the context of their construction, it is these operative schemes that constitute the mathematics of children.

As Cobb has indicated in the above quote, even when starting with a single instructional activity like his candy factory, the children clearly differentiate themselves in their interactions. This is similar to what Maturana must have been alluding to by his comment that "the physiology of the organism generates its behavior." We should expect children to differentiate themselves in their interactive mathematical communication and I regard it as our goal to abstract the schemes of action and operation of the children that constitute their "psychology." Clearly, these schemes are second-order models.

Teachers who are interested in formulating a model of learning would be interested also in abstracting patterns of interaction among and with children and coordinating them with the mathematics of children so as to form categories or types of interaction. I will for the moment leave open any consideration of what might constitute properties of these categories, but it should be clear that knowledge of how one might interact with children of certain types, including how one might control and monitor those interactions and what the results of those interactions might be currently, retrospectively, and prospectively, would be very useful to a mathematics teacher.

3.3 The mathematics of education

Regarding the mathematical knowledge of children as the mathematics of education rather than conventional adult knowledge has far reaching consequences for educational practice. Rather than starting with concepts like place value numeration and paper and pencil algorithms (a first-order model), the designer would start with a knowledge of the mathematics of children (a second-order model), which includes the constructions that children make as a result of interacting. This shift in understanding of what constitutes the mathematics of education changes mathematics education in the most dramatic way possible. No longer would instructional designers consider paper-and-pencil algorithms or even place value numeration as starting points. Rather, the operative schemes like those children construct when reasoning with composite units would be of primary interest in mathematics teaching. These operative schemes can be modified by children through interaction, social and otherwise, and would be a constitutive part of the mathematical practices established by the classroom community.

The mathematics of children (Cobb & Steffe, 1988; Steffe, 1988) must be learned by teachers and other mathematics educators through interacting with children and constitutes a major aspect of what I envision to be the culture of the classroom. When the teacher's focus is on the mathematical practices that evolve from children's using their schemes of action and operation in a medium, the teacher must learn to participate in the practices of the mathematical culture of children, as well as reciprocally.

The mathematics of children may not make sense when the mathematical meanings and practices institutionalized by a wider society are taken as a point of reference. At appropriate times, however, teachers may encourage legitimate modifications of children's mathematical practice in the direction of place value numeration or paper-and-pencil algorithms, among other conventional topics. The key here is that these conventional topics must be reformulated as second-order models before I would consider them to be part of the mathematics of education. What this means to me is that children would need to *construct* them as reorganizations of powerful schemes involving composite units in a way similar to what Wertheimer (1959) called productive thinking. But we would not expect the products of those constructions to be isomorphic to the conventional adult conceptions nor at the same level of abstraction. Reconstituting the mathematics of education to consist of the mathematics of children respects the hard core principle of Piaget's genetic epistemology as it was stated by Piattelli-Palmarini and casts mathematics education as a developmental as well as sociocultural field.

3.4 Enculturation vs. acculturation

As I have defined acculturation, it is inappropriate to retain the idea of a mathematical apprenticeship because that idea is the result of viewing learning as a process of enculturation. When mathematical practices are produced through the recursive interactions of individual children with respect to *their* mathematics, children serve as *actors* with a great deal of autonomy rather than as *apprentices*.

Casting children as mathematical apprentices is not appealing to me for any one of several reasons. First, it implies that there is a master present whose practices are to be internalized or interiorized, not copied, but reconstituted as one's own practice. This essentially shifts the locus of what is to be learned to the conventional mathematical knowledge of the teacher. It serves to suppress the mathematics of children and the spontaneous ways and means they have of operating. It might also serve to suppress modifications of those spontaneous ways and means of operating into more adequate spontaneous ways and means.

Considering the mathematics to be learned by a group of children as consisting of the mathematics that other children have learned who are like the current children still does not adequately express how I see the relation between the knowledge of the teacher and the knowledge of the children. The teacher needs a starting point, and starting with the mathematics that other children have learned who are like the current children is certainly appropriate. But because children are *self*-organizing rather than instructable systems and because teaching and learning are not causally related, the modifications that children make in their current schemes as a result of interacting with the teacher and with other children may not be what the teacher expected. In these cases, it is the teacher who must learn what the children have learned.

These adaptations by the teacher is one thing that I mean by acculturation. By learning what the children learn, the teacher can chart the children's itineraries of construction and, at the same time, keep a record of what she has learned as a result of teaching. The teacher can continually compare and contrast what she learns about the children's constructions with what else she knows about the mathematical practices of a "wider society", and I use quotations to indicate that I consider a wider society to include what the teacher knows about what other children have learned. Through these comparisons and contrasts, the teacher can make decisions about where she might try to take the children.

If children are considered to be mathematical apprentices, they would not become members of a "mathematical guild" until their practices were sanctioned by their teachers. It would not be the goal of the teachers to learn the spontaneous ways and means of operating mathematically of the children and how those ways and means might be modified through appropriate interactions. Rather, it would be the goal of the teachers to engage in those mathematical practices that they believe their students should learn. In those cases where mathematical practices to be learned are those of other children like the current children, considering the current children as apprentices is still inappropriate because they could at best be retrospectively aware of the modifications they make in their ways and means of operating.

Perhaps my concern about casting the children as mathematical apprentices can be best communicated by an example. Cobb (this volume) cited two children as forming the "equivalence" of 1/2 and 2/4 by cutting up two pizzas, one into two equal parts and one into four equal parts (p. 42). Based on Richard's comment that in the case of the pizza cut into four equal parts, "you'd get two pieces, or you'd get a big half", Cobb commented that:

> The issue of the equivalence of different partitionings emerged naturally in the sense that the question of whether a person would receive the same amount of pizza in each case appeared to be both relevant and personally meaningful to the children (p. 42).

On the face of it, I certainly agree. But other investigators have found that such a comparison can be based on operations that are much lower powered than those operations that are involved in fractional equivalence (Saenz-Ludlow, 1990; Ning, 1992). In fact, there may be substantial differences in the operations of children that enable them to comment as did Richard. The issue here is that if a teacher focused on her own mathematical operations rather than those of the children, she may impute much more to the children than is perhaps warranted. In that case, inappropriate interactions may be initiated by the teacher and the consensual domain of interactions may be ruptured.

Another issue is that even if the teacher had a model of children's reasoning in this consensual area, could Richard understand what such children do or say any better than he might understand what his teacher might do or say? Some would say "yes," but in my experience, children cannot observe more advanced children operate and then intentionally modify their own ways and means of operating so as to be like those of the more advanced children unless they become consciously aware of what the other children are doing. To become consciously aware means that there are sufficient assimilatory mechanisms available which are activated to interpret the actions of the other. In that case, it is possible that the assimilating children would modify their assimilatory mechanisms on the spot, but we should not expect these modifications to be major modifications. In any case, the assimilating children would be involved as both actor and observer. However, there is no guarantee that the modified ways and means of acting could be construed as being at the same level of abstraction as the activity of the other children.

3.5 Realistic mathematics vs. mathematical realities of children

I have been fascinated with the work of the people in the Freudenthal Institute ever since I read Freudenthal's (1973) *Mathematics as an Educational Task*. One thing that has fascinated me is their emphasis on realistic mathematics (Streefland, 1991). One reason that this is fascinating is that it is compatible with my own emphasis on experiential mathematical realities of children, which are *produced* through interactions of either one of the two types in constructivism. That is, an experiential mathematical reality is the result of using one's mathematical schemes of action and operation in a medium. For example, to be regarded as two, a pair of perceptual items must be reconstituted as a composite unit by the acting individual using unitizing and uniting operations. We don't find mathematics *in* realistic situations without *putting it there.*

Because of my belief that mathematics is a contribution of the individual, I have a certain ambivalence regarding experiential situations except that they be of interest to children and that they have the possibilities of engaging children in mathematical activity with a playful orientation (Steffe, & Weigel, 1994). Nevertheless, I believe one of the most important contributions of the sociocultural emphasis in early childhood mathematics education resides in what can be said about the experiential mathematical realities established by children in the context of experiential situations.

Stressing the experiential mathematical realities of children rather than the experiential situations is crucial though, because it brings the experiencing teacher into left center stage in sociocultural approaches to mathematics education. As difficult as it is, it is much easier to formulate experiential situations like The Candy Factory than it is to account for the experiential mathematical realities of the children as they work in The Candy Factory from the point of view of the experiencing teacher.

4. FINAL COMMENTS

What I have just said may seem to be a little unsettling, but children's mathematical realities are second-order models in that they are models of self-organizing systems that an observer constructs as a result of extensive interactions in a consensual domain. It is these second order models that should be of primary concern to us in mathematics education and they clearly differentiate mathematics education from the field of mathematics.

Second-order models are of distinctly different types. Most basic are those models of the children's spontaneous ways and means of operating mathematically and of the children's accommodations of those ways and means. These models become useful to the teacher as she plans experiential situations and situations of learning, and as she contemplates how she might interact with her students using these situations. They are also useful to the teacher in the context of actually interacting with her students. In this, it is important for the teacher to expect to be surprised and to be always on the lookout for novelties in the children's constructions.

Another type of second-order model concerns the teacher as a second-order observer. Ackermann (1995), when speaking of how designers of artifacts proceed, commented that they "focus on how they establish a conversation with their own expression or externalizations ... . They switch roles from being producers to being critics of their own production. Every now and then, they 'stop and think,' removing themselves from messing around with the materials" (pp. 348-349). I think this quotation captures what teachers need to do as second-order observers. Being able to predict the outcomes of interacting in a certain way is a heady experience.

A model of learning should be about a teacher bringing forth, sustaining, and modifying her own interactions with the children she is charged with teaching. Because these interactions are with other individuals, they must include an account of the mathematical activity of those other individuals and how it may or may not change as a result of interacting. The teacher must interpret the mathematical activity of those other individuals with whom she is interacting and control her own interactions in such a way that she may engender predictable modifications in the knowledge of the interacting others. I would not characterize the use of second-order models in mathematics education as either a "top-down" or a "bottom-up" approach because the former emphasizes the knowledge of the teacher, whereas the latter emphasizes the knowledge of the children. Emphasizing the knowledge of the children from the point of view of the teacher includes the frame of reference of both in an interactional way.

How second-order models can be constructed and used in mathematics education is an issue that needs to be dealt with throughout the field. The experience of the theoreticians is a major issue because, returning to the caption that I chose for the paper, knowledge implies interactions, and we cannot step out of our domain of interactions, which is closed. Living in a domain of subject-dependent knowledge and subject-dependent reality applies to researchers just as it does to teachers and to children. This is important to keep in the forefront, because the most essential aspect of claiming to have established a second-order model is that the model exists in a living, experiential form. I have never claimed that the second-order models I have been fortunate enough to establish are to be taken as absolute truths. But because I have found them to be useful and modifiable as I work with children, I have continual confirmation that children's mathematics is indeed a living subject—a human activity—and that it is possible to understand its ontogeny.

REFERENCES

Ackermann, E. (1995). Construction and transference of meaning through form. In L. P. Steffe & J. Gale (Eds.), *Constructivism in education* (pp. 341-354). Hillsdale, NJ: Lawrence Erlbaum, Associates.

Bauersfeld, H. (1995). The structuring of the structures. In L. P. Steffe, & J. Gale (Eds.), *Constructivism in education* (pp. 137-158). Hillsdale, NJ: Lawrence Erlbaum, Associates.

Cobb, P. (this volume). Constructivism and activity theory: A consideration of their similarities and differences as they relate to mathematics education. Vanderbilt University.

Chomsky, N. (1980). On cognitive structures and their development: A reply to Piaget. In M. Piattelli-Palmarini (Ed.), *Language and learning: The debate between Jean Piaget and Noam Chomsky* (pp. 35-54). Cambridge, MA: Harvard University Press.

Confrey, J. (1995). The relationship between radical constructivism and social constructivism.In L. P. Steffe & J. Gale (Eds.), *Constructivism in education* (pp. 185-226). Hillsdale, NJ: Lawrence Erlbaum, Associates.

Davydov, V. V. (1975). Logical and psychological problems of elementary mathematics as an academic subject. In L. P. Steffe (Ed.), *Children's capacity for learning mathematics* (pp. 55-108). Chicago: University of Chicago Press.

Freudenthal, H. (1973). *Mathematics as an educational task.* Dordrecht, Holland: D. Reidel Publishing Company.

Guthrie, E. R. (1942). Conditioning: A theory of learning in terms of stimulus, response, and association. In L. B. Henry (Ed.), *The psychology of learning.* Chicago: University of Chicago Press.

Maturana, H. R. (1978). Biology of language: The epistemology of reality. In G. A. Miller & E. Lenneberg, (Eds.), *Psychology and biology of language and thought: Essays in honor of Eric Lenneberg.* New York: Academic Press.

Ning, T. C. (1992). Children's meanings of fractional number words. Unpublished Doctoral Dissertation, University of Georgia.

Piattelli-Palmarini, M. (1980). How hard is the 'hard core' of a scientific program? In M. Piattelli-Palmarini (Ed.), *Language and learning: The debate between Jean Piaget and Noam Chomsky* (pp. 1-20). Cambridge, MA: Harvard University Press.

Piaget, J. (1962). *Play, dreams, and imitation in childhood.* New York: W. W. Norton & Company.

Piaget, J. (1964). Development and learning. In R. E. Ripple & V. N. Rockcastle (Eds.), *Piaget rediscovered* (pp. 7-20). Cornell University, NY: Ithaca.

Piaget, J. (1971). Genetic epistemology. New York, NY: Columbia University Press.

Piaget, J. (1980). *Adaptation and intelligence.* Chicago, IL: University of Chicago Press.

Piaget, J. & Inhelder, B. (1963). *The child's conception of space.* London: Routledge & Kegan Paul.

Renshaw, P. (this volume). A sociocultural view of the mathematics education of young children.

Renshaw, P. (1992). The psychology of learning and small group work. In *Classroom oral language: Reader.* Geelong, Victoria, Australia: Deakin University Press.

Saenz-Ludlow, A. (1990). Michael: A case study of the role of unitizing operations with natural numbers in the conceptualization of fractions. In G. Booker, P. Cobb, & T. N. de Mendicuti (Eds.), *Proceedings of the fourteenth PME conference.* Mexico City: Program Committee for PME International.

Shotter, J. (1995). In dialogue: Social constructionism and radical constructivism. In L. P. Steffe, & J. Gale (Eds.), *Constructivism in education* (pp. 41-56). Hillsdale, NJ: Lawrence Erlbaum Associates.

Sinclair, H. (1990). Learning: The interactive recreation of knowledge. In L. P. Steffe & T. Wood (Eds.), *Transforming children's mathematics education: International perspectives* (pp. 19-29). Hillsdale, NJ: Lawrence Erlbaum Associates.

Steffe, L. P. (1983). The teaching experiment methodology in a constructivist research program. In M. Zweng, T. Green, J. Kilpatrick, H. Pollak, & M. Suydam, (Eds.), *Proceedings of the fourth international congress on mathematical education.* (pp. 461-471). Boston: Birkhauser.

Steffe, L. P. (1988). Children's construction of number sequences and multiplying schemes. In J. Hiebert & M. Behr (Eds.), *Number concepts and operations in the middle grades* (pp. 119-140). Hillsdale, NJ: Lawrence Erlbaum Associates.

Steffe, L. P. (1991). The learning paradox: A plausible counterexample. In L. P. Steffe (Ed.), *Epistemological foundations of mathematical experience* (pp. 26-44). New York: Springer-Verlag.

Steffe, L. P. (1991). Operations that generate quantity. *Learning and Individual Differences, 3*(1), 61-82.

Steffe, L. P. (1992). Schemes of action and operation involving composite units. *Learning and Individual Differences, 4*(3), 259-309.

Steffe, L. P. (1995). Alternative epistemologies: An educator's perspective. In L. P. Steffe & J. Gale (Eds.), *Constructivism in education* (pp. 489-524). Hillsdale, NJ: Lawrence Erlbaum Associates.

Steffe L. P., & Cobb, P. (1988). *Construction of arithmetical meanings and strategies.* New York: Springer-Verlag.

Steffe, L. P., von Glasersfeld, E., Richards, J., & Cobb, P. (1983). *Children's counting types: Philosophy, theory, and application.* New York, NY: Praeger Scientific.

Steffe, L. P., & Wiegel, H. G. (1994). Cognitive play and mathematical learning in computer microworlds. In P. Cobb (Ed.), *Learning mathematics: Constructivist and interactionist theories of mathematical development* (pp. 7-30). Boston: Kluwer Academic Publishers.

Streefland, L. (1991). *Realistic mathematics education in primary school.* Utrecht University, Netherlands: Freudenthal Institute.

Steier, F. (1995). From universing to conversing: An ecological constructivist approach to learning and multiple description. In L. P. Steffe & J. Gale (Eds.), *Constructivism in education* (pp. 67-84). Hillsdale, NJ: Lawrence Erlbaum Associates.

Treffers, A. (1987). *Three dimensions: A model of goal and theory description in mathematics instruction—The Wiskobas project.* Dordrecht, Netherlands: D. Reidel Publishing Company.

von Foerster, H. (1984). On constructing a reality. In P. Watzlawick (Ed.), *The Invented Reality* (pp. 41-61). New York, NY: W. W. Norton & Company.

von Glasersfeld, E. (1980). The concept of equilibration in a constructivist theory of knowledge. In F. Benseler, P. M. Hejl, & W. K. Köck (Eds.), *Autopoiesis, communication, and society: The theory of autopoietic systems in the social sciences* (pp. 75-86). New York: Campus Verlag.

von Glasersfeld, E. (1981). An attentional model for the conceptual construction of units and number. *Journal for Research in Mathematics Education, 12*(2), 33-96.

von Glasersfeld, E. (1989). Constructivism in education. In T. Husen & N. Postlethwaite (Eds.), *International Encyclopedia of Education* (Supplementary Volume, pp. 162-163). Oxford: Pergamon.

von Glasersfeld, E. (1991). Abstraction, re-presentation, and reflection: An interpretation of experience and Piaget's theory. In L. P. Steffe (Ed.), *Epistemological foundations of mathematical experience* (pp. 45-67). New York: Springer-Verlag.
Vygotsky, L. (1986). *Thought and language.* Cambridge, MA: MIT Press.

L. P. Steffe
University of Georgia,
United States of America.

CONTRIBUTIONS TO PART THREE

Contributors to this section were asked to focus on concept formation, including the factors influencing formation and conceptual change in the mathematical development of children.

Fischbein and Brun present us with strong theoretical developments. Brun begins by acknowledging Vergnaud's (1992) premise of conceptual fields as his starting point and expands on this theory. For Vergnaud, conceptual fields are sets of situations linked by interconnected concepts; it is the child who must construct the interconnections.

Fischbein reviews some earlier work on concept development and then breaks new ground by linking current theories in mathematics education with cognitive psychology—the ideas of prototypicality and fuzzy boundaries that first emerged in the seventies. Briefly put, these ideas indicate that hierarchical classification does not emerge as logically as might be expected from adult perspectives—for example, children see some breeds of dogs as more "doglike" than others!
The other contributors to Part Three first set out their own particular view of concept formation and then give details of specific curriculum approaches based on those views.

The Editors.

THE PSYCHOLOGICAL NATURE OF CONCEPTS

1. INTRODUCTION

There is no commonly accepted definition for the term *concept* in psychology, as with all psychological terms. Some definitions are, simply, unacceptable. "A concept consists of a set of objects, symbols or events (referents) which have been grouped together because they share some common characteristics" (Merril & Wood, 1974, p. 19). A concept is a mental entity, an *idea*.[1] It *cannot* be a group of objects. One may claim that a concept is an idea *representing* a class of objects or events, which is completely different. In classical logic textbooks, a concept was said to be determined by two properties: its extension and its intension (*comprehension* in French). The *extension* is the totality of elements (objects, events, etc.) to which the concept refers. The *intension* is the totality of common, essential properties which characterize the concept. By knowing the intension of a concept we possess the criteria by which we are able to identify those objects which are represented by the concept and distinguish them from those which are not.

A concept is the product of mental conception according to Herron (1983; cf. Hershkowitz, 1989). If we consider the term *conception* as equivalent with *mental production* (in both senses as the act and the product) we do not learn anything specific about the term *concept*. A sensory representation, a solution to a problem, or a theory are all *conceptions*. When is a conception a concept?

A better definition has been given, in my opinion, by the French psychologist H. Piéron in his "Vocabulaire de la Psychologie":

Symbolic representation (almost always verbal) used in the process of abstract thinking and possessing a general significance corresponding to an ensemble of concrete representations with regard to what they have in common (Piéron, 1957, p. 72; my translation).

A more concise definition is that of the Russian psychologist Menchinskaya. "By *concept* we mean a *generalized cognition which reflects the essential properties of objects or of phenomena*" (Menchinskaya, 1969, p.75, emphasis in original; cf. Hershkowitz, 1989, p. 2). In this definition, two main aspects are emphasized: (a) a concept is a generalized cognition; and (b) a concept expresses the essential properties of objects or phenomena. This description is, in my opinion, correct but not sufficient. A physical law like F = ma also represents a general cognition and expresses an essential property (an essential relationship between force, acceleration

---

[1] When dealing with concepts we usually deal with *classes*: categories of objects, events, properties, phenomena. A category is a collection of elements characterized by some common properties. The *idea* representing that category—its potential exemplars and the common properties uniting them - constitutes the concept.

H. Mansfield et al. (eds.), Mathematics for Tomorrow's Young Children, 102–119.
© 1996 *Kluwer Academic Publishers. Printed in the Netherlands.*

and mass). The above law expresses a basic relationship between conceptualized magnitudes but it is not, by itself, a concept.

Concepts are never isolated mental entities. A concept has no meaning and no functional validity by itself. A concept simply does not exist as an isolated entity. The genuine nature of a concept is to be able to entertain various dynamic relationships with a vast network of other concepts. The term *number* for example expresses a concept only in relation to numerous other concepts like cardinality, order, one-to-one correspondence, measure, unit of measure, or the invariance of cardinality with respect to the position of elements. As the child grows older, he or she learns about natural numbers, fractions, real numbers, and about the infinity of various sets of numbers and various levels of infinity. The term *number* becomes the potential predicate of an infinity of potential statements in which the various particular numbers are the subjects: five is a number, 1/2 is a number, and so on.

A fundamental fact which should be understood in discussing the cognitive and behavioral role of concepts is the *impact of society in shaping them*. Most of our concepts constitute collective representations made possible by language. The enormous superiority of human beings, in comparison with other animals, has been made possible by the fact that we are able to share the results of our experience with others - other individuals, other groups of people and other generations. Acquisitions are compared, verified, selected according to their efficiency, refined and socially accumulated. The concepts produced are collective representations which, from generation to generation, improve themselves, reflecting with more and more accuracy the essential similarities of realities. The cognitive and the behavioral efficiency of a concept are functions of the genuine essentiality of the common characters on which the concept is based.

Certainly, a distinction has to be made between the elaboration of concepts on the basis of everyday life experience and concepts produced by the scientific community[2] on the basis of systematic and consistently verified investigation. In fact, the distinction is not absolute. Many scientific concepts represent refinements of concepts produced and used originally in everyday conditions. Terms like *force, energy, motion, distance, speed, number*, and *life* are commonly used by ordinary people. In scientific representations they have special meanings, fixed by the scientific community as an effect of systematic investigation and thought. But in both everyday life and science, concepts express socially accumulated experience.

This affirmation is of fundamental importance for the instruction process. Children do not construct concepts only as an effect of their own experience, by processes of induction and generalization[3], as is sometimes erroneously depicted. Cer-

---

[2] Tall and Vinner have used the terms *concept definition* and *concept image* for distinguishing between the meaning of a concept as it is established by the scientific community, and the subjective interpretation of the meaning by a person. The concept image describes "the total cognitive structure that is associated with the concept which includes all mental pictures and associated properties and processes. It is built over years through experiences of all kinds, changing as the individual meets new stimuli and matures" (Tall, 1991, p.7). The term *concept image*, though referring to a genuine mental reality, has an important drawback. The reader may assume that *concept image* means basically a conglomerate of mental pictures, but this is not the intention of Tall and Vinner.

tainly, children learn to recognize similarities in the environment. But it is through language, which is a product of socially accumulated experience, that they learn the main categories in which the surrounding world is organized.

The distinction between naive and scientific concepts, though not absolute, is also important from a didactical point of view for another reason. The teacher should be aware of the fact that pupils bring with them information acquired from everyday life with regard to concepts learned in school. The information is usually incomplete, distorted, or even erroneous in comparison with scientific concepts, and the teacher has to take this fact into account. A term like *animal* has in the child's mind a much smaller extension and a much richer intension than in the scientific interpretation. The term *number* expresses originally only a name for a collection of objects, while in mathematics its meaning is much richer. The effect of these differences is that basic cognitive obstacles may appear which render difficult the complete and correct assimilation (or reconstruction in the constructivist view) of concepts.

This constructivist approach however does not imply that children are able to build alone their own scientific and mathematical knowledge. The main task of the instructional process is to create conditions in which the child *assimilates actively* the knowledge elaborated by the scientific community. The school provides the information, the questions, the problems, and the environment which stimulate children's mental efforts by which they will reach the concepts, the interpretations, the algorithms, elaborated by society in general, and the scientific community in particular.

From children we may learn how they understand, what they understand, how they solve, what are their difficulties. Consequently, we try to adapt our didactical means to that important information. But to claim that we have to watch passively how children react to certain situations and learn to cope with them (discovery approach) and to call this constructivism as is sometimes done in a naive way would be mere nonsense.

2. CONCEPT FORMATION

A problem which has attracted the interest of psychologists has been how concepts are formed. We distinguish here between different categories of concepts.

Concrete and abstract concepts. This distinction is artificial because a concept is, by its very nature, an abstraction, an idea. Mathematical concepts (numbers, geometrical figures and the other mathematical concepts) are always of an abstract nature.

This distinction emphasizes the fact that some concepts represent categories of concrete realities such as objects, living beings and events, while other concepts

---

[3] In the last few years, the metaphorical term *encapsulation* has been used for expressing the process of concept attainment. This seems to say that by attaining a certain meaning, for instance by induction, we encapsulate the meaning, or fix the meaning as we would solidify a substance into a capsule. But the idea of a capsule expressing the nature of the concept is sheer nonsense. A bottle of capsules is a conglomerate of totally separated, isolated, perfectly solidified objects. A concept is, by its very nature, the effect of a living interaction between the meanings of a dynamic network of meanings.

refer mainly to properties abstracted and mentally isolated from these concrete realities, such as density, energy, vectorial magnitudes, point, line, plane, right, beauty and justice. The distinction is not absolute. As Howard mentions, "It is better considered a continuum than a dichotomy" (Howard, 1987, p. 23). Nevertheless, it is usually considered that concrete concepts are earlier acquired than abstract ones in the mental development of the child.

Conjunctive, disjunctive and relational concepts. A distinction usually referred to in the research literature is that between conjunctive, disjunctive and relational concepts. For instance, the concept of square is a *conjunctive* concept. Its intension consists in a number of attributes which all have to be considered. A square is a quadrilateral with equal sides and equal (right) angles. A *disjunctive* concept is based on a disjunctive relationship between attributes. An instance is a member of the concept if either of the features is present. For instance, a real number is either a rational or an irrational number. Disjunctive concepts are relatively rare and much more difficult to identify. Concepts that express a relationship are termed *relational concepts*. For instance, the concept of equivalence represents a relationship between two entities if this relationship is symmetrical, reflexive and transitive. A ratio is a class of equivalence because all the ratios a/b ($b \neq 0$) obtained by multiplying or dividing a and b by the same number are equivalent. The term *ratio* is itself a relational concept. It expresses a comparison between two magnitudes. All concepts based on ratios are relational concepts. Density, specific weight, and velocity are examples of relational concepts as are the concepts of measure, derivatives, trigonometric functions, the classical concepts of probability.

Earlier studies have been oriented according to three main directions: inductive concept formation, deductive concept formation, and inventive concept formation.

2.1 Inductive concept formation

Most of the studies following this direction have been experiments of classification. The main idea has been that the subject observes one thing after another and, grasping common features in a number of objects, groups them together. It has been reported that often subjects may not be aware of the common features considered when classifying objects selected into one category.

Introspective reports show that subjects commonly employ specific strategies in the process of concept elaboration. They form hypotheses, test them against further instances, and revise them. The difficulty in interpreting behavior in this type of research is that subjects may themselves not be aware of all the features influencing their choice and classification. An interesting finding has been reported by Hanfmann (Hanfmann & Kasanin, 1934; Hanfmann, 1941) using the well-known Vygotsky test of concept formation. The materials used in the Vygotsky (or Hanfmann-Kasanin) test of concept formation consists of blocks of different shapes and colors (Leeper, 1951, pp. 740-741). There are cylinders and prisms (hexagonal, trapezoidal, triangular) colored white, yellow or green. The subject had to identify a concept by testing various instances (that is, combinations of properties).

Two types of behavior could be identified. Abstract thinkers tried to classify objects according to one criterion (the color of the objects) and many failed. Others, who relied more on global, perceptual factors, performed better. Their scores were twice as good as those of subjects who used a verbal-abstract approach. Certainly, as Hanfmann herself observed, the superiority of one group of subjects over the other depends on the experimental situation. Nevertheless, the best results have been reached by subjects who were able to combine or alternate the two modes of approach. The main idea to be stressed from the above findings is that, in the process of inductive concept formation, verbal-abstract and figural-perceptual modes of approach both play an important role. Success in solving geometrical problems, for instance, depends on harmonic, productive cooperation between the two aspects.

2.2 Deductive concept formation

Though generalization plays an essential role in concept formation, deduction has also been considered as contributing to the formation of concepts. For instance, may one claim that the result of the subtraction 5-7 *is* a number? Using the primitive model of numbers as representing the common property of equivalent collections, the result of 5-7 does not exist as a number. But if one can prove that, with entities of the type a-b where b > a, one may define some basic operations like addition and multiplication, then a-b may also be accepted as a number. In this case, the concept of negative numbers has been created mainly by deduction.

By deduction, concepts may be enriched. This situation is often encountered in mathematics. The theorem stating that in a triangle the altitudes intersect in the same point is proved by deduction. In this way we learn a general property of triangles.

2.3 Inventive concept formation

Concepts like *siren* or *centaur* do not correspond to any objective reality. They are mentally created hybrids, but, nevertheless, they have been accepted at one time by the human mind as existing realities.

In fact, the scientific inventory of invented concepts is very rich. Such concepts do not correspond to directly observable realities, at least up to a certain time. They are invented in order to explain or to justify observable phenomena, in order to confer on such phenomena a reasonable interpretation. Terms like *black holes*, *quarks* and even *electron*, *positron*, *proton*, *photon*, *neutron*, and *neutrino* do not correspond to observable physical entities. They have been invented by scientists. Some deductive processes have played a role, but deduction does not explain, by itself, the production and acceptance of the above concepts.

What distinguishes inventive concept formation in everyday reasoning and in science is that in science, including mathematics, new concepts are not arbitrarily chosen. They are imposed by the development of science, by requirements of completeness and coherence. The invention of complex numbers was imposed by the necessity and the possibility of conferring on the symbol $\sqrt{-1}$ a mathematical meaning. If this meaning does not lead to contradictions, it becomes a mathematical concept.

The distinction between the deductive and the inventive way of concept formation in science and in mathematics is artificial. Both strategies merge in one constructive process in which invention and deduction totally cooperate. For a detailed description of the inductive, deductive and inventive processes in concept formation in earlier studies, see Leeper (1951).

3. CONCEPTS, MEANINGS AND LANGUAGE

Are concepts learned from experience or from words? This is a fundamental question with broad theoretical and didactical implications.

Laboratory investigations are based usually on the tacit or explicit assumption that concepts are the effect of inductive and hypothesis-testing procedures. Subjects start from certain instances which possess some common features and decide that they belong to the same category. Through generalization, the category is represented, mentally, as a concept. New instances are examined and their connection with the category is tested. Or alternatively, in order to test the legitimacy of the assumed concept, new instances are tested by referring to some kind of feedback[4] (positive and negative instances) and the selection of relevant features is improved. See, for instance, the research of Bruner, Goodnow, and Austin (1956).

But what is true for laboratory investigations may not be exactly applicable to real life situations. The fundamental reason is that concepts are generally treated and imposed by society. Language conserves and transmits meanings. Concepts are, usually, the meanings of words. Learning the language from the cultural environment, the child learns, at the same time, a very complex system of conceptual hierarchies which would shape the child's own conceptualization experience.

The conclusion is not that the individual's experience does not participate in the process of conceptual elaboration and development. The child does not assimilate passively the categories built by society. On the contrary, the child builds actively his or her own concepts, but under the strong impact of social experience.

4. PROTOTYPES AND EXEMPLARS

As we have seen, the classical view with regard to concept formation is mainly based on induction and hypothesis-testing processes. More recent theories highlight the role of prototypes and exemplars. The two terms are often confused, but Howard (1987) offers different descriptions of the two. The prototype theory "proposes that a category is represented by some measure of central tendency of some

---

[4]   Many experimental investigations have been devoted to concept formation. We will mention especially one of them, often quoted in the literature. Bruner, Goodnow, and Austin (1956) organized a systematic study in order to detect the main strategies used by subjects in the process of concept identification. They used images varying on four dimensions. Subjects had to identify a concept defined by some values of the attributes. In a group of stimuli, the subject had to identify the concept by learning (by successive feedback) which stimuli were instances of the concept. In principle, subjects had to test successively their hypotheses and adjust them according to the feedback received. Bruner, Goodnow and Austin describe several strategies used by the subjects:(*See bottom next page.*)

instance which ... can be a highly typical instance or an idealization. Stimuli are then categorized as exemplars or non-exemplars by reference to the prototype..." (Howard, 1987, pp. 93-94). The prototype, then, does not necessarily contain all the characteristic features and only them. Sometimes the prototype is an idealized composition of certain more salient, more common characteristic features of the category. Sometimes the prototype is concentrated in a certain highly typical instance. A bird is usually considered to possess the following features: lays eggs, has feathers, flies, sings (Howard, 1987, p. 94). Consequently it is somehow difficult to accept a penguin as a bird. An animal is usually thought of as represented by mammals and therefore one feels some difficulty in accepting insects or fish as animals. A metal, in the prototypical view, includes the property of being solid and, therefore, we are surprised to learn that mercury is a metal.

According to the exemplar theory, "a learner simply remembers one or more exemplars of a given category without abstracting anything from them" (Howard, 1987, p. 100). For instance the category *dog* is mostly represented by a familiar dog.

The difference between the prototype view and the exemplar view is that a prototype expressly emphasizes a collection of characteristic features, while an exemplar is simply one instance of the category with which other possible instances are compared.

5. THE PARADIGMATIC VIEW

I have used the term *paradigmatic models* for describing a situation in which a concept is structured around a certain exemplar or a particular sub-class of exemplars of the respective concept (see Fischbein, 1987).

The above distinction between the prototype view and the exemplar view is artificial. In practical terms, when trying to retrieve, use or define a concept, we refer either to a typical instance or a sub-class of the category. We do not refer to a formal composition of characters, but rather to an instance or a sub-class which is most familiar or common, and the salient characters are a relatively good approximation of the defining characters of the concept. Such a representative of the entire class is not an abstraction but a concrete, structured reality. As a consequence, it usually includes characteristics which seem to fit well together and which, in addition to some defining relevant features, include also specific features which are not critical for the entire category. Such a structured representation is then a model and not a formal composite of features. It is a model because we use it instead of the representation of the entire class in our attempts to describe or define the concept or to distinguish exemplars and non-exemplars of the concept.

The term *paradigm* is, in my opinion, more appropriate for such a model because it is a combination of concreteness and representativeness such as, for instance, the particular verbs we use in learning the inflexions of an entire category of verbs.

(cont.) Conservative focusing: Subjects start with one instance assuming all its attributes are defining features. They then test out each feature by selecting stimuli that differ in only one attribute.
Focus gambling: Subjects test more than one attribute at a time.
Scanning strategy: Subjects test attributes either one at a time or a few at a time.

The term *prototype* emphasizes the idea of first, of primitive, an exemplar which precedes in our experience all the other exemplars of the same category. Things are usually so, but they are not always and not necessarily so. A child may learn first about squares, but nevertheless an oblique parallelogram may become later on the representative, the paradigmatic model, of the class of parallelograms. Finally, while a prototype is by definition one, a concept may be supported by a number of paradigms. When we think of the concept of metal, we may refer equally to iron, steel, or gold with their common, salient properties such as solid, heavy, and shiny.

But it is not the term which is especially important. The important thing is that we deal here with a particular type of model and, using the term *paradigmatic model*, we want to emphasize that specific instances are used, very often tacitly, instead of the original category, with all its features, whether relevant or irrelevant. The theory of paradigmatic models becomes part of a broader theory, that of mental models with all its psychological and didactical implications. We use models in our reasoning processes for various reasons. They are generally more familiar, more accessible, simpler, better structured, easier to manipulate, practically or mentally, than the original.

An instance or a particular class of instances becomes a paradigmatic model for the above reasons. When asked "What is a liquid?" a child usually says, "A (kind of) water" (Stavy & Stachel, 1985). Water is the most familiar liquid. Its properties are the best known. Nobody would think of clouds as representing liquids. Nobody will mention mercury as an example of a liquid.

Thinking of numbers, trying to understand what numbers are and the properties of numbers, we usually have in mind natural numbers. If somebody is asked to give an example of a number, he will generally not mention i or e or π or even $\sqrt{2}$, but will mention a natural number. When new categories of numbers have been created in the history of mathematics, such as irrational, negative, or complex numbers, the first question was whether the laws concerning the natural numbers and the operations with them fit also the new classes of numbers. The difficulty of accepting these new entities as numbers derived from the fact that the natural numbers were originally associated with collections of objects. With such a model in mind, it is impossible to accept irrational, negative or complex numbers as true mathematical objects. If the concept of number is related to the operation of measuring, the difficulty remains.

In her doctoral thesis, Rina Hershkowitz found that "even in *instantaneously formed* concepts where an *invented concept* was given by a verbal definition without out presenting a single example, subjects (students and teachers) produced mostly the same prototypical examples" (Hershkowitz, 1989, p. 4). For instance, a "dushlash" was defined as being "a geometrical figure built from two triangles having a common vertex (the same point is the vertex for both triangles)" (Hershkowitz, 1989, p. 63, my translation). The subjects had to draw a "dushlash" or to choose one from several drawings. It was found that at all age levels the same figure was the most popular from various possible figures corresponding to the definition (Figure 1 below).

Figure 1: Examples 1 & 2 used by Hershkowitz.

The conclusion is that for certain figural-structural reasons, a certain instance is considered the most representative for the entire concept. Example 1 obtained the highest percentages (30-40%), while Example 2 obtained the lowest ones (1-2%). In Example 1 the two triangles are absolutely distinct and the common vertex is striking while in Example 2 it is apparently only one triangle which is immediately perceived. The larger one absorbs, perceptively, the smaller one.

6. EXPLICIT AND IMPLICIT MODELS

Sometimes, models are purposely and consciously chosen or built in order to facilitate the finding of a solution. One produces, for instance, preliminary sketches or other types of simulation in order to study in simplified conditions the possible behavior of projected devices. Graphs, diagrams, histograms are deliberately drawn. In geometry, we use drawings or materially built objects which are models of the ideal, genuine geometrical figures. In physics the scientist, considering the structure of the atom, uses an imaginary model analogous to a planetary system. Children build their number concepts starting from collections of objects to which they learn to associate certain names by one-to-one correspondence. The understanding of arithmetical operations is, primarily, based on practical operations in which operations with sets of objects such as marbles or children's fingers are used as models.

In the above examples, models are produced and used consciously. They play an important role in concept formation, in problem solving, and in interpretations of phenomena. But very often models may play an active, even decisive, role in the reasoning process in a tacit way. Individuals are not aware of the fact that their concepts, interpretations and solutions are manipulated from behind the scenes by certain implicit models. Sometimes individuals are aware of the model, but not of its influence and sometimes individuals are not aware at all of the presence and nature of the model.

We know, for instance, that in geometry a point is an entity without dimensions. Such an entity cannot be manipulated mentally as such. Therefore it is represented as a small dot. When we affirm that a line is determined by two points, we imagine a drawn line with the two dots on it. So far, things are simple and clear mathematically and psychologically.

But let us imagine the following situation. Two line segments of different lengths are compared. Are the sets of points on the two segments equivalent or not?

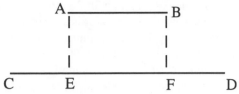

Figure 2: Different length line segments.

Intuitively, two contradictory answers seem to be acceptable. Either the two sets are equivalent, and both consist of an infinity of elements, or there are more points on the segment CD. If we draw the perpendiculars AE and BF, the sets of points of the segments AB and EF are obviously equivalent. The segments CE and FD are additional fragments of the segment CD. What about these points? The source of this apparent contradiction consists in the fact that we continue to rely tacitly on the intuitive representation of the point concept as a small dot.

Let us consider some more examples concerning the tacit influence of models in structuring our concepts. In a recent study, Alessandra Mariotti (unpublished manuscript, 1992) has discovered the following interesting phenomenon. Subjects of different ages are shown a tetrahedron and asked to observe and analyze the structure of the object. After the tetrahedron is taken away, the subjects are asked to draw its net. Many subjects at different age levels draw a pyramid with a square base. It seems that the tetrahedron and the preliminary discussion about it have triggered in the subject's mind the concept of pyramid. But the concept of pyramid is related in the subject's mind to a certain paradigmatic model, the pyramid with a square base. It is the model which determines the answer and not the original perception! It seems that we remember not what we perceive, but the main representative of the particular category. The pyramid with a square base acts, in this case, as a tacit model in the sense that the subject is not aware of its influence.

Another example is drawn from a previous study of mine (Fischbein, Deri, Nello, & Marino, 1985). Consider the following two problems:

1   From 1 quintal of wheat, you get 0.75 quintal of flour. How much flour do you get from 15 quintal of wheat?

2. 1 kilo of a detergent is used in making 15 kilos of soap. How much soap can be made from 0.75 kilo of detergent?

These two questions, among many other questions, were asked of 628 pupils in grades five, seven and nine from 13 different schools in Pisa, Italy. The students were asked only to choose the correct operation without performing the computation. We quote the percentages of correct answers, according to grades:

Problem 1: 79 (Gr. 5); 74 (Gr. 7); 76 (Gr. 9)
Problem 2: 27 (Gr. 5); 18 (Gr. 7); 35 (Gr. 9) (Fischbein et al., 1985, p. 10.)

For both problems, the solution requires the multiplication 15 x 0.75. Formally and procedurally the solution is the same. What makes the difference?

As one may observe by reading carefully, in the first problem the operator is a whole number, while in the second the operator is a decimal. From a formal point of view, this should not make any difference: multiplication is a commutative operation. But *intuitively* things look totally different.

Let us imagine that behind the operation of multiplication lies an intuitively acceptable model, the one in fact taught in elementary classes: multiplication is repeated addition. The model is adequate, but only as long as one deals with whole numbers. Three times five means, in this interpretation, 5 + 5 + 5 = 15. But what does 0.75 times 5 mean? *Formally*, "0.75 times 5" and "5 times 0.75" lead to the same result. But intuitively they do not, and 0.75 times 5 does not have an intuitive meaning. It cannot be represented in terms of the repeated addition model.

In a multiplication A x B, verbally expressed as "A times B", A is the operator and B the operand. If the operator A is a decimal, the multiplication has no intuitive meaning. As a consequence, when addressing a multiplication problem in which the operator is a decimal, the student will not grasp directly or intuitively the solution procedure. The repeated addition model, operating tacitly behind the scenes, will prevent the right solution instead of facilitating it. As an effect of this situation, the student is led to believe, intuitively, that "multiplication makes bigger" and "division makes smaller". These statements are true, are intuitively acceptable, but only if the operator is a whole number. It is important to emphasize that such tacit models continue to remain active even in adolescents and adults who have already acquired the formal knowledge which should have eliminated their impact.

7. MATHEMATICAL CONCEPTS

7.1 Empirical and mathematical concepts

Many of the basic mathematical concepts have their historical and ontogenetical origin in our experience. Numbers are related to operations of comparing by one-to-one correspondence two sets of objects or by comparing a certain magnitude to a unit, the operation of measuring. Geometrical shapes are, originally, inspired by real figures or solids. The straight line, the circle, the cube, and the parallelepiped are all inspired by real objects. Higher order mathematical concepts have also, very often, their origin in our practical activities such as the concepts of function, derivative, or integral. Nevertheless, there is a fundamental difference between empirical and mathematical concepts.

Empirical concepts tend always to approximate a certain given reality. The process of enriching and refining an empirical concept, so as to express in the most exact and complete way a given reality, never comes to an end. With mathematical concepts, the situation is different. A mathematical concept is totally controlled by its definition. In principle, one does not improve the structure and the understanding of a mathematical concept by confronting it with reality, but by rendering its definition as precise and rigorous as possible in the realm of a certain axiomatic system. In mathematics, a concept is an absolute expression of its definition, while in empirical domains concepts tend to express reality by adapting their definitions to that reality.

Certainly there are and there must be some undefined terms and some unproved propositions from which to start. The fundamental term *set* in mathematics is accepted as undefined though it is explained as a collection of objects. But, generally speaking, the meanings of mathematical terms are fixed unequivocally by definitions.

These comments mean that mathematical concepts have usually a constructive, operational nature. A circle is defined as the locus of all the points in a plane the distance of which to a certain point, the center, is constant. In fact, we describe the properties of the circle by describing how it is built. The same is true for other geometrical concepts like ellipse and parabola. A natural number is an entity built by successively adding units, while the term *unit* is undefined. An irrational number is obtained by comparing two incommensurable magnitudes like the side and the diagonal of a square. A function describes the dynamic relationship of two or more variables.

Mathematical concepts refer to ideal entities. The term *ideal* means, in the present context, both mental (an idea) and ideally perfect. In objective, material reality, there are no perfect straight lines, circles, planes, cubes, or tetrahedra. Mathematical concepts are, strictly speaking, pure mental constructs. This explains the fact that mathematical concepts may be *entirely* controlled by definitions. This also explains the fact that mathematical statements may be proved only by logical, formal means and never by practical facts. It follows then that mathematical entities are always of an abstract nature. The objects to which mathematics refers—basically numbers and figures—have no material properties. A point, a line, a surface, do not exist as such in reality. A cube or a sphere are not supposed to possess any material properties, like weight, mass, density, or color.

Geometrical figures are a special situation. Though abstract ideal entities, they reflect, in their intrinsic structure, spatial properties like shape, magnitude, position. They are entirely conceptualized entities without abandoning their spatiality. Because of their double nature—both figural and conceptual—we term geometrical figures *figural concepts*. The absolute symbiosis between figure and concept in a geometrical figure is, psychologically, only an ideal limit. The two facets remain relatively under the influence of both systems, the conceptual and the figural ones.

7.2 The duality process-object

As Anna Sfard has shown, there is an inherent process-object duality in the majority of mathematical concepts. The operational (process-oriented view) emerges first and the mathematical objects (the structural view) develop afterwards through reification of the processes (Sfard, 1991; Sfard & Linchevsky, in press).

This conception is important for understanding both the nature and the formation of mathematical concepts. A number is first based on processes of comparing, by bijection, two sets of elements and on processes of counting. But, after these processes have been learned, numbers are manipulated as objects. The acquisition of the elementary arithmetical operations follow the same path. When asked to perform an addition, for instance 5 + 3, children will first use fingers for counting successively five fingers and then three fingers. After they have learnt by heart through association that 5 + 3 = 8, the numbers become again objects which have to be added to yield the known result. Later on, when learning the properties of addition (like closure, associativity) addition is again treated mentally as an object characterized by various properties. For a description of how children develop elementary mathematical solving strategies, see the succinct paper of Resnick (1989).

The notion of function was born initially from the operational view in which variable quantities depend upon one another. In the expression $y = f(x)$, x is the independent variable and y is the dependent variable. In modern mathematics the static view prevails. A function is defined as the correspondence between the elements of two sets A and B such that to each element of A there corresponds one and only one element of B. The original intuitive, dynamic idea of two magnitudes, the variation of one of them influencing the variation of the other, is replaced by an abstract, static view (a mapping) by which the elements of B (the co-domain) are said to be images of the elements of A (the domain).

7.3 Levels of formalization

Piaget (1967) has spoken of first and second degree operations. A first degree operation deals with concretely represented realities. Five marbles and three marbles yielding a set of eight marbles is a first degree operation because one deals, practically or mentally, with marbles. This does not imply that the child, when performing an operation of addition has necessarily to combine concretely two groups of marbles or some other material, such as fingers. An operation is in Piagetian terminology a mental act, composible and reversible, which may be either related or not related to a concrete reality.

A second degree operation is an operation which is performed with operations. Its relation to reality is indirect or, simply, does not exist. The multiplication or division of fractions is, usually, a second degree operation. Each fraction expresses an operation (for instance, considering a certain part of a whole) while the division of two fractions is an operation performed with these fractions.

According to Piaget, a concrete-operational child (ages 7-12) is able to understand and manipulate abstract concepts if these concepts are directly related to concrete realities. This is true for natural numbers and the operations of addition and multiplication of such numbers. Simple fractions like 1/2 and 1/3 are also in this situation. But when considering a multiplication of fractions like 5/7 and 3/4 we deal with an operation of the second degree, the direct concrete representation of which is no longer possible. In this case we have to rely on a formal definition:

$$\frac{a}{b} \times \frac{c}{d} = \frac{a \times c}{b \times d}$$

Such a second degree operation and the related concept of multiplication of fractions, may acquire a meaning only at the formal operational level after the age of 12.

Let us summarize what has been said above about mathematical concepts. Mathematical concepts are ideal, abstract entities, totally controlled by definitions. They may be related to concrete realities directly, as first degree operations, or indirectly, as second degree operations. They possess a double process-object nature with the process aspect being the primordial one. All these properties confer on mathematical concepts a specificity when compared with empirical concepts which plays a decisive role in their evolution both historically and ontogenetically and in the processes of teaching and learning. Let us now consider the basic aspects already described with regard to the formation of concepts and apply them to mathematical concepts.

Induction plays an important role especially at the initial stages in acquiring the number concept. The property of cardinality can be acquired first by comparing sets of various types of elements and identifying what they have in common, disregarding the spatial arrangements of the elements in the sets. But, at the same time, the one-to-one principle has to be put into action because this is the procedure for extracting and defining cardinals. Learning the number concept implies also counting activity. The induction process does not have any role in this case. Names in a fixed order have to be assigned to cardinals also considered in a fixed order, the "stable-order principle" according to Gelman and Gallistel (1978, p. 79). One-to-one correspondence is necessary also in assigning names to cardinals, but the schema of order intervenes. According to Piaget, the schema of order is established during the concrete operational period, but other authors consider that this ability appears earlier, at the age of 4 - 5 (Gelman & Gallistel, 1978). Thus, while induction plays a certain role in the elaboration of the concept of number, this role is limited and has to be considered in a broader mental context.

Though induction may be used as a basic heuristic in problem solving, as Polya has shown, it may block the emergence of genuine mathematical concepts when used inadequately. The reason, as suggested earlier, is that a mathematical concept is entirely controlled by its definition and not by its appropriateness for representing a class of real objects. Squares, rhombuses, rectangles, and oblique parallelograms belong to the same class of parallelograms, not because of salient figural similarities (they seem to be figurally so dissimilar!) but because they respond to a certain formal definition. Certainly, we run here didactically into a conflict. The natural didactical way would be to familiarize the child first with various figures like squares and rectangles, and afterwards to extract the common features. But this is not the main way by which mathematical concepts are produced and corresponding exemplars identified. Starting from a generic example, one extracts a definition and builds or identifies subclasses which correspond to this definition. A parallelogram is defined by the parallelism or the equality of its opposite sides. Consequently, a square is also a parallelogram, no matter how strange this conclusion may appear. Because children learn first to call squares, rectangles, and rhombuses by different names, it becomes very difficult to change their attitude and to teach them to apply definitions and not to resort to figural similarities when classifying these objects.

This problem is also related to the hierarchical structure of mathematical concepts. Conceptual hierarchies may be found everywhere in scientific systematizations, but in mathematics the hierarchies are strictly, explicitly, and formally determined by definitions, even if apparent similarities or dissimilarities may conflict with the formal organization.

As suggested earlier, we run here into a didactical difficulty. Many mathematical concepts have their origin in everyday life situations and in what is taught in elementary classes. At this intellectual level, the natural way to form concepts is the inductive one. Later on, the inductive attitude and the resulting empirical classifications and hierarchies become an obstacle for developing a genuine mathematical approach. This fundamental change of attitude has represented an intellectual revolution in the history of mathematics and it should constitute a revolution in the child's mathematical reasoning too. I consider that the teacher should prepare children for this moment and should help them to overcome the difficulties of this fundamental change of perspective.

Deduction is essentially a method of proving in mathematics. On the other hand, it is by deduction that very often we assign properties to newly acquired concepts. After proving a certain theorem by using a generic example, we conclude via deduction that the same property holds for the entire class. Though this appears to be an inductive process, it is not induction with which we deal here. Let us consider an example. We prove that in a triangle the altitudes intersect in a single point. The proof is made on one particular triangle. But through the respective exemplar, we consider in fact all triangles, no matter the magnitude of angles and sides. The particular triangle is in principle a model through which one discovers properties of the entire class. We get a theorem, a general statement. The basis of this kind of reasoning is not induction in the sense of empirical induction but a formal proof which guarantees the generality of the statement. After the theorem has been proved, we apply it deductively to various types of triangles. We learn by deduction, for example, that in a right triangle, strangely enough, AB, AD and AC are the altitudes with A the common point (see Figure 3).

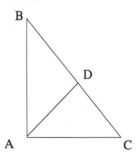

Figure 3: Altitudes of a right triangle.

A specific way for producing new concepts in mathematics, termed by me the *constructive way*, is a combination of invention and deduction. I have already mentioned, as an example, the extension of the concept of number so as to include negative, irrational and complex numbers. The essential point here is that the new concept is an entity appearing, originally, as an artifact but which is afterwards accepted as a genuine mathematical concept if one proves that it obeys a certain set of laws. For the concept of number defined by a set of laws, see Knopp (1952) and Gelman and Gallistel (1978, pp. 180-201). The formal interpretation of the production of the number system raises a fundamental didactical problem.

What has been said about the inductive method refers also to the role of models in the reasoning process. The first models, ontogenetically and didactically, on which the concept of number is based are necessarily concrete ones, namely collections of objects and operations with them. This fact creates an essential cognitive obstacle which hinders the further development of the concept of number. One may continue with fractions expressing the part-whole interpretation, but negative, irrational and complex numbers are essentially counter-intuitive. As I have already said, a change of perspective has to take place in the student's mind, similar to the revolution which took place in the history of mathematics, in order for the student to accept these entities as numbers. That is, one has to give up the primitive, intuitive models on which the concept of number has been initially based and to resort to a totally different conception. The existence and meaning of mathematical entities are not established by their correspondence with some aspects of reality, but by purely formal constraints, that is by consistent systems of formal propositions (axioms and definitions).

Unfortunately, this fundamental modification of perspective is not tackled seriously by the actual theory of mathematics education. Textbooks, teachers and curriculum writers continue to make use, sometimes excessively, of concrete didactical means to teach elementary mathematics, without any effort to prepare the child for a genuine understanding of the nature of mathematical concepts in higher classes.

8. SUMMARY AND CONCLUSIONS

A concept is the general idea we hold about a category of objects or phenomena united by a number of common attributes. Concepts play an essential role in our reasoning processes because they express the results of a selective and organizing activity based on socially shared experience. Usually, a concept is crystallized by means of paradigmatic models which fix the common features in coherent structures and facilitate the explicit definition of the particular concept.

Essentially, children learn systems of concepts from their social environment via language, but it is their own experience which endows the concepts with behavioral and practical meanings. In the ontogenetical construction of a concept, the child starts with pre-concepts—global representations in which the particular and the general are not yet well distinguished. As an effect of personal experience and socially-verbally fixed categories, the child learns—between the ages of 2 and 4—to distinguish the particular and the general.

Empirical concepts and their implicit or explicit definitions are mainly approximations of objectively existing realities. Empirically based concepts improve and refine themselves—historically and ontogenetically—by a continuous confrontation with reality. Mathematical concepts—though often inspired by reality—are essentially established by formal constraints, by axioms, theorems and definitions. The improvement of mathematical concepts—with regard to coherence, clarity, rigor—and the creation of new concepts take place not through confrontations with reality, but by analyzing, improving, and enriching their formal foundations.

This situation creates a fundamental dilemma for the didactics of mathematics. During the first stages of intellectual development, children's intelligence is concretely oriented. The concepts which they are able to learn, to build and to manipulate have a concrete, practical meaning. It is the only way in which they may learn mathematical concepts too. Numbers and elementary arithmetical operations and geometrical figures are, and should be, taught initially in relation to concrete models.

But an undesirable phenomenon happens: these models become deeply rooted in children's minds and continue to influence their mathematical concepts and operations later during the formal operational stage. Sometimes they may be helpful, but very often they may distort the reasoning process. Mathematical concepts, as already emphasized, should become strictly controlled, formally independent from the constraints of reality.

This transformation of perspective represents a very complex didactical task. So far, the pedagogy of mathematics has paid little attention to it. We do not know, yet, how to tackle this problem.

REFERENCES

Anderson, J. R. (1990). *Cognitive psychology and its implications.* New York: W. H. Freeman.

Bruner, J. S., Goodnow, J., & Austin, G. A. (1956). *A study of thinking.* New York: John Wiley.

Fischbein, E. (1987). *Intuition in science and mathematics.* Dordrecht, The Netherlands: Reidel.

Fischbein, E., Deri, M., Nello, M. S., & Marino, M.S . (1985). The role of implicit models in solving verbal problems in multiplication and division. *Journal for Research in Mathematics Education, 16* (1), 3-17.

Gelman, R., & Gallistel, C. R. (1978). *The child's understanding of number.* Cambridge, MA: Harvard University Press.

Hanfmann, E. (1941). A study of personal patterns in an intellectual performance. *Character and Personality, 9,* 315-325.

Hanfmann, E., & Kasanin, J. (1934). A method for the study of concept formation. *Journal of Psychology, 3,* 521-540.

Herron, D. (1983). *Concept learning.* Unpublished manuscript.

Hershkowitz, R. (1989). *Geometrical concept images of students and teachers.* Unpublished doctoral thesis (In Hebrew, with an English summary), The Hebrew University of Jerusalem, Israel.

Howard, R. W. (1987). *Concepts and schemata: An introduction.* London: Cassel.

Knopp, K. (1952). *Elements of the theory of functions.* New York: Dover.

Leeper, R. (1951). Cognitive processes. In S. S. Stevens (Ed.), *Handbook of experimental psychology.* New York: John Wiley.

Mariotti, M. A. (1992). *Concepts and definitions.* Unpublished manuscript.

Menchinskaya, N. A. (1969). The psychology of mastering concepts. Fundamental problems and methods of research. In J. Kilpatrick & I. Wirszup (Eds.), *Soviet studies in the psychology of learning and teaching mathematics,* Vol. 1 (pp. 75-92). Chicago: University of Chicago.

Merril, M. D., & Wood, N. D. (1974). *Instructional strategies: A preliminary taxonomy.* Columbus, OH: ERIC/SNEAC.

Piaget, J. (1967). *La psychologie de l' intelligence.* Paris: Armand Colin.

Piéron, H. (1957). *Vocabulaire de la Psychologie.* Paris: Presses Universitaires.

Resnick, L. (1989). Developing mathematical knowledge. *American Psychologist, 44* (2), 162-169.

Sfard, A. (1991). On the dual nature of mathematical conceptions: Reflections on processes and objects as different sides of the same coin. *Educational Studies in Mathematics, 22,* 1-36.

Sfard, A., & Linchevsky, L. (in press). The gains and the pitfalls of reification. The case of algebra. *Educational Studies in Mathematics.*

Stavy, R., & Stachel, D. (1985). Children's conception of changes in the state of matter: From solid to liquid. *Archives de Psychology, 53,* 331-344.

Tall, D. (1991). The psychology of advanced mathematical thinking. In D. Tall (Ed.), *Advanced Mathematical Thinking* (pp. 4-21). Dordrecht, The Netherlands: Kluwer Academic Publishers.

Efraim Fischbein
Tel Aviv University
Israel

WHAT CONCEPTS ARE AND HOW CONCEPTS ARE FORMED[1]

1. INTRODUCTION

With respect to the question of how mathematical concepts are formed by children, we can draw upon several theoretical positions, going from the most general point of view, relative to the universal subject, to the most specific point of view, relative to the didactic subject. In this chapter I will rely on the theory of conceptual fields, whose originator, G. Vergnaud, describes it thus: "The theory of conceptual fields is a cognitivist theory, which sets out to provide a coherent framework and some basic principles for the study of the development and learning of complex competencies, notably those which arise in the sciences and technologies" (Vergnaud, 1991, p. 135). I shall try first to show the necessity of that theory for the didactics of mathematics in relation to that of genetic epistemology; in the second section I shall elaborate on what the theory of conceptual fields contributes, with the notion of *scheme-algorithm*, to questions on the cognitive sources of observable errors in written calculations.

2. THE FORMATION OF CONCEPTS AND THE THEORY OF CONCEPTUAL FIELDS

2.1. The Piagetian question on the transformation of knowledge

A decisive stage, preliminary to the study of the formation of mathematical concepts, is overcome with Piaget through the epistemological dimension of his work. His project concerns in effect a new discipline, genetic epistemology; genetic psychology is its instrument and serves as a method for studying the formation of knowledge and for constructing a theory of knowledge. Let us recall that in the Preface to volume 1, devoted to mathematical thought, of his *Introduction to genetic epistemology* (Piaget, 1973a), Piaget defines his object of study by the following question: how is knowledge developed? That is to say how do its successive organisations evolve? It is a renewal of the question of epistemologists of that time who had been considering the very nature of knowledge and not its genesis.

I borrow from the work of Inhelder, Cellérier and their collaborators the definition of Piagetian work:

---

[1] The first part of this chapter was originally published in French as Brun, J. (1994). Evolution des rapports entre la psychologie du développement cognitif et la didactique des mathématiques. In M. Artigue, R. Gras, C. Laborde, & P. Tavignot (Eds.), *20 ans de didactique des mathématiques en France* (pp. 67-83). Grenoble, France: La Pensée Sauvage. It is reprinted here by kind permission of La Pensée Sauvage, 20 rue Humbert 11, BP 141, 38000 Grenoble, France. English translation by H. Mansfield with assistance from N. Bednarz. The second part of this chapter is based on the work of Brun et al (1993). It was translated from the French by La griffe d'or culturelle.

H. Mansfield et al. (eds.), Mathematics for Tomorrow's Young Children, 120–136.

The deep-seated originality of Piaget has been to orientate right away his work towards the study of categories of knowledge, without which no adaptation to reality and no coherent thought would be possible; this has allowed him to create a fundamental psychology dealing with the construction of constituent notions such as space, time, causality, etc. It is in this sense that the epistemic subject appears above all as the subject of normative knowledge (Inhelder et al, 1992, pp. 20-21).

This is in the same sense as the Kantian question of categories of knowledge.

In concerning himself with the epistemology of mathematics, Piaget has surely been driven towards the pedagogical terrain, with the intention of which he has accompanied his epistemological writings with some considerations and recommendations for the teaching of mathematics; see in particular Piaget (1960, 1973b). However, none of his writing is presented as experimental scientific work on teaching. Genetic psychology maintains, therefore, from the beginning, an exterior position with respect to research on the teaching of concepts, but its originality when it ventures on this terrain is in *the affirmation of the necessity of a point of epistemological departure to questions of teaching.*

However works which rely on Piagetian ideas have not been lacking in the field of mathematics teaching and we have seen some "applications" of Piagetian theory appear. The "applicationist" position considers teaching as a field shaped at the whim of advances in sciences of the child which then become the norms for teaching. Ricco (1992) has made in his study a profound analysis of the different attempts of programs which have sought to follow the evolution of genetic psychology. These attempts are characterised by changes in the purpose of teaching, excluding mathematical knowledge from it, and this in at least two ways.

One way consists of substituting for the mathematical objects of teaching content relevant to operative structures (*structures opératoires*) defined by means of logic (the logic of classes and relations). We take advantage of teaching mathematics to introduce a kind of program for developing mental operations, sometimes called elementary logic. In so doing, we are led to introduce experimental settings and the clinical interview method of genetic psychology to teaching situations. For example experiments on the genesis of number will serve as a model of didactical progression: classification, seriation, and number as the synthesis of the two. Experiments which taken together on the basis of an experimental design intended to decide between different epistemological positions concerning number have been wrongly used for a different purpose: describing progression in the development of individual learning.

Another way of rejecting knowledge in these programs has its origin in concern with following the evolution of Piagetian work. In the 1970s, issues were related to the mechanisms of development and the emphasis put on structures was displaced towards the study of cognitive functioning. The transfer of this work into teaching aims at "the learning" of operative mechanisms (*mécanismes opératoires*) themselves (cognitive conflict, reflective abstraction, equilibration), independently of their specific content. We have there similarly a good example of the impasses to which an applicationist view of the psychology of cognitive development leads: the very sense of the work of genetic psychology is again diverted. For example, that on the learning of structures of knowledge (Inhelder, Sinclair & Bovet, 1974) is understood as if it were concerned with a general theory of learning able to provide rules for school programs.

Without talking about the significance which the introduction of such programs would have for the school as an institution, we forget here that the work being referred to does not lead to the construction of a general theory of learning but seeks to make a *detour* by experimental methods around learning in order to understand better the big mechanisms of development, themselves the objects of the theory. The authors describe it well:

> The very general theoretical problem concerns the existence and the explicative power of the factor of equilibration in cognitive learning. This mechanism is difficult to understand given transversal behaviors which do not take account of development except by discontinuities of time. On the other hand, the method of inquiry that allows the tracing over a certain time period of the successive acquisitions of a child in a precise experimental context will allow, we hope, the gathering of clearer manifestations of this essentially dynamic mechanism. (Inhelder, Sinclair & Bovet, 1974, p. 32).

The major diversions of meaning spelled out previously should not, however, make us forget certain questions which to me appear common to genetic epistemology and the didactics of mathematics. For my part, I understand in fact that the didactics of mathematics is in its turn a fundamental attempt to respond to the question of transformations of knowledge. In the process it takes responsibility in these transformations for what amounts to the phenomenon of cultural transmission, which embodies the purpose of teaching, through the intermediary of institutions, in particular the school.

If one really wants to admit that the transformation of knowledge, at the most general level, participates in that realm of possibilities that includes the "epistemic subject" in the guise of the universal knowing subject, it is reasonable to affirm, at the start of all didactic questions, the necessity of taking an epistemological position concerning the connection between the knowing subject and the object of knowledge. It is this that the didactics of mathematics is doing in adopting for its own reference framework a constructivist and interactionist position in the footsteps of genetic epistemology. Didactics will reinforce the interactionist point of view, in particular in relying on Vygotsky (Vergnaud, 1990). This position is summarized in this way by Vergnaud:

> Activity in context is, for an increasing majority of psychologists, both the source and the criterion of conceptual thought. Language plays, certainly, a fundamental role, since it alone allows for theoretical discourse and since, without this discourse, there is hardly any concept, but it does not constitute, in the eyes of psychologists, the most decisive criterion. The most decisive criterion remains action in context (Vergnaud, 1977, p. 53).

For Piaget, knowledge, including mathematical knowledge, derives from the adaptation of the individual to his or her environment and constitutes a particular case of a more general biological process which is itself an interplay between assimilations and accommodations. Action is the principal factor in the process of knowing; it is progressively interiorized and becomes an operation. Action is transformed in mathematical knowledge by abstraction of the properties and relations characteristic of the actions and operations of the subject.

From this fundamental position, it is evident that some new questions arise, questions to which knowledge about the epistemological subject is not sufficient to respond, which is the most general form of the knowing subject. At this point, a new reference becomes indispensable, that of properly constituted mathematical knowledge[2], historically and socially elaborated; mathematics under discussion in genetic epistemology concerns principally, as some see it, the study of big categories of knowledge (number and space are the big chapters of volume 1 of the *Introduction to genetic epistemology*) seen from a structural point of view (see Note 1).

2.2 The question of mathematical content: Logico-mathematical structures and conceptual fields.

Vergnaud is the first psychologist to have addressed this question of the content of instruction at the heart of a psychology of cognitive development, a question that he repeats in the following manner: "Cognitive psychology is confronted by the double problem of taking close account of socially constituted knowledge (scientific, technical, cultural, practical...) and at the same time not remaining restricted by their actual description, so as to analyse closely the formation and functioning of the knowledge of individual subjects" (Vergnaud, 1985, p. 251). This sentence contains, in my eyes, the double-sided and powerful demand of all work on knowledge in didactics. This work demands that the description of properly constituted knowledge be readdressed; it is a new beginning for the psychologist, used either to relying on general models and not to starting with properly constituted knowledge, or accepting in advance the description which is given him at the moment he refers to it.

The first claim, taking account of constituted knowledge, marks therefore a difference from the strictly Piagetian point of view which was re-organising knowledge into general logico-mathematical structures. Vergnaud in elaborating the theory of conceptual fields points out clearly this difference:

With regard to a cognitive psychology based on logical structures like that of Piaget, the theory of conceptual fields seems above all like a psychology of concepts, even when the term "structures" is involved in the very designation of the conceptual field under consideration: additive structures, multiplicative structures. (Vergnaud, 1991, p.147).

That is an important point which marks a decisive stage in the manner of envisaging the links between the psychology of cognitive development and the didactics of mathematics. The second claim requires that one considers seriously with respect to individual subjects a cognitive organisation which does not allow itself to be locked at once into descriptions of knowledge but which takes account of activities in formation from the point of view of the subject knowing *in relation to situations*. Let us not forget that action in situations is the source of the formation of concepts.

A conceptual field is explained therefore through two means, through concepts and theorems on the one hand, through situations on the other. *Situation* is taken at

---

[2] The term *knowledge* has two meanings in French: *savoir* which refers to knowledge elaborated historically and socially, and *connaissance* which refers to knowledge from the point of view of elaboration by the subject. We speak here of the first meaning.

this level of analysis in the broad sense of problem-context and not of didactic situation.

The conceptual field of additive structures is at the same time the whole set of situations whose treatment implies one or several additions or subtractions, and the whole set of concepts and theories that allow the analysis of these situations as mathematical tasks. (Vergnaud, 1991, p. 147).

The narrow bond between context and concept has as a consequence that one makes original and quite large classifications in knowledge, taking account of the fact often mentioned by Vergnaud that a concept does not take its meaning from a single class of situations and that a situation is not analyzed by means of a single concept. Research is then engaged on the process of the "continuities and discontinuities" between the knowledge required by the transformation of situations in the long term. The basic unit of this structure of continuities and discontinuities is the *scheme,* "invariant organization of behaviour for a class of given situations" (Vergnaud, 1991, p. 136). It is the scheme which organizes and at the same time gives sense to actions, to contexts and to symbolic representations which accompany them; it changes meaning and is transformed during actions.

Schemes, generally speaking, are characterized by being both structural and functional units (Inhelder, Cellérier et al, 1992). They are organizations, the products of cognitive activity, and organizers, the tools of assimilation. The theory of conceptual fields values these two characteristics of the scheme: on the one hand it takes account of the structural aspects of schemes in analyzing them in terms of operative invariants and this *from the point of view of constituted knowledge itself* (central point of the theory); it is at least the sense which I give to the notions of concept-in-action and theorem-in-action. *With invariant operatives one seeks to give a mathematical content to organizations of behaviour that can be detected in context.* On the other hand from the functional point of view genetic epistemology places schemes at the center of the general process of adaptation of cognitive structures; the theory of conceptual fields makes precise the functionality of schemes for the process of transformation of knowledge across a series of situations centered on concepts (see the didactic sequences on the notion of volume, Vergnaud at al, 1983). One can thus understand the mutual movement of transformation of situations and of transformation of knowledge in relation to concepts.

This research approach has shown its great fruitfulness through work in the classification of situations, problems, procedures and representations, work which constitutes one of the major achievements of research on the didactics of mathematics. I quote here at length from Vergnaud to emphasize the originality of his approach:

The classification of situations results at the same time in mathematical considerations and psychological considerations. Certain distinctions are only interesting because they entail significant differences in the manner in which pupils set about dealing with the situations thus differentiated; mathematicians themselves take no more care of these distinctions and, if we limit ourselves to properly constituted mathematics, we neglect distinctions which are important for mathematics education. However a classification which did not have mathematical sense would be inadmissible. One of the challenges which must engage psychology that is interested in the learning of mathematics is to establish classifications, describe procedures, formulate the knowledge-in-action, analyse the structure and function of expressions and symbolic representations, in terms which have a mathematical meaning. (Vergnaud, 1991, p. 156).

And further, with respect to didactic situations this time:

The underlying thesis of the theory of conceptual fields, however, is that a good didactic intervention is itself based necessarily on knowledge of the relative difficulty of scholarly tasks, of obstacles habitually encountered, of the repertoire of available procedures, and of possible representations. (Vergnaud, 1991, p. 157).

In this structure, the concept of *representation* is, as will already have been noted in these quotations, equally important. To what necessities does it respond? First of all to a developmental necessity: if we follow the functioning of schemes according to the development of the child, the appearance of the semiotic function at some moment in this development provides new elements for this functioning; these are representations of a semiotic nature. Subjects rely on the signifiers which they can distinguish from the signified. Semiotic representations therefore play an eminently functional role, even if they remain subordinate to operations.

In the process of the *formation of knowledge in situation*, representation is a tool and is used to designate objects, to analyze aims and means, to build a strategy to answer problems of communication and validation which can be posed in context:

However operative action (*action opératoire*) is not the whole of the conceptualisation of reality, far from it. One does not debate the truth or the falsity of a totally implicit statement, and one does not identify the aspects of reality to which it is necessary to pay attention, without the help of words, statements, symbols and signs. The use of explicit signifiers is indispensable to conceptualisation. (Vergnaud, 1991, p. 145).

In the resolution of particular problems this time, representation involves knowledge in relation to a precise situation; it serves to choose and evoke schemes useful for achieving the fixed goal and for choosing an approach to use; it works then as an intermediary between schemes and situation in order to make meaning precise (Brun & Conne, 1990). In this context, I understand schemes in fact less as states of knowledge (even if they tend to generalization) which will be actualisable on demand, but rather as *possibilities,* unconscious, which must always be formed and re-formed in the face of a new situation. A subject's scheme is only at a state of potentiality and it is only action in context which will decide in some way the individualization of the scheme (Inhelder et al, 1992); the function of representation then plays its role.

I stress this point: to recognize in the schemes of the subject a structural character which can be described in the terms of properly constituted mathematics does not have as a goal to determine the "acquisitions" of the subject, even in an implicit form, but to seek to establish how organizations and cognitive processes structure mathematical knowledge. It seems to me that we thus turn away seriously from a conception of representations viewed as mental entities which are stores of acquisitions available on demand.

Conceptual fields, their organization on a lengthy temporal ladder (for example additive and multiplicative structures), as well as their formation across sequences of situations (for example didactic sequences on the concept of volume, Vergnaud et al, 1983), constitute a decisive wealth of knowledge in response to the question of the place of the content of teaching in cognitive structures. We can equally well invoke the functioning of schemes in algorithmic tasks as in written calculations. Certain errors can be reconsidered as traces of the progressive construction of a *scheme-algorithm* (Vergnaud, 1991). We think we are able to carry arguments in that perspective by proposing analysis of errors observed in tasks requiring the implementation of algorithms for the operation of division (Brun et al, 1993).

To conclude this section on conceptual fields, it is good to recall the research program which underlies them:

-Analyze and classify the variety of situations in each conceptual field;
-Describe precisely the variety of behavior, procedures, and reasoning that students exhibit in dealing with each class of situations;
-Analyze mathematical competencies as organised schemes and identify clearly the invariant properties of situations on which the invariant properties of schemes rely (concepts-in-action and theorems-in-action);
-Analyze how language and other symbolic activities take place in such schemes, how they help students, and also how teachers use such symbolic intermediaries;
-Trace the transformation of implicit invariants, as ways to understand and act, into well-identified objects, which become progressively as real as physical reality; and
-Trace the way by which students become conscious that procedures have a relationship of necessity both to the goals to be reached and to the initial conditions and subsequently that theorems can be proved (Vergnaud, 1990, pp. 23-24).

3. SCHEMES, ALGORITHMS, AND COMPUTATIONAL ERRORS[3]

The aim of this section is to open a debate on the notion of schemes in relation to computational algorithms. Vergnaud's theory of conceptual fields is of central importance to schemes, and we feel that we can provide further arguments in this direction by analyzing mistakes made in tasks requiring the application of computational algorithms; more precisely, we want to know whether the mechanical character of the algorithm is compatible with the dynamic character of the scheme. In this chapter, we are discussing the algorithm for division. In order to clarify the framework of our analysis, Vergnaud is quoted at length, below:

Children make sense of concepts through situations and through problems to solve (...) Two kinds of situations can be distinguished: types of situations for which the subject possesses, at a certain point in his or her development and under certain circumstances, the necessary skills to be able to deal almost immediately with the situation; types of situations for which the subject does not possess all the necessary skills, and therefore must take time to reflect and explore, undergoing hesitations and making aborted attempts before eventually succeeding or failing. The concept of scheme is significant for both types of situations, but it works in different ways in each respective case. In the first case, in the same type of situation, largely mechanical behaviour, organized in one scheme only, is observed. In the second case, what is observed is the successive introduction of several schemes, which can be in competition with each other, and which must be adapted, decombined, and recombined to arrive at the desired solution; this process necessarily involves discoveries. We define "scheme" as *the invariant organization of the behaviour for a given type of situation* (Vergnaud, 1991, p.136).

---

[3] This text is an extension of our research work carried out with the help of a grant from the Fonds National de la Recherche Scientifique (no. 11-25448.88). Richard Schubauer and Jean Portugais also took part in different stages of this work.

And, further on:

The pupil's cognitive procedure comprises operations which progressively become mechanical (the changing of a sign when a side is changed, the isolation of an x on one side of an equals sign) and conscious decisions which allow the particular values of the variables of the situation to be considered. In the end, the reliability of the scheme depends on the subject's explicit or implicit knowledge of the relation between the algorithm and the characteristics of the problem to be solved.

The mechanical aspect is obviously the most remarkable manifestation of the invariant character of the organization of the action. But a series of conscious decisions can also be subject to an invariant organization in a given type of situation. Moreover, the mechanical aspect does not prevent the pupil from having control over the conditions in which an operation is appropriated or not. Let us take as an example the algorithm for the addition on decimal numbers; its execution is largely mechanical for most children at the end of elementary school. However, the children are able to generate a series of different actions which depend on the characteristics of the situation: carrying over or not, an intercalated zero or not, decimals or not. In fact, all of this behaviour includes both mechanical actions and conscious decisions. It can also be seen from these examples that algorithms are schemes, or that schemes are objects of the same logical type as algorithms: what they are missing is possibly "effectiveness", that is, the certainty of arriving at a correct answer in a limited number of steps. Schemes are often efficacious, but not always effective" (pp. 137-138). This closeness between schemes and algorithms should be revealed in the analysis of pupils' errors in written computation tasks. This is what we hope to show in the case of the algorithm of division.

In the teaching context, errors in written computation are spontaneously viewed as departures from the algorithm which has been taught. The teacher usually seeks the error within a step of the algorithm procedure to then bring in the necessary elements to correct it. Most of the time, the teacher isolates or centres on the particular step and carries out a brief remedial teaching session concerning it. That this practice is widespread has been clearly shown by the analysis of the framework established for teachers and pupils to work together on written computation tasks, and by the analysis of questionnaires filled out by teachers.

To understand the errors observed, the emphasis on correction should be put aside, and the pupil's work should be considered as an organized whole occurring in time, and therefore subject to adaptations. It then becomes possible to infer the implicit interpretative framework within which the pupil has carried out the computation. Thus, understanding the errors requires locating both the cognitive and the didactic dimensions of the pupil's interpretative framework.

We should specify here that our objective of understanding pupils' errors is a research objective and the content of our study is not at all intended as a recommendation regarding teaching. For a critical review of English-language research on mistakes in arithmetic, see Belanger (1991).

Studies by Brown and Van Lehn (1980, 1982) and Van Lehn (1990) have constituted an important step in the understanding of pupils' errors: they have shown their organized character by detecting *systematic errors*, that is, regularities between different individuals and in the same individual at different points in time. These errors are characterized by an internal logic which can be reproduced, as they "make up a system". The production models developed by these authors have a real predictive value. Their theory can also be seen as correctly, or at least partially correctly, describing the processes implemented by the pupils, by providing clues indicating the interpretation and the use that the pupils have made of the rules that they have been taught (repair theory). However, as Resnick (1982) has remarked, these models focus only on the *syntactic* aspects of the algorithmic rules. The conceptual and numerical aspects present in the computations should be considered. Here, the notion of the scheme is necessary to account for these errors. We should add that the dynamic character of the computation process needs to be studied more thoroughly: how do pupils invent adjustments for their calculations as they go along? Do they remain on a mechanical level devoid of anticipation and inference?

The computations for written operations of *division with remainder* that we collected from six classes of fifth and sixth grade pupils provided us with a great variety of errors. We will now verify if it is possible to understand them by means of the conceptual framework explained above.

A description of these errors allowed us to classify them in three main categories (Conne & Brun, 1991):

- Controls of the numerical relations between dividend, divisor, quotient, remainder

```
1575   | 15
  15   | 1   4   1
0075   |
  60   |
  15   |
  15   |
   0   |
```

-Intermediary operations, subtraction in particular.

```
2740   | 14
  14   | 1   9   8
 134   |
 126   |
 120   |
 112   |
   8   |
```

- Placing the data in the written operation diagram.

```
1636   | 18
  36   | 23
  60   |
  54   |
  16   |
```

The first category was the fullest and the most interesting for our purposes. Exactly which "controls" or "lack of controls" are being exercised? Which conceptualizations are present? Let us return to the task required of the pupils: "carry out a written operation of division with remainder." Such a task involves a veritable enacted knowledge (*connaissance-en-acte*) (Vergnaud, 1991) and not the simple ordered application of the conventional rules. Within the computational situation, the pupil must anticipate, make choices, plan and control his or her actions, even if this becomes increasingly mechanical with experience. The pupils do all this based on their own numerical knowledge and not only on their mastery of the algorithm's sequence of steps. In the case of the written division algorithm, we consider the totality of the behaviors necessary to carry it out as one scheme; we will call it the *scheme-algorithm* (Vergnaud, 1991, p. 139), which comprises: operatory invariants (*concepts-en-acte, theoremes-en-acte*: enacted concepts and enacted theorems); anticipation of the goal to be reached; rules of action; inferences (Vergnaud, 1991, p. 159).

This scheme-algorithm, *as it is being constructed by the pupil*, presents different (provisional) organizations that we can pinpoint by analyzing the errors collected: the *sub-schemes* which constitute it, instead of being combined logically, can simply be juxtaposed without being adapted to the situation; they can also be in actual conflict with each other, according to the way the pupil breaks down the situation and the references that are retained. In other words, we consider the pupil's computations as active attempts to adapt to the variety of division situations presented; the choice and the organization of the knowledge applied to these situations should lead to the successful completion of the task. The errors are inventions corresponding to different variations of these choices and organizations.

If we are insisting on the conceptual meaning, in the didactic context, of these computation errors, it is because we have found, as have other researchers before us, that if many errors relate to the mechanical aspect of the algorithm (or to the procedure as a sequence of pertinent actions), they are far from accounting for the totality of the errors observed. On the contrary, many errors strictly respect the order of the steps to be carried out, but can be attributed to original combinations of knowledge and rules, combinations which, instead of controlling each other, justify each other and therefore create their own sequence. We will give several examples of this. Let us return to the category of division errors corresponding to the different degrees of control of the relations between dividend, divisor, quotient, and remainder. In this category, we can distinguish several organizations of the scheme-algorithm in construction; we include the *diagram* (as defined by Conne, 1992) within which the algorithm functions in these organizations. Indeed, the operations cannot be dissociated from the system of signifiers: the graphic disposition of the operation determines and even organizes the action. At the same time, it also masks the meaning of the sequence of actions necessary to carry out the operation.

Our principal finding based on the errors observed is that a basic scheme works very well for pupils and helps them assimilate the whole of the division situations. This scheme can be described as the *splitting-up and distributing* scheme. It seems that for the pupils division basically consists of splitting a quantity into parts. This splitting is defined by another quantity: that of the parts to be distributed. Division, therefore, would be in one sense a splitting-up from the point of view of the dividend, and a distribution from the point of view of the divisor, with the dividend and the divisor relating to each other as container and contained. This refers to the scheme of action for situations which are presented at the beginning stages of learning to divide.

This scheme then corresponds to the numerical situations described by Condorcet:

For example, having the number 2124, you may want to know how many times the number 6 must be repeated to make 2124; how many times the number 6 is **contained** in 2124; or, to know the number which, repeated 6 times, is equal to 2124, and which is contained six times in 2124 (Condorcet, 1751/1988, pp. 74-75).

By their variety, the computation situations presented to the pupils offer a certain number of obstacles to this assimilating scheme; it is then that the different errors relating to the characteristics of the situations and the ways of adapting the scheme to the situations are committed. This is shown by the following analysis of the errors resulting from the different situations. Note that we consider each step of the algorithm as a new computational step for the pupil; the carrying out of the computation can be understood as the mutual control that the steps have over each other. "Control" should be understood essentially as placing skills in relation to each other, and not simply as an a posteriori evaluation.

A. Situations in which the dividend is equal to the divisor

The *splitting-up and distributing* scheme works for some pupils only when the dividend is greater than the divisor. The situation in which the dividend is "only" equal to the divisor cannot be assimilated by the scheme because, according to these pupils, the quantity to be split up should be greater than the parts to be distributed or the dividend cannot be split up; therefore, the pupils bring down a number from the next column to arrive at the situation in which "the dividend is greater than the divisor". Thus, in these situations, it is impossible for the pupils to divide when the breakdown of the dividend is equal to the divisor (the first step of the algorithm; here, 9 ÷ 9). In the following examples, a numeration rule is coordinated with the *splitting-up and distributing scheme*: in every position of the written quotient, the highest number is 9.

9009	9		7147	7
81	9 9 9		63	9 9 9
90			84	
81			63	
99			217	
81			63	
18			154	

Example 1a   Example 1b

This restrictive function of the scheme can be seen in the following case, where the remainder is equal to the divisor.

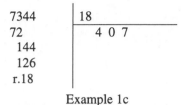

```
7344    │ 18
72      │  4  0  7
144     │
126     │
r.18    │
```

Example 1c

B. *Situations in which the (partial) remainder is greater than the divisor*

The *splitting-up and distributing* scheme works very well; it can be coordinated with a constraining rule related to numeration: "9 is the highest possible number for the quotient"; so that when it becomes possible to control the computation by the remainder/divisor relation, the pupils do not solve this problem of the control of the remainder/divisor relation. Rather, they carry it with them until they reach the indication of the end of the computation (the last column). We then have a succession of nines in the quotient; this is the case in the above examples, or again, in the following:

```
60363   │ 9
45      │   5999
153     │
81      │
626     │
81      │
5453    │
81      │
5372    │
```

Example 2a

(We are not taking subtraction errors into account in this analysis. This error is dealt with in another category of the typology.) The *splitting-up and distributing* scheme can, on the other hand, impose itself quite strongly in the resolution of the problem of the remainder/divisor relation, to the point of overriding the associated rules of numeration. Two-digit numbers are observed in the quotient, thus:

```
60363   │ 7
56      │  8  5  12  3
43      │
35      │
86      │
84      │
23      │
21      │
```

Example 2b

Instead of the two-digit number, there is also a succession of numbers for the same dividend; the dividend is split up successively:

```
13117    | 13
13       |    1008  1
0117     |
104      |
13       |
```

Example 2c

In this form of the scheme, the search for a remainder smaller than the divisor leads to another way of dispensing with the rules of place value. This treatment can take the form of adding a succession of ones to the quotient, corresponding to a series of successive subtractions.

```
25125    | 125
125      |    111
126      |
125      |
125      |
```

Example 2d

```
540060   | 901
901      |    11111
4499     |
901      |
3598     |
901      |
2697     |
901      |
1796     |
901      |
8956     |
```

Example 2e

3. Situations in which the dividend is smaller than the divisor
In these cases, the *splitting-up and distributing* scheme is not fed into, with the following results:
   a. Passing to the next column and an absence of the zero in the quotient

```
7344     | 18
72       |    48
144      |
```

Example 3a

b. In the absence of the next column, the computation is halted

18202	901
1802	2
182	

Example 3b

4. Situations with a remainder smaller than but close to the divisor
The scheme still works here, even though the computation is halted; it is fed into by
the fact of a large remainder, in two ways:
  a. a supplementary zero in the quotient

568	368
368	10
200	

Example 4a

b. the entry of 1 into the quotient

7829	39
78	21

Example 4b

Our explanation in terms of schemes seems well justified by our analysis of pupils'
errors above; what stands out clearly is the dynamic, organized character of these
errors: dynamic in the sense that the computation forms a whole, and is carried out
according to an internal logic which is used to negotiate the different constraints of
the algorithm, some of which are considered inviolable while others are considered
negligible, in order to complete the computation without mishap. The errors are
systematic, but more than that, their systematic nature comes from an organization
of the pupil's numerical knowledge in adaptation to the particularities of the situation, and not simply from the syntactic dictates of the algorithm.
  Certainly, when analyzing the example–

60363	9
45	5999
153	
81	
626	
81	
5453	
81	
5372	

Example 4c

we could easily have said the error was to have chosen 5 x 9, 45 instead of 6 x 9, 54. This is true, but we would have missed what effectively constitutes the computation; indeed, the pupil considered the computation as a whole: she could continue "as long as it works", go back, or wait until the end for verification. Furthermore, certain pupils in this same situation corrected themselves: after having put 5, they then put 6. Other pupils, like this one, continue their computations by adopting rules which are meant to respect the algorithm, and they adapt their knowledge to the situation.

If we do not try to capture these moves in thinking, we would be limited to a disparate catalogue of listing and locating the errors and would be further removed from understanding them. As a whole, the computations that we have reviewed here all show a common *splitting-up and distributing* scheme; this knowledge works. We can even say that it works so strongly that in certain situations it overrides other knowledge and rules that should be applied (for example, rules due to the fact that the algorithm splits the number into the largest possible successive parts, taking place value into account; see example 2b. In other situations, it comes up against place value rules; see example 1.

We were also struck by the fact that these adaptations mainly affect the *written forms* of computation. The attentive reader will have noticed that in many of the errors presented here, the proof "Dividend = Divisor x Quotient + Remainder" remains true (see examples la and lb). Simply, the algorithm was not respected: the *effectiveness* of the algorithm was missing from the *efficaciousness* of the scheme, to use Vergnaud's terms. Moreover, perhaps we should not use the word *errors* any more, and should only refer to *failures*.

Certain forms of computation observed here appear to be a mixture of different figures of the algorithm taught during what are considered the intermediary stages of the learning of the algorithm. We have called them *hybrid* forms (Conne & Brun, 1991). For example, the pupils mix additive procedures (successive subtractions) with the multiplication notations required by the decimal position numeration. We have shown examples of this above (see 2b, c, d, e). The way that the pupils borrow from the different reference situations that they have learned clearly indicates the process of an active search for adaptations to the computational situation.

4. CONCLUSIONS

To conclude, let us return to the different theoretical positions: first, our results show that the errors do not correspond to an absence of semantic control; on the contrary, we are tempted to say that sometimes there is an excess of it; but pupils' errors stem from the lack of *regulation of this control*. As we said above, the pupil negotiates different constraints without reaching the equilibrium that the scheme-algorithm constitutes. The fluidity of execution of the operation is more evident than its segmentation, and its character as an organized whole does not comply with the idea of a pot-pourri of different rules. We see it as the result of the pupil's attempts at active adaptations to the situation.

Note 1: However, we should not forget the meeting of Piagetian positions with Bourbakist mathematics (Piaget, 1960). These positions must always make us attentive to the facts of observation of genetic epistemology which make evident the pre-constructs of the child in relation to the most abstract structures of mathematical thought. It is Jean-Jacques Ducret (1993) who has reminded me of this aspect of Piagetian work and I thank him. Without doubt it is always useful to examine in depth the thinking Piaget displays concerning the "inductive" approach to the discovery of mathematical structures: "But this somewhat inductive approach to the discovery of structures is to the contrary very revealing about the relations which support the structures with the various elements that they place in order. If, historically, these elements seem given before the discovery of structure, and if this last thus plays essentially the role of a reflexive instrument intended to sort out their most general characteristics, it is necessary not to forget that, psychologically, the order of metacognitive consciousness reverses that of development: what is first in the order of construction appears last in reflexive analysis, because the subject becomes conscious of the results of mental construction before attaining the innermost mechanisms. Far from constituting a decisive argument in favor of the independence of "structures" in relation to the work of intelligence, their belated and quasi-inductive discovery tends therefore on the contrary to make us suspect their primitive and generative character " (Piaget, 1960, p.14). The link with mathematical knowledge, and most particularly logic, can thus be established: "Psychology offers, in fact, assistance to logic by showing that intelligence is orientated spontaneously towards the organisation of certain operative structures (*structures opératoires*) which are isomorphic to those or parts of those that mathematicians put at the beginning of their construction or that logicians recognise in the systems that they elaborate" (Piaget, 1960, p.31).

REFERENCES

Belanger, M. (1991). Les erreurs en arithmétique. Un siècle de présomption américaine. *Petit x, 26*, 49-71.

Brown, J. S., & Van Lehn, K. (1980). Repair theory: A generative theory of bugs in procedural skills. *Cognitive Science, 4*, 379-426.

Brown, J. S., & Van Lehn, K. (1982). Toward a generative theory of bugs in procedural skills. In T. Carpenter, J. Moser, & T. Romberg (Eds.), *Addition and subtraction: A cognitive perspective* (pp. 117-135). Hillsdale, NJ: Lawrence Erlbaum.

Brun, J. (1993). Evolution des rapports entre la psychologie du développement cognitif et la didactique des mathématiques. In M. Artigue, R. Gras, C. Laborde, & P. Tavignot (Eds.), *Vingt ans de didactique des mathématiques en France* (pp. 67-83). Grenoble: La Pensée Sauvage.

Brun, J., & Conne, F. (1990). Analyses didactiques de protocoles d'observation du déroulement de situations. *Education et Recherche, 3*, 261-285.

Brun, J., Conne, F., Floris, R., Lemoyne, G., Leutenegger, F., & Portugais, J. (1993). Erreurs systématiques et schèmes-algorithmes. In M. Artigue, R. Gras, C. Laborde, & P. Tavignot (Eds.), *Vingt ans de didactique des mathématiques en France* (pp. 203-209). Grenoble: La Pensée Sauvage.

Condorcet, M. J. A. (1988). Moyens d'apprendre à compter sûrement et avec facilité. Paris: A.C.L. Editions. (Original work published 1751)

Conne, F. (1988). Comptage et écriture en ligne d'égalités numériques. *Recherches en didactique des mathématiques, 9*(1), 71-116.

Conne, F. (1992). Savoir et connaissance dans la perspective de la transposition didactique. *Recherches en didactique des mathématiques, 12*(2/3), 221-270.

Conne, F., & Brun, J. (1991). Analyse de brouillons de calcul d'élèves confrontés à des items de divisions écrites. In F. Furinghetti (Ed.), *Proceedings of 15th Annual Conference of the International Group for the Psychology of Mathematics Education* (Vol. 1, pp. 239-246). Assisi, Italy.

Ducret, J. J. (1993). Savoirs généraux et spéciaux en intelligence artificielle et en psychologie génétique des conduites. In J. Wassmann & P. Dasen (Eds.), *Les savoirs quotidiens* (pp. 181-202). Association Suisse des Sciences Humaines, Université de Fribourg.

Inhelder, B., Cellérier, G., & Ackermann, E., Blanchet, A., Boder, A., de Crapona, D., Ducret, J. J., Saada-Robert, M. (1992). *Le cheminement des découvertes de l'enfant. Recherche sur les microgenèses cognitives*. Neuchâtel, Switzerland: Delachaux et Niestlé.

Inhelder, B., Sinclair, H., & Bovet, M. (1974). *Apprentissage des structures de la connaissance*. Paris: PUF.

Piaget, J. (1973a). *Introduction à l'épistémologie génétique, vol. 1. La pensée mathématique* (2nd ed.). Paris: PUF.

Piaget, J. (1973b). Remarques sur l'éducation mathématique. *Math-Ecole, 58*, 1-7.

Piaget, J. (1960). Les structures mathématiques et les structures opératoires de l'intelligence. In J. Piaget, E. W. Beth, J. Dieudonne, A. Lichnerowicz, G. Choquet, & C. Gattegno (Eds.), *L'enseignement des mathématiques. Vol. 1: Nouvelles perspectives* (pp. 11-33). Neuchâtel, Switzerland: Delachaux & Niestlé.

Resnick, L. B. (1982). Syntax and semantics in learning to subtract. In T. Carpenter, J. Moser, & T. Romberg (Eds.), *Addition and subtraction: A cognitive perspective* (pp. 136-155). Hillsdale, NJ: Lawrence Erlbaum.

Ricco, G. (1992). *Psychologie cognitive et didactique. Constitution d'une nouvelle approche théorique concernant l'appropriation des connaissances scolaires*. Unpublished doctoral dissertation, Université Pierre Mendès-France, Grenoble.

Van Lehn, K. (1990). *Mind bugs. The origins of procedural misconceptions*. Cambridge, MA: MIT Press.

Vergnaud, G. (1977). Activité et connaissance opératoire. *Bulletin de l'Association des Professeurs de Mathématiques, 307*(2), 52-65.

Vergnaud, G. (1985). Concepts et schèmes dans une théorie opératoire de la représentation. *Psychologie Francaise, 30*(3/4), 245-252.

Vergnaud, G. (1990). Epistemology and psychology of mathematics education. In *Mathematics and Cognition: A research synthesis by the International Group for the Psychology of Mathematics Education* (pp. 14-30), ICMI Study Series, Cambridge, MA: Cambridge University Press.

Vergnaud, G. (1991). La théorie des champs conceptuels. *Recherches en didactique des mathématiques, 10*(2/3), 133-170.

Vergnaud, G., Rouchier, A., Desmoulieres, S., Landre, C., Marthe, P., Ricco, G., Samurcay, R., Rogalski, J., & Viala, A. (1983). Une expérience didactique sur le concept de volume en classe de cinquième (12 à 13 ans). *Recherches en didactique des mathématiques, 4*(1), 71-120.

Jean Brun
University of Geneva
Switzerland

with F. Conne
Service de l'Enseignement Spécialisé, Lausanne, Switzerland

and G. Lemoyne and J. Portugais
University of Montreal
Canada

K. C. IRWIN

YOUNG CHILDREN'S FORMATION OF NUMERICAL CONCEPTS: OR $8 = 9 + 7^1$

1. INTRODUCTION

The ways in which young children develop mathematical concepts have been of interest to many writers. Theories related to children's development of mathematical concepts have been developed by such diverse writers as Case (1985), Fuson (1989), Gelman and Gallistel (1978), Inhelder and Piaget, (e.g., 1958), Resnick (e.g., 1989), and Steffe, Cobb, and von Glaserfeld (1988). All of these authors work within a broadly constructivist framework which examines the ways in which children build their own understanding. This view of learning is put well by Lindfors, when writing about children's language (Lindfors, 1987, page x). She says, 'I see children as shapers of their own knowing....I see children's learning in all areas as an active sense-making process–necessary and inevitable and individual.'

This chapter looks at some of the evidence for this active sense-making process. It looks at the numerical concepts that children have constructed, or are constructing, when they start school. It examines the numerical activities that are only partially understood by the children, in order to see what principles they appear to be applying as they tackle numerical tasks. Examples are taken from children between four and six years of age.

The process of constructing understanding can never be fully understood because it happens within the minds of individual learners. These learners do not always share with us what is going on in this sense-making process. What they can do is give us windows into the process of forming concepts through their behavior and their discussion about what they are doing.

In New Zealand, children enter school on their fifth birthday. This means that they may join classes on any day during the school year. Several consequences arise from this constant arrival of 'new entrants' in schools. One consequence is the need for teachers in the first years of school to be responsive to individuals with a wide variety of numerical concepts. Another consequence is the extent to which students use one another as resources, with younger children being apprenticed to slightly older children both for learning school routines and for learning the content of school knowledge. It may be that young children's activity in making sense of numerical concepts is affected by this apprenticeship to slightly older children.

2. A FRAMEWORK FOR NUMERICAL CONCEPTS

The theoretical framework within which I will discuss children's concepts derives from that of Resnick (e.g., 1989, 1992). Resnick has discussed children's knowl-

^{1} This research was supported by a grant from the Ministry of Education. I am grateful to Janita Craw and Dianne Burgham for collecting the counting samples.

137

H. Mansfield et al. (eds.), Mathematics for Tomorrow's Young Children, 137–150.
© 1996 Kluwer Academic Publishers. Printed in the Netherlands.

edge of counting and their protoquantitative schemas or pre-numerical knowledge about quantity. She has indicated that a primary challenge for children in the early school years is that of integrating these areas of knowledge in the development of numerical understanding. My interviews with children confirm the presence of counting and protoquantitative concepts as separate areas of knowledge, understood separately before they are integrated into an ability to reason with numerical quantities.

The data presented come from interviews that my students and I have had with young children. They include evidence of the things that children in this age bracket can do, as well as what their errors tell us about their developing logic. The comments from children who have recently turned five, or are younger, are seen as particularly interesting because these children provide their own logic in explaining their schemas and explanations, rather than the answers that they believe teachers expect of them.

2.1 Counting

The knowledge that children hold principles about counting before they count accurately was established by Gelman and Gallistel (1978) in their now classical study. They demonstrated that preschool children used several principles in counting. They identified these principles as one to one matching, including tagging each item with a count name and partitioning those items still to be counted from those that had been counted; the need for a stable order of the words used in counting; cardinality, or appreciation that the final numeral in a counting series represents the numerosity of the whole set; abstraction, or the understanding that different types of objects, or objects that can not be pointed to, can be counted; and order irrelevance, or the understanding that objects in a set can be counted in any order without affecting the cardinality. This work has stimulated several related studies, as well as reinterpretation of the original data. Of Gelman and Gallistel's principles, most are related to meaning, or semantics. The principles of stable order and cardinality have additional importance that could be considered syntactic, or related to the structure of words and sentences. Both of these principles draw attention to the order in which words are used and the fact that this order contributes to meaning.

The terms syntax and semantics are used primarily in the analysis of spoken and written language, including the analysis of language development (e.g. Bloom & Lahey, 1978). However they are useful concepts for examining the development of children's use of numbers (see Resnick, 1982). While semantics clearly relates to meaning, syntax relates to word, phrase, clause or sentence structure. Syntax should not be seen as a meaningless order of words: it reflects underlying meaning. Children's understandings of the syntax of counting numbers in English becomes more important as they work with numbers over 20, which, using the children's terminology, we call "big numbers." For big numbers, the syntax reflects the meaning of the base-ten place value system.

One of the general learning tasks of early childhood is learning to count. One sample of parents of three-year-olds reported that their children enjoyed counting, had done so with their parents from at least age two, and did so without prompting as they practiced this new skill (Bairstow & Irwin,1989). This counting skill is described by Ginsburg and Allardice (1984) as an example of "System 2 knowledge," culturally derived and socially transmitted, by adults, older children, television, and books.

A study carried out in New Zealand by Young-Loveridge (1989a, 1989b) examined the counting skills that a cohort of 81 New Zealand children had at age five, within one month of their entry to school. This was part of a much larger study of numerical competence. It was a longitudinal study in which children were reassessed annually, until they were nine years old. She reported the following errorless counting at ages five, six and seven:

Accurate counting string	Age 5 (N=81)	Age 6 (N=80)	Age 7 (N=75)
up to 10	74	99	100
up to 20	28	78	95
up to 30	10	54	83
up to 100	04	18	60
up to 110	00	05	31

Table 1: Percentages of children counting forward by ones, to each level.

Thus the majority of these children could count without error to 10 by their fifth birthday. By age six the majority could count to 30 without error, and by age seven the majority could count to 100 without error. This study did not examine what processes children went through in order to develop this fluency. It did not examine the semantic or syntactic knowledge that children used. Two New Zealand studies, with different children, demonstrate what principles for counting are used by children of four and five when they attempt to count to 100. Their counting displays the use of other principles in addition to those given by Gelman and Gallistel (1978).

Counting to 100 is a goal of many young children. In the first example given below, a four-year-old child was asked to count six objects. This activity served as a prompt, for her, for rote counting. The episode was videotaped, and transcribed

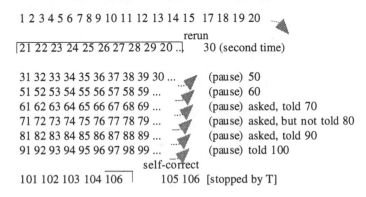

Figure 1: The counting sequence of a four-year-old child.

with rises and falls in the child's voice. For this child the numbers 1 through 20 were a single string, or sentence. Thereafter she counted in sentences of ten numerals, with each decade being followed by a lift in her intonation, and a pause. Sometimes she followed this pause with the name of a next decade, and sometimes she followed it by asking what number came next. Note that she did not stop at 100, but was finally stopped by the interviewer, who was also her teacher.

This sample could be analysed to emphasize the errors made, for example omitting '16', repeating the decade that started with 21, and so forth. Alternatively it could be analysed in terms of the percentage of correct responses in the way that early reading behaviour is in this country (Clay, 1991). This child said 90 numbers in the correct order, made 3 errors, and needed prompting on 3 occasions, or was correct 94% of the time. Her errors, with the exception of leaving out '16' were all related to not knowing which decade name came next. She used five decade names correctly (10, 20, 30, 60, and 80) and did not use four others (40, 70, 90, and 100).

Counting patterns were also collected in a different study from six children aged 5 years 4 months to 5 years 8 months (Irwin & Burgham, 1992). These children had been given the activity of first taking iceblock sticks from a large collection and bundling them in groups of ten. The counting was recorded when the children were asked to tell the teacher how many sticks they had. This was enumeration, not rote counting. Each child chose to unbundle his or her groups of 10 sticks and count them by ones. Five of the six had close to 100 sticks, and used a counting pattern that got them nearly to 100. Two examples are typical of their counting patterns:

Brett:
1 2 3 4 5 6 7 8 9 10
11 12 13 14 15 16 17 18 19 20
21 22 23 24 25 26 27 28 29 40   T correction
31 32 33 34 35 36 37 38 39 40
41 42 43 44 45 46 47 48 49 50
51 52 53 54 55 56 57 58 59 70   T correction
61 62 63 64 65 ... 67 68 69 40   T correction
71 72 73 44 45 46 47 48 49 20   T correction
81 82 83 84 85 86 87 88 89 70   T correction
91 92 93 94 95 96 97 98 99   Appeal, T prompt

Kim:
1 2 3 4 5 6 7 8 9 10
11 12 13 14 15 16 17 18 19 20
21 22 23 24 25 26 27 28 29 30
31 32 33 34 35 36 37 38 39   Told by a peer
41 42 43 44 45 46 47 48 49   Told by a peer
51 52 53 54 55 56 57 58 59 70   Appeal to T, T correction
61 62 63 64 65 66 67 68 69 70
71 72 73 74 75 76 77 78 79 80
81 82 83 84 85 86 87 88 89 90
91

Figure 2: Five-year-old children counting ice block sticks that they had bundled in groups of 10.

One error made by Brett was in saying 44 after 73. There was a disruption in the classroom at this point, and it appears that Brett lost his place in terms of the decade, but was able to start again because of his knowledge that 4 came after 3. This was probably only a decade difficulty. However, for a conservative estimate we considered all seven of his next numbers incorrect. Analysed in terms of the percentage of correct responses, Brett was correct on 89% of the numerals. He knew four decade names, and needed correction on five. Kim was correct for 97% of the numerals. She did know six decade names and did not know three decade names, but was aware that she needed to be told what they were.

The counting of both of these five-year-olds and the four-year-old whose counting appears in Figure 1 follows clear logical principles. This logic was evident before the children displayed full accuracy in their counting. There appear to be several counting principles, in addition to those proposed by Gelman and Gallistel (1978), that these young children applied when they used big numbers, which demonstrated their understanding of the language of counting. These are largely syntactical skills, but reflected an emergent knowledge of place value. For the four-year-old child who was engaged in rote counting without enumeration it was not possible to say what meaning she attached to the numerals, and whether, for example, she could tell whether 48 or 84 was larger. The five-year-old examples were of enumeration, and it could be expected that these children did have a clear idea of the relative size of the names of the big numbers that they used.

The syntactic principles that these children followed were:

1. In counting big numbers, block them in "sentences" of 10. The exception to this is the first 20 numbers, which may be grouped as a single "sentence."
2. The first word of a big number (>20) is always in the form of x-ty.
3. This same word is repeated at the start of each number in that decade.
4. Each decade follows the pattern of x-ty-1 to x-ty-9.
5. The last number, x-ty-9, must be followed by a new decade name.
6. There is a special set of decade names, which need to be used in a standard order.

This counting had high status in the classroom and was practiced voluntarily on the playground. Yet this skill was rarely used in New Zealand classrooms at the time of the study. Classes for five- and six-year-old children worked from a syllabus which introduced children to working with numbers only up to nine in their first two years of school (Department of Education, 1986). The children in this study came from homes in which parents were largely unskilled workers or unemployed. There was every temptation to see them as disadvantaged, without recognizing the counting skills that they were developing outside of the syllabus.

What these children did not know was the decade names, and when to use which one. See Fuson (1988) for a further discussion of this. Muira (1987) noted that in Chinese, Korean and Japanese these decade names are predictable, in that they say "ten-one" for eleven, and "two tens" for 20. Maori counting uses the same conventions, and New Zealand's new mathematics curriculum (Ministry of Education, 1992) suggests introducing children to Maori counting of big numbers, as a way of controlling this early difficulty in counting. It has yet to be shown if this will overcome the difficulties demonstrated above. It is possible that in concentrating on the one aspect of counting that these children have difficulty with teachers will fail to acknowledge the six principles given above that they do use, when counting big numbers. They will emphasize errors rather than the high proportion of counting that is correct.

Of particular concern for this group of children was that unless their teacher had been curious about their counting skills and presented them with this opportunity to count large quantities, she and other teachers in the school could well think that they had lower levels of understanding than they actually had, or than middle class children of a similar age had. The children in turn would be justified in believing that some areas of knowledge that they controlled belonged to outside school, and other areas of knowledge, which perhaps they did not control, belonged to school, and that there was little continuity between the two.

2.2 Protoquantitative concepts

Resnick (1989, 1992) identified three main protoquantitative schemas which relate to the development of numerical concepts, as comparison, increase/decrease, and part-whole schemas. For all of these areas, young children go through a process of making sense of their experience. Several researchers have written about the comparison schemas that children use from an early age. One aspect of this work refers to the words for comparative quantity that children may use in an egocentric manner. These egocentric meanings are themselves part of the construction of meaning, or active sense-making. Walkerdine (1989) wrote of the context-dependent meaning that children from working class families had for "more", the opposite of which was "no more." Durkin (1980) discussed children's concept of "near" which tended to mean 'near to me' rather than near to another focus that the interviewer presented.

In my interviews with young children, described below, I found a similar egocentric use of the word "fair." Desforges and Desforges (1980) had reported that children as young as three and a half could demonstrate a number-based concept of fairness in sharing tasks. I had used the term to provide a basis of comparison for changes to one quantity, while the other quantity remained constant. This was done by using a pair of dolls and having a child divide toffees between them so that it was "fair," then making changes to the quantities of one of the dolls' toffees and asking if the distribution was still "fair." Several four-year-olds and one five-year old child told me that it was fair if the dolls had the same amount or if the doll focused upon had more, but not fair if the the doll focused upon had less.

All of these instances emphasize the child-centered nature of meaning for words as they are being learned. They all relate to words which have a mathematical meaning as well as a meaning in general parlance. In concept formation, it is clear that words are learned first in relation to what is important to the child.

Increase/decrease schemas relate to entities that grow or shrink. These will be discussed later in relation to part-whole schemas, and their application to numerical quantities.

My work has looked into children's part/whole schemas (Irwin, 1990). I interviewed over 100 children between the ages of four and eight. Using various situations, I asked them whether the whole quantity had altered after a change had been made to one of the parts. Some of these situations involved uncounted quantity, and elicited protoquantitative schemas. Other involved counted quantity, to demonstrate quantitative concepts. The task which looked at quantitative schemas required children to have both counting and protoquantitative schemas, so that protoquantitative schemas, including increase/decrease schemas, could be applied to changes in counted quantity. I wanted to see if children understood that an increase or decrease in one part would lead to covariant change in the whole, or a change to one part which was compensated for by a change to the other part led to no change in the whole quantity.

A brief description of the protoquantitative and quantitative tasks is needed so that children's responses can be interpreted. The task which turned out to be most useful in getting children to use and explain their protoquantitative schemas involved presenting a child with two dolls, called "Red" and "Yellow" because of the colour of their hair. The child was asked to divide a pile of toffees between Red and Yellow so that it was fair. Then boxes with lids were brought out, two boxes for Red and two boxes for Yellow, for the dolls to keep their toffees in. These boxes became the "parts" of the dolls' "whole" quantity of toffees. As the interviewer I then put each doll's pile of lollies into the two boxes provided, without attending to the number that went into each box. After the child had told me that the distribution between the two dolls was still fair, I added a toffee to one of one doll's boxes, removed a toffee, or moved a toffee from one box to the other and asked about the effect on the whole. Each of these transformations was done in the context of a story. Transformations were presented to each child in a counter balanced order, and each question was preceded by separating all the toffees between Red and Yellow "so that it was fair." After children gave their answer, they were asked for a reason. This was followed by counter-suggestion in which another doll, "Ernie," disagreed with the child.

A typical section from the protocol of a four-year-old is given below. This was the condition in which a toffee was shifted from one of the parts to the other, and the child was asked if this affected the whole (I is the interviewer.).

I: Now Red *and Yellow have all these lollies to share. Can you share them so it's fair?...Is it fair now?*
Caroline: *Yes.*
I: *Okay, now Yellow puts her lollies in these boxes and puts the tops on.* [Inteviewer does so] *Now Red puts her lollies in those boxes and puts the tops on them.* [Interviewer does so] *Is it still fair between Red and Yellow?*
C: *Yep.*

I: *Yellow's having a good look at the ones in her boxes and she says, 'I'm going to put that one in my other box'. Is it still fair between Red and Yellow?*

Child: *Yes.*

I: *Why?*

C: *'Cause there is still just the same amount.*

I: *But Ernie says ,"I don't think so, I think it is different." Is he right or wrong?*

C: *He's wrong.*

I: *Oh Ernie. Why?*

C: *Cause they've got the same amount.*

On this task, 72% of the four-year-old children showed a firm understanding of protoquantitative changes to part-whole relationships, 81% of five-year-old children understood this relationship, and 92% of six-year-old children showed understanding. Reasons for failure on the task differed, but were often because children attended to the changes to the part when they were being asked about changes, or lack of change, to the whole. This led to the suspicion that more children might have been successful in demonstrating protoquantitative understanding of part/whole relations if their personal need to have the whole stay the same had been stronger. Overall there was strong reason to believe that children understood this relationship of parts and wholes before they started school. This knowledge provides a very important basis for the understanding of nearly all the aspects of the early mathematics curriculum. Yet the teachers of the children whom I interviewed were not making use of this understanding.

2.3 Quantitative concepts: Integrating counting and part/whole schemas

The task in which I investigated understanding of quantitative part/whole relationships involved having a child count out for me a set number of buttons, then seeing me close my fist on these, and then seeing me pour some buttons into the other closed fist. The buttons in each fist became the "parts" of the counted "whole." The child then added a button to one of my fists, removed a button, or slipped a button out of one fist and into the other. The child was asked to tell how many buttons there were in both hands altogether after the transformation. This task required them to combine their understanding of part/whole changes with their ability to increase or decrease the total number by one. This task was considerably more difficult that the protoquantitative task. The percentage of children succeeding on this task at each age was: five-year-olds: 58%; six-year-olds: 66%; six-year-olds: 88%; and seven-year-olds: 95%.

The children's answers, and their reasons when they used numbers, provide a window for observing their developing concepts, and particularly for observing their integration of counting and protoquantitative understanding. A few children had little idea of how counted quantities increased or decreased despite having an understanding of what happened when uncounted quantities increased or decreased.

Other children understood how numbers went up but had difficulty knowing how they decreased, an activity similar to counting backwards. Other children had a firm concept and could relate it to other quantities that increased or decreased. An additional group of children tried to keep in mind how many buttons were in each hand (or part) and then work out how many there would be altogether, with varying degrees of accuracy. Responses from four-year-old children that give examples of all of these concepts are given below.

Zeb was a child with protoquantitative understanding but no apparent understanding of quantitative changes. He was the one child who had not counted conventionally either by rote or in enumerating during interview, but did enumerate when asked to do so by his kindergarten teacher.

I: Well actually *you have given me four Zeb. I'm going to shut my hands and then you give me another one. How many do I have now?*
Zeb (4): *Two.*

Anna found it easier to go up her mental number line than down, but recognized a correct downward move, as in the following conversation. She had put four buttons in my hand and then removed a button from one of my hands:

I: *You take one out. You sneak one out of my hand. How many do I have now?*
Anna (4): (pause) *This is hard.*
I: *It is hard. And a lot of four-year-olds don't know. You gave me four and now how many do I have?*
A: *I know what comes after four. Five.*
I: *You think I have five?*
A: *Yes.*
I: *Why?*
A: *'Cause I sneaked one out.*
I: (in counter suggestion) *Ernie thinks I have only three. Is he right or is he wrong?*
A: *He's right.*
I: *Now who's right, you or Ernie? You thought five and he thinks three. Who's right really?*
A: *I think Ernie's right.*

Daniel showed clear understanding which involved both protoquantitative understanding and a mental number line. He had been presented with a protoquantitative task but chose to deal with it quantitatively. He attended to the whole and not to the component parts. When an object was added, he said:

Daniel (4): *There will be five now and that's how old I will be when I have my birthday.*

When one object was removed he said:

D: *There's only three now and that's how old I was before I had my birthday.*

Francis was a child who tried to work out how many buttons might be in each hand, and, on the basis of that, how many there might be altogether. There was no way in which he could see the buttons in each hand. After he had added an additional button to one of my hands he reviewed the situation:

I: *So how many do I have altogether?*
F (4): *There's one in this hand and one in that hand and three in the other.*
I: *So how many is that altogether?*
F: *Four.*
I: *Why is it four?*
F: *Cause there's three in that hand and two in that hand.*

Several children appeared to be trying to keep in mind the number that was in each of the hands, or parts. This appeared to be a more complex task as it required understanding of additive combination of numbers, not just how the total increased or decreased. Children who failed on the tasks were prone to attend to the size of the parts while those who were successful attended to the change or to the total. Because this attention to the size of the parts, or number of buttons in each fist, interested me, I ran an additional series of interviews in which I asked five- and six-year-old children what they thought the number of buttons in each fist might be.

Children's answers to this question fell into five categories, all of which showed some understanding of numbers, if not the additive concept required. The chart below shows the percentage of children whose answers fell into each category. Percentages equal more than 100 as the same child gave more than one answer and these answers sometimes fell in different categories. For these children the original number of buttons was either six or eight.

Answer	Age	
	5	**6**
Parts are number names each larger than the possible total, e.g. 8 made up of 10 and 20	08	09
Parts are a counting string, e.g. 7 is made up of 8 and 9	17	09
Parts = total or the total $\pm$ 1 e.g. 6 = 6 and 6 or 8 = 7 and 9	75	18
Parts are reasonable estimates e.g. 6 = 3 and 2	17	36
Parts are possible e.g. 8 = 8 and 0	25	55

Table 2: Categorisation of children's answers in guessing the size of parts of a known whole, given as percentages.

In making sense of this question, all children gave an answer involving numbers. For the first category above, that appears to have been their only criterion. The second category of answers showed the emphasis that children in this age put on forward counting—if the interviewer gave one number and asked you for others, one possibility was to produce the forward string that you know. Responses in these two categories suggest that these children had not yet integrated their protoquantitative concepts with their counting concepts in order to understand quantitative part/whole relationships.

The third category of answers, which was adopted by the majority of the five-year-olds, suggested that they believed that each part was the same as the total before a transformation. The transformation changed the parts in the same way that it changed the whole, so if a part had increased it became the whole plus one, and if it had decreased it became the whole minus one. It is possible that they were applying increase/decrease schemas to the numerical quantities and, at this point, ignoring their part/whole schemas. The fourth and fifth categories showed an understanding of potential parts, or the additive nature of the quantities. By age six the majority of children had an idea of the additive way in which numbers combined, even if they were not always accurate. The children whose responses fell in the fourth and fifth category appeared to be using quantitative part/whole schemas which integrated their counting skills and their protoquantitative part/whole schemas. This third category is particularly interesting in the five-year-olds. It is obviously transitory, as very few children in the next age bracket used it. Examples of this response are given below:

I: You *put 6 in my hand.... How many do I have?*
Julie (5). *6.*
I: *I'll put some of them in each hand, but I still have them all. How many do I have in in my hands?*
J: *6 each.*
I: *6 each. Tell me, if you were to count them, how would you count them? Put your finger on and pretend you are counting the buttons.*
J: *1,2,3,4,5,6. 1,2,3,4,5,6.*
I: *You counted 1 to 6 in my left and 1 to 6 in my right hand. OK, I want you to sneak one out of there, and stick it in the other hand. How many do I have altogether, in both hands?*
J: *7.*

Another five-year old was given 8 buttons.

I: *You take those green buttons. Put 8 in my hand...So how many do I have in my hand now?*
Sam (5): *8.*
I: *I'm going to put some in each hand. How many do I have altogether in my two hands?*
S: *8.*

I: *You take one out of that hand and put it in the other hand. Now how many*
       do I have in my two hands together?

S: *8.*

I: *8.* [discussion about one part getting smaller and one part getting bigger]...
       and it's still the same. How many do you think it might be? You can't see
       them, but guess how many might be in this hand.

S: *7* [point to one hand].

I: *Could be 7 in that hand. And how many would be in the other? I've got 8*
       altogether.

S: *9.*

I: *Could be 9 in that hand. Is that because you moved one from one side to*
       the other?

S: *Mmm.*

These children could have been displaying the difficulties of class inclusion discussed by Piaget, in that they appeared to be unable to bear in mind both the size of
a whole and the imagined size of parts at the same time (Vuyk, 1981). However, it
seems more likely that they are attending strongly to an increase/decrease schema,
at the expense of a part/whole schema. These increase/decrease schemas are probably easier to apply to numerical problems than part/whole schemas, because they
are supported by a counting sequence.

It was quite clear that these young children had schemas which helped them to
make sense of the ways in which numerical quantities worked. They had the roots
of number sense which teachers could build upon, although their teachers were
usually unaware of these underlying concepts.

3. CONCLUSIONS

This evidence, derived from listening to children, suggests that children already
understood many principles related to counting, quantity and numerical relations
when they started school, at five, and were actively making sense of the aspects that
were not quite clear to them as yet.

These children were developing concepts in a way which suggests that they were
formulating underlying principles. Examples of this were evident in their use of
syntactically correct counting of big numbers which reflected an understanding of
the place value system. Their development of these principles appeared similar to
the ways in which young children learn language.

These underlying principles were evident in the high proportion of four-, five-
and six-year old children who demonstrated understanding of part/whole relationships in a protoquantitative context. While Piaget (as referred to by Fischbein, this
volume) indicated that the part/whole relationship was not well mastered by children of four and five, it appeared that in this case, the principle of part/whole relations was mastered before the specific instance of applying it to numerical relationships was mastered. The children's development of increase/decrease schemas, which

are related to seriation, initially interfered with, rather than contributed to, their ability to apply part/whole schemas to numerical reasoning.

The evidence from counting big numbers confirms the role that the larger community plays in developing skills even though these skills were not valued in New Zealand schools. The wider community provides frequent opportunities for practice, prestige for accomplishment, and help with what is not yet known. It is also evident that children developed concepts in relation to what was important to them, a process which might lead initially to egocentric meanings and confusions in communicating with adults who intended different meanings. Children may not share a teacher's understanding of what is meant by terms used in early mathematics classes.

In solving novel numerical problems in which they are asked to speculate on numerical part/whole relationships, children actively used what they knew about the counting string. The principles that they used appear to follow a developmental pattern from use of any number, to forward use of a number line, to both forward and backward movement on this line, to understanding the possible additive composition of numbers.

As children develop concepts, we cannot always understand what they are doing. In some instances children do not complete a numerical operation accurately, but do have the requisite underlying logic. Both teachers and researchers may underestimate children's knowledge. This might be because we have not found a shared language or because we have not observed with adequate care. It is safe to assume that children are actively trying to make sense of numerical relationships, that these developing relationships are important for them, and that it is worth our time to try to understand, so that instructional activities can build upon the understanding that children already have.

REFERENCES

Bairstow, R., & Irwin, K. C. (1989). Counting skills of three-year-old children. *The New Zealand Mathematics Magazine, 26* (3), 4-7.

Bloom, L., & Lahey, M. (1978). *Language development and language disorders*. New York, NY: Wiley.

Case, R. (1985). *Intellectual development: Birth to adulthood*. Orlando: Academic Press.

Clay, M. M. (1991). *Becoming literate: The construction of inner control*. Auckland, New Zealand: Heinemann Educational.

Department of Education. (1986). *Beginning school mathematics, Cycles 1 - 6*. Wellington, New Zealand: Department of Education.

Desforges, A., & Desforges, C. (1980). Number based strategies in sharing in young children. *Educational Studies in Mathematics, 6*, 97-109.

Durkin, K. (1980). Developmental changes in the comprehension of near. *Papers in Linguistics: International Journal of Human Communication, 13*, 739-758.

Fischbein, E. (This Volume). The psychological nature of concepts.

Fuson, K. C. (1988). *Children's counting and concepts of number*. New York, NY: Springer-Verlag.

Gelman, R. & Gallistel, C. R. (1978). *The child's understanding of number*. Cambridge, MA: Harvard University Press.

Ginsburg, H., & Allardice, B. S. (1984). Children's difficulties with school mathematics. In B. Rogoff & J. Lave (Eds.) *Everyday cognition: Its development in social context* (pp. 194-219). Cambridge, MA: Harvard University Press.

Inhelder, B., & Piaget, J. (1958). *The growth of logical thinking from childhood to adolescence*. New York: Basic Books.

Irwin, K. C. (1990). *Children's understanding of the principles of compensation and covariance in the context of wholes and their component parts.* Report to the Ministry of Education, Auckland NZ: Education Department, University of Auckland.

Irwin, K. C., & Bergham, D. (1992). Big numbers and small children. *New Zealand Mathematics Magazine, 29* (1), 9-19.

Lindfors, J. W. (1987). *Children's language and learning.* Englewood Cliffs NJ: Prentice Hall.

Muira, I. T. (1987). Mathematics achievement as a function of language. *Journal of Educational Psychology, 79,* 79-82.

Ministry of Education. (1992). *Mathematics in the New Zealand curriculum.* Wellington, New Zealand: Learning Media.

Resnick, L. B. (1982). Syntax and semantics in learning to subtract. In T. P. Carpenter, J. M. Moser, & T. A. Romberg (Eds.), *Addition and subtraction: A cognitive perspective.* (pp. 136-155). Hillsdale NJ: Lawrence Erlbaum Associates.

Resnick, L. B. (1989). Developing mathematical knowledge. *American Psychologist. 44,* 162-169.

Resnick, L. B. (1992). From protoquantitative to operators: Building mathematical competence on a foundation of everyday knowledge. In G.Leinhardt, R. Putnam, & R. Hattrup (Eds.), *Analyses of arithmetic for mathematics for teachers.* (p. 27-53) Hillsdale NJ: Erlbaum.

Steffe, L. P., & Cobb, P. (with E. von Glaserfeld). (1988). *Construction of arithmetical meanings and strategies.* New York, NY: Springer-Verlag.

Vuyk, R. (1981). *Overview and critique of Piaget's genetic epistemology 1965 - 1980.* London: Academic Press.

Young Loveridge, J. M. (1989a). The development of children's number knowledge: The first year of school. *New Zealand Journal of Educational Studies, 24,* 47-64.

Young Loveridge, J. M. (1989b). The development of number knowledge in five to eight-year-olds. *Delta, 42,* 25-37.

Walkerdine, V. (1989). *Counting girls out.* London: Virago.

Kathryn C. Irwin
University of Auckland,
New Zealand

CONCEPT FORMATION PROCESS AND AN INDIVIDUAL CHILD'S INTELLIGENCE

1. INTRODUCTION

Let us ask ourselves a seemingly simple question: why do we teach pupils? Do we want to give them profound and thorough knowledge? But only a small part of the digested information remains in their memory after education is complete, and knowledge may quickly become obsolete.

Do we want to teach the skills of logical reasoning? But using the methods of logic is by no means the most reliable instrument of cognition when solving non-standard problems. This would be sufficient if after long years of studying pupils became free individuals able to make choices in life. This presupposes that pupils develop a broad outlook; analytical capacity; generality and flexibility of estimations; readiness to perceive unusual information, and interpret it in a variety of ways; an ability to explain and predict events; to differentiate obvious aspects of things from the ones not easily observed; and so on. In other words, at the end of teaching we would like to have a sensible person with developed intellectual abilities. And what do we understand by intelligence?

Intelligence is, from our point of view, a complex system of cognitive mechanisms, allowing efficient perception and comprehension of reality. The higher a person's intellectual potential, the richer and more structured appears an individual's speculative "picture of the world", then the more competent is that person. This view of the aim of teaching poses other questions. Is a child's intelligence formed spontaneously? Can a teacher promote its development? To what extent is a teacher equipped with techniques that directly develop pupils' intelligence? In particular, are textbooks oriented towards the goal of increasing intellectual potential? What should the teacher's pedagogical influence be directed to first and foremost?

The answers to all these questions may be found in the psychology of cognition. In the works of the well-known Russian psychologist Vygotsky (1983) there is the idea that conceptual thinking plays a central guiding role in the development of children, in particular their cognitive development. From a psychological point of view, the formation of notions is a process of converting definite units of objectively existent knowledge into subjective cognitive structures. Individual cognitive resources, forming the basis of an individual's intellect, appear to be represented in these structures in an integrated form (Vekker, 1976; Kholodnaja, 1983).

Thus, following Vygotsky, one can promote children's intellectual growth by purposefully developing their conceptual thinking, successively setting forth subjective images of notions. But how can this process be realized?

We faced this problem when we started to create a series of school textbooks on mathematics. We began to think what stages pupils should go through in forming various concepts and what sets of tasks should be used to stimulate pupils' con-

H. Mansfield et al. (eds.), Mathematics for Tomorrow's Young Children, 151–163.

ceptual development. It seemed possible to identify five stages in the process of formation of notions.

1. **Motivation** is the realization by pupils of the need to describe their experiences—everyday, arithmetical, and geometrical—in new ways.

2. **Categorization** is a gradual build-up of the degree of generalization of visual and symbolical "languages" representing the meanings of the initial concept and separating essential from inessential aspects.

3. **Enrichment** means accumulating and differentiating experiences of the given concept. These processes include recognizing additional signs of the initial concept, thus introducing it into the pupils' conceptual framework and extending the *context* for understanding the *content* of the initial concept.

4. **Transference** is the realization of the possibility of applying concepts in new situations.

5. **Contraction** is an urgent reorganization of the whole complex of a pupil's knowledge associated with a given concept and the conversion of that knowledge into a generalized informational structure.

To realize these stages successfully, the teacher supported by a textbook must offer tasks which by their logical structure may activate the development of certain components of conceptual thinking. So, for instance, our textbooks contain the following kinds of tasks:

(a) those aimed at the formation of sign-image transfer skills (children's ability to use simultaneously and interchangeably their verbal and imaginative experiences);

(b) those singling out signs of a concept to be mastered (finding out a set of all possible signs, their differentiation and comparison according to the degree of generalization and importance);

(c) those including an initial concept into the system of connections with other concepts (within mathematics and with concepts from other fields of knowledge);

(d) those developing basic thinking operations (analysis, synthesis, comparison, generalization, and concretization); and

(e) those dependent on everyday experience of pupils.

We shall give several examples, based on the following story (Gelfman et al, 1991), showing how we develop the concept of the "place value in numeration."

2. A STORY ENGENDERING CONCEPT DEVELOPMENT

"For example, what is the length of the pole you found?" asked Muskrat with a touch of irony. Snufkin was confused by the question.

"Measure it properly. It will comfort Muskrat and then we shall all be able to build the weathercock," said Moominmamma.

There lay in the kitchen a smooth rod which nobody really needed. It was kept in memory of a soup ladle, which Moomintroll had put into the Hat and the Hat had turned it into the rod forever. Moominmamma decided to use this former soup ladle as a measure for measuring the pole. She also decided to give Snufkin an apple.

"The problem of the pole we found is settled," Snufkin said, returning into the cave. "We shall make a pole for the weathercock out of it. Only Muskrat wants us to measure this thing. Otherwise he will not step into the cave." "And will it not spoil the beauty?" asked the Snork Maiden cautiously. "Why care about Muskrat's beauty?" murmured Snork. "I mean the beauty of the pole," answered the Snork Maiden in icy tones.

Snufkin interrupted these biting remarks. "I will measure and you count!" He took the measure, put it carefully onto the sand near the pole and drew a line in the sand with a piece of wood. Like this:

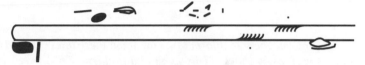

Figure 1

And Moomintroll bent his finger. Looking at Moomintroll, the Snork Maiden did the same. Meanwhile Snufkin replaced the measure, putting its end to the first line and drew one more line in the sand. Like this:

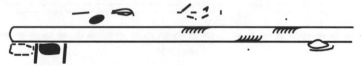

Figure 2

And Moomintroll and the Snork Maiden bent one more finger each. Then Snufkin replaced the measure once more and drew with a piece of wood in the sand and Moomintroll and the Snork Maiden again bent their fingers.

Everybody was busy: Snufkin was measuring the pole, the Snork Maiden and Moomintroll bent their fingers, Thingummy and Bob were running around the pole thinking how to help, and Snork and Sniff were talking about the weathercock and the pole going to be the best things in the Moominhouse. Sniff also was keeping an eye on Snufkin so that he would not scratch the shining surface of the pole with the measure.

When quite a big piece of the pole had been measured and quite a number of lines appeared in the sand, the Snork Maiden suddenly got worried.

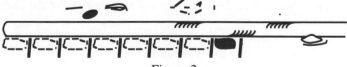

Figure 3

"How are we going to count further? I have no more fingers," she exclaimed, looking with embarrassment at her paws, clutched into fists. "Never mind. Carry on, Snufkin," Moomintroll comforted everybody. "I have several more fingers."

Snufkin drew two more lines in the sand, and Moomintroll had no more fingers left. And the pole had not yet been measured. (Don't be surprised. The Snork Maiden, like all the Snorks, has only four fingers on each paw and the Moomintrolls have five fingers on each paw.)

Nobody knew what to do further. Even Thingummy and Bob stopped running and were just turning their heads, sitting on the sand. Snufkin was determined to finish his work one way or another.

Figure 4

"I wonder, how are you going to inform Muskrat about these lines?" asked Snork. "Well," Snufkin was taken aback. "This is quite a problem. Nobody has enough fingers. Who would think that this pole is so long!"

"We may put a pebble in front of every line. We have so many of them lying around," Moomintroll suggested helpfully.

"This is much better," Snork agreed.

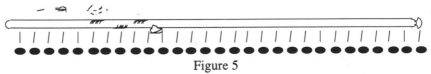

Figure 5

"Ahem, how is it useful for Muskrat?" asked Sniff. "We shall collect all these pebbles and somebody will take them and the measure into the Moominhouse. Mamma will see and know the length at once," exclaimed Moomintroll. "My Mamma is very clever. She will take this measure and lay it off as many times as there are pebbles. This will give the length of the pole."

Thingummy and Bob volunteered to go and take the pebbles. Unfortunately they had no strength to do it.

"Let me help you," said Sniff to the kids. Burning with the desire to participate in such an important venture and hoping to earn apples, they squeaked in their own language:

"No, only we! We shall carry!" "O.K. you will carry," said Snork. "Just wait a bit."

Saying this he picked up several branches and broke off their ends. Now he had light and equal sticks, which Snork put on the sand in front of the lines, which could still be seen in the sand.

Sniff got into the bushes, trying to find suitable branches. At last the required number of sticks was put down along the pole.

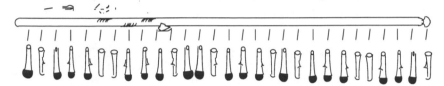

Figure 6

They gave a bundle of sticks and the measure to Thingummy and Bob. The kids ran home, but when they were just passing the first bush, they found Sniff's ill-fated tail. After a short discussion, the sticks were split and mixed with branches prepared by Sniff. Thingummy and Bob were a poor sight and nobody reproached them. "Don't cry," said the Snork Maiden tenderly. "We shall collect all the sticks." They collected the sticks, but nobody was sure that they collected as many as they had before.

"These are definitely not those sticks which I was personally carrying when these gawks bumped into me," stated Sniff. "Nothing can be done," Snufkin said. "We'll have to put the sticks again in front of the lines." "If they still exist, these lines," grumbled Sniff. "I'm afraid we'll have to measure everything again." "Quickly to the pole," Snork gave a command.

Near the pole Moomintroll was walking on his front paws, nobody knew why, and was singing something cheerful.

"Watch you don't tread on these lines!" cried Snork. "We'll have to count them again." "I am just counting them," said Moomintroll, unruffled. "Counting with my fingers. Look, it turns out so easy. Fingers, that's something! You can't spill them."

All of them crowded around the pole. Near the lines in the sand were the prints of Moomintroll's paws.

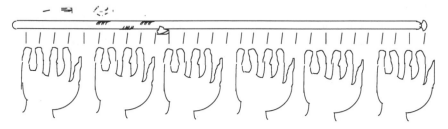

Figure 7

"Paw, paw, paw, paw," Snufkin began to count. "Paw and one more paw, only without the finger. Aha, it means that the number of measures gone into the pole is five Moomintroll's paws and four fingers more." "And I counted in a different way," argued Moomintroll. "I think there is the following number of measures in the pole: both of my paws taken twice and nine fingers more, just look! "

And Moomintroll, having covered the prints with sand, walked on the sand on his front paws. It turned out like this:

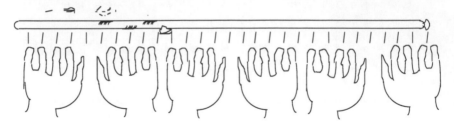

Figure 8

"Aha, we may say it also like this," said Snork. "All the fingers of the front paws of Moomintroll, taken twice, plus nine fingers. We need to check it again. And then into the Moominhouse."

Moomintroll walked again along the pole on his front paws, only this time he began from the other end of the pole. The prints in the sand looked like this:

Figure 9

"Now look," said Moomintroll, satisfied, turning to Snork. "Again we have nine fingers plus all my fingers, taken twice."

Thingummy and Bob, who watched the events attentively, volunteered to inform Muskrat about the results of the measurements. In spite of the failure with the sticks they did not lose hope of having prize apples.

"Just wait, I have to count the lines myself with my paws." Snork stopped them and left prints in the sand like this:

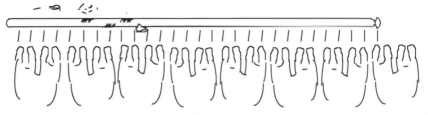

Figure 10

The result was all the Snork's fingers taken three times and five fingers more. The Snork shook the sand off his paws, satisfied, and gave a command to go.

In raptures Thingummy and Bob ran to the Moominhouse. But because they were running so fast and had such a strong desire to eat apples, they forgot who got which of the results. It was good that they came up to Moominmamma first and not to the Muskrat. Moominmamma, who had been dreaming of a weathercock, could not imagine the pole from their information. After thinking a bit, she drew a picture, and asked Thingummy and Bob to write down the number of ladles in the pole digits in the picture.

Figure 11

Sniff found a piece of paper and a pencil. Everybody wrote down the results of his measurements, and drew his face near them so that Moominmamma would know to whom the results belonged.

The last notes were made by Snufkin. (You, the reader, must remember that Snufkin has six fingers on each paw, a dozen, that is twelve, in all.)

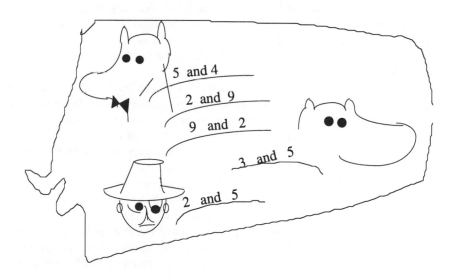

Figure 12

While the document was being composed the pole was not wasting time. It was trying to react. And how! Numbers "3 and 5", "2 and 5" he greeted with a bra-

*vura march, "5 and 4" he accompanied with "ahem", "9 and 2" he awarded the
exclamation "Oh!", and "2 and 9" he accompanied with solemn chords.*

Wonders in the Moominhouse are not rare things.

*Take 29 sticks or other objects and explain the pole's behavior while making up
the "document".*

3. CONTINUING WITH POSITIONAL NUMERATION

Pupils, together with the characters who have different number of fingers on their
paws, come to the notion of a natural number and of a positional number system.

In the first part they want to find a way of describing the results of measurements. As a matter of fact, the characters follow the historical evolution of natural
numbers. They come to the idea of correspondence; they realize the necessity of
searching for a set, a means of transferring information; come to the conception of
grouping or making into bundles; and so on. It seems to us that not only by telling
a story of a number, but also by involving children's practical experiences, drawing them into a purposeful game, we raise the pupils' interest, motivating the introduction of natural numbers.

An especially important thing is that pupils themselves should work with 29
objects, gradually singling out the signs of a positional number system. So, for
instance, analyzing "3 and 5", they can notice that the bundles are counted in the
same way as the sticks. While doing it, the same words are pronounced and the
same figures are written.

Examining "2 and 9" and "9 and 2" pupils will be able to single out one more
feature of the positional number system. The figure denoting bundles has to be
written to the left of the figure denoting sticks, otherwise this notation will not be
clear. It is good if during this activity a teacher will add one more stick. This
additional stick will make it possible to discuss the role of zero for constructing
the positional number system.

In the course of this work and in later activities the teacher needs to ensure that
pupils master a full set of symbols of these natural numbers and of the positional
numeration system. They themselves must enumerate these signs, name them, realize which of these properties are important and which of them are not. And finally they must comprehend that an unimportant sign may become an important
one in a definite situation (for example, the numeral system base).

Thus, pupils gradually study the generalization and enrichment stages. Just constant work on converting the substance of verbal-symbolic expressions into corresponding iconic ideas is, in our opinion, a condition of successful notion formation. It seems important to see to it that images of a different degree of generalization are born in pupils' minds starting with concrete object impressions and finish-
ing with generalized schemes. Pupils should choose which materials to study in
the iconic form and in the verbal-symbolic form. (See Figure 13.)

Why is this kind of work with natural numbers and the positional numeration
system going on in the book "Decimal Fractions in the Moominhouse" from which
the preceding extract is taken?

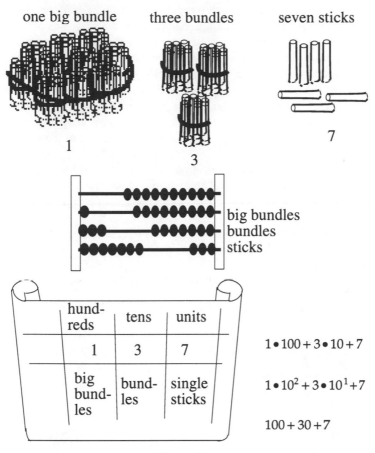

Figure 13

We suggest the combined study of decimals and natural numbers following the introduction of natural numbers enriches the content of the concept of place value. Decimal numeration is a logical extension of natural number numeration. Operations with decimals are considered in comparison with natural number operations. It seems to us that such interconceptual connections (consecutive study of natural numbers and decimals) make pupils' knowledge about both number sets more structured and flexible. Pupils are convinced of the necessity to transfer knowledge of natural numbers onto decimals, refining by this their knowledge about natural numbers.

It ought to be noted that, as a rule, in each of the first four stages (motivation, categorization, enrichment, transference) all the main types of tasks are used. However, using children's experiences (everyday and educational) becomes most imresult, a subjective image of a notion, preliminarily detailed in the preceding stages, turns out to be presented in a condensed and concentrated form.

The psychological nature of such individual cognitive experience reorganization is not yet clear. However, in all probability, just the existence of this experience in the form of contracted cognitive structure provides the possibility of a qualitatively new way of understanding a corresponding object field, which is typical for experts' intellectual activity (Glaser, 1981; Hejny, 1988; Sternberg, 1986).

One may assume, for instance, that one of the examples of the tasks, promoting contraction of the information concerning positional numeration systems is decoding the record "5 and 4" in the story extract. It is impossible to answer the question there without thoroughly understanding the essence of the positional numeration system.

We would like to stress the following circumstance. In subsequent grades the concept of the "positional system of numeration" should be constantly developed because it can serve as a reliable basis for the introduction of a number of mathematical concepts.

Below you will be able to see some such tasks offered to learners at later stages of their mathematical education.

4. TASKS FOR LATER STAGES

Example 1. *Explain the following drawings:*

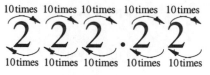

hund-reds	tens	ones	•	tenths	hund-redths
2	2	2	.	2	2

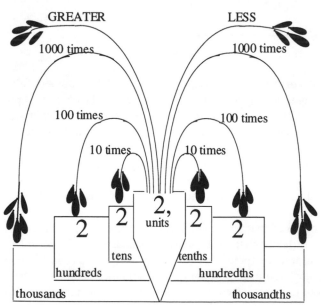

Example 2 (from Gelfman, Demidova et al, 1991).

Three dressmakers were given 16 m of cloth each. Each of them was asked to make five similar dresses. The first dressmaker wrote the problem down as follows:

$$16 \text{ m} \div 5 = 3 \text{ m (rem. 1 m)}$$

3 m   3 m   3 m   3 m   3 m   and 1 m

The second one wrote it down in a different way.

$$160 \text{ dm} \div 5 = 32 \text{ dm} = 3.2 \text{ m}$$

3.2 m   3.2 m   3.2 m   3.2 m   3.2 m

The third one wanted to make waist-bands besides. She wrote it as follows:

$16 \div 5 = 3.2$

$$
\begin{array}{r|ll}
16 & \div 5 & = 3 \,|\, .2 \\
-15 & & \\
\hline
1 & \text{units} & \\
-10 & \text{tenths} & \\
\hline
0 & &
\end{array}
$$

3 m   3 m   3 m   3 m   3 m | 0.2 | 0.2 | 0.2 | 0.2 | 0.2 |

If you were to make several similar dresses, which way of cutting the cloth would you choose?

Example 3 (From Gelfman et al, 1993).

While carrying out the following multiplications someone wrote it this way:

(1)   41   (2)   206
          x 8   x 3
           8   78
          32
          40

Do the results of the multiplications carried out this way seem suspicious to you? Explain how they came about and do the given calculations yourselves.

Study the table describing multiplication of numbers and a monomial by a polynomial.

Try to formulate the rules of this type of multiplication.

Numbers	Algebraic expressions
20·234	$2x \cdot (2x^2 + 3x + 4)$
$= 2 \cdot 10(2 \cdot 10^2 + 3 \cdot 10 + 4)$	
$= 2 \cdot 10 \cdot 2 \cdot 10^2 + 2 \cdot 10 \cdot 3 \cdot 10 + 2 \cdot 10 \cdot 4$	$= 2x \cdot 2x^2 + 2x \cdot 3x + 2x \cdot 4$
$= 4 \cdot 10^3 + 6 \cdot 10^2 + 8 \cdot 10$	$= 4x^3 + 6x^2 + 8x$
$= 4680$	

Consider the way in which the numbers 24 and 234 are multiplied.

$$
\begin{aligned}
24 \cdot 234 \ & = (20 + 4) \cdot 234 = 20 \cdot 234 + 4 \cdot 234 \\
& = 20 \cdot (200 + 30 + 4) + 4 \cdot (200 + 30 + 4) \\
& = (4000 + 600 + 80) + (800 + 120 + 16) \\
& = 4680 + 936 = 5616
\end{aligned}
$$

Compare the multiplication of these numbers with the multiplication of the numbers 20 and 234.

We hope you will easily understand how the following numbers and polynomials are multiplied.

1.
$$(2x + 4) \cdot (2x^2 + 3x + 4)$$
$$= 2x \cdot (2x^2 + 3x + 4) + 4 \cdot (2x^2 + 3x + 4)$$
$$= (2x \cdot 2x^2 + 2x \cdot 3x + 2x \cdot 4) + (8x^2 + 12x + 16)$$
$$= 4x^3 + 6x^2 + 8x + 8x^2 + 12x + 16$$
$$= 4x^3 + 14x^2 + 20x + 16$$

2.

234	$2x^2 + 3x + 4$
x 24	X 2x + 4
936	$8x^2 + 12x + 16$
4680	$4x^3 + 6x^2 + 20x + 0$
5616	$4x^3 + 14x^2 + 20x + 16$

5. CONCLUSION

A child's conceptual growth in the teaching technique we have proposed is controlled by two aspects: stage by stage mastery of process dynamics and major psychological characteristics of conceptual thinking. Is taking into account the psychological preconditions of the mastery of notions the only guarantee for developing a child's intellectual resources?

We think that in this aspect it is necessary to keep a number of other requirements in mind. A teacher using a textbook in our opinion should:

- create conditions for developing such intellectual qualities of an individual as inquisitiveness, criticism, discipline, self-control, and ability to carry on a dialogue;

- provide a psychologically comfortable context of intellectual activity, that is making it possible for a child to choose the most suitable strategy of learning as well as learning pace, creating an atmosphere of optimistic and friendly communication within the subject context of a textbook, and so on.

All of the above-mentioned general conditions of teaching must assist its effectiveness. But there arises a problem: how to match these general requirements with a unique pupil's individuality? We see the solution, to some extent, in that on the one hand, a teacher should be able to use a set of instruments for determining pupils' individual characteristics and on the other hand, the teacher should form an opinion about pupils' metacognitive awareness. Thus the teacher needs the ability to realize, estimate, and take into account individual intellectual characteristics.

REFERENCES

Gelfman, E. G., Wolfengaut, J. J., Demidova, L. N., Zhilina, E. I., Lobanenko, N. B. & Kholodnaja, M. A. (1991). *Decimal fractions in the Moominhouse.* Tomsk, Russia: Tomsk Univ. Publishing House.

Gelfman, E. G., Demidova, L. N., Grinshpon, S. Ya., Wolfengaut, J. J., Zhilina, E. I., Kseneva, V. N., Lobanenko, N. B., Malova, I. E., Matushkina, Z. P., Nepomnjashchaya, L. V., Novikova, G. A., Slobodskoi, V. I., Panchishchina, V. A. & Flescher, T. M. (1991). *Practical studies. Natural numbers and decimal fractions.* Tomsk, Russia: Tomsk Univ. Publishing House.

Gelfman et al. (1993). *Making friends with algebra,* Tomsk, Russia: Tomsk Univ. Publishing House.

Glaser, R. (1981). A research agenda for cognitive psychology and psychometrics. *American Psychologist, 36*(9), 923-936, 1981.

Hejny, M. (1988) Knowledge without understanding. *Proceedings of the International Symposium on Research and Development in Mathematical Education,* (pp. 63-74). Bratislava, Slovakia.

Kholodnaja, M. A. (1983). *Integrated structures of conceptual thinking,* Tomsk, Russia: Tomsk Univ. Publishing House.

Sternberg, R. (1986). Inside intelligence. *American Science, 74*(2), 137-143.

Vekker, L. M. (1976). *Psychic processes. Thinking and intelligence, Vol. 2..* Leningrad, Russia: Leningrad State Univ. Publishing House.

Vygotsky, L. S. (1983). *Thinking and speech.* Complete works, Vol. 2. Moscow, Pedagogika.

Walters, J., & Gardner, H. (1986). The crystallizing experience: Discovering an intellectual gift. In R. Sternberg (Ed.), *Conception of giftedness.* (pp. 306-331). Cambridge, UK: Cambridge University Press.

E. G. Gelfman, L. N. Demidova, N. B. Lobanenko, J. J. Wolfengaut
Tomsk State Pedagogical Institute, Russia

M.A. Kholodnaja,
Kiev State University, Ukraine

CONTRIBUTIONS TO PART FOUR

The charge given to contributors in this section required them to articulate the roles of culture and social interactions within classrooms and also to make an attempt to account for the role in learning of the broader cultural context within which classrooms are situated. There is now a growing appreciation of the connected influences of both the microcultures of the classroom and the cultural traditions that different students bring to the classroom.

The first three chapters follow well-established research frameworks to investigate classrooms; Nunes gives us a chapter investigating the influence of different linguistic backgrounds on numeration systems. This chapter links nicely with Masanja's historically-located discussion of the effects of colonialism and different African cultures on the development of number representation, and the connection of number and space through intricate diagrams with cultural origins. Nunes and Masanja both are concerned with how broad cultural traditions influence the mathematics that is learned.

Our other two contributions to this section describe in detail the development of microcultures within classrooms and the powerful influence these have on the learning process. Reynolds and Wheatley investigated the learning of measurement, while Poirier provides a case study of children's interactions in their exploration of number ideas.

The Editors.

INTERACTIONS BETWEEN CHILDREN IN MATHEMATICS CLASS: AN EXAMPLE CONCERNING THE CONCEPT OF NUMBER

For the last several years our studies have been concerned with the social analysis of the development of mathematical knowledge in children. (Bednarz & Dufour-Janvier, 1988; Dufour-Janvier, Bednarz, 1989; Bednarz, Poirier & Bacon, 1992; Bednarz, 1991; Bednarz, Janvier, Poirier & Bacon, 1993).

The different learning situations created in the framework of these studies, aiming at the formation of elementary mathematical concepts in children, are based on a view of learning in which collective activity plays an important role. (See Garnier, Bednarz, Ulanovskaya, 1991; Bednarz & Garnier, 1989). In what follows we shall briefly present the theoretical foundations of such an approach before moving on to the social interactions put into place during an experiment with young children (6, 7 years old). The relations between the social dynamic and the conceptual framework will then be elaborated.

1. FOUNDATIONS OF THE APPROACH: THE SOCIO-CONSTRUCTIVIST PERSPECTIVE

The social dimension of the development of mathematics has taken on greater and greater importance recently in reflections brought to bear on the teaching of mathematics (Ernest, 1991; Bauersfeld, 1988). It forms a theoretical framework for activities carried out in classes with children (Cobb, Yackel &Wood, 1992; Garnier, Bednarz & Ulanovskaya, 1991; Bednarz & Garnier, 1989). The social interpersonal process of dialogue and critique, at the base of the development of mathematics itself, plays a role of primary importance (Lakatos, 1976; Ernest, 1991).

Inscribed in the social paradigm of the elaboration of mathematical knowledge, our studies draw their theoretical foundations in the socio-constructivist perspective stemming from the Geneva school (Doise, Mugny, Perret-Clermont, 1976; Mugny, 1985), and in the theory of learning situations (Brousseau, 1986). Social experience plays a fundamental role intervening as a component of individual dynamics participating in the cognitive development of children and in their construction of mathematical knowledge.

From this perspective, "individual dynamics are conceived as being founded on social experience they are called upon to structure" (Mugny, 1985, p. 18). These dynamics are viewed in different forms in the studies that subscribe to the socio-constructivist perspective. *At the origins* they refer to the interactions among children putting into place a socio-cognitive conflict, that is, "a structuring conflict, the source of change in the individual. This conflict is possible only in interactions where simultaneously there are expressed several actions, solutions, discourses ... in which there is manifested a system of opposing cognitive centerings" (Garnier, Bednarz & Ulanovskaya, 1991, p. 15). Having socio-cognitive conflict as their

H. Mansfield et al. (eds.), Mathematics for Tomorrow's Young Children, 166–176.

point of departure, the studies will little by little move away from this to gradually include other social dimensions. In this way studies interested in the role of social variables in cognitive development will gradually be undertaken:

In these studies social experience is viewed beyond conflict, under significant aspects attached to the content of tasks and situations. This social nature of the situation presented to subjects rejoins the preoccupation of certain didacticians on the "didactical contract" that relates the teacher, the students and knowledge within a pedagogical situation (Brousseau, 1986; Schubauer-Leoni, 1986). (Garnier, Bednarz & Ulanovskaya, 1991, p. 15.)

Other studies focus on the role of cultural and social factors on the construction of knowledge (Nunes, 1991; Janvier, 1991; d'Ambrosio, 1989). A final type of studies emphasizes the dynamic social interactions between students carrying out the same task. This is the perspective we will take here.

These confrontations between students, put into place in the classroom that will contribute to the evolution of individual mathematics knowledge, as well as to the solution procedures used by the children, can take several forms: action situations between subjects (the division of the same problem task between two subjects); communication situations between two subjects, or two groups, concerning different social roles (Laborde, 1991, Brousseau, 1986); and validation situations in which different positions will be expressed and confronted. These diverse confrontations between students play an important role in the theory of situations developed by Brousseau (1986).

In the first phase of the process of mathematisation, termed the "dialectic of action", the child is called upon to elaborate certain mental models of relations connecting the elements present in a situation, and that regulate his or her action. It is by starting from these models that the learning processes will be articulated. In order for mathematisation to take place, the child should be brought to make his or her model explicit by means of an appropriate language. This is part of a fundamental phase, termed the "dialectic of the formulation," where the interactions between students play a role of the first order in the communication situations put into place between subjects or groups of subjects.

During these interactions, children should make explicit the language they use, their conventions, and justify their choices—thereby leading to debate between them, where the different positions will be exteriorized. These debates enable the students to clarify their thinking, to analyze the different models elaborated, to question these, to modify them as needed, and to reject them if appropriate.

We see in these different phases of the process of mathematisation the importance accorded to the interactions between students, as well as the process of social negotiation described by Ernest. The studies we refer to here concern the interactions between students in class in the construction of early arithmetic concepts in young children.

2. THE PROCEDURE

The intervention put into place, that lasted five months (from September 1991 to January 1992), was conducted in a first grade class with six years olds at the beginning of their schooling. Centered about the first arithmetic learnings it aims in particular at the construction by the child of the concepts of number and operations, the development of the skill of mental calculation and problem solving. In order to illustrate the procedure we shall focus below on one of the aspects worked on in this intervention in relation to the early arithmetic learnings - number and counting.

The teaching of the concept of number, that we usually find in first year school textbooks, is centered on the coding of collections, and the decoding of a symbolism (written numbers) starting from well-structured small collections less than ten. These are followed by collections between ten and twenty. After this work on units the work on regroupings begins for the purpose of coding. In the case of larger collections, the tens are placed on the left, and the ungrouped units on the right. In school textbooks we give little opportunity for children to organize their tasks or their ways of proceeding.

The objective in textbooks is generally centered on the reading and writing of numbers based on the learning of the rules and conventions of writing. Our intervention, on the other hand, is in another perspective. It aims at certain essential skills in the acquisition of the number concept: the counting of collections, putting them in order, to the early operations on collections. This implies, as we shall discuss, an organization of increasing complexity for children to resolve the tasks proposed. The sequence of activities presented to students is based on a conceptual analysis of number and on the underlying skills required for understanding. To illustrate the procedure we focus on the activities of counting and comparison.

2.1 Conceptual framework

One of the first acquisitions of the young child in regard to number is the number sequence (the recitation of a numerical sequence). However, a child who knows the number sequence does not necessarily know "counting" or "enumeration", that is, how many objects are in a collection. For this, the child needs not only to know the names of the number sequence, but also how to apply this sequence correctly to the objects counted by counting each element one and only one time and coordinating the sequence with the object counted. Counting requires the knowledge of the number sequence (memorization), its organization (in order to make sure that each element is named only once), and coordination (in order to correctly associate the sequence to the object pointed).

A series of activities of increasing complexity is then used partly in view of encouraging a better organization. In this way, after having counted a small collection of real objects, the students are brought to the counting of a larger collection that is drawn on paper. The counting strategies first put into place for small collections should be refined to respond to the requirement for the counting of larger collections and to the passage to drawn collections.

By focusing in this way on a mathematical reality of increasing complexity, forcing the children to an organization of increasing sophistication, the intervention should contribute to their conceptual evolution. This evolution is closely tied, as we shall see, to the child's need to treat and communicate concerning collections of increasing demands. This intervention suggests the presence of interactions between children. We shall now illustrate this mode of intervention.

2.2 Social interactions and the construction of counting schemes by children

Among the situations presented to the students touching the development of the number concept and the construction of number schemes of increasing efficiency, we find at the beginning of the intervention activities of counting and the comparison of collections.

The situations presented in what follows are spread over a period of about a month. At the start of this period, the students had already developed certain procedures more or less efficient to count small collections (those from 10 to 20). We will see in the following example how increasing the size of the collection to count forces a more efficient organization, and how work in groups encourages an evolution of the counting schemes.

2.21 Counting tasks with a collection of real objects. The initial activity proposed to the children consisted of individually counting small collections (approximately sixteen wood rods). The directions given by the teachers were as follows: "I will give a bag to each of you, containing rods. You have to find a way so that you can know, when I will take back all the bags, how many rods are in your bag. You can organized yourself anyway you want, but you have to be able to tell me how many elements were in your bag."

When all the children have finished this activity a second activity is undertaken. This time the children are put into teams of two. Each team has to count all the rods in the two bags, thus confronting them with a larger collection; the directions given by the teachers are always the same: "Arrange yourselves together in order than we can know how many elements there are in your collection." Two by two the children engage in the counting of their new collection giving rise to diverse interactions between them.

For some children, the solution is essentially individual. Clement and Alexandra, after having united their rods, start counting. This work is done individually, each working separately. The teacher intervenes and repeats the directions: they should find a way, as a team, so that we may know how many rods there are in their collection. Alexandra then carries out the counting alone, putting aside the objects counted. When Clement tries to take a rod, she takes it back to place it in her pile. The activity is thus carried out by only one child; there is no collaborative interaction.

For others, an organization allows control of the counting. Valerie and Emmanual, in contrast to the preceding pair, work as a team. Valerie holds the packet of rods in her hand and places them one by one on the table so that Emmanual can count them. Emmanual takes the rods one by one counting each and then puts it aside. He continues thus until the whole collection is counted. In order to verify their result they repeat the counting reversing their roles. We see in this team cooperation taking place on a shared task, developing a certain efficient organization in order to count the given collection.

Some students divide up the task. Another team exhibits another manner of co-operation. The work this time is done by alternating. William and Sebastian divide up the collection to be counted, each taking up a handful of rods. Taking their turn they each put a rod on the table, taking care to line them up, and counting out loud. When Sebastian hesitates before saying a number he looks at William who approves, and the sequence can continue.

We see in this example, in addition to team work in the division and carrying out of the tasks, how interaction enables one of them to reinforce his knowledge of the number sequence. In fact, Sebastian hesitating could perhaps not have been able to go on by himself. Encouraged by the help of William, he carries it out. In the interaction between children different modes of organization take place to carry out counting. How will the schemes previously elaborated be adjusted to respond to a new task?

2.22 The task of counting a collection drawn on paper. The task of counting a collection, this time drawn on paper, should provoke a modification of the schemes previously used. Given the greater complexity of the task, the objects drawn cannot be displaced and put aside, a strategy that the children use spontaneously with real objects. By using a drawn collection we force a progressive readjustment of their counting scheme, obliging the children to have recourse to new organizations and strategies.

Figure 1

In this new situation, the teacher first shows the children a cardboard, for only a few seconds, on which there is a drawing of 21 scattered bows (see Figure 1). She asks the children to quickly say how many bows there are on the cardboard. Some children will try to give an approximate answer stating "I looked carefully," or "I think there are a lot," without being certain of their answer.

In order to encourage division of the work into a larger organization the children are once again put into teams of two, and are given a reproduction of the cardboard and a pencil. The teacher proposes finding "ways that once the task is finished (retaking the paper) we can quickly tell how many bows there are on the card-board." The children have access to different strategies more or less organized. While some count the bows without leaving any marks on the paper, others put a check mark beside each counted bow, or connect the bows to each other with lines (Figure 2). This strategy, effective for small collections, is much less effective when the student has to count a large scattered collection, because there is a greater risk to forget or to pass over the same bow more than once.

Figure 2

Other students numbered each bow, the last bow numbered indicating the cardinal number of the collection (Figure 3). This procedure is effective for this task, but risks causing problems when the objects to be counted are more numerous leaving less space for the child to write all the numbers.

A final strategy used by some children regroups the objects to be counted by 2, 3, or 5. In Figure 4, the child used grouping by threes then counted by 3, 6, 9....

Figure 3

Figure 4

However, the use of this organization is not without difficulties. The following extract illustrates, in part, the complexity of counting a drawn collection and the support of interaction between children on the evolution of counting schemes. When Clement (recall he had not counted in his first activity) writes his name, Benjamin starts counting the bow by twos. After Clement has finished writing his name, Benjamin restarts counting:

Benjamin:	"Two" (he points to two bows with his pencil, then looks at Clement.) "I counted some, now it's your turn."
Clement:	(he points to two other bows with his pencil) "Two" (at this point he imitates Benjamin)
Benjamin:	"No !"
Clement:	"Four" (there is here an adjustment in the counting already carried out by Benjamin)
Benjamin:	"Four, two, four, six" (Benjamin continues adding two more to the four, the place where Clement had reached.)

The two children continue in this way. Furthermore, Benjamin seems to follow a certain pattern in his counting of the objects on the box in order to avoid forgetting or repeating. Benjamin starts counting in the upper left hand corner of the sheet then continues by a systematic sweeping. This is confirmed when Clement points to bows far from the last objects counted. This will be taken up by Benjamin who explains to him that the bows should be counted in a certain order "because if not, we'll get all mixed up." After having divided the sheet into two parts, they then correctly count by alternating the first part of the sheet, then the second.

As we have seen, counting a drawn collection is a complex task. Clement does not seem to use a strategy to make sure that all the bows have been counted one and only one time, risking forgetting some or counting the same one twice. Benjamin suggests a sweeping strategy. Working in a team allows an evolution of the counting scheme for Clement, an evolution that manifests itself in the following situation.

2.23 Comparison task of two drawn collections. The teacher shows the children two cardboards representing flowers from two florists, Mr. Green and Mrs. Red. She states, "you will have to tell me quickly who has more flowers. Can you organize your work so that we can quickly see who has more." Each child receives two sheets one showing Mr. Green's flowers the other Mrs. Red's. When the task is finished the whole takes part in a discussion of the various solutions that were proposed.

Catherine (Figure 5) proceeded by connecting Mrs. Red's flowers with red lines, and Mr. Green's flowers with green lines. Being careful not to forget counting any of the flowers, she is, however, unable to respond to the direction of showing quickly "Who has more flowers?"

Clement, on his part, explains that he put a mark on each flower (Figure 6). The teacher asks the class, "If I look at Clement's papers can I find very quickly which one has the most?" The class answers no. Alexandra explains that Clement "has put

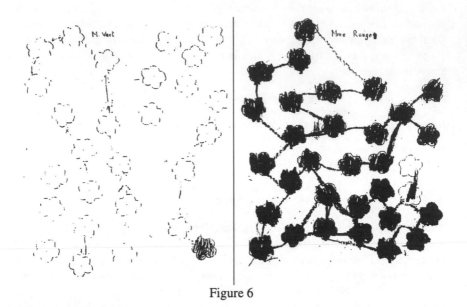

Figure 6

marks to make sure he has counted everything." The teacher repeats her question, "Can I know very quickly who has the most?" Fanny replies, "No, you have to count them yourself because if there are just little checkmarks that won't tell you." The teacher says, "When I look at Clement's paper I see that he has made all his little checkmarks. I'm sure he hasn't missed any. But, to know who has more, as Fanny says, I have to count them all again."

Eve-Marie then suggests, "To start, I put colors [on the counted flowers], but I found that wasn't a good idea, then I put numbers" (Figure 7). After discussion the class agrees that this is a better way to quickly determine which of the two florists has more flowers.

This extract shows us there was an evolution of the counting scheme for Clement. Whereas at the start he counted in a disorganized way with a high risk of making an error, his work with Benjamin (preceding extract) shows him the necessity of ensuring that the elements are counted only once. This is what he does in checkmarking the counted flowers. However, this verifies only one part of the task. Clement's strategy does not provide for others a way to see quickly who has more flowers. Eve-Marie goes further by writing as she goes along in counting each flower, and thus determining the total quantity to which she arrives.

3. CONCLUSION

These few extracts illustrate how the increasing complexity of the proposed tasks, and the social interactions between children, were able to contribute to the evolution of the counting schemes. In presenting to children tasks of increasing complexity (passage from a small collection to a larger collection of real objects, then

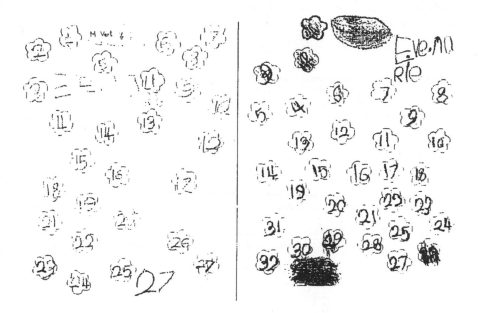

Figure 7

passing to a drawn collection, task 2, and finally bringing the children to compare two drawn collections, task 3), we oblige, in this way, the children to organize themselves, to modify and to adjust the strategies developed.

An efficient strategy used by some children in the first task consisted of putting aside the counted objects; however, in presenting them with a drawn collection (task 2) this strategy had certain limitations. The drawn objects not being able to be moved or to be put aside forces the children to modify their organization. Some students identified the counted objects by checkmarks thereby making sure of counting each bow only once. This strategy, efficient for solving the problem of counting a drawn collection, is not efficient, as we have seen in task 3, where we need to compare two drawn collections in to order to determine quickly which is greater. The children had to adjust their strategy as a function of the task. This adjustment was made via the social interactions put into place during their work in teams, and during the discussion with the entire class, making it eventually possible to develop these new cognitive tools. The child was in effect brought to adjust his or her way of doing in accordance with his or her team mate, in the carrying out of the task itself, in making explicit his or her procedure or strategy, bringing about a clarification of thinking. Confronted with the different ways of others, the child is brought to progressively restructure his or her thinking and to refine the procedures developed.

Such an evolution implies a real engagement on the part of each partner on the task, in regard to a situation that should be significant to them. In parallel, it suggests to researchers the need to reflect on situations that are susceptible to contribute to such an evolution.

REFERENCES

Bauersfeld, H. (1988). Interaction, construction and knowledge: alternative perspectives for mathematics education. In T. Cooney & D. Grouws (Eds.), *Effective mathematics teaching.* Reston, VA: National Council of Teachers of Mathematics.

Bednarz, N. (1991). Interactions sociales et construction d'un système d'écriture des nombres en classe primaire. In C. Garnier, N. Bednarz & I. Ulanovskaya (Eds.), *Après Vygotski et Piaget. Perspectives sociale et constructiviste. Écoles russe et occidentale* (pp. 51-67). Bruxelles, Belgium: Éditions de Boeck.

Bednarz, N., & Garnier, C. (Eds.). (1989). *Construction des savoirs: obstacles et conflits.* Montréal, Canada: Agence d'Arc.

Bednarz, N., Janvier, B., Poirier, L., & Bacon, L. (1993). A socioconstructivist point of view on the use of symbolism in the teaching and learning of mathematics. *Alberta Journal of Educational Research, 39*(1), 41-58.

Bednarz, N., & Dufour-Janvier, B. (1988). A constructivist approach to numeration in primary school: Results of a three year intervention with the same group of children. *Educational Studies in Mathematics, 19,* 299-331.

Bednarz, N., Poirier, L., & Bacon, L. (1992). Apprendre à penser en mathématiques: un exemple d'intervention pédagogique auprès de jeunes enfants. *Vie pédagogique, 79,* 35-36.

Brousseau, G. (1986). *Théorisation des phénomènes d'enseignement des mathématiques.* Thèse de doctorat d'État, Université de Bordeaux.

Cobb, P., Yackel, E., & Wood, T. (1992). A constructivist alternative to the representational view of mind in mathematics education, *Journal for Research in Mathematics Education, 23*(1), 2-33.

D'Ambrosio, V. (1989). What can we expect from ethnomathematics? In C. Keitel (Ed.), *Science and technology education: mathematics, education and society.* Paris, France: UNESCO.

Doise, W., Mugny, G., & Perret-Clermont, A.N. (1976). Social interaction and cognitive development: Further evidence. *European Journal of Social Psychology, 6*(2), 245-247.

Dufour-Janvier, B., & Bednarz, N. (1989). Situations conflictuelles expérimentées pour faire face à quelques obstacles dans une approche constructiviste de l'arithmétique au primaire, In N. Bednarz & C. Garnier (Eds.), *Construction des savoirs: Obstacles et conflits* (pp. 315-333). Montréal, Canada: Agence d'Arc.

Ernest, P. (1991). *The philosophy of mathematics education.* Hampshire, UK: The Falmer Press.

Garnier, C., Bednarz, N., & Ulanovskaya, I. (Eds.). (1991). *Après Vygotski et Piaget. Perspectives sociale et constructiviste. Écoles russe et occidentale.* Bruxelles, Belgium: Éditions de Boeck.

Janvier, C. (1991). Contextualisation et représentation dans l'utilisation des mathématiques. In C. Garnier, N. Bednarz & I. Ulanovskaya (Eds.), *Après Vygotski et Piaget. Perspectives sociale et constructiviste. Écoles russe et occidentale..* Bruxelles, Belgium: Éditions de Boeck.

Laborde, C. (1991). Deux usages complémentaires de la dimension sociale dans les structures d'apprentissage en mathématiques. In C. Garnier, N. Bednarz & I. Ulanovskaya (Eds.), *Après Vygotski et Piaget. Perspectives sociale et constructiviste. Écoles russe et occidentale..* Bruxelles, Belgium: Éditions de Boeck.

Lakatos, I. (1976). *Proofs and refutations: The logic of mathematical discovery.* Cambridge, MA: Harvard University Press.

Mugny, G. (1985). *Psychologie sociale du développement cognitif.* Berne.

Nunes, T. (1991). Systèmes alternatifs de connaissances selon différents environnements. In C. Garnier, N. Bednarz & I. Ulanovskaya (Eds.), *Après Vygotski et Piaget. Perspectives sociale et constructiviste. Écoles russe et occidentale..* Bruxelles, Belgium: Éditions de Boeck.

Louise Poirier and Lily Bacon (Translated by Maurice Bélanger)
CIRADE, Université du Québec à Montréal
Canada

WHAT IS THE DIFFERENCE BETWEEN *ONE, UN* AND *YI?*

1. INTRODUCTION

Learning to count is an important acquisition for young children anywhere in the world. Numeration systems increase our power to represent quantities in sets and create the possibility of carrying out calculations. English, French, and Chinese speaking children profit equally from these advantages. In all three languages, when young children start learning to count, they need to memorize the number words in a fixed order. In all three languages they also need to come to understand the way number labels are generated in order to surpass simple memorization of labels. However similar the task of memorizing number labels may be across languages, the task of understanding how number labels are generated is not the same for English, French, and Chinese children.

Chinese children have to learn a regular system. There is a basic set of labels in the system, those for 1 to 10. From 11 to 99, children do not need to learn new labels. The number words are combinations of the basic labels generated through a simple set of rules in a completely regular system (for a description, see Miller & Stigler, 1986). A number label (say the word for 2) placed before the word for 10 indicates a decade-that is, "two-ten" refers to 20. A number word placed after the 10 indicates the number of units to be added to whatever number of tens precede it.

English children, in contrast, have to learn a system that contains both regularities and irregularities. There are twelve unrelated labels to start with, three more than the number of words that will be used as stems to generate other labels in the system. The decade words can give children a clue to the existence of a system because they share a common ending, "-ty." But the decades also comprise some irregularities because some of the stems suffer changes when they become part of a decade label (eg., two-twenty; three-thirty, five-fifty). A basic number word, like the word for 2, placed after the decade word means that that number of units should be added to whatever number of tens precede it, just as in Chinese.

French children have to learn the most difficult of the three oral numeration systems. They start out by having a larger set of unrelated words to memorize than both the Chinese and the English children. Like the English children, they use a system that has regularities and irregularities. However, there are fewer regularities in the French decade-labels. It is hardly worth it to attempt to learn a rule for generating them. One might as well memorize the nine decades and use some of the similarities between decade-labels and the basic number words (eg., trois-trente; quatre-quarante; cinq-cinquante; six-soixante) as *aide memoire*. Finally, the last aspect of the French system does not differ from that of English and Chinese: a basic label, like the word for 2 (or the word for 12 also, in French), placed after a

177

H. Mansfield et al. (eds.), Mathematics for Tomorrow's Young Children, 177–185.

decade word means that the number of units it indicates has to be added to whatever decades precede it.

In this chapter, I want to review some studies which analyze the understanding of the numeration system by British, French, and Chinese children. The similarities and differences described above will be used in exploring the distinction between counting and understanding the numeration system. They will also allow for a discussion of the roles of cognitive and linguistic factors in children's understanding of number.

The next section of this chapter discusses a general analytical approach to the study of children's understanding of numeration systems. The following section reviews the cross-cultural evidence. In the last section, a summary of the findings and educational implications are presented.

2.WHAT IS THE DIFFERENCE BETWEEN COUNTING AND UNDERSTANDING A NUMERATION SYSTEM?

2.1 Conceptual problems in understanding a numeration system with a base

A numeration system with a base is rather complex semantically. The base in a numeration system involves the idea of units of different values being counted and added. In a base ten system, like the one we use in English, there are three orders— ones, tens, and hundreds—in each class (units, thousands, millions, and so on). Each time we count ten units of one order, we group them together, and this group becomes one units of the next order. Thus to understand a base system we need at least two concepts: (1) we need to understand that units may have different values—that is, we need to understand the concept of *relative value*; and (2) we need to understand that different value units can be put together in one single value by addition—that is, we need to understand the *additive composition of number*.

Children who can count up to high values—for example, 40 or 50—seem to have understood how number labels are put together. It is unlikely that they would be producing this long sequence of number labels in the correct order without any idea of the rules generating labels in the system. Several investigators (for example, Ginsburg, 1977; Fuson, Richards & Briars, 1982; Siegler & Robinson, 1982) have pointed out aspects of children's counting behavior that suggest the understanding of some of the rules generating number words. For example, children are most likely to stop counting and say they do not know what comes next when they reach a decade plus nine. Also, children may repeat a decade or skip a decade altogether, without disrupting the pattern of decade plus 1, plus 2, plus 3, and so on. Children seem to realize this addition rule in the number labels early on. But do they understand additive composition?

It is possible that children produce the strings of numbers as a linear sequence, the order of which is facilitated by this pattern of introducing one, two, three after decade words without understanding relative value and additive composition. When they count objects like jelly beans or marbles, these are not regrouped into tens and ones. How then can we investigate whether children realize that *twenty-two* means *twenty plus two*?

Some years ago, together with a colleague, I developed a set of tasks to investigate children's understanding of relative value and of the additive composition of numbers (Nunes Carraher, 1985; Nunes Carraher & Schlieman, 1990). In order to distinguish between children's counting and their understanding of relative value and additive composition, we had to find a situation in which children would need to use these concepts to solve problems. The situation we chose involved counting money. Two types of tasks were developed. In the *Relative Values Task,* children were presented with two arrays of money, one belonging to the child and the other belonging to the experimenter, and we asked the children who would be able to buy more sweets if they went to a shop[1]. Table 1 contains a description of the types of items we used. The crucial items in this task involved presenting the children with arrays in which attending only to the number of coins would not provide the correct response.

Who can buy more sweets if they go into a shop, A or B, or can they buy just as much?

Type 1: Simple counting of coins as objects give the right answer.
　　　　　Example: A has ten 1p coins and B nine 1p coins.
Type 2: Same number of coins, different denominations.
　　　　　Example: A has four 1p coins and B has four 10p coins.
Type 3: Different number of coins and different denominations.
　　　　　Example: A has nine 1p coins and B has one 10p coin.

Table 1. Three types of items used in the Relative Values Task.

In the *Additive Composition Task,* children were asked to pay certain sums of money for their pretend-purchases using either coins of one denomination only or coins with different values. Some examples of items in this task are presented in Table 2. The significant items are those in which the children have to count money in sums that involve mixed denominations.

Children are asked to pay certain sums of money for their pretend-purchases using the coins they have. The experimenter does not have any change.

Type 1: Composition using 1p coins only
　　　　　Example: The child has twenty 1p coins and is asked to pay 13p, 8p, ….
Type 2: Composition using 5p and 1p coins
　　　　　Example: The child is given three 5p and four 1p coins and is asked to pay 6p, 8p, ….
Type 3: Composition using 10p and 1p coins
　　　　　Example: The child has two 10p and nine 1p coins and is asked to pay 22p, 24p, ….
Type 4: Composition using 20p and 1p coins
　　　　　Example: The child is given two 20p and nine 1p coins and asked to pay 22p, 24p, …

The first type of item is referred to as counting/paying with singles only; the latter three types are referred to as counting/paying with mixed denominations.

Table 2. Four types of items used in the Additive Composition Task.

[1] Children were always tested with the appropriate currency. The identification 1p, 5p and so on, is used here as shorthand for the different denominations of coins irrespective of country. Some of the children were tested with coins and others with play money but this difference does not affect performance.

This task was initially carried out with pre-school children and, in a modified version, with illiterate adults in Brazil (Nunes Carraher, 1985) to investigate whether it was necessary to master the written numeration system to understand relative value and additive composition, as Luria (1969) had suggested many years ago. *The results clearly indicated that children and adults who did not master the written numeration system could understand both concepts.* The performance of the adults was almost perfect in the version of the tasks that was developed for working with them. About one third of the pre-school children showed performance at ceiling level although none of them could write multi-digit numbers.

These studies indicated that counting and understanding the numeration system are not identical abilities. Two thirds of the pre-school children could not compose sums of money as small as 13p by using one 10p and three 1p or even a sum like 6p by using one 5p and one 1p.

Nunes, Bryant, Falcão, and Lima (1993) later investigated the factors that could possibly explain young children's performance in these tasks in a sample of British 5 and 6 year old children. The British children were given the three types of items in the Relative Values Task described in Table 1. In the first type of item, the arrays were composed of coins with the same value; only the number of coins differed. To succeed in these items, children only had to count the number of coins in the arrays. In the second type of item, the number of coins was the same but their values differed. Children could succeed in these items without counting by reasoning in terms of one-to-many correspondences. In the third type of item, children had to coordinate the number of coins with their value to provide a correct response.

The results indicated that British 5-6 year old children had no difficulty with items that simply required counting the number of coins. Their performance was almost at ceiling level, with a mean number of correct responses equal to 2.82 out of 3 items. However, it was clearly difficult for them, especially for the 5-year olds, to take relative value into account. An analysis of variance with number of correct responses in each type of item (repeated measures design) and age (as a between groups factor) revealed a significant effect of age and type of item with no significant interaction. Both type 2 and type 3 items were rather difficult and no significant difference was observed between these two types of item.

Further analysis of these results was carried out by looking at the correlations across types of items. Whereas performances in type 2 and type 3 items were significantly correlated, children's performances in these items did not correlate with their performance in type 1 items, which only required counting the number of coins. These results bring support to the distinction between counting and understanding the numeration system brought forth on the basis of the initial set of data with Brazilian children.

Nunes, Bryant, Falcão, and Lima (1993) also presented the British children with the *Additive Composition Task.* In this task, a shopping game was played in which the children had coins that they were asked to use to pay for their pretend purchases. All four types of item described in Table 2 were used. The comparison between 1p only and the remaining types of items could bring further support to the distinction between counting and understanding additive composition of number.

The comparison between items involving 5p, 10p and 20p coins in combinations with 1p coins were set up to investigate whether children merely followed the linguistic cues or whether they had a genuine understanding of additive composition of number. If they succeeded with the items involving 20p coins and 1p coins but were unsuccessful with the others, they could be simply following the linguistic cues—that is, in order to pay "twenty-one p," they would take out one 20p coin and one 1p coin. However, if there were no significant differences across these types of items, we could be more confident that they were relying on the understanding of additive composition.

The results of this study were rather clear. The children's performance when counting money in 1p coins was close to perfect (mean correct response 4.62 out of 5) and differed significantly from their performance on all other types of item. This result confirms once again the distinction between counting and understanding the numeration system. In contrast, there were no significant differences across the other types of item, a result that is consistent with the notion that the successful children were not simply following the linguistic cues from the number labels but had genuinely understood additive composition.

In an attempt to explain further children's performance in the additive composition task, we also gave them a series of three addition problems to solve (with the support of tokens, if they so wished). We expected that there would be significant correlations between performances on the addition problems and on the numeration system tasks if the children effectively had to think of a number as the additive composition of parts.

Composite scores were obtained for the *Relative Values Task* (including all items that required taking relative value into account) and for the *Additive Composition Task* (including all items that involved mixing coins of different values). The intercorrelations between these tasks showed no significant relationships between counting and the other tasks whereas the correlations between solving addition problems, on the one hand, and relative value (r = .53) and additive composition (r = .72) on the other, were significant. *These intercorrelations suggest that there is much more shared variance between understanding of the numeration system and addition than between counting and understanding the numeration system.* However, it must be recalled that there was little variation in children's counting ability in the counting task used here and these correlations may underestimate the commonalities between counting and understanding the numeration system.

In short, the results of the Brazilian and the British studies indicate that counting and understanding the numeration system are two distinct forms of knowledge. They also indicate that additive composition is not taken simply from the linguistic labels nor from knowledge of the written numeration system.

3. DOES THE REGULARITY OF THE NUMERATION SYSTEM FACILITATE ITS UNDERSTANDING?

Whereas the previous studies demonstrated that children are not simply mapping number labels onto coins as objects when they perform well in the *Additive Com-*

position Task, it seems unlikely that the linguistic forms have *no* impact on children's understanding of numeration systems. When comparisons are carried out across systems, effects of the linguistic system are found. But they seem to take place at the level of understanding the system rather than through to a mapping of labels onto values.

Research already available suggests that regularity confers on learners some advantages. Miller and Stigler (1986) have already shown that it is easier to learn the number words in a regular counting system, such as the Chinese one, than in a less regular system, such as the English one. Chinese 5- and 6-year-old children count up to higher numbers than American children and count sets of objects more successfully. However, Miller and Stigler point out on the basis of an error analysis that the Chinese children's greater success in counting objects can be attributed to their better knowledge of number labels rather than a better understanding of one-to-one correspondence.

Understanding the numeration system involves a different issue. The question is whether the greater regularity of a system facilitates the understanding of additive composition that is present in all three systems. Chinese is perfectly regular; English contains some irregularities but fewer than those observed in French; French is the most irregular of the three systems. Does this order matter or is the difference between regular and irregular more significant?

Miura, Kim, Chang, and Okamoto (1988) investigated number representation among children who used regular systems (Chinese, Japanese, and Korean children) and others who did not (American children). They used an optional paradigm in which children were asked to give the experimenter certain numbers of blocks and could do so by counting out units or by using tens from base ten blocks material. They also verified whether children could represent the same number in a variety of ways. The Asian children showed a preference for using base ten blocks whereas the American children showed a preference for using ones only. Further, more Asian than American children were able to construct the number representation in two ways. These results clearly indicate that the Asian children, all learners of regular systems, are likely to understand the concept of *base* earlier. Two aspects of these results require further investigation. First, optional paradigms do not always induce subjects to use their best capacities. Second, base ten blocks are essentially a pedagogical device and may have little significance to children. Further investigation with significant material in another paradigm could be productive.

Lines and Bryant (1993) analyzed the performance of Chinese and English children (16 in Taiwan and 16 in Britain, mean age = 5.8 years in the *Additive Composition Task* described above, which uses significant materials. The children were given the *AdditiveCcomposition Task* with three types of item: coins of 1p only; 10p and 1p coins; and 5p and 1p coins. No significant differences were found between the Chinese and the British children in the trials where only 1p coins were used. For values under 20, British and Chinese children counted equally well. In contrast, the Chinese children did significantly better than the British children in the items where coins of different denominations were mixed—that is, those items that required additive composition. Although Chinese children made more errors in the additive composition items that involved 5p than in those items that involved 10p mixtures with 1p coins (20% errors versus 6%, respectively), this difference does not indicate that Chinese children were simply following a linguistic pattern in the *Additive Composition Task.* They still performed rather well in the additive composition items with 5p and 1p mixtures, where no linguistic cues were available, and significantly better than the British children.

In summary, the greater regularity of the Chinese counting labels appears to facilitate the understanding of additive composition of number. It now remains to be seen whether different levels of irregularity are also reflected in the understanding of additive composition from the comparison between British and French-speaking children.

Nunes, Bryant, Falcão, and Lima (1993) carried out a comparison between 20 French and 40 English children in the *Additive Composition Task.* Both samples of children were of two age levels, 5- and 6-year-olds, but the British 5-year-olds were in their first term in school and the French 5-year-olds were in pre-school. In spite of this difference, the samples of 5-year-olds were still considered comparable because the British children were seen in their first term in school. All children answered, among other tasks, the *Additive Composition Task* with two types of item, those that used only 1p coins and those that mixed 10p coins and 1p coins.

In addition, the French 6-year-olds and a further group of 7-year-old French children answered items where the children were asked to pay amounts of moneybetween 80p and 90p either using mixtures of 20p and 1p coins or using mixtures of 10p and 1p coins. These items were introduced in order to ascertain whether French children would show greater ease in composing these sums of money by using four 20p coins (a composition that parallels their "quatre-vingt" level for 80) or by using eight 10p coins (a composition that is distanced from the label but is coherent with the understanding of additive composition of number built from values under 80). If children used additive composition rather than a direct mapping from labels onto coins as objects, we should not find a significant difference between paying values in the 80s with four 20p coins versus eight 10p coins.

The results of comparing across types of item for the French children demonstrated once again the significance of the distinction between counting and understanding the numeration system. Items that only involved 1p coins were significantly easier than all of those that involved combinations of coins of different denominations although the value of the sums of money was controlled for.

The comparison between French and English children did not produce significant differences. The greater irregularity of the French counting labels does not make the task of understanding additive composition any more difficult for French than for English children. Finally, French children did not find it any easier to compose sums of money in the 80s by using four 20p coins rather than eight 10p coins. In other words, if children understand additive composition, the particular values that go into the composition do not affect their performance of the task significantly.

4. CONCLUSIONS

To summarize briefly the studies described above, I wish to point out the importance of distinguishing between children's knowledge of counting words and their understanding of the numeration system they are learning. Young children may be able to say the number words as strings but fail to understand the base system that is part of the meaning of counting words. Thus they may not realize the importance of the relative value of the units and so do not think of numbers as the result of the additive composition of units of different values.

Counting systems vary with respect to their regularity in the generation of number words. A perfectly regular system, such as the Chinese one, appears to be so transparent that 5-year-old children can be quite successful in understanding additive composition, significantly more so than those children who are learners of less regular systems. However, within the limits of the differences between English and French, the degree of irregularity did not matter.

The work reviewed here (also in Nunes, 1992) stresses the significance of representational systems for children's development. There are occasions when the same concepts can be represented in different ways. Sometimes the different systems are found across cultures and sometimes across situations in the same culture. The tasks we developed for the analysis of children's understanding of additive composition constitute an example of different representations of number. In order to count money, children need to use their oral counting system and also the knowledge they have about the value of coins. Thus there are in the same culture different representations of numerical value that children can be familiar with. Although we used these tasks here in the investigation of children's understanding of additive composition, it is likely that they can be profitably used to promote understanding in the classroom.[2]

REFERENCES

Fuson, K. C., Richards, J., & Briars, D. J. (1982). The acquisition and elaboration of the number word sequence. In C.J. Brainerd (Ed.), *Children's logical and mathematical cognition* (pp. 33-92). New York: Springer-Verlag.

Ginsburg, H. P. (1977). *Children's arithmetic. The learning process*. New York: Van Nostrand.

Lines, S., & Bryant, P. E. (1993). Counting in English and Chinese: Linguistic effects on number understanding. Unpublished manuscript.

Miller, K. F., & Stigler, J. W. (1986). Counting in Chinese: Cultural variation in a basic cognitive skill. *Cognitive Development, 2,* 279-305.

Miura, I. T., Kim, C. C., Chang, C. M., & Okamoto, Y. (1988). Effects of language characteristics on children's cognitive representation of number: Cross-national comparisons. *Child Development, 59,* 1455-1450.

Nunes, T., Bryant, P. E., Falcão, J., & Lima, M. F. (1993). Understanding additive composition: Cross-cultural findings. Unpublished manuscript.

Nunes, T., Silva, Z. H., & Miranda, E. M (1993). Improving children's learning of addition and subtraction algorithms. Unpublished manuscript.

---

[2] Nunes, Silva, and Miranda (1993) have provided some evidence of the pedagogical value of these tasks in teaching children about the addition and subtraction algorithms. This work could not be reviewed here for reasons of space.

Nunes Carraher, T. (1985). The decimal system: Understanding and notation. In L. Streefland (Ed.), *Proceedings of the Ninth International Conference for the Psychology of Mathematics Education* (pp. 288-303). Utrecht: University of Utrecht.

Nunes Carraher, T., & Schliemann, A. D. (1990). Knowledge of the numeration system among pre-schoolers. In L. P. Steffe & T. Wood (Eds.), *Transforming children's mathematics education: International Perspectives* (pp. 135-141). Hillsdale, NJ: Lawrence Erlbaum.

Siegler, R. S., & Robinson, M. (1982). The development of numerical understandings. In H. Ress & L. Lipsitt (Eds.), *Advances in child development and behaviour* . New York: Academic Press.

Terezinha Nunes
Institute of Education, London
United Kingdom

HOW DO SOCIAL INTERACTIONS AMONG CHILDREN CONTRIBUTE TO LEARNING?[1]

1. INTRODUCTION

The question we are concerned with makes the assumption that interactions between students in the social setting of the school do contribute to the learning of individual students. This assumption is itself controversial in that the predominant model for the teaching of mathematics, in the United States at least, has been one of explain and practice, with, as Romberg and Carpenter (1986) document, the teacher assuming a role that is managerial or procedural. Research studies by Slavin et al. (1985), Webb (1989), and others have emphasized the cooperative learning environment with students working in small groups; however the predominant view of the student's role in the learning setting has been one which militates against this environment. The student continues to be viewed as in need of " practice" of teacher demonstrated procedures. Small groups which may be established in the classroom are frequently seen as opportunities for more able peers to tutor those in need of further practice in these procedures rather than as opportunities for students to interact collaboratively as they construct their mathematical ideas.

In this chapter we raise theoretical issues about the collaborative learning environment (Wheatley, 1991) and illustrate the potential for learning by analyzing a particular activity that uses this approach. We focus on the mathematics class while recognizing that learning also takes place in other social settings of the school.

2. THE LEARNING OF MATHEMATICS

Steffe, von Glasersfeld, Richards and Cobb (1983) speak of the way in which students actively construct mathematical meaning for themselves through interaction with the environment and through the reorganization of their own mental constructs. Learners actively construct meaning for mathematical ideas and relationships and are not passive receivers of a body of knowledge that has been ontologically realized by someone external to them (Wheatley, 1991). The sense learners makes of their experiences is strongly influenced by interactions with others. As social beings interacting in a cooperative environment we make sense of our experiences not in isolation but through a process of negotiating meaning with others (Pepitone, 1980). It is through this negotiation that we come to certain taken-as-shared meanings. Thus to learn mathematics is to construct mathematical relationships, to negotiate mathematical meanings with others, and to reflect on our mathematical activity (Wheatley, 1991; Wheatley, 1992).

[1]   The research in this chapter was supported by the National Science Foundation under grant No. MDR 885-0560. The opinions expressed do not necessarily reflect the views of the funding agency.

H. Mansfield et al. (eds.), Mathematics for Tomorrow's Young Children, 186–197.

2.1 The scene

This research was conducted in a third grade class in the South-Eastern United States. The students were representative of the normal social pattern of the city in which they lived. During their second and third grade years these students were involved in a problem-centered learning environment (Wheatley, 1991). During this time we were involved in the classroom on a continuing basis, developing with teachers and students social norms with the potential to enhance students' mathematics learning. We continued to be involved with the same students as they moved into fourth grade, where the predominant learning setting was explain/practice.

2.2 The activity

We focus on an activity developed for the grade three students as part of a unit on measurement. It is our belief that young children need to experience mathematical activities in a setting that allows them to give viable meaning to the mathematical concepts they are constructing. On occasion the confines of the classroom inhibit this sense making process. This is particularly so in the realm of measurement. Classroom activities restrict students' experiences of measurement to a domain constrained by the dimensions of the classroom and by the objects it can contain. Within the classroom we can pose tasks that allow students to experience the development of smaller units of measure, for example centimeter and to some extent meter. However, what does it mean to the child to talk about 100 meters or one kilometer? These are experiences that may not become meaningful to the child within the confines of a 15 x 10 meter room. In dealing with number, it is much easier to help the child give meaning to 13 than it is to give meaning to 1 013. Similarly in the realm of measurement it is easier to give meaning to small units than to larger units. It is thus imperative that students be given the opportunity to develop some meaning for these larger units.

Measurement of units of time pose an added difficulty for the child. In measuring the distance from one place to another, the area of a particular space, or the volume of a three dimensional object, it is possible for the child to use concrete materials to lay along the length, to cover the space or to fill the inside of a container. The boundaries can usually be experienced simultaneously through the various senses. This is not possible in measuring time. How does one hold two moments of time in one's experience *at the same time* in order somehow to relate them? Yet the child is expected to give some meaning to measuring time—be it weeks, days, hours, minutes or seconds. Days and hours can at least be marked by the motions of the earth around the sun, but minutes and seconds are more ephemeral. Teachers must provide opportunities for students to segment their experiences and construct meaning for time.

2.3 The social climate of the mathematics class

How can the teacher and students together create an environment for potential mathematics learning in the classroom? If our goal is to foster the induction of students into the mathematical community and towards doing mathematics, then the conventional social environment will not do. Wheatley (1991) proposes a problem centered learning environment whose components are tasks, groups and sharing. Tasks are chosen (by the teacher or the student, c.f. Grundy, 1987) such that they have the potential to engage students mathematically. It is important to recognize that the types of tasks that provide opportunity for mathematical learning for students are not necessarily tasks that would be used in a conventional mathematics class. In the conventional learning environment mathematical ideas are " packaged" in such a way that tasks are completed by the end of the lesson period. The sort of tasks being suggested in the problem centered learning environment are such that a group of students isengaged for a lengthy period of time, or a task may suggest another line of investigation for a group of students or an individual. Mathematical " content" cannot be packaged up into smaller bits and taught as isolated units. Several related mathematical ideas will be developing as the students engage with the tasks. Thus the teacher needs to think in terms of a more open approach to the completion of tasks.

In the problem centered learning environment students work in small collaborative groups rather than in isolation. This interaction process encourages students to construct meaning through negotiation. Students are encouraged to develop meaningful ways of working with a problem rather than given specific procedures to use. Thus students are in charge of their learning. They are encouraged to use whatever is appropriate to aid them in working with the task.

The sharing time involves the whole class. During this time students present their solutions to the class. This is an extremely important time in the learning process. During their small group activities students have had the opportunity to construct meaningful ways of looking at the task and finding solutions. Now the students must be able to present their solutions to a wider mathematical community and be prepared to defend their thinking. It is also an opportunity for students to hear how others have given meaning to the task, and possible different approaches to its solution.

We propose the following social norms to enhance mathematical learning in the classroom:

> *students expect a task to require investigation and to require time;*
> *students expect to be puzzled, to develop their own methods, to work together, to negotiate, and to explain their solutions.*

It will be argued in the section that follows that:

- these norms encourage students to *construct* mathematical relationships;
- through small group interaction students will be encouraged to *collaborate and negotiate* meanings;
- the norms of the group develop whereby the students *intend* to engage in mathematical activity;

- through the communicating of ideas students have the opportunity to *image* their mathematical thinking;
- in this setting students have the opportunity to *reflect* on their mathematical activity;
- through whole class discussion students are encouraged to *defend* their mathematical thinking.

A. *These norms encourage students to construct mathematical relationships*. It is increasingly being recognized that students learn mathematics when they have the opportunity to construct that mathematics (von Glasersfeld, 1987). Thus the mathematical task needs careful consideration.

Conventional classroom tasks discourage students from constructing mathematical relationships, from acting as developing mathematicians— they stress a procedural orientation to mathematics learning. Research by Cobb and Wheatley (1988) and Kamii and Lewis (1991) has shown that, though students may show proficiency in standardized tests, these same students have little understanding of the mathematical relationships involved in the procedures they are using. In investigating second grade students' understanding of *ten* Cobb and Wheatley (1988) found that children whose prior instructional experience consisted of typical textbook instruction in which rules were taught for assigning value to digits based on their position, "did not construct ten as a structure composed of ones when they operated in the school context—ten was, for them, one thing which was not itself composed of units" (p.1). These students were thus not in a position to construct viable meaning for the standard addition algorithm which was subsequently taught.

In the course of our research, we have interacted with a group of students for three years, as these students moved from grade two, through three and into four. In grade two and three the social norms of the classroom emphasized giving meaning to the mathematical ideas. In their grade four year, these students experienced a rule oriented approach, where many of the tasks focused on practicing procedures. About midway through the grade four year one of these students, Kristin, was asked by the researchers to solve a non-routine problem (as she had been doing consistently in grade two and three). She very quickly decided on a procedure to apply. In doing so she switched from a *sense-making* mode to a *procedure-oriented* mode and as a result made little sense of the task. Two weeks later she expressed her thoughts about her mathematical activity in this way:

Now I realize, I didn't realize, you could have like, um, the point isn't, before I thought the point was for you to get the answer right, now I realize it's not; it's for you to figure out these kind of problems; but these kind of problems (pointing to the vertical arrangement of 64 + 23 which she had written previously while discuss ing the type of problems she did in class) is for you to get the answer right.

While no one would question the ultimate importance of a mathematically "correct" answer, in this interaction Kristin has highlighted the difference in the mathematical challenge posed by the contrasting classroom norms.

For a task to provide students with the potential opportunity to construct mathematical relationships it needs to invite students to make decisions and encourage them to use their own methods, ask "what if" questions, and lead somewhere mathematically. The measuring activity to be described was designed for the school playground, a fenced area of approximately 40 x 36 meters. The playground is irregularly shaped and contains several tall trees, two slides of differing length, swings, climbing equipment, tables and seats, and tires spaced at irregular distances. Questions were designed to give students the opportunity to explore time and linear measure. For a list of questions used see the appendix.

Some questions concerning time allowed students to compare results by completing tasks simultaneously. For example the question "Who can make it down the slide the fastest?" could be answered by pairs of students using the slide which was wide enough for both students to slide down at the same time. They could thus set race conditions for themselves in deciding the answer without necessarily considering an independent unit of time for comparison. However, the majority of the questions using measurement of time required students to devise some way of keeping track of time as each student completed the task individually. For example, it was impossible for students to climb through the tires at the same time since the tires allowed room for only one student at a time to maneuver through the space provided. The few students who had been wearing watches that day had been asked to leave them in the classroom before the class moved to the playground for this activity. Thus, in order to complete these tasks students had to devise some way in which they could count the lapsed time in completing the activity, a way that was accurate enough to use as a standard for comparison.

Most of the linear measurement tasks could be completed by students using improvised measuring devices like sticks or body parts. However, one task (measuring the height of a ten meter tall oak tree) could not be completed in this manner.

The climate is set for rich mathematical constructions by the choice of appropriate tasks. The dynamics through which the tasks are completed provide the opportunity for the doing of mathematics and the making of these constructions.

*B. Through small group interaction students will be encouraged to **collaborate** and **negotiate meaning**.* In problem-centered learning students work in small collaborative groups rather than in isolation. These groups usually consist of pairs of students whose mathematical constructions are developmentally compatible. Pairs, rather than larger numbers in a group, are formed to provide opportunities for each individual to express her/his view and negotiate action plans with a partner. The interaction encourages students to construct meaning through their negotiations. Students are encouraged to develop meaningful ways of working with a problem rather than being given specific procedures to use. Thus students come to take charge of their own learning. They use whatever is appropriate to aid them in solving a problem rather than being directed to use specific manipulatives or procedures. The actual pairs, which remain relatively stable over time, are determined by the teacher with input from students in a way that will appropriately enhance collaboration. On some occasions, such as in this setting, it is appropriate for students to work in larger groups. Thus, on this occasion several students formed groups of three.

2.4 What we observed as the students collaborated on these tasks

Measuring time: As we had anticipated most students used some form of rhythmic counting in order to measure the time it took to complete the activity. One student counted on from one as the other completed the task. Several groups were observed rehearsing this procedure so that each person would count at the same speed in order to make a fair comparison. These students were thus considering the issue of " standard" unit as they invented ways of solving their problems.

Interestingly, one group of three students used a variation on this counting procedure as they tackled the question, "Who can make it through the tires in the shortest time?" The tires were spaced out individually in one section of the playground, fixed upright into the ground. This arrangement made it necessary for the students to take turns completing the task. These three students solved the problem of making a fair comparison in the following way. On the signal to start, one student made his way through the tires as quickly as he could. As he was proceeding through the tires another student continuously circled the tire at the starting point while the third student counted the number of times he did this. These students had thus eliminated the problem of " standard" inherent in the rhythmic counting procedure used by the other students. However, they had introduced another variable, that of the differing speeds at which each of them could circle the tire. It became obvious to us as we watched these three students that they were aware of this problem. They spent considerable time negotiating a solution. They eventually decided that the same boy would do the circling for each of the other two. Then the slower of the other two boys would be used as the circler while the faster of those two competed with the third boy. In this way they could fairly decide who was fastest. Such an approach required logical thought as they negotiated a standard unit of measure.

Measuring length: Many of the students completed these tasks by using some parts of their bodies as a unit of measure (usually their foot). The task of measuring the length of the playground thus became a long and tedious process for them, providing them with the opportunity to count into the thousands. It takes a considerable number of children's sized feet to traverse that distance. However, their choice of such a small unit of measure provided us with the opportunity later to discuss the appropriateness of this choice. The class was thus discussing the need for different units of measure depending on the object to be measured.

Several groups of students attempted to solve the problem, "How tall is the tree near the fence in the playground?" (the ten meter oak)—but could not devise a way to measure it. Two groups of students interpreted the question as asking how far the tree was from the fence. However, one pair of students found a creative way of measuring the height of the tree. Joe stood against the tree trunk while Jim positioned himself about five meters away. He then used his hand as a sighting instrument and found that at that distance it took two of his hands to mark off the height of Joe standing against the tree. He then continued using his hands to measure to the top of the tree. Each time he counted off two hands he converted those units to the unit of Joe's body length and reported that the height of the tree was five times

Joe's height. Though the actual measurement might be in question, the way in which it was devised shows considerable sophistication. As we watched them using this procedure we could not help but think of the manner in which a surveyor and her assistant might go about the task of measuring distances.

The question, "Who can jump the longest distance?" created much discussion among several pairs of students as they negotiated the best and fairest way to measure this distance. It thus became an opportunity for mathematical reasoning and negotiation. The most common solution for pairs of students involved drawing a starting line on the ground. On several occasions this method stimulated more negotiation as students decided if both students must start from behind the line. Also entering into the discussion was the question of where to measure the "end" of the jump. Does one measure from where the person's toes or heels land? Most, but not all, groups agreed that the appropriate place to measure to was where the heel landed. We watched one pair of students discussing this issue in detail. They eventually compared the length of their feet and decided that since their feet were different lengths they had to measure to the heels in order to be "fair."

We were also intrigued by two groups of students who found it necessary to complete this task by both students jumping simultaneously. This was one task that did not require students to act simultaneously, yet these students felt a necessity for doing so. This very act was a source of discussion for the whole group later as students debated whether this action was necessary to the particular task. Students were thus discussing the issue of appropriate constraints needed in defining a task.

As we observed students completing this task, what came to mind was the difficulty some students encounter when they use rulers as measuring devices - where to position the ruler to begin measuring, or where to line up a ruler in order to measure the distance between two objects. Reynolds (1993) noted the difficulty students had in using the ruler appropriately when they attempted to solve various measurement tasks. For example, when using a ruler in which the zero point did not correspond with the end of the ruler, Kristin, a mathematically gifted student, did not distinguish between these two starting points. On several occasions she puzzled over inaccuracies in her drawings which had been caused by her use of the end of the ruler instead of the zero point as her initial point of measurement. Although she *identified* discrepancies in her drawings she was unable to identify the cause of those discrepancies (see also Kamii, 1991). In attending to details like that of measuring to the toes or the heels these third grade students were thus dealing with quite sophisticated concepts relating to measure as they completed and discussed the task.

*C. The norms of the group develop whereby the students **intend to engage** in mathematical activity.* The students' intentions have a significant influence on the social climate of the mathematics classroom. If their intentions are to make sense of their mathematical experiences, then the focus will be on the task. If their intentions are to get the task finished or do it the way the teacher wants, then their attention is not on the mathematical thinking and formulating of ideas, but on "playing the game called school." Kristin's comment about the differences between her intentions when solving a non-routine problem and when engaged in her fourth-grade classroom work highlight the importance of a student's intentions in this regard.

Two students in this setting decided very early that they could not measure either time or distance units without having standard measuring devices available to them. For example, they stated that without having a ruler to use, all they could say about the length of the playground was that it was "very long." They discussed the impossibility of the task as other students worked around them, measuring in various non-standard units. At one point they were standing in the middle of the playground as a pair of students, Jane and Karen, who were completing the question "Find some way to measure the length of the playground. How long is it?" by using their foot as a measuring device, approached them from behind. Jane asked these students to move out of the way (they were standing on their direct line from one end of the playground to the other) so that she and Karen could continue to measure this distance. Jane and Karen continued on their way while these students watched them; however, these two students did not rethink their stance on the impossibility of the task. These two girls were quite capable of devising valid methods but did not do so. It was a matter of intentions.

It is difficult to surmise the intentions of these two students. Perhaps they knew a more sophisticated method and saw no reason to use a primitive method. For whatever reason this did not appear to be a meaningful task for them even though it was for the other students in the class. Many factors, including some over which the classroom community has little control, influence students' intentions as they engage in mathematical activity. However, it is possible, and necessary, that the classroom community negotiates social norms whereby the focus is on the doing and the learning of mathematics.

D. Through the communication of ideas students have the opportunity to image their mathematical thinking. We often communicate with one another through imagery. In mathematics classrooms it is important that the development and use of imagery is fostered through encouraging the expression of ideas among students. Our language is laden with images (Johnson, 1987; Lakoff, 1987). Students will also form images as they attempt to make sense of mathematical ideas and express those images particularly in diagrams as they attempt to explain their thinking to one another. In the small group setting, imagery will develop and be enhanced by explaining, negotiating, sense making. In the whole class setting, students experience a rich variety of ways of imaging a situation as different students present their solutions to a problem. Our current research highlights the importance of imagery, both in the giving of meaning to mathematical ideas, and in the communication of those ideas with others (Reynolds & Wheatley, 1992; Reynolds, 1993).

On this occasion, the way in which Jim and Joe measured the height of the tree was the source of much discussion and replete with imagery. Two of the students who had interpreted the task as measuring the distance from the tree to the fence were challenged by the class to reread the question and thus interpret it differently. The sharing time occurred in the classroom; thus it became a challenge for Jim and Joe to explain their procedure. They attempted their explanation by using a diagram on the chalkboard. In doing so they, and the students who attempted to make sense of this procedure, were trying to interpret on a two dimensional surface an event from a three dimensional world. Their method prompted several students to ask questions of clarification and to make judgments about the viability of this method. Jim and Joe attempted to elaborate on their diagram by a physical demonstration. This led another student to make suggestions about how to change the drawing on the board to clarify their presentation.

E. In this setting students have the opportunity to reflect on their mathematical activity. Wheatley (1992) stresses the importance of reflection as students construct their mathematics. In a classroom where emphasis is placed on speed and accuracy there is little time for reflecting on mathematical patterns and relationships and formulating possible explanations for these. Reflection is actually discouraged in such a setting.

   In the problem centered learning environment much of the small group interaction is spent alternately talking, listening and reflecting on the problem. It is also important to plan reflection time. During this time in small groups students are encouraged to reconstruct their ideas and come to some decision about the viability of their solutions. If they feel comfortable about their solutions, then they need to plan a presentation to the whole class. If they decide that they are not comfortable with the viability of their solutions, then this reflective time will help them identify areas of concern. Thus they will be more focused when another student is presenting a solution and will have the opportunity to rethink the problem through listening and asking questions.

F. Through whole class discussion students are encouraged to defend their mathematical thinking. A key component of discourse in the mathematics community is the formal presentation of proofs and defense of mathematical ideas previously formulated. Lo, Wheatley, and Smith (1994) found that the potential for mathematics discourse as students engaged in whole class sharing in a problem centered learning environment was considerable. At the completion of small group negotiation and collaboration on mathematical tasks, students profit from being given the opportunity to present and defend their thinking to the class. The social norms to be negotiated for this time are somewhat different from those operating in small groups. At this time students present to the class solutions that they have discussed with their partners and reflected on as being viable. This does not mean that the students presenting a solution have necessarily solved the problem - however it does mean that those students believe, because of their discussion and reflection, that they have a viable solution. They are encouraged to present their thinking in a logically coherent way. They argue their case to the mathematical community consisting of their peers.

   This demands a particular responsibility on the part of peers to listen and to challenge ideas if those ideas appear to not make sense to them. It is their responsibility to bring to this whole class sharing their own constructions regarding a particular problem so that they have some means of attempting to evaluate the ideas of the presenting student.

It is important that several students present different solutions to a particular task. This encourages a variety of ways of giving meaning to the mathematical ideas reflected in the task. This is one reason why it is important that these tasks be such that different ways of reaching a viable solution are possible. Students should be encouraged to develop their own strategies in attempting to solve a problem. Thus a rich variety of strategies will be presented by students in the whole class sharing time, and students will have the opportunity to experience these different solutions.

In the particular activity being reported here, students were quite interested in sharing how they completed the various tasks and in listening to what others had done. Several of the methods provided an opportunity to talk about the appropriateness of the selected measurement unit. For example, in answering the question "Find some way to measure the length of the playground. How long is it?" many students had used their feet as units of measure. Considering the length of the playground, students found that keeping count as they measured this length was quite taxing. The whole class discussion gave students the opportunity to think about other ways of measuring this distance. For example, one student suggested that it would have been easier to use her stride. Also, the question arose about how students could compare answers in order to judge the accuracy of a reported answer. This led to a discussion in two parts: (1) how to convert the count of one student who had used her foot as a measuring device to that of another student who had used his foot which was a different size; (2) the need for some standard measuring units so that comparison is made easier.

Another issue arose in this discussion of the length of the playground. Several students noted that, even allowing for the different sized feet used as measuring devices, some answers being reported were much larger than other answers. As students discussed this it became evident that three groups of students had interpreted this question to mean measuring the distance around the perimeter of the playground, hence their larger answer. This led to discussion about the interpretation of the word "length." Thus these students were constructing meaning for various terms used in the measurement of plane figures.

The teacher becomes a facilitator during this whole class sharing and must not act as the judge of the viability of solutions being presented—this is the responsibility of the students. If they are to be encouraged to act as a mathematical community then they need the opportunity to make sense of the arguments of their peers and challenge where appropriate. This does not mean that the teacher is not considering the constructions that students have made. However, the teacher's communication with the class must be non judgmental. Through listening to solutions and the responses and challenges of the students, the teacher has the opportunity to learn about students' thinking, so that decisions may be made about subsequent mathematical tasks for these students. The teacher's responsibility here is to encourage the students to challenge and ask questions—to facilitate the social interactions. In taking this stance, the teacher is encouraging intellectual autonomy among students (Kamii, 1985). The focus shifts from a "performance" with the hope of praise on the part of the students, to one of involvement in the mathematical task.

3. FINAL THOUGHTS

It is possible for elementary school classes to become mathematical communities where students engage in mathematics discourse. It requires the negotiation among teacher and students of the social norms that encourage the doing of mathematics, the expression of mathematical ideas, the building of theories and the holding up of those theories to the scrutiny of peers. Social norms that enhance the learning of mathematics encourage students to spend time investigating the mathematical nuances of a task, to puzzle its meaning in negotiation with others, to develop their own methods for dealing with a task, to reflect on the viability of their mathematical constructions, and to explain their solutions to their peers. The classroom thus becomes a mathematical community where the development of mathematical ideas is valued.

REFERENCES

Cobb, P., & Wheatley, G. (1988). Children's initial understandings of ten. *Focus on Learning Problems in Mathematics, 10* (3), 1-28.

Grundy, S. (1987). Curriculum: Product or praxis. New York: Falmer Press.

Johnson, M. (1987). *The body in the mind: The bodily basis of meaning, imagination and reason.* Chicago: University of Chicago Press.

Kamii, C. (1985). Young children reinvent arithmetic. New York: Teachers College Press.

Kamii, C. (1991). Children's readiness for measurement of length. In *Proceedings of the Thirteenth Annual Meeting of the North American Chapter of the International Group for the Psychology of Mathematics Education, vol. 2,* (pp. 113-118). Blacksburg, VA.

Kamii, C., & Lewis, B. (1991). Achievement tests in primary mathematics: perpetuating lower-order thinking. *Arithmetic Teacher, 38*(9), 4-11.

Lakoff, G. (1987). *Women, fire and dangerous things: What categories reveal about the mind.* Chicago: The University of Chicago Press.

Lo, J., Wheatley, G., & Smith, A. (1994). The influence of mathematics class discussion on the beliefs and arithmetic meaning of a third grade student. *Journal for Research in Mathematics Education, 25*(1), 30-49.

Pepitone, E. (1980). *Children in cooperation and competition.* Lexington, MA: Lexington Books.

Reynolds, A. (1993). *Imaging in children's mathematical activity.* Unpublished doctoral dissertation. Florida State University.

Reynolds, A., & Wheatley, G. (1992). The elaboration of images in the process of mathematics meaning making. In *Proceedings of the Sixteenth Annual Conference of the International Group for the Psychology of Mathematics Education. Vol. 2,* (pp. 242-249). Durham, NH.

Romberg, T. A., & Carpenter, T. P. (1986). Research on teaching and learning mathematics: Two disciplines of scientific inquiry. In M. C. Wittrock (Ed.), *Handbook of research on teaching,* (pp. 850-873). New York: Macmillan Publishing Company.

Slavin, R., Sharan, S., Kagan, S., Lazarowitz, R., Webb, C., & Schmuck, R. (Eds.). (1985). *Learning to cooperate, cooperating to learn.* New York, NY: Praeger.

Steffe, L., von Glasersfeld, E., Richards, J., & Cobb, P. (1983). *Children's counting types: Philosophy, theory and application.* New York, NY: Praeger.

von Glasersfeld, E. (1987). *The construction of knowledge: contributions to conceptual semantics.* Seaside, CA: Intersystems Publications.

Webb, N. (1989). Peer interaction and learning in small groups. *International Journal of Educational Research, 13,* 21-39.

Wheatley, G. (1991). Constructivist perspectives on mathematics and science learning. *Science Education, 75*(1), 9-21.
Wheatley, G. (1992). The role of reflection in mathematics learning. *Educational Studies in Mathematics, 23*, 529-541.

Anne Reynolds
The University of Oklahoma

Grayson H. Wheatley
Florida State University

United States of America

Appendix

Tasks given to the students as they engaged in an outdoor measuring activity:

(Students were asked to leave watches in the classroom and to bring with them only pencils, clipboards and a sheet on which the questions were written to the playground.)

1. Who can jump the highest?
2. Who can make it down the slide the fastest?
3. How fast can you walk around the edge of the playground?
4. Who can jump the longest distance?
5. Who can stand the longest time on one foot? How long was that?
6. Who can make it through the tires in the shortest time?
7. Find some way to measure the length of the playground. How long is it?
8. How high is the fence?
9. How tall is the tree near the fence in the playground?
10. Find two other things to compare in the playground.

CULTURAL AND SOCIAL ENVIRONMENTAL HURDLES A TANZANIAN CHILD MUST JUMP IN THE ACQUISITION OF MATHEMATICS CONCEPTS

1. INTRODUCTION

In Tanzanian traditions every adult member of a community was in one way or another a teacher and every child a pupil. When formal education was introduced by colonial powers a gap between the education process at home and that at school was created. Parents and community had nothing to do with the formal type of education process. In particular, mathematics education as it was presented by foreigners was exclusively a white man's creation and ability. There were absolutely no African indigenous ideas in mathematics education. This made the subject divorced from the children's reality. Children, teachers, and parents alike found the subject to be unrelated and irrelevant.

Theories on acquisition of mathematical concepts (for example by Dienes and Piaget) assert that learning mathematical concepts is aided by a variety of experiences and proceeds from a cluster of experiences to logical analysis. Also logical or analytical abstract ordering is preceded by concrete or physical experiences (Mmari, 1973). When Tanzanian children went to school they learnt different mathematics from that experienced at home. Thus children lacked experiences on which to base their mathematics learning. How could these children easily conceptualize and acquire abstraction of ordering in the absence of concrete experiences? Children learn best when they take an active part in the learning process. Can children take active parts in something completely foreign?

The fundamental principle of learning, as put forward by Harris (1980) (quoted by Clements, 1984), must always begin with that which is known and proceed from the known to the unknown. At entry to school, Tanzanian children initially possessed no knowledge as far as school mathematics is concerned. How could they proceed to the unknown?

Based on research findings, Sinclair (1990) argues that children struggle from a very early age to create meaning for mathematical concepts when they encounter them in their day to day lives. Mathematics education in Tanzania was not a continuous process from infancy to adulthood because of the cultural gap between informal and formal education. There existed no interaction between the two education processes. The goals, content and methods of mathematics education were not compatible with the original Tanzania civilization. The majority of Tanzanian children lived in rural areas. What they encountered in day to day life differed tremendously from the mathematics they met in school. How could these children create meaning for concepts in the type of mathematics they met in school?

H. Mansfield et al. (eds.), Mathematics for Tomorrow's Young Children, 198–215.

According to Gagné and White (1978) (quoted in Clements, 1984), in attempting to accommodate new information, children call upon various kinds of information already in their memory structure. Such information is stored in the form of factual knowledge, intellectual skills, imagery and episodes. What memory structures did Tanzanian children possess when they first encountered mathematics in school? Gagné and White further claim that to grasp a new concept, the stimuli that motivate thinking about the concept must help to establish appropriate links between existing information in the children's cognitive structures. How could Tanzanian children make necessary links with foreign concepts?

To these children information remained a mystery of unconnected facts. When children lack experience, their knowledge cannot be sorted into a system and a previously constructed one seems unnatural and artificial to them. Content and methods should be influenced by some practical motives, as stressed by Kagan et al (1979) (quoted in Clements, 1984).

Mason, Burton and Stacey (1982) stress that conceptualization in mathematics is improved by practice with reflection and it is supported by an atmosphere of questioning, challenging and reflecting. Tanzanian children had nothing to reflect on and could not practice school mathematics in the home environment. It became very difficult for them to improve their conceptualizations. As Ki-Zerbo (1990) puts it, ever since slavery and the colonial periods, African people have had their foundations removed from them. Tanzania has not been spared this.

The attainment of political independence did not result in bridging this gap. Instead, in a hurry to alphabetize the entire society, teachers and literature from all over the world were brought into the country. Instead of fighting the battle of one foreign culture, one had to struggle to understand the instructors who had difficulty with English, one had to cope with the different cultures of the teachers and in the books, one had to cope with different units and systems in the books, and so on. This created more serious problems in the conceptualization of mathematics.

Africanisation, nationalism and socialist policies that followed independence, unilateral decisions without prior proper planning such as Universal Primary Education (UPE), as well as disproportionate budget allocations to education have resulted in even bigger problems in learning in general and in learning mathematics in particular. Today, over 30 years after gaining independence, the conceptualization problems in mathematics faced by primary school children, with social, cultural, and environmental causes, are enormous.

Is there room for improvement? Apart from reasonable budget allocations to education, reform in educational policies must be made. Traditional mathematical knowledge must be integrated in the instruction of mathematics.

Do Tanzanian traditions possess any mathematics? As in many ethnic groups of sub-Saharan Africa, Tanzania has enormous reserves of traditional mathematical knowledge, creativity and capacity. Ethno-mathematics researchers such as Gerdes (1988, 1990), D'Ambrosio (1985), Shirley (1986) and Zaslavsky (1973) have pointed out a variety of mathematics which is embedded in African traditions. What Tanzania (and Africa in general) needs is a culture-oriented mathematics education. This means that we have to incorporate African mathematical heritage into the curriculum. Then according to Ki-Zerbo (1990), mathematics education is apt to generate the self-confidence from which imagination springs.

2. LEARNING MATHEMATICS IN THE TANZANIAN ENVIRONMENT

2.1 Education before foreign intervention

Let me discuss the learning of mathematics in the social-cultural environment of Tanzania starting from the historical point of view. That way I will be able to point out in a transparent way the serious problems which primary school children face today in learning mathematical concepts.

During the pre-colonial era there was no formal education in Tanzania. Children learnt various traditions from their parents and community from early childhood. Children watched, participated in and experienced the day-to-day activities of the community. They learnt skills such as farming, construction of huts and granaries, basket making, ornamentation, hair plaiting, making pots and other crafts, making long trips, looking after the animals, hunting, guarding crops against animals, making drums and other musical instruments, and so on.

Children watched adults play complicated games and make expert drawings. They were involved in puzzles, riddles and fables from infancy. Children were told fairy tales and stories, they learnt counting rhymes and rhythms. They learnt and experienced how time was reckoned, how weather forecasts were made, how expected yield was estimated, how war strategies were planned. They were actively involved in traditional dances where they learnt formation of different patterns and learnt communication by drums and other means.

From infancy, children experienced and learnt numeration, both oral and by gesturing. For example when women are making decorations using beads or making mats or baskets, they count the beads to form patterns using different colors. Children used to mimic female members of the family and in so doing they got involved with counting as well. Animals were counted before being taken out for grazing and when brought back. Boys mimicked male members of the family and so got involved in counting.

From early childhood children experienced counting, locating, measuring, designing, playing games, explaining, classifying, sorting, and time reckoning as they occurred naturally in day-to-day activities. From an early age, children started to develop very good visual discrimination and visual memory in order to master their environment.

2.2 Mathematics education in the wake of foreign intervention

As travelers started to invade the country, they introduced their mathematics in our traditions. Portuguese traders introduced their currency (peso). One of the Kiswahili words for money is *pesa* and originates from peso. Then came the Arabs. These were slave traders, rulers and missionaries. They introduced Arabic measures of length and capacity, measures of time and the calendar, as well as currency. The numeration system in Kiswahili comprises many Arabic words. Later came the Asiatic traders (Indians, Pakistani and people from Sri Lanka). These introduced business mathematics into our school system (Mmari, 1980).

German Christian missionaries followed by German colonizers came to the then Deutsch Ost Afrika (Tanganyika, now Tanzania minus Zanzibar; Rwanda; and Burundi) and introduced formal schools. They brought school curricula as well as books with them. They also brought their systems of measure, currency, and calendar. Teachers were Germans and later Tanzanians trained by Germans. Slowly the Germans introduced, in schools, the Kiswahili language (which was widely spoken along the coast of the Indian Ocean and along the slave trade tracks). Kiswahili and the German language were used as the medium of instruction.

After World War I, the Germans were replaced by the British in Tanganyika. Overnight, the German language was replaced by English, the metric system by the imperial system, German books and teachers were replaced by English ones.

All this foreign intervention took place within a few decades. In this short period one had to absorb Arabic, Asian, German and British traditions. One had to learn to switch currencies and other measures, for example from *simbi* (Bantu) to *pesa* (peso, Portuguese) to *fedha* (Arabic) to *rupia* (rupee, Indian) to *hela* (heller, German) to *shilingi* (shilling, British). Also from metres, kilograms, and litres to yards, furlongs, farthings, stones, half crowns, and gallons.

How do children who underwent such upheavals compare with those who have to cope with a single set of measures in their own language and culture?

3. KIHAYA AND KISWAHILI

Tanzania has about 150 different ethnic groups with different languages; of these 60% belong to the Bantu group of languages. As the Kiswahili language spread throughout the country, it was adopted as a medium of instruction for primary grades one to four and later German/English was used. Though the grammar is similar to that of the Bantu group of languages, Kiswahili has a lot of foreign words, notably Arabic, in its mathematical terminologies. Even the Kiswahili words for mathematics and arithmetic, **hisabati** and **hesabu** are Arabic.

Children who until seven years of age had gathered some concrete experiences at home and spoke in their mother tongue, went to school and started to learn in Kiswahili. At school these children were confronted with totally different ideas even in those areas where they had already gathered some knowledge. I will give two examples, one of counting and numeration and the other of time reckoning at home and at school. I will consider a child from the Bahaya ethnic group which uses a Bantu language.

3.1 Counting and numeration in Kihaya and in Kiswahili.

A child learns to count 1 to 10 by heart both in Kiswahili and Kihaya. At home where Kihaya is spoken, the child has been hearing the numerals in everyday activities since infancy. Switching to Kiswahili creates some problem in the numerals 6, 7 and 9 which differ very much from those in Kihaya because they are in Arabic.

	1	2	3	4	5
KIHAYA	emoi	ibili	ishatu	ina	itanu
KISWAHILI	moja	mbili	tatu	nne	tano

	6	7	8	9	10
KIHAYA	mukaga	mushanju	munana	mwenda	ikumi
KISWAHILI	sita (Arab.)	saba (Arab.)	nane	tisa (Arab.)	kumi

Further counting is as given below:

	11	12	…………	19
KIHAYA	ikumi na emoi	ikumi na ibili…………		ikumi na mwenda
KISWAHILI	kumi na moja	kumi na mbili…………		kumi na tisa

The additive composition for 11, 12,...,19 is similar in both languages. These numbers follow the system of the Bantu languages and not the Arabic system. Let us now look at more numerals.

	10	100	1 000	10 000	
KIHAYA	*ikumi*	*kikumi*	*lukumi*	*kakumi*	

	10	100	1 000	100 000	1 000 000
KISWAHILI	kumi	mia	elfu	laki	milioni
	(Bantu)	(Arab)	(Arab)	(Indian)	(European)

From the table we note that in Kihaya ten, hundred, thousand and ten thousand have a common stem -KUMI. A child needs only to learn the pre-fixes standing for 10, 100, 1 000, 10 000, which are i-, ki-, lu-, ka-. Higher numerals such as 100 000 and 1 000 000 are combinations of these. From the same table we see that in Kiswahili the numerals have names whose origins are from different languages, that is Bantu, Arabic, Indian and European. Let us consider further numerals.

	5	50	500	5000
KIHAYA	*itanu*	*gatanu* bi*tanu*	lu*tanu*	
KISWAHILI	tano	hamsini	mia tano	elfu tano

In Kihaya, we see that FIVE (-TANU) is a common stem with different prefixes. The prefixes for ten, hundred and so on take on their plural forms which are i-, ga-, bi-, li-, and ka- respectively. In fact, plural forms are not learned by heart. Children know them automatically just as they know plurals of other words. In Kiswahili, however, things look different. Five and 50 are totally different, one originating from Bantu and the other from Arabic. On the other hand 500 is made out of a composition of 5 and 100; 5 000 is made out of a composition of 5 and 1 000, and so are 500 000 and 5 000 000.

A child learning to count in Kihaya needs to know how to count 1, 2, 3, 4, 5, 6, 7, 8, 9, and 10, and also the additive composition for 11, 12, ..., 19, as well as the prefixes for ten, hundred, thousand, ten thousand and their plural forms. Then all other numerals are very easily constructed. For example, the set of numbers 2, 20,

200, 2 000, 20 000 has two (-BILI) as a common stem. Similarly, the set 3, 30, 300, 3 000, 30 000 has 3 as a common stem and so on up to the set 9, 90, 900, 9 000, 90 000 which has nine as a common stem with the relevant prefix. Numbers like 206, 348, 9 765 can be easily constructed using additive composition. One is basically dealing only with the numbers 1, 2, ..., 10; the stem of 10; the prefixes for ten, hundred, thousand, ten thousand and their plural forms. Once children know this they can construct numbers up to 99 999 in a short time even without knowing what the numbers mean.

That is not the case with counting in Kiswahili. This is demonstrated by considering more numbers.

KISWAHILI:

20	30	40	50	60	70
ishirini	thelathini	arobaini	hamsini	sitini	sabini

80	90	100
themanini	tisini	mia

10	100	1 000	100 000	1 000 000
kumi	mia	elfu	laki	milioni
(Bantu)	(Arabic)	(Arabic)	(Indian)	(European)

4	40	400	4 000	400 000	4 000 000
nne	arobaini	mia nne	elfu nne	laki nne	milioni nne

We note that members of the sets 6, 60; 7,70; 9,90 have similarities. Both members of the set have the same Arabic origin. The rest of the sets, that is 2,20; 3,30; .... 8,80 have absolutely nothing in common. The units originate from Bantu languages and the tens from Arabic. All the tens have to be learnt by heart. A child would never have heard of them at home. From the same table we see that 100s, 1 000s and so on have names from several other foreign languages. The composition, though, follows the Bantu system. A child has to learn new names at many stages. In Kiswahili a child has many totally new names of numerals to learn by heart, and cannot logically construct more numerals without assistance at many stages of counting.

Children learn counting in Kihaya very fast and have the opportunity of composing new numbers on their own. This makes counting very interesting to children. Besides, children start learning to count at home as it occurs in every day activities. Children see the relevance of counting. Then children go to school and learn to count in Kiswahili where Bantu, Arabic, Indian and English numerals are mixed. They also learn this in quite a different way from learning at home. Assistance is needed at many stages but children can not be assisted at home. Parents and other relatives have no idea of this type of mathematics. The child does not feel that the knowledge from home has anything to do with school mathematics.

Since infancy children have been using their mother tongue. Now they have to learn a new language and learn mathematics in this new language. Children can not communicate with their relatives in this language either. So they have to battle with the language as well as the subject matter which is completely alien from former experiences.

3.2 Reckoning time in Tanzania

Problems faced with counting are faced in other areas as well. Another interesting example is that of daily time reckoning. Time reckoning in Tanzania (actually in East Africa) is different from that of western countries. We are near the equator so we have almost 12 hours daylight and 12 hours darkness all year round. We start counting hours when the sun rises. We count 12 hours of daylight and then we start counting 12 hours of darkness at sunset. For example if it is 8 am and I am asked the time, I will say 8 am or 8 hours to an English speaker and at the same time I will say 2 o'clock to a Kiswahili or any Tanzanian vernacular language speaker.

This means one has to know both time reckonings and be able to transform them from one system to the other in an instant according to needs. Clocks and watches are set in the non-East African time. One reads 10 on the clock but pronounces 4 in Kiswahili, or one reads 5 and pronounces 11. One has to relate, simultaneously, non-African languages to the non-East African time and African languages to the East African time. To children and indeed many adults this is very confusing.

Children see the East African time to be logical and easy to follow. Children see the sun rising and time starts to be counted. As the sun goes up hours increase until after 12 hours when it starts to set. It becomes very difficult for children to understand that the day begins at midnight when it is extremely dark. The name *day* is associated with daylight. The non-East African time reckoning brings a lot of confusion and makes learning time a very hard task. To children this makes the school activity have no relation to their need to know the time. Learning time appears to be a purely abstract activity.

3.3 The general school process

Having singled out these two examples let us go back to the general formal school process during the colonial period. After four years in school children had to switch from learning in Kiswahili into learning in English. Just when children were about to be comfortable with Kiswahili they had to change and learn in yet another language, English. Kiswahili, though full of foreign words, has the same grammatical structure as the Bantu languages. Kiswahili is an African language. But English is entirely different. Language semantics, pronunciation and word order are quite different. Children had to fight an even harder battle.

They had to fight again with new English mathematical terminologies. Their English books used examples based on European experiences and traditions which had absolutely no meaning to the children, the teacher, or parents and relatives. Children could not rely on help at home. The learning of mathematics became a very gruelling task. Young pupils found the going tough and disliked mathematics even more than before.

In general children had no chance to feel that the knowledge of life they broughtwith them to the class wasworthwhile.

3.4. Any improvement after attaining political independence?

Tanzania attained political independence in 1961. With it came an increase in school enrollment. This necessitated an increase in the number of teachers, books and materials. Volunteers and other donors from all over the world came in to assist in different sectors, including teaching. I went to school at this time. In primary school we were taught by American Peace Corps vcolunteers, and volunteers from Britain, German, Denmark, Sweden, Cuba, the Soviet Union, akistan, Ireland, Israel, Canada and from everywhere people volunteered to come. In my school time, I was taught by teachers of 13 different nationalities, each with its own culture, its own English language problems (accent, slang, jargon), and with its own types of prejudice.

All sorts of books were used provided they were in English. They were donated by different people from different nations. Their contents contained different systems of measures and units, with examples from different socio-cultural environments. Not only did children have to battle with the language and subject matter but also with the distance between them and their teachers, as well as the literature. The confusion that resulted from this caused apathy on the part of many towards mathematics.

Shortly after independence, the colonial educational policies began to undergo reform. Efforts to remove colonial vestiges and to improve curricula to suit our needs were under way. Immediately after independence Kiswahili became the national language and efforts to spread it were intensified. Towards the end of the 1960s Kiswahili became the medium of instruction in all classes of primary school (standards 1-7) in all subjects except English. By the end of the 1970s only indigenous teachers were teaching in primary schools. The Kiswahili language spread rather fast and widely and now many Tanzanians are native Kiswahili speakers.

In 1967 a major political reform took place. The ideology of the so-called African socialism (*ujamaa*) and self-reliance (in the Arusha declaration) was introduced in Tanzania and so were major reforms in the educational policy. The objectives of education were changed, the main objective being education for self-reliance and creating awareness in the population as regards their dignity and long-denied rights. Therefore self-reliance projects (mainly manual labor based) and politics were introduced into the curriculum. Western (referred to as *colonial, capitalist, oppressive*) types of ideas and examples were replaced by socialist based ones with a touch of pre-colonial Africanism. These were even more inconceivable to the teachers, pupils and society in general. At least living with missionaries and colonial masters for more than 80 years had given some bleak idea of western norms. But the socialist norms mixed with a no longer existing African way of life were much more foreign than the western ones.

With independence and socialism the common ethnic bonds gave way to nationalism. Tribalism was being fought with all possible means. Teachers from one part of the country had to teach in other parts where they lacked knowledge of local customs and traditions as well as the ethnic language spoken there. The country was being unified rather fast. Because of this unification and so-called African socialism, books for primary schools were replaced with those containing examples related to the life of a given ethnic group mixed with socialist ideas. Children (and adults as well) from other ethnic groups had tremendous difficulty in comprehending these examples. Again this did not ease children's learning of mathematics—it only compounded the problems of conceptualization.

In 1977, Universal Primary Education (UPE) was introduced. This meant that all children must go to school, by law. This was not done gradually but was introduced abruptly. There was no transition period. There was a sudden big rise in enrollment and thus a very big shortage of teachers, classrooms and all other facilities. The teaching was in Kiswahili and was to be done by indigenous people. To meet the demand unqualified and semitrained teachers were employed. These teachers lacked confidence and interest in mathematics and could not teach the subject properly. They were absolutely unable to bring any innovative ideas to the instruction of mathematics.

3.5. The current problems of conceptualization

Socialist ideologies were introduced 25 years ago. Now many people are conversant with those ideas. Primary school children of today have been born and are growing up amidst those ideas. They have no problems with the Kiswahili language or with mathematical terminologies in Kiswahili. But the problems of conceptualization in mathematics emanating from the socio-cultural environment have taken another form.

Budget allocations to education have been declining year after year. This has resulted in lack of maintenance of buildings and other school properties, lack of expansion, lack of requisite materials and poor salaries for teachers. Ideologies coupled with poor planning have also played a major role in making the learning of mathematics difficult. I will mention some of the existing causes of poor conceptualization of mathematics by primary school children today.

3.51 Classroom social-cultural environment. Classrooms are very few indeed, particularly in the urban areas. This results in a classroom which should hold 45 pupils holding 130 and even up to 150 pupils. The classrooms are fully packed. A teacher managing such a class has no time to identify each child's individual problems. S/he cannot give sufficient exercises to the class. It is difficult for the teacher to assess individual learners' level of attainment.

In Tanzania age group is not synonymous with class level. Children in standard 1 (the first year in primary school) have ages ranging between 5 years and 11 years (Basic Education Statistics, Tanzania, 1986-1990). Effective conceptualization goes by age group and ability level. Our classes are heterogeneous in age and ability levels. Again this poses much difficulty in mathematics concept formation.

3.52 School location. In learning mathematics, school location plays a role as well. Urban schools are better equipped than those in rural areas in terms of both the quantity and quality of teachers, materials and morale. Children in urban areas have more time for self study and extra tuition whereas their peers in rural areas, after school time, must help their parents to collect fire-wood and water or to work on the farm. Children in rural areas have long distances to walk to school whereas in urban areas they take buses or are within short walking distances. Pupils have so-called self-reliance projects at school in order to generate extra income to run the schools. For those in rural areas they have very large farms and animals such as pigs and cattle. They spend a lot of time and energy working on these farms and tending to animals.

3.53 Other sources. Most schools lack teaching aids and mathematical instruments, and are poorly stocked with books. Pupils and teachers do not have money to buy their own books and instruments.

It is difficult to attract people to the teaching profession because of numerous unfavorable conditions. It is also difficult to retain those recruited. Students who perform well in mathematics do not join the teaching profession. We end up with those weak in mathematics teaching the subject at primary level. They themselves lack confidence and interest in the subject but have got to teach it. They have limitations in designing relevant mathematical examples. Most of the teachers are semi-trained or untrained. Even the few who are trained have hardly any chances to refresh their knowledge and keep abreast of new developments.

Girls have special problems in mathematics. Even though they perform equally well as boys up to the age of 10-12, their performance drops rather sharply after that as can be seen from The National Examinations Council of Tanzania (NECTA) results of 1968-1990 for standard IV and VIII. Poor attainment by girls is largely attributed to societal injustice in the distribution of labor, gender stereo-typing and prejudice.

Despite all the problems, some children succeed very well in mathematics. Just as Mmari (1973) said, children who take all this in their stride must be a matter of pride for themselves and of wonder to those who fail to cope but are from a homogeneous ethnic group, are learning in their own language, are in classrooms of the same age group and ability level, and in ideal classroom conditions with a well-trained and well-motivated teacher.

3.6. Can something be done to alleviate the problem?

Priorities in educational policies are required. Good teacher training, good remuneration for teachers, increase in the number of classrooms and provision of materials can be implemented if reasonable budget allocations are made by governments.

Various organs in Tanzania like the Mathematical Association of Tanzania, The Tanzania Teachers Association, and various non-government organizations are producing materials, conducting seminars and in-service courses to mathematics teachers and many other activities to improve the quality of teachers, instill mathematics interest in teachers and pupils and boost their morale.

3.7. What about the cultural gap?

Curricula reforms have to be made. It is not sufficient to translate into children's own languages materials and concepts which are basically Euro-centered or social-ist-centered. First, the traditional mathematical knowledge as we now experience it should be integrated in the teaching of mathematics. Second, efforts should be made to incorporate indigenous mathematics in the curriculum, that is, the indigenous mathematics in African traditions has to be uncovered. On-going research activities in ethno-mathematics have revealed that Africa is very rich in mathematics. This fact remained hidden until recently.

Efforts made by colonizers to relegate indigenous knowledge to a low position resulted in racial and cultural prejudices. The knowledge of how rich African tradi-tions are in mathematics is a big stimulus to African children and scholars in gen-eral. The apathy in colonialism and whatever is associated with it has played a role (consciously or subconsciously) in the dislike for mathematics, as it is seen as a white man's creation. In addition to mathematics in African traditions being com-patible with the original civilization, knowing that mathematics belongs to African cultures as well will act as a catalyst for people to become interested in the subject and to be proud of it. This knowledge has to be enhanced in order for children to gain self-confidence in the subject.

4. MATHEMATICS IN AFRICAN CULTURE

Many mathematical ideas and activities in African culture are often intertwined with art, craft, riddles, games, graphic systems and other traditions. The mathemat-ics is often hidden. Researchers such as Gerdes (1985) and Ascher (1988) have developed methods to uncover the hidden mathematics and suggest possibilities of using them in classroom. I will mention some of the research findings on the Afri-can traditions rich in mathematics.

Gerdes (1991) gives an overview of the history of mathematics in sub-Saharan Africa. He presents findings by many researchers on a variety of African traditions in which mathematics is embedded.

Numeration symbolism: (Written, spoken and gesture counting) in different ethnic groups of Africa.

Number symbolism: Most of these are associated with superstition and taboos, with counting, in sand drawings and networks, and in objects of African art such as basketry where even and odd numbers come into use.

Riddles and puzzles: Different types of puzzles from different peoples of Africa are presented (see Gerdes, 1991). They require mathematical logical aspects and some-times solutions have to be found using auxiliary drawings.

Art and symmetry: A lot of symmetry appears in African craft work and art. Mathematicians have analyzed symmetries in some African art such as in decorative patterns that appear on clothes, ornaments, smoking pipes, calabashes, weaving of hand bags, hats, baskets and brooms.

Gerdes (1990) analyzed geometrical forms of traditional objects such as baskets, mats, pots, houses and fish traps. He was able to discuss the properties and relations of circles, angles, rectangles, squares, regular pentagons and hexagons, cones, pyramids, cylinders and symmetry.

Games: Many games of different peoples in Africa have been reported in the literature (see Gerdes, 1991). They include counting rhymes and rhythms, "three in a row" games, arrangements, games of chance and board games, games involving strategy, games of alignment, struggle for territory and the mathematical principles underlying them. Doumbia (1989) analyzed some African traditional games by classifying them, finding the solution of mathematical problems posed by the games and analyzing the possibility of using them in classrooms. What is now being looked into is the possible relationship between visual memory and concentration as a necessity for success in many African games and the development of mathematical ideas behind them.

Geometry and architecture: There are studies on geometric shapes and ornamentation of traditional African architecture. Description of house decorations and rural paintings and geometric patterns used on house walls is given. Gerdes (1985) described the geometrical knowledge used in laying out circular or rectangular house plans whereas Mahajane (1989) uncovered geometrical knowledge applied in the construction of traditional granaries of maize and beans.

Time reckoning: A bone discovered in Zaire by De Heinzelin dated at 9 000-6 500 BC contains notches which have been interpreted by Marshade as an early lunar phase count. De Henzelin however interpreted this as some sort of game whose inventors had a number system based on 10 and knowledge of duplication of prime numbers (Zaslavsky, 1973, pp. 17-19).

Another bone found between Swaziland and South Africa, marked with 29 clearly defined notches, resembles calendar sticks carried by Bushmen. The bone dates from approximately 35 000 BC and is considered to be perhaps the oldest artefact (see Gerdes, 1991).

Lynch and Robbins (1983) analyzed evidence of a calendar that was in use in eastern Africa at around 300 BC. Numerous other analyses of concepts of time, time-reckoning and cosmology among various ethnic groups in Tanzania and sub-Saharan Africa are presented in Gerdes (1991). Research carried out at the Ahmadubello University in Nigeria has also revealed a lot of the mathematics hidden in African traditions (see Gerdes, 1991).

Networks, graphs or sand drawings: Networks from different African groups have been discussed. For example, Gerdes (1988) described the *sona* (sand drawings of the Tchokwe of Angola). In drawing the sona, experts first set out an orthogonal net of equidistant points. One or more lines are drawn that embrace the points of the reference frame. This is an example of an early use of a coordinate system. The expert uses dimensions of the reference frame and a geometrical algorithm.

Most drawings belong to a long tradition. They refer to tables, games, riddles, animals and so on and played a very big role in the transmission of empirical mathematical knowledge from one generation to the other. This knowledge was mostly secretly transmitted from father to son. The underlying geometry in the sona drawings is non-Euclidean.

Ascher (1988) uncovered the topological aspects of sona with symmetries, extension, enlargement through repetition, and isomorphy. Gerdes (1988) on the other hand analyzed symmetry and monolinearity, classes of sona and corresponding geometry algorithms for their construction, systematic construction of monolinear base patterns, chain rule and elimination rule for the construction of monolinear sona. He suggested that the experts who invented the rules could prove the truth of theorems that the rules express. Gerdes further showed the possibility of using sona ideas in the classroom. Let me cite two of his suggestions.

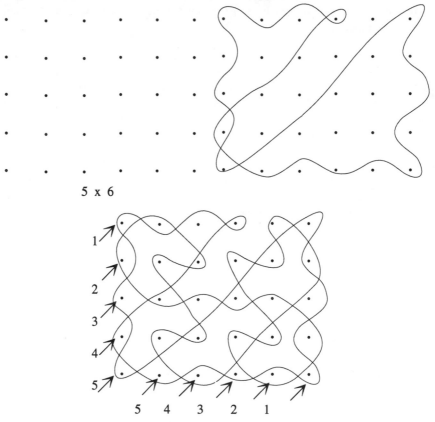

Figure 1: Sona representation of the proverb, "Creeper
is the firewood of old people."

(1) On Arithmetic Progressions: From the symbolic representation of the proverb "creeper is the firewood of old people" as shown in Figure 1, Gerdes (1988, pp. 7-8) analyzes this mathematically to be: $5.6 = (1 + 2 + 3 + 4 + 5) + (5 + 4 + 3 + 2 + 1) = 2 . (1 + 2 + 3 + 4 + 5)$

He suggests this can be used as a starting point for the study of sums of the arithmetic progression. This can be generalized to: $n(n + 1) = 2 . (1 + 2 + 3 + ... + n)$.

Gerdes analyzes the representation of "Kalunga (God)", Figure 2, as $6^2 - 6 = 2(1 + 2 + 3 + 4 + 5)$ which can be generalized: $(n + 1)^2 - (n + 1) = 2 \times (1 + 2 + 3 + ... + n)$.

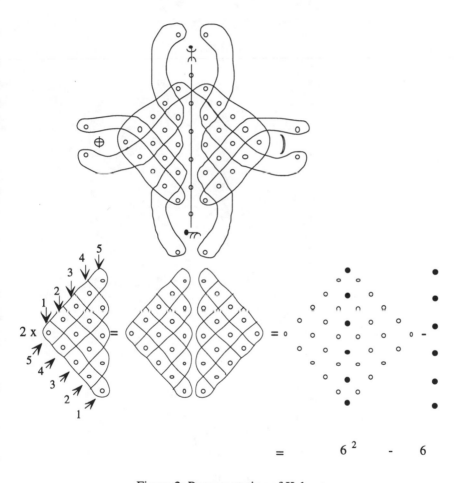

Figure 2: Representation of Kalunga.

(2) On the highest common factor. The sona of a tortoise, a head of an elephant and a head of an antelope have been used to give a geometrical determination of the highest common factor of two natural numbers (Gerdes, 1988, pp. 14-15).

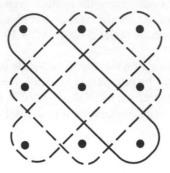

Figure 3a: Tortoise.

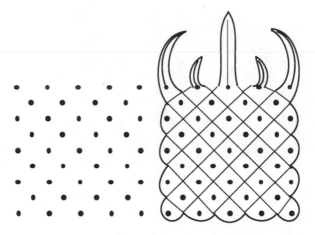

Figure 3b: Elephant.

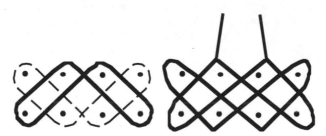

Figure 3c: Antelope.

To draw the tortoise one starts with a 3 x 3 reference frame and needs three closed curves, as in Figure 3a. The number of curves to embrace all the network points is the highest common factor. For the elephant's head a 5 x 5 frame is laid down and five curves are necessary, so the highest common factor is five (see Figure 3b).

Figure 3c shows the antelope's head. The frame is 2 x 4 and two curves are necessary to embrace all the network points. Figure 4 shows a 4 x 6 frame. A closed curve embraces two points of each of the initial six columns and three points of each row. There are four rows, so 4/2 = 2 curves are necessary and for the six columns 6/3 = 2 curves are necessary. The highest common factor is two.

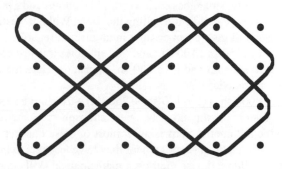

Figure 4: A 4 x 6 frame sona.

Gerdes (1988) suggests further possible uses to show similarity; $5^2 = 4.6 + 1$; the Pythagorean triples; bilateral, double bilateral, point and rotational symmetry; as well as Euler graphs.

5. CURRICULUM REFORM FOR THE 21ST CENTURY IN AFRICAN CULTURE

The Ethno-mathematics Research Project of Mozambique has carried out experiments on how to incorporate traditional African cultural elements into mathematics education. They have demonstrated alternative constructions of Euclidean geometrical ideas developed from the traditional culture of Mozambique. They have also shown how diverse African ornaments and artefacts may be used to create a rich context for the discovery and the demonstration of the Pythagorean Theorem and of related ideas and propositions. They analyzed some possibilities for the incorporation of sona drawings into education and produced a booklet for 10-15 year olds on sona sand drawings. They are expanding this research and are preparing for a mathematics curriculum reform which will be based on African traditions and socio-cultural environments (reported in Gerdes, 1991). The Mozambican experience should be extended to other parts of Africa.

Certainly African traditions and cultures are constantly undergoing changes. We have, in Tanzania alone, a big diversity in traditions. As such the traditions on which mathematics is based may be unknown to many pupils. Efforts to incorporate indigenous mathematics in the curriculum may not deliver the desired results. The manner in which mathematics is presented must take into account traditional mathematical knowledge as we now experience it. If children and indeed adults see the relevance of mathematics in their day-to-day activities they learn it well and are enthusiastic in devising their own skills in computations and construction of mathematical ideas and formulae.

For example in most Tanzanian societies of today it is common to see pre-school and primary school children selling items like groundnuts, ice cream, buns, fruit and so on. They handle cash in hundreds of shillings. They must give back change in an instant. Since they cannot afford to delay change, the children devise their own methods of combining addition, multiplication and subtraction in order to give change depending on the denominations they have. Consider someone with a 1 000 shilling note who buys two mangoes each worth 110 shillings and a pineapple worth 250 shillings from a ten year old child selling the fruits. Without wasting time, most children of that age will give exact change in an instant, regardless of their class level. If they have only 50 sh., 100 sh., and 500 sh. notes it is just common for the child to ask for a 20 sh. coin and give 550 sh. as change. Here the child does the following mental arithmetic:

$$1\ 000\ \text{sh.} - (2 \times 110\ \text{sh.} + 250\ \text{sh.}) + 20\ \text{sh.} = 550\ \text{sh.}$$

Nothing other than the competitive business atmosphere has taught these children how to do the arithmetic. Surprisingly, most of these children have tremendous difficulty in arithmetic at school where they have teachers to instruct them to do the arithmetic. Children devise their own mathematical skills in games such as hair plaiting. They do the mathematics with interest and continuously devise better skills to outwit their peers.

6. CONCLUSION

The problems of conceptualization of mathematical ideas faced by children might be reduced to a minimum, if (1) instructions are delivered by a teacher very conversant with, or of the same ethnic origins and socio-cultural environment asthe child; (2) using the language of the child; and (3) if emphasis is put on the development of mathematical concepts where the role of the teacher is to create a meaningful cultural framework in which children might construct their mathematics, taking into consideration the mathematics they bring with them to school.

REFERENCES

Ascher, M. (1988). Graphs in cultures (II): A study in ethno-mathematics. *Archive for History of Exact Sciences, 39*(1), 75-95.

Clements, K. (1984). The origins of conceptual difficulties that young learners experience in mathematics. In United Nations Educational Scientific and Cultural Organization, *Studies in mathematics education, Vol. 3,* (pp. 107-127).

D'Ambrosio, U. (1985). Ethnomathematics and its place in the history of mathematics. *For the Learning of Mathematics, 5* (1), 44-48.

Doumbia, S. (1989). Mathematics in traditional games. In C. Keitel, P. Damerow, A. Bishop, & P. Gerdes (Eds.), *Mathematics education and society*, (pp. 174-175). Paris: UNESCO.

Gagné, R. M., and White, R. T. (1978). Memory structures and learning outcomes. *Review of Educational Research. 48*(2), 187-222.

Gerdes, P. (1985). *Zum erwachenden geometrischen Denken*. Eduardo Mondlane University, Maputo, 267 p (mimeo).

Gerdes, P. (1988). On possible uses of traditional Angolan sand drawings in the mathematics classroom. *Educational Studies in Mathematics, 19*, 3-22.

Gerdes, P. (1990). *Ethno geometrie, kultureanthropologische Beitrage zur Genese und Didaktik der Geometrie*. Bad Salzfurth, Germany: Verlag Barbara Franzbecker.

Gerdes, P. (1991, August). *On the history of mathematics in sub-Saharan Africa.* Paper presented at the 3rd Pan-African Congress of Mathematicians, Nairobi, Kenya.

Harris, P. (1980). *Measurement in tribal Aboriginal communities.* Darwin, Northern Territory, Australia: Northern Territory Department of Education.

Institute of Education (1979). *Evaluation of mathematics teaching in primary schools.* Dar es Salaam, Tanzania.

Kagan, J., Klein, R. E., Finley, G. E., Rogoff, B., &Nolan, E. (1979). A Cross-cultural study of cognitive development. *Monographs of the Society for Research in Child Development, 44*(5).

Ki-Zerbo, J. (1990). *Educate or perish: Africa's impasse and prospects.* Dakar/Abidjan: UNESCO-UNICEF.

Lynch, B. M., & Robbins, L. (1983). Namoratunga: The first archaeo-astronomical evidence in sub-Saharan Africa. In *Blacks in science* (pp. 51-56). New Brunswick, NJ and London, UK: Transaction Books.

Mahajane, S. (1989). On geometrical knowledge applied in the construction of traditional granaries for maize and beans in southern Mozambique. Eduardo Mondlane University, Maputo (unpublished course paper), 10 p.

Mason, J., Burton, L., & Stacey, K. (1982). *Thinking mathematically.* New York, NY: Addison Wesley.

Mmari, G. (1973). *The study of the understanding of mathematical ideas and concepts among Tanzania secondary school pupils.* Unpublished PhD thesis, University of Dar es Salaam, Tanzania.

Mmari, G.(1976). Teaching mathematics through a foreign language. *Science Teacher, 19.*

Mmari, G. (1980). Secondary mathematics in the United Republic of Tanzania. In *Studies in Mathematics Education,* Vol. 1, (pp. 106-126). UNESCO.

Mpama, R. A. (1990). Factors contributing to poor performance in secondary school mathematics. *The Tanzanian Mathematical Bulletin, 20*(2), 20-27.

Omari, I. M., & Mosha, H. J. (1987). *The quality of primary education in Tanzania.* Nairobi, Kenya.

Seka, B. R. (1990a). Evaluation of mathematics teaching. *The Tanzanian Mathematical Bulletin, 20*(2), 52-73.

Seka, B. R. (1990b). *Problems of teaching and learning mathematics in Tanzania.* The Mathematical Association of Tanzania research paper, Dar es Salaam, Tanzania.

Shirley, L. (1986, March). *Ethnomathematics and the history of African mathematics.* Paper presented at the 2nd Pan African Congress of Mathematicians, Jos, Nigeria.

Sinclair, H. (1990). Learning: The interactive recreation of knowledge. In L. P. Steffe & T. Wood (Eds.), *Transforming children's mathematics education: International perspectives* (pp. 19-29). Hillsdale, NJ: Lawrence Erlbaum Associates.

Zaslavsky, C. (1973). *Africa counts: number and pattern in African culture.* Boston, MA: Prindle, Weber & Schmidt.

Verdiana G. Kashaga Masanja
University of Dar es Salaam
Tanzania

CONTRIBUTIONS TO PART FIVE

Language and its rôle in concept formation is the centerpiece of the contributions to Part Five. A broad view of language was taken, ranging from young children's drawings to their spoken interactions and written symbolic forms. Semadeni writes about connecting physical manipulation with written and spoken representation, while Bednarz shares similar concerns but focuses more directly on verbalization.

Khisty provides insights into how teacher language and written texts may influence children's available speech for talking about their concepts in mathematics. The other dimension to this chapter is its consideration of multilingual classrooms where the mathematical discourse may be carried on in a language that is not the first language of all participants in the discourse.

The first three chapters in this part of the book focus mostly on language and provide us with both theoretical views and classroom perspectives. The final chapter, that from Jaime, looks very specifically at one content area, geometry, and warns against the confused language engendered in children by inappropriate language of geometry in textbooks. Her claim is that confusion in language is associated with confused ideas and ill-formed conceptual knowledge.

The Editors.

LIMITATIONS OF ICONIC AND SYMBOLIC REPRESENTATIONS OF ARITHMETICAL CONCEPTS IN EARLY GRADES OF PRIMARY SCHOOL

1. INTRODUCTION

The purpose of this chapter is to point out and discuss certain problems concerning the language used for teaching mathematics in the early grades of primary school[1]. Language is understood here as a means of communication, that is, of giving and receiving information by talk, gestures, writing, and drawing pictures. The oral or written language used to exchange information during the lesson is a natural language (for example, everyday English) augmented with words or phrases coined by mathematicians and educators. In this paper, the term *language* also includes:
- •gestures enriching words (e.g., showing: "from here to here");
- •various drawings (e.g., picture of a number of apples), graphic schemata (simple schemata, like an arrow, or more highly sophisticated schemata); and
- •formal symbols (they are of three categories: standard symbols, like those in the formula 2+3=5; symbols devised for educational purposes and not used otherwise; symbols introduced *ad hoc*).

These last two components of the language, drawings and symbols, will be at the core of our arguments. It should be emphasized that the phrases, pictures and symbols used by the teacher should make sense to the child. This crucial principle is obvious. A perplexing problem is how to achieve the desired effects of this principle.

Let us also stress the importance of using the natural, spontaneous language of the child. However, the way the language is used for communication in the classroom cannot be identical with that used at home or during play. Two important questions are: (1) how to help children adopt the language, conventions and requirements of the school instruction? and (2) how to do this in a "mild" way by fostering the development of children's natural powers rather than teaching them certain techniques?

2. THE PROBLEM OF OPERATIONAL REASONING AT THE BEGINNING OF SCHOOLING

In many countries, in curricula and textbooks for grade 1 it is tacitly assumed (although perhaps not by the textbook authors) that the learner has already attained a certain level of operational thinking. The term "operation" means here *concrete operation* in Piaget's sense. However, a significant number of school beginners fail standard tests of conservation of (cardinal) number. Typical preoperational chil-

---

[1] This chapter is based on research partially supported by Polish KBN grant 2 1221 91 01.

H. Mansfield et al. (eds.), Mathematics for Tomorrow's Young Children, 218–227.
© 1996 *Kluwer Academic Publishers. Printed in the Netherlands.*

dren may count six items, for example, stones, and see them spread out immediately afterwards, and yet they do not understand that there is no need to recount the items, for there must be still six. These children are in danger of failure in school mathematics; rote learning is often seen as the only remedy. For more about this problem, and for further references, see Gruszczyk-Kolczynska and Semadeni (1990).

Children who do not yet understand the invariance of cardinal number have not, of course, acquired the ability to use the abstract context-free concept of "six". Still more difficult are statements involving numbers. For instance, the statement 6+2=8 means that abstract 6 plus abstract 2 equals abstract 8. Put differently, this statement is a symbolic expression of the following: if we take any 6 items and then take any 2 items and join them together, then there will be 8 items. But for preoperational children it is not clear that after moving the objects in order to bring them together their number remains the same. If they find out that 6 apples and 2 apples is 8 apples together, then they still have to count how many it would be if 6 pencils and 2 pencils were put together. Attempts to explain to them that it does not matter what items they count are in vain. They have to mature into this understanding.

Consequently, if the level of operational thinking of the child is too low, he/she may recognize and even write the digit 6 and be able to use it in simple situations, for example, by responding appropriately to the written instruction "Color 6 circles," but may not yet be able to handle numbers and arithmetic operations at the symbolic level in a meaningful way. The conservation of number is indispensable if a child is to regard a number (say 6) as an object in its own right—an object which can be part of larger symbolic structures, such as part of the statement $6 + 2 = 8$, or of that in a much more difficult task: $6 + \square = 8$.

At the same time, many preoperational children can count items well beyond the school-assigned limit of 10 or 20 and can sometimes solve arithmetical problems regarded as too difficult for their age. More precisely, they can solve problems that are formulated in a way meaningful to them, provided that they are encouraged to use manipulatives. The gap between what children can do if a mathematical problem is presented in a form meaningful to them (in natural language, with adequate motivation) and what the same children can do with exactly the same problem formulated in an apparently simple but more abstract way is much deeper than most teachers and educators would admit (see, for example, Carraher, Carraher, & Schliemann, 1985).

We should note that if a child is given such a conversation task to determine the level of operational thinking, then his/her performance depends heavily on the context of the task and on the language used. In special situations, even four-year-olds can give the so-called pseudoconservation responses (Szeminska, 1977); for instance, if they are given toy roofs and houses without roofs and are asked whether there are enough roofs for the houses, they are not deceived by spreading out roofs (or houses) and are able to give correct answers.

In standard conservation tests the counters are semantically neutral, that is, the child deals with green blocks and red blocks, or with small blocks and big blocks. Sometimes the counters may suggest non-conservation responses, for example if 6 small and 6 large blocks are used. Usually there are no hints given to help the child to understand the meaning of the experimenter's question: "Are there as many ... ?" The level of abstraction should correspond to the purpose of the test; the task is not too abstract (for example, blocks are concrete) and not too easy.

3. LEARNING TO HANDLE SYMBOLS

The child first learns the simplest mathematical symbols, the digits. Much more difficult are sequences of symbols: multidigit numbers (e.g., 27) and formulas (e.g., $8 - 3 = 5$).

As an example of the passage from concrete manipulations and everyday language to symbolic expressions, let us analyze possible ways of mastering addition with carrying ($7 + 5$, say) by the child:

1 Finding the results by using manipulatives (counters, fingers). This is an excellent way at the beginning, but sooner or later the child has to perform the computations more efficiently.
2 Learning number facts. This is an elegant euphemism for learning sums by heart. Of course, nothing is wrong with remembering sums as a result of practice with manipulatives. However, this approach often degenerates into rote learning.
3 To compute the result by the standard decomposition method. The method is apparently simple and natural. The problem is how to write it down. Note that if the instruction is based on textbooks then the problem of how to write something becomes crucial.

There are many possible ways of presenting the decomposition method. The worst can be found in some textbooks for children from the new-math era:

   Example A: $7 + 5 = 7 + (3 + 2) = (7 + 3) + 2 = 10 + 2 = 12$

Examples like this are sometimes accompanied by reference to the associativity of addition); for an analysis of Example A see Whitney (1973). One of the arguments against Example A is that using parentheses is too difficult for children who have yet to learn the addition $7 + 5$. We may try to simplify the sequence in Example A by omitting any bracketing, e.g.,

   Example B: $7 + 5 = 7 + 3 + 2 = 10 + 2 = 12$.

This method or a variant of it is quite popular in European textbooks. Many educators take it for granted that it is the most suitable approach. However, the difficulty of Example B can be understood better if we take into account the following possible reasons.

First, we should bear in mind that many of the children who are taught to add numbers such as $7 + 5$ are still preoperational or otherwise may not have a sufficiently clear understanding of the symbols, 7, +, or =. So any way of writing computations of the type in Example B may be too sophisticated for them.

Second, suppose we want to avoid symbols and replace them by oral description of successive steps of the decomposition method, assuming that the child will perform them mentally, uttering (or writing) only the final result. Let us try to figure out how many mental operations are to be performed: (1) keep numbers 7 and 5 in memory (unless they are given in written form); (2) find the complement of 7 to 10;

(3) decompose the other summand 5 as 3 + 2; (4) add 3 to 7 and then add 2, getting 12. It must really be difficult to learn to deal with so many operations in a row!

Third, the argument used in Example B, though apparently simple, requires good command of manipulating such strings of abstract symbols. The child must think not only of one, single, next step of computation, but must also keep the whole procedure in mind, and remain in control of it. Most children who are learning addition of the type 7 + 5 are not yet capable of this degree of control.

Undoubtedly, one of the reasons for the difficulty children experience in handling symbolic expressions in Example B is their limited understanding of the equality sign. As a result of inflexible teaching ("doing sums") children have a strong tendency to interpret the "=" symbol as the command "compute and complete the equation by writing down the result on the right." Consequently, the reverse order such as 8 = 5 + 3, and identities such as 5 + 3 = 6 + 2, are hard for pupils to accept as legitimate expressions (see Behr, Erlwanger, & Nicholls, 1980; Kieran, 1981; Hughes, 1986; Sfard, 1991). Similarly children may reject Example B as making no sense to them.

Authors of textbooks devise various ways of avoiding multiple equality symbols while presenting the regrouping method of addition. For instance, children may find two separate lines written:

$$7 + 3 + 2 =$$
$$7 + 5 =$$

The order of these lines is later changed (e.g., first 8 + 6 = and then 8 + 2 + 4 =) children may also see two oblique lines joining the digit 6 with the 4 + 2. Such a variant of Example B, if it is properly explained, may help learners. Otherwise the task is still hard. Children have to grasp the structure of two lines of symbols, rather than just one line, and to identify the relations between them.

All these methods have the same serious shortcoming. If they are to be shown in a book, they are usually static, appearing ready-printed, and hence difficult for the child to comprehend. This is the chief obstacle to the children's understanding.

In her ontological-psychological study, Sfard (1991) stresses the dual nature of mathematical conceptions, which has been discussed by many authors from different perspectives and described in various terms (see also Piaget & Garcia, 1989). She argues that basic mathematical notions can be conceived of in two complementary ways: *operationally* as processes, and *structurally* as objects. Operational conception, a product of certain processes or the process itself, precedes the structural conception, a mathematical entity conceived as a static structure, as if it were a real object. Passage from the former conception to the latter is a long and inherently difficult process, accomplished—according to Sfard—in three steps: interiorization, condensation, and reification. The stage of reification is the point where an interiorization of higher-level concepts begins. Processes can be performed in which the new-born object is an input.

Applying her ideas to the problem considered here, we may say that the child first conceives of addition, 3 + 2 say, as a process. The equality 3 + 2 = 5 means that 5 is the result of the computation. The ability to regard 3 + 2 as an entity is a later step in the development of mathematical thinking. If children have already reached this level, they may regard 3 + 2 as an object which may be part of more complex structures. This ability is at the core of carrying out operations such as those in Example B.

If Example B or its modifications are too difficult for the child, is memorizing the addition table the only solution to this educational dilemma? The answer is no. Proper organization of the work with concrete material may help the child. For instance, sticks may be used. This can be done in various ways. Educators often think of the so-called cardinal approach to the concept of the sum of natural numbers and represent 7 + 5 by two arrays of counters:

The child is expected to join them together and to count all. This gives the result, 12, but still leaves a large gap between this action and general, efficient methods of computation. However, the child may be told to take sticks one by one from the right-hand array and keep moving them to the left-hand one until there are ten on the left:

There are now 10 sticks and 2 more, that is, 12 together. After some practice, the child may be aware how many sticks are needed to get ten in the left array and will take the whole group at once. The crucial difference between this approach and the former (joining all sticks together) is that now the child enacts the computation as symbolized in Example B. The mathematical idea of regrouping sticks is the same as in decomposing numbers but the above enactive representation of this idea is natural for a child, while Example B is symbolic and difficult. Moreover, this kind of manipulation is a good starting point to learn later the symbolic expression Example B, which may be regarded as a record of what the child has actually done.

Of course, after dozens (or hundreds) of such regroupings the child will eventually remember the addition table. But mastering the table is not the only reason why such activities are recommended. Another, equally important, goal is to deepen the understanding of numbers and operations. Handling the operations in an algorithmic way should be a later step in education.

Let us now point out some popular misconceptions, which can be identified in many textbooks.

4. SEVERAL OVERSIMPLIFICATIONS OR MISCONCEPTIONS

4.1 First oversimplification: representations form a one-way sequence: enactive, iconic, symbolic

In a series of papers (see, for example, Bruner, 1966), Bruner distinguished three well-known types of representation: *enactive* (by doing something); *iconic* (a schematic picture), and *symbolic* (which includes not only mathematical symbols but also spoken words). There is a lot of evidence that the child learns first enactive representation, then iconic and finally symbolic[2]. In the 1970's iconic representations of numbers and operations became popular with certain groups of educators as an intermediate between the concrete and the abstract. However, the concept of "representation" was used in a sense somewhat different from Bruner's. For him the concept was psychological. He referred mainly to the way thoughts are made manifest externally, though he also considered representations as a way of transferring ideas. The làtter meaning is predominant in educational publications.

Bruner's ideas were often oversimplified by thinking of them as a simple progression: enactive, iconic, symbolic. While it is true that iconic representations of a mathematical concept should result from earlier enactive ways of dealing with concrete problems, it does not mean that at a certain moment the child can pass to iconic representations and there is no need to return to enactive representations of the same concept any more. Children should be accustomed to using iconic or enactive representations if they encounter difficulty while dealing with a problem at a symbolic level. If they cannot add two numbers, they may use fingers or other manipulatives. If a word problem is not understood, they should be helped to use counters to simulate the given situation. In this way the child acquires a sound knowledge of basic arithmetical operations (see also James & Mason, 1982).

In many schools, iconic and symbolic representations are used too early, without adequate introduction and motivation. One of the reasons is that only these two types of representations can be shown in textbooks. Textbooks are the easiest way of organizing classroom instruction. Organizing manipulation of concrete objects requires much more effort on the part of the teacher—it is technically more complicated, requires flexibility, individualization, coping with clumsiness of certain children, and so on. Therefore, while enactive representations often dominate in preschool education, they are not used so much in the primary school. What children need is a proper balance of various types of representation, depending on the topic, age of the children, and their level of understanding.

4.2 Second oversimplification: iconic representations are easy for children

Iconic representations are generally easier than symbolic ones; yet, we should bear in mind that "easier" does not imply "easy". Children may have serious difficulties with inadequate or ill-timed iconic representations.

Authors of textbooks often jump from one interesting representation to another, without giving the student a chance to become familiar with them. Numerous examples of ill-devised or doubtful pictures could be found even in the textbooks displayed in the exhibition at the International Congress on Mathematics Education in Quebec in 1992. Consider the following typical example of a simple idea obscured by an over-complicated graphic schema. (See next page.)

---

[2] Note that Hughes (1986, pp. 57-60) in his description of children's invention of written arithmetic, distinguished "pictographic representation," "iconic representation," and "symbolic representation"; he noted that Bruner used the term "iconic" somewhat differently.

In a task of this kind, there is a number of items (for example, apples, cars; in the above example there are 5 hearts). These items are drawn inside a rectangle in the left part of picture. The rectangle is joined to a box by a line. Another rectangle with a number of (similar or different) items, joined with another box, is drawn in the right half. Either box is the place where the child fills in the number of items. Finally, between the two boxes one of the symbols <, >, = is to be written.

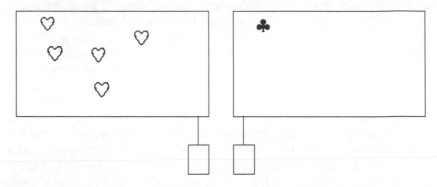

The task seems easy. However, it is quite hard as it appears in a book, ready-made and static. The child has to analyze a fairly complicated graphic schema and grasp the meaning of various parts of it. What are the big rectangles? What are the boxes? Much effort is needed to come to the conclusion that 5 < 7. For many pupils it is obvious that 5 is less than 7 and yet they are likely to be puzzled by the illustration. A purely symbolic expression 5 < 7 would perhaps be easier than such a complicated drawing. In some textbooks a graphic schema of this kind may be further obscured by 5 lines that are intended to represent a one-to-one correspondence between 5 elements of one set and 5 elements of the other.

Conceivably, the purpose of the task is to show that 5 < 7 even in cases where we count different objects. For example, there may be 5 apples on the left and 7 plums on the right (rather than hearts and clubs). But preoperational children will not be convinced by carrying out the task (even if the teacher doesher best to explain it). They know that 5 apples is more to eat than 7 plums. If they are told to fill in the symbol < they may do this peremptorily, just to satisfy the teacher.

Another serious problem is that many authors change (without warning) the meaning of graphic schemata. As an example of this phenomenon, let us consider arrows. They may serve as symbols of many different concepts in the same textbook. Before the concept of a number is introduced, a bunch of (straight or curved) arrows denotes a one-to-one correspondence. Some pages later an arrow is used to indicate motion, perhaps to show that a number of counters are moved away in a concretization of subtraction. The meaning is changed again when an arrow becomes a symbol of the operation of adding 3, say; it joins two points on the number line and "+3" is written above it. The line itself has a pointed end and looks like a long arrow.

This lack of consistency is a result of deep belief that arrows are so simple and well known that their meanings must be obvious. It is taken for granted that iconic representations facilitate the learning. However, many drawings in textbooks are a hindrance rather than a help to students. Decoding the meaning of a graphic symbol (like an arrow)—especially when it is a part of a larger graphic schema—may be harder for the child than grasping the arithmetic idea itself. It is a paradox that some of the pictures in textbooks can be decoded only by those who are familiar with rudiments of methods of teaching mathematics; in order to perform a task the learner should be aware of the didactical goals of it. Also note that coding is always easier than decoding, even if it is done by the same person. It is still harder to analyze designs made by somebody else.

Some iconic representations are natural and easy. This applies to most pictures used in textbooks to illustrate addition or multiplication. However, we should be aware of the possibility of various difficulties. Lay (1982, p. 263) points out that for some persons the picture:

is a mental model for "six" rather than "five." I have heard some children claim the number to be both of these, but also to claim that there are four, perhaps ignoring the endpoints.

Serious problems arise when iconic representations of subtraction are considered. For instance the following, apparently obvious, picture is supposed to represent the difference between 6 and 2, that is, taking two dots from 6.

However, many people, both children and adults, respond to such a picture by subtracting 2 from 4, that is, calculating 4 - 2. They act seemingly as if the representation were of 4 + (-2).

Generally, in a graphic schema representing the difference of two numbers, the discarded items may be crossed out, or encircled by a line with an arrow indicating that they are taken away, or some other convention may be used. However, none of these devices should be regarded as a self-evident representation of subtraction. Each such schema should be carefully explained (or, better, its meaning should be negotiated with children). Moreover, at the beginning of learning it may be not enough to explain the first example of subtraction by showing one single picture; many children need at least two pictures in a row: one showing the situation before taking away and one showing the situation after. It requires some practice to imagine the whole story while looking at just one illustration.

Still more difficult are pictures which require inverting (in the mind) an arithmetical operation. For instance, a picture may intend to represent addition with unknown addend and the student is expected to interpret it as subtraction. Similar remarks apply to multiplication and its inverse operation division. For instance the picture:

* * * * | * * * * | * * * * | * * * * | * * * * | * * * *

may represent multiplication, 6 x 4, or division, either 24 ÷ 6 or 24 ÷ 4.

Generally, if a single operation with two numbers given and one unknown to be determined is to be represented by a graphic schema, there are usually two easy options: either all three numbers are given in the picture (in the sense that items can be simply counted), or only one number can be found in the picture and the other two numbers cannot be determined. In the latter case, one of the other numbers must be given as either written or oral information.

The above comments do not mean that iconic representations should be abandoned. Their role in the learning of arithmetic should be appreciated, but at the same time their limitations should be recognized and their use should be carefully considered. Such a representation may appear obvious to an adult and obscure to children. The effect of using it must not be taken for granted. No graphic schema works by itself.

Iconic representations are suitable for instruction if they result from the children's experience. A child understands a picture if it depicts what he/she has already done. See Semadeni (1992) for examples of activities (tossing dice and moving pawns on a piece of number strip) that help children conceive the idea of representing addition and subtraction by arrows and also activities that help them to draw trees of operations.

4.3. Third oversimplification: if only small numbers are involved, the task is easy.

Of course, a problem involving ten items is generally easier for children than the same problem for a hundred items (sometimes the increase of difficulty is enormous). However, it does not mean that any task concerning only a few items is easy. The numbers in a task may be small and yet it may be quite hard if it is combined with the need to decode the symbols (picture, wording) used to present it. In the above task with 5 hearts and 7 clubs the numbers are less than 10 and the main obstacle is the graphic language.

In the 1960s, the idea, "if only small numbers are involved the task is easy," was one of the key arguments for teaching non-decimal systems of numeration, base three, for example. It was hoped that some transfer of knowledge would help children to understand better the decimal system. What was not taken into account were social and cultural constraints. Such obstacles may turn out to be much more important than numbers themselves.

In fact, for school beginners one of most difficult is the smallest whole number: zero. One may cause similar troubles (especially in problems involving multiplication). And yet in some textbooks for grade 1 the symbol "+" is introduced immediately after the numbers 1 and 2, with only one possible example: 1+1=2, because the digit 3 has not yet been taught!

There are a lot more questions concerning the problems considered in this chapter. Let me point out one of them. Teachers often are told: *from the concrete to the abstract.* What about the reverse: from the abstract to the concrete? Children should be taught to illustrate abstract operations with concrete examples; yet, this is easy neither for them to perform nor for the teacher to organize.

REFERENCES

Behr, M., Erlwanger, S., & Nichols, E. (1980). How children view the equals sign. *Mathematics Teaching, 92*, 13-15.

Bruner, J. S. (1966). On cognitive growth. In J. S. Bruner, R. R. Oliver, & P. M. Greenfield, (Eds.), *Studies in cognitive growth*. New York: Wiley.

Carraher, T. N., Carraher, D. W., & Schliemann, A. D. (1985). Mathematics in the streets and in schools. *British Journal of Developmental Psychology, 3*, 21-29.

Gruszczyk-Kolczynska, E., & Semadeni, Z. (1990). The child's maturity to learn mathematics in the school situation. In *Developments in School Mathematics Education Around the World*, Proceedings of CUSMP International Conference, (pp. 210-232). Reston, VA: NCTM.

Hughes, M. (1986). *Children and number: Difficulties in learning mathematics*. Oxford: Basil Blackwell.

James, N., & Mason, J. (1982). Towards recording. *Visual Language, 16*(3), 249-258.

Kieran, C. (1981). Concepts associated with the equality symbol. *Educational Studies in Mathematics,12,*, 317-320

Lay, L. C. (1982). Mental images and arithmetical symbols. *Visual Language, 16*, (3), 259-274.

Semadeni, Z. (1992). Arrow graphs and trees as iconic-enactive representations. [in Polish; English summary], *Annales Societatis Mathematicae Polonae, Series "Dydaktyka Matematyki", (14)*, 115-120.

Sfard, A. (1991). The dual nature of mathematical conceptions: Reflections on process and objects as different sides of the same coin. *Educational Studies in Mathematics, 22*, 1-36.

Szeminska, A. (1977), De l'identification à la conservation opératoire. *Bulletin de Psychologie*, Groupe d'Etudes de Psychologie de l'Universite de Paris, 369-375.

Whitney, H. (1973), Are we off the track in teaching mathematical concepts? In *Developments in Mathematical Education–Proceedings Second International Congress on Mathematical. Education* (pp. 283-296). Harvard, MA: Cambridge University Press.

Zbigniew Semadeni
University of Warsaw
Poland

LANGUAGE ACTIVITY, CONCEPTUALIZATION AND PROBLEM SOLVING: THE ROLE PLAYED BY VERBALIZATION IN THE DEVELOPMENT OF MATHEMATICAL THOUGHT IN YOUNG CHILDREN

1. INTRODUCTION

The model for official discourse in mathematics that can be traced in books, textbooks or teaching practice, is often characterized by ideas of clarity, rigor, precision, and purity. From this conception of discourse, among others, originates the increasing formalization of the language used in the classroom.

A systematic analysis of mathematics textbooks reveals the preponderance of symbolic over natural language wording. Moreover, when the support of natural language is used as well, it is interwoven into the symbolic code and deformed in favor of the symbolism (Laborde, 1982). Our observations at a variety of school levels showed that from a very early age, children today are faced by the ever-increasing use of symbolism in school manuals and other material (Dufour-Janvier, Bednarz, & Bélanger, 1987). This trend, a relatively recent phenomenon in mathematics teaching practice, leads to the impoverishment of natural language as a learning support. If we look at old textbooks that were used in elementary schools, we can see that for a long time natural language played a significant role in transmitting a certain kind of mathematical knowledge to pupils. These textbooks were mainly written in natural language and used very few symbols, mostly the standard mathematical symbols.

The abandonment of natural language in favor of a growing use of symbolic notation took place gradually in programs and textbooks, particularly under the influence of the new math movement in the 1960s. The consequences of this increased use of symbolism has been amply demonstrated. Several studies have shown the difficulties children encounter at various school levels due to the excessive use of often inappropriate multiple external representations for example, schemas, diagrams, and symbols (Dufour-Janvier, Bednarz, & Bélanger, 1987), and the increasingly dominant insertion of this symbolism into natural language, to the latter's detriment (Laborde, 1982).

Our analysis shows that language activity, when it does occur, plays at most the role of communicating a certain mathematical content by the teacher, whereas oral explanations or speaking required of pupils is generally limited to providing the teacher with an oral or written explanation of the solution of a problem. Moreover, these studies reveal that when students are in the position of having to produce a symbolic code in contexts in which this activity is meaningful, the code rarely appears spontaneously. Throughout their oral and written work, one can observe the solidity of their resistance to the use of symbolism and their spontaneous preference for natural language in writing solutions or communicating them to others

228

H. Mansfield et al. (eds.), Mathematics for Tomorrow's Young Children, 228–239.
© 1996 Kluwer Academic Publishers. Printed in the Netherlands.

as, for example, when they are asked to construct messages that will allow other students to reproduce drawings which they have not seen (Laborde, 1982).

When faced with the task of describing geometrical figures without any labeled elements, students made long and tedious descriptions of geometric relations between the elements of the figure in natural language and did not spontaneously decide to denote the key elements for the description of the figure by letters.   (Laborde, 1991, p. 6.)

Without denying the importance of symbolism in mathematics, and its necessary consideration for learning mathematics (see Laborde 1991; Bednarz, Dufour-Janvier, Poirier, & Bacon, 1993), the studies mentioned above show that natural language is a privileged tool in pupils' spontaneous mathematical activity. Natural language may be present in the way pupils express a problem's solution for themselves or for others, in their description of geometrical figures or other situations in order to understand or solve them.

The question arising from this analysis is the following: How can the construction of meaning in mathematics rely more heavily on the natural language used spontaneously by students? What role can language activity play in the learning of mathematics and the development of mathematical thinking in children?

Some of our studies have pointed to the contribution which could be made by natural language which, although it is increasingly neglected in the teaching of mathematics, is spontaneously used by pupils in the context of their mathematical activities. For example, our research on the learning of arithmetic in primary schools revealed the important role played by oral or written verbalization in the construction of mathematical knowledge by children and in the development of signified/signifier relationships (Bednarz, 1992; Bednarz et al, 1993).

Focusing on another domain, that of problem solving, we will, in this chapter, examine more closely the role that language could play in the development of the child's mathematical thought within the context of the teaching and learning of mathematics. Before getting into our teaching experiment with young children on which we will base our explanations of the possible contribution language activity can bring to learning, we will briefly review the theoretical foundations of this approach.

2. THE ROLE OF LANGUAGE IN THE DEVELOPMENT OF CHILDREN'S MATHEMATICAL THOUGHT

The learning of mathematics is a strongly socialized activity (Ernest, 1991; Bednarz, Garnier, 1989; Garnier, Bednarz, & Ulanovskaya, 1992). It takes place in the classroom through a negotiation process between the subjects (pupils and teacher, pupils with each other) who have mutual expectations and who mutually interpret each other's messages. It is through this didactic contract, a system of reciprocal expectations (Brousseau, 1986; Schubauer-Leoni, 1986), that children attach a certain meaning to the content that is being taught. *As a social process* involving a specific content, the teaching of mathematics is concerned with this classroom dynamic in which *the language used by the teacher or the children* plays an important role, as well as with the resulting construction of mathematical knowledge .

In this classroom process, language not only fulfills the generally recognized function of communication, but also, in relation to this function of communication, plays an essential role in the children's development of concepts. This view of the development of language and the formation of mathematical thought, in which the two functions of communication and conceptualization are intimately linked, has been supported by Vygotsky, who clearly showed the interaction between conceptual, social, and linguistic aspects.

Real concepts are impossible without words, and thinking in concepts does not exit beyond verbal thinking. That is why the central moment in concept formation, and its generative cause, is a specific use of words as functional "tools". (Vygotsky, 1986, p. 107.)

As an element of communication and of mutual understanding among children, language plays a decisive role in the process of mutual comprehension and in the development of concepts.

Without this functional moment of mutual understanding, no one group of sounds would ever become a bearer of meaning, and no concept would ever appear.
(Uznadze, 1966, p. 76, from Vygotsky, 1986, p. 101.)

As we have seen above, this important role of natural language as a verbal and written support in learning seems to have been ignored, and language has been used at best in the teaching of mathematics simply for the purpose of communicating a certain mathematical content. What was ignored was its function as an aid in the pupil's mathematical thinking. Language is also a means of understanding oneself. Here, we agree with the ideas of several mathematics "educators" (Laborde, 1991; Vergnaud, 1990; Brousseau, 1986).

It is common to say that language has a double role of communication and representation. But this may lead us to underestimate its supportive role in thinking which is only partially considered when we speak of its representative and communicative functions.
(Vergnaud, 1990, p. 159. Transl. by authors.)

In the process we initiated with a group of school children, and to which we will refer in this article, it will become apparent that language was an essential tool. The experiment in class was organized around communication situations between two subjects or between two groups of subjects, the "transmitting" group and the "receiving" group (Brousseau, 1986), in which the dialectic set in motion (the decoding of the message by a receiving group and confrontation) played an extremely important role in helping the conceptions the children developed become explicit. These were subject to conflicts of opinion, expressed in debates between the pupils. The (oral) explanations and arguments which developed gradually contributed to the emergence of new conceptions and strategies. It was from this perspective and in continuity with our past work, that our teaching experiment took place (Dufour-Janvier & Bednarz, 1989; Bednarz, 1991). Language's dual functions of communication and conceptualization appear to be strongly linked here. The children's communication of solutions, or of a symbolic notation together with its regulatory conventions, already requires a certain development on the part of the communicator. Furthermore, for a certain functional communication to take place between the subjects, a modification is required, an adjustment of the child's first attempts at communication. Thus, the adjustment of these formulations to the conceptualizations of others, in the interpretation that they construct of the messages, makes it possible for conceptions to evolve. Reasoning occurs through language; language allows access to, and facilitates an evolution of, the underlying signified.

To clarify the role that language is capable of playing in the construction of mathematical knowledge by young children, we shall present an experiment conducted in a class of 6- and 7-year-old first graders at the beginning of the school year.

The main objectives of the experiment were the development of concepts of number and of operations, and the development of abilities related to the understanding and solution of problems by the child, such as a critical attitude towards the problem statement, leading to questions regarding the data, the relationships between the data and the question asked, and the search for different solutions. We will discuss some of these later in the chapter.

2.1 Procedure

The approach was situated within a socio-constructivist current (Bednarz & Garnier, 1989; Garnier, Bednarz, & Ulanovskaya, 1992) in that it tackled the question of the construction of meaning in problem solving from the angle of conjectural situations in which the children's responses emerge and give rise to observable group interaction.

Classroom sessions were video taped regularly for the entire duration of the project (November to January for the problem solving part). The video taping allowed us to focus on a few children as they worked together and they constitute the source of data used in the analysis of the children's mathematical learning and their classroom interactions.

Overall the approach emphasizes the analysis of problems with children, that is, discussing them together, questioning the terms of a problem or having them make some up without necessarily solving them. A collection of appropriate problems was built up. It contained problems with missing, superfluous, or contradictory data, intended to make the children reflect on the problem. The procedure also included complex and open-ended problems which left the children to make several possible conjectures. These problems were presented with the aim of developing certain critical abilities which would help the pupils understand a problem and embark thoughtfully in the solving process.

Here, language played a role in the discussions about the problems: in the children's verbalizations of their reasoning while working on solutions in small groups; in explaining the solution to others; in the group discussion of the solutions; in the critique of the different strategies developed by the children; in the discussions about the problems proposed; and in their reformulation into their own words. Language was also present as an essential element in the children's own formulations of problems for the others to solve. We will now concentrate on these different aspects.

3. FORMULATION, CONCEPTUALIZATION AND SOLVING OF A MATHEMATICS PROBLEM

Three examples will illustrate the role played by language in the conceptualization of a problem.

3.1 Discussion of problems

The following extract from a classroom session illustrates the supporting role of language activity in the critical argumentation established in the case of an "impossible" problem. The following problem was given to the class: *"You have 10 stickers in your desk. Your friend has 5. How many children are there in the class?"* The teacher first asks the children to reformulate the problem, "Can someone tell me the story I have just told?"

Benjamin reformulates the problem this way: "Well, you have 10 stickers in your desk and your friend has 5. And then how many children are in the class?" Certain children begin a solution; others are critical. A discussion of the problem begins.

The children's arguments are varied:

Clément: No because you didn't give us anything to help us guess what is the children in the class. (He means how many children are in the class.)

Teacher: I didn't give you anything to help you guess how many children are in the class. You say that is the reason. Are there other reasons?

Marie-Claude: No because the children in the class... Well at first you said stickers But there were no children in what you said … stickers.

Fannie: Well because you said I have 10 stickers in my desk. Then you said my friend has 5. So then when you say how many students are in my class, we can't say 2. (2 children because we refer to 2 children in the story)... We don't know, perhaps there are more or less ... We don't know... we can't solve it.

The children are then encouraged to correct the problem so that it can be solved. "We can't solve it. As Clément said, I don't give you any indication in my story that allows you to know how many children are in the class. What can we do, what can we change in the story so it will work, so that you will be able to work on this little problem?"

The children then modify the problem statement in various ways, changing the data or the question:

Eve-Marie: Well you need to say I have 10 stickers, my friend has 5, there are as many pupils in the class as there are stickers altogether.

Teacher: Okay, you say I have 10 stickers, my friend has 5, and here Eve-Marie changed, she said there are as many children in the class as we have stickers altogether. Now do you find the problem works?

Class: Yes.

Teacher: Any other ideas...?

Ariane: We could do I have 10 stickers in my desk, my friend has 5, we could do ... I have ... altogether how many are there?

The preceding process, repeated for other problems, contributed, with the other experimental activities, to progressively help develop reflective problem solving competence. In the future the children had a much more critical approach to solving problems. Language, as we see here, plays an important role in the thinking that arises.

3.2 Children's rewording of a problem presented to the whole class.

Once a problem had been presented, reformulating the problem *in the children's own words* seemed to be an important step. This allowed access to the children's interpretations of the problem, bringing out their representations, and (in the interaction which occurred in the class) the reformulation allowed the children to better understand the terms of the problem. An example will illustrate this. The following problem was presented to the whole class: A florist must prepare bouquets of flowers for Mother's Day. He wants to make the bouquets *different from each other: some bigger, some smaller (with a different number of flowers in each one). He has 18 roses. What kinds of bouquets can he make? Can you help him find different ways of making them?*

First, the children were asked to describe the situation in their own words, to see what they had understood. One child (Marc) began with the following formulation: "There was a florist. He had to make bouquets of flowers for Mother's Day. So then, he wanted to make a bouquet with 18 flowers."

A discussion, started by the teacher ("Does that really tell my story?") ensued, involving the other children in the class:

Benjamin: No, he has to make bouquets with the 18 flowers...
Teacher: What do you mean?
Benjamin: Well, there's a florist who is preparing flowers for Mother's Day... So then... the flowers
            have to be arranged... so that... the florist... it has to make 18, but in different ways...
This was corrected by another pupil:
Fannie: It's a florist, he is going to make bouquets of flowers for Mother's Day; there are 18 flowers
            in his store. He has to make bouquets, but he says I'm going to make them in different
            ways...
Another child (Marie-Eve) asked: What does that mean, in different ways?...
Fannie: Many bouquets, but they can't be the same...
Guillaume: You mean, with different flowers...
Fannie: Uh, no... there are only roses in his store... but the bouquets can be small or big...

The dynamics of the above discussion show how the children's re-formulation of the problem gradually clarified its structure.

3.3 The children's formulation of problems for the other children to solve.

This time, the children had to formulate a problem given a context, so that the other children in the class would be able to solve it. At first the children were grouped in pairs with different problems to solve. Each team was given a different card depicting a certain context accompanied by a question. The teams then set out to solve these problems.

Next the teams presented their problems orally to the rest of the class who had not seen their cards so that the other children could begin solving the problems based on this oral presentation. The difficulty here was to provide all the pertinent information and to adequately explain the structure of the relationships between the data so that the other children could effectively solve the problem.

This context, requiring communication between the children, provides evidence of the children's formulations of the problem: it is a way of provoking their expression, it allows one to follow their evolution and to explore the links between this verbal activity and conceptualization activity in problem solving

These formulations are more than a simple transposition of an already formed image, they constitute an authentic conceptual activity. The description of a problem situation which allows the problem to be solved requires an analysis of the problem that extracts the characteristic elements (the data and the relationships linking the data). In their formulations of the problem the children will privilege certain elements, certain relationships.

3.4. What was the nature of the children's first problem formulations?

Some of the children *reformulated the context only,* without including any numerical information. For example, Arnaud (referring to the context pictured below): There is a person with a tower of blocks. Then his dog comes and knocks down the blocks. How many blocks were left standing?

Figure 1

Other children *focused on a single element of the data*, formulating an incomplete problem, as did Marie-Eve (for the above context):

It's someone who has made a tower of 22 blocks. Then suddenly, his dog runs in and topples the tower over, and we want to know how many blocks didn't fall over.

This *focus on a single element of the data* was quite frequent in the children's spontaneous formulations and was often accompanied by a description which *focused on the context and the details*. Thus, Ariane, on the context, depicted in Figure 2, said: *There's a little girl who is putting...14 buns on the table. Then, the little girl lays the whole table for her mother and her father... maybe she has brothers and sisters... the little girl's name is Marie... so she puts a whole lot of buns on the table... then, the problem is... how many buns were on the table in all?*

The child centered on the final result, giving the answer to the problem in her formulation of it.

Figure 2

Marie-Claude for the context pictured next said: *There's a train... and we want to know... the little problem is that we want to know how many children are in the train, but in the cars of the train, there are two children... then, the train... isn't very big, but... there are also children from different countries in it. Then, we want to know how many children are in the train.* Here, again the focus was on the context and its details, and in particular, on one bit of the data.

These first formulations revealed how difficult it was for the children to cope with all the data, to retain only the essential data from the situation, and to express the relation between the data and the question. Moreover, these formulations stuck very close to the context under consideration, and to the contextual details of the situation.

These same characteristics could be found in the first symbolic notations the children developed when a method was introduced which encouraged the children to construct such notations and which was built around their notations (Dufour-Janvier, & Bednarz, 1989).

For children, a good representation includes the actions or transformations made on the collections as well as the contextual details of these actions or transformations.

(Dufour-Janvier, Bednarz, 1989, p. 320. Transl. by the authors.)

Figure 3

The dynamics of the method which was built around the children's first problem formulation, helped assure a progression of their formulations so that, no matter how descriptive, incomplete, awkward, or contradictory they may have been at the beginning, the formulation gradually became coherent, taking into account all the relevant data and its relationship to the question.

The approach is illustrated by the following chart::

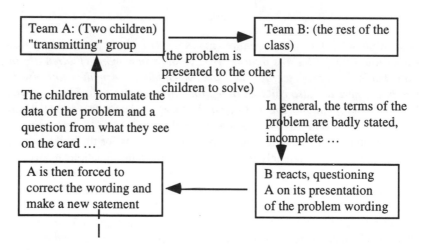

Thus, an interactive process took place between the A and the B groups, as shown in the example below:

When Marie-Claude's formulation of the train problem was proposed to the other children in the class, their reactions were quick:

Yes, but how many cars are there?
We don't know, we can't answer...
We don't know... you don't talk about the cars...

The team at the front of the class, after consultation, tried a new formulation:

There's a train, and there are some children in it... there are 6 cars, then there are children from different countries in them. So we want to find out how many children there are in the train...

Here again, the children only provided one element of the data (the other one), adjusting their formulation to the reactions of the other children; and once again focusing on the context and details. Again, we can see the difficulty that the children had in structuring the complete terms of the problem, and in integrating the relationships between the various data elements.

A new reaction was then heard from the rest of the class: "How many children are there? ... We don't know..."

Marie-Claude answered spontaneously: "There are 2 children in each car," and Etienne (her team partner) reformulated the problem as follows: "There are 6 cars. There are 2 children in each car. There are children from different countries. We want to find out how many children there are."

At this point, the way in which the problem was formulated, clearly specified the relationships among the data, and asked a question that was coherent with the data. As this formulation seemed to satisfy the rest of the children in the class, they then proceeded to try to solve the problem in teams. This was followed by a group discussion of the different strategies that had been used.

4. CONCLUSION

The preceding examples briefly illustrate the dynamic exchange that took place, and the role that it played in leading to a complete formulation of the problem. The process led the "transmitting" group to reflect upon the terms of the problems (data, relations among the data, question...) while the other children, who eventually had to solve the problem, were led to develop a certain critical sense with respect to the problems presented.

The social stakes in the task were very important. The finality of their formulations meant they had to consider their decoding audience and vice versa (the children invested a lot in the task, a general concern for good communication with the decoders). The social nature of the task is a factor which favors the children's reflection on the choice of relevant data, of their relationships, and their expression. Problem reformulation arises from constraints and offers a specific response to the difficulties that arise. It is the focus of discussion among the children and the object of subsequent modifications. The improvement of problem formulations to remedy ambiguities leads gradually through the various activities to a critical view of their work or even to throw it all into question. These activities provide a way of raising an awareness of the essential characteristics of a problem statement, the relation-ships between the givens.

Through the experimental sessions and the classroom interaction, we were able to identify an evolution in the children's skills in understanding a problem: a criti-cal attitude towards the problem statement, leading to questioning the data, the relationship between the data and the question asked. One can observe the strength of the social elements in this evolution through the children's increasing discussion of the problems and their rejection of the validity of certain statements.

Interviews with each of the children before and after the experiment, in Novem-ber and February, show the evolution that occurred both in formulating problems and solving them. The children developed increasingly clear formulations of the problems, using varied and rich contexts and various meanings for operations. Lan-guage, as we have seen, played an essential role in this development.

It appears that the language activity used here, both in the children's formulation of the problems and in their subsequent critical debate, encouraged the discovery of the pertinent relationships, their temporal organization and their control, thus prompt-ing an evolution in the understanding of the problem statement in relation to its solution.

We have used the approach illustrated here in a specific context, that of problem solving, in other contexts (the construction of number and operations or the con-struction of meaningful symbolism by the children themselves). It shows clearly the interactions which occur between conceptual, social and linguistic aspects in the development of mathematical thinking.

REFERENCES

Bednarz, N., Dufour-Janvier, B., Poirier, L., & Bacon, L. (1993). Socioconstructivist viewpoint on the use of symbolism in mathematics education. *The Alberta Journal of Educational Research, 39*(1), 41-58.

Bednarz, N., & Garnier, C. (Eds.). (1989). *Construction des savoirs. Obstacles et conflits.* Montréal, Canada: Agence d'Arc.

Bednarz, N. (1991). Interactions sociales et construction d'un système d'écriture des nombres en classe primaire. In C. Garnier, N. Bednarz, & I. Ulanovskaya (Eds.), *Après Vygotsky et Piaget. Perspectives sociale et constructiviste. Ecoles russe et occidentale* (pp. 51-67). Bruxelles: Editions de Boeck.

Brousseau, G. (1986).*Théorisation des phénomènes d'enseignement des mathématiques.* Thèse de doctorat d'état, Université de Bordeaux 1.

Dufour-Janvier B., & Bednarz, N. (1989). Situations conflictuelles expérimentées pour faire face à quelques obstacles dans une approche constructiviste de l'arithmétique au primaire. In N. Bednarz & C. Garnier (Eds.), *Construction des savoirs: Obstacles et conflits* (pp. 315-333). Montréal, Canada: Agence d'Arc.

Dufour-Janvier, B., Bednarz, N., & Bélanger, M. (1987). Pedagogical considerations concerning the problem of representation in the teaching and learning of mathematics. In C. Janvier (Ed.), *Problems of representation in the teaching and learning of mathematics* (pp. 109-122). Hillsdale, NJ: Erlbaum.

Ernest, P. (1991). *The philosophy of mathematics education.* London, UK: The Falmer Press.

Garnier, C., Bednarz, N., & Ulanovskaya, I. (Eds.). (1992). *Après Vygotsky et Piaget. Perspectives sociale et constructiviste. Écoles russe et occidentale.* Bruxelles, Belgium: Éditions de Boeck.

Laborde, C. (1982). *Langue naturelle et écriture symbolique: deux codes en interaction dans l'enseignement mathématique.* Thesis, Université Joseph Fourier, Grenoble: IMAG.

Laborde, C. (1991). Students' reading and writing of mathematics. *Proceedings of the Annual Meeting, Canadian Mathematics Education Study Group*, Fredericton, Canada, (pp. 3-15.).

Schubauer-Leoni, M. L. (1986). *Maître-Elève-Savoir: analyse psychosociale du jeu et des enjeux de la relation didactique*. Thèse de doctorat en Sciences de l'Education, Université de Genève.

Vergnaud, G. (1990). La théorie des champs conceptuels. *Recherche en didactique des mathématiques, 10*(23), 133-170.

Uznadze, D. (1966).*Vyrabotka poniatii v doshkolnom vozraste* [Concept formation in preschool children]. In D. Uznadze, (Ed.), [Psychological investigation]. Moscow, Russia: Nanka.

Vygotsky, L.S. (1986). *Thought and language*. Cambridge, MA: MIT Press.

Nadine Bednarz
CIRADE, Université du Québec à Montréal

CHILDREN TALKING MATHEMATICALLY IN MULTILINGUAL CLASS-ROOMS: ISSUES IN THE ROLE OF LANGUAGE[1]

1. INTRODUCTION

In the United States and in many other countries, our assumptions as to what constitutes acceptable mathematics teaching and learning recently have changed dramatically. We now recognize that communication about mathematics plays an important role in the learning of the subject, and consequently, that a language rich classroom facilitates learning among children see, for example, NCTM, 1989). As we have started to create such classrooms, we also have begun to recognize various factors related to language which affect children's learning such as teachers' discourse (Khisty, McLeod, & Bertilson, 1990) and the language of mathematics itself (Pimm, 1987).

At the same time, as we move toward more emphasis on instructional strategies that utilize communication constructs, classrooms in many instances are becoming much more multilingual. For example, in the United States, the National Center for Educational Statistics (1981) has projected that the school population of language minority students (LMS)[2] will reach 3.4 million in the year 2000, or one in four teachers will have students for whom the dominant language of instruction (English) is their weaker or nonexistent language. However, students from homes where English is a second language are 1.5 times more likely to drop out of school than their English-only counterparts (Cardenas, Robledo, & Wagonner, 1988). More importantly, the learning of mathematics plays a significant role in equity in schooling for language minority students since there is a strong relationship between doing well in mathematics and staying in school; students seldom drop out while enrolled in courses such as Algebra or Calculus (Cardenas, Robledo, & Wagonner, 1988).

In light of these demographic factors, it is critical to examine issues surrounding language use or talk in mathematics in a multilingual context and from the various perspectives (linguistic, social, and cultural) that this suggests. The purpose of this chapter is to identify and discuss such issues that arize among students whose dominant language is not the language of instruction particularly as they engage in col-

---

[1] The research reported in this paper was supported in part by National Science Foundation Grant No. MDR-9196124. Any opinions, conclusions, or recommendations are those of the author and do not necessarily reflect the views of the National Science Foundation.

[2] The target student population of this paper is commonly referred to as limited-English proficient (LEP). I have chosen to use the term language minority student (LMS) instead in order not to imply a deficit among these children and to be more inclusive of the broad range of language characteristics that pertain to this population. The reader is referred to the following book for additional discussion of this topic: Arias, B. & Casanova, U. (Eds.). (1993). *Bilingual education: Politics, practice, and research*. Chicago, IL: The National Society for the Study of Education, University of Chicago Press.

H. Mansfield et al. (eds.), Mathematics for Tomorrow's Young Children, 240–247.
© 1996 *Kluwer Academic Publishers. Printed in the Netherlands.*

laborative work with other students who may or may not speak the same language. These situations, which I am collectively calling *groupwork*, can include two children tutoring each other or a group of three or more children solving a problem. The discussion is drawn from preliminary findings from a larger qualitative investigation of the general nature of mathematics teaching with Hispanic bilingual students. Furthermore, while what follows comes from a study of instruction with a particular language group and in a particular country, the implications of the study applies to any language minority group in a multilingual context.

The present study is based on naturalistic observations conducted in one upper level and two primary level elementary classrooms which were part of the larger study. The classrooms have native English speakers and significant numbers of students whose abilities in English range from no proficiency to much proficiency in two languages. The particular classrooms for this study were selected because groupwork was commonly used as an instructional strategy. Each classroom was videotaped intermittently for seven to ten hours over a year. In addition, each classroom was videotaped for one whole week (some of the hours mentioned previously are included in this period) in order to get a sense of consistency of the mathematics lessons across time. Field observations were conducted intermittently in each classroom for one year and various artifacts, such as completed student worksheets, were collected to supplement the videotapes which are the primary source of data. Triangulation among three independent observers was used to provide validation of the items deemed to be linguistically troublesome. Lastly, formal interviews with a prepared set of questions regarding professional training were conducted with each teacher. Informal interview were conducted with each teacher as necessary in order to identify and clarify reasons for instructional decisions which occurred during a lesson. Informal interviews also were conducted with randomly selected students to assess their grasp of the mathematics presented in the lesson and to enhance the observations. From these data, patterns emerged suggesting the issues and recommendations which follow.

2. ISSUE 1: JUNKY INPUT

One of the primary functions of language is to represent the world and to make it one's own. In fact, the thing is not known until it is named, discussed, and put into relationship with other things. Language is how the transformation of information into knowledge is accomplished (Goodman, Smith, Meredith, & Goodman, 1987). However, coming to know does not happen in isolation, but rather, it happens in social situations where language is used in dialogic processes (for example, Vygotsky, 1978). In mathematics, we have responded to this conceptual framework by incorporating learning situations that allow for children to work and talk with other children. However, simply having students talk with each other may not be sufficient in itself.

In the classrooms which were observed, children used the language they were used to which was not always mathematically (or linguistically if the student was especially new to English) correct or appropriate. Many words and phrases could be considered "junky input" in that children used with each other terms that were incorrect or sentences that were disconnected or imperfect, and what they heard (that is, the input data) soon became internalized. In these particular instances, this was more a result of simply not being accustomed to speaking mathematically in any cultural language rather than due to difficulty in using a second language since the same types of "junkiness" appeared in both English and Spanish. However, it also was a result of the little attention teachers paid to this junky input to students' cognitive structure and to the lack of modeling by the teachers of how to speak mathematically. Consequently, virtually the only mathematics students heard spoken came from others who used the language of mathematics poorly and/or who spoke English poorly.

The following is an example of how the ambiguous or "junky" speaking of mathematics can affect students' learning. In a discussion between two young girls on how to solve the problem $3.12 - 0.49$, one of the students frequently used the phrase "this one" meaning "this particular thing." However, the phrase made the discussion confusing because it could also refer to the various other "ones" in this problem such as the "one" in the tenths group or the "one" which was written to indicate borrowing. The student who listened to this had a difficult time following the explanation and comprehending how to work out a solution, and when given similar problems to solve independently, made many errors. Unfortunately, this peer tutoring situation was the major activity for learning how to solve such problems. In another situation with different students, a decimal point was always referred to as a "dot" and the significance of its meaning was overlooked as both students continuously made errors in combining whole numbers with tenths and hundredths.

In the third classroom, the teacher paid close attention both to developing students' mathematics vocabulary and their ability to speak mathematically. Before beginning a unit on fractions, the teacher wrote on the board a list of the key words that would be used in the following weeks. Students were asked to copy the words in a notebook. Then the teacher proceeded to teach the new vocabulary by providing examples of what the words meant and how the words were used in sentences. These examples were also copied in notebooks along with examples students were asked to generate themselves. As the unit progressed and students worked with each other to solve problems, the teacher not only monitored how problems were solved but how students used language to communicate mathematical ideas. There were several instances when a student used a phrase such as "the number on top" and the teacher interrupted the discussion and encouragingly asked what this is called mathematically. If the student could not recall the term, she/he was asked to refer back to the notes that had been written earlier. Very soon, students were heard using mathematical terms and phrases correctly and also assisting one another when someone did not know a word. More importantly, when the students were asked why, for example, a number was called a *numerator*, they could explain it in terms of how it related to the overall concept of a fraction.

The role of language suggested by these examples is one where language has a certain control over thinking. In the situations where students used the limited language they had for describing their strategies or processes, their grounding in the meanings they were dealing with also seemed limited. Errors of various kinds were more prevalent in the first two classrooms than in the third classroom. In addition, where students were allowed to use "junky" expressions with one another, their collective or public descriptions persisted and became fossilized. These students seemed resistant to adjusting their strategies or correcting any errors. The misconceptions they developed at the beginning of the year were still evident toward the end of the year. In other words, they had not yet appropriately named the world, and consequently, the world of mathematics was not theirs.

3. ISSUE 2: OPERATING IN A SECOND LANGUAGE

Language is part of the ideating phase of learning where new objects, events, or ideas are conceptualized and brought into a personal schema. Talk, consequently, allows for the public monitoring of how ideas and concepts are developing and what misconceptions may be occurring. However, when students are using their second language, it is not always easy to know if children are having difficulty developing mathematical ideas or having difficulty expressing themselves in their weaker language. The teachers who were observed sometimes took a misstatement, mispronounced word, or even a hesitation in speaking in a group as indicating that the child did not comprehend the mathematics when, in fact, there was nothing at issue mathematically. When the child was encouraged to express his/her understandings in the home or primary language, it was more often than not found that there was no misconception.

While this was not always true, in that sometimes there indeed was a mathematical misconception or misunderstanding, the point is that interpreting language minority students' use of language and the process of ideating is not so simple. Using the students' primary language for monitoring the development of mathematical meanings helps reduce the influence of the second language factor.

Furthermore, groupwork which is specifically organized around clusters of children who reflect various levels of mathematics and language abilities has clear benefits for LMS as suggested by DeAvila (1984). However, observations from some of the classrooms suggested that there can be other factors which need to be considered if this instructional strategy is going to be as beneficial as it can be. First, in groupwork, language use was very chaotic. Children, in their eagerness, spoke very fast and very loudly. In some instances, LMS found it hard to distinguish what was being said in their own group from what was being said in another group. For a student listening to talk in a second language, such a spoken language environment may make it even more difficult to comprehend meanings or to hear accurately what is being said. Second, some LMS were very quiet during groupwork and appeared not to be engaged. This seeming passiveness caused teachers to question how motivated or able the students were actually. In this situation, it is important to bear in mind that second language learners go through a silent period where they use "observer" and "comprehender" strategies (Wong-Fillmore, 1976). During this period, they are not talkative but rather are quiet and hesitant to speak. Nevertheless, they comprehend what is said in the second language and are actively engaged in learning. This non-production stage of second language development can be misinterpreted as being "passive," "slow," or "uncooperative," and can mislead teachers to make erroneous evaluations of a student and faulty instructional decisions in light of them.

Some of the teachers in this study overlooked these factors and did not always adequately accommodate the needs of students; they did not consider arranging seating so that there was sufficient space between groups to minimize the overlap of sound between them or did not spend time to set class norms of etiquette while talking. As a result, language minority students appeared to have to work extra hard to concentrate on what was being said. In essence, learning was made unnecessarily more difficult for the students. More importantly, the students' understanding and ability with mathematics was not enhanced accordingly since they did not always garner critical conceptual aspects of what was said. Also, it is important to keep in mind that not all children are talkative regardless of whether they are second language learners or not. As Lindfors (1990) points out, some children are not inclined to talk either in a whole class situation or in a smaller group of peers. These students may feel more comfortable in talking and learning with only one other person. Consequently, classroom organizations should be sufficiently varied to provide opportunities for children to talk in whatever way–and in whatever language–they are comfortable.

4. ISSUE 3: COMING TO KNOW

The third and last issue regarding the role of language in groupwork with language minority students has to do with the relationship between knowing and the process of experiencing. As stated earlier, language may be seen as a link between these two in that a thing which is experienced is not known or understood until language embodies it. Therefore, there is a critical interplay between experiences and language. However, just as language is pivotal in a person's learning through experience, the experience can influence language. What students experience and embody through language comes to be what they know.

The classrooms that were observed provided examples of this influence of experience on language and what one knows. In one classroom, students worked collaboratively on decontextualized problems such as adding several decimal numbers (e.g., 13.75 + 11.035 + 5.6) or on very simply worded problems (e.g., Pedro had $1.55 and earned $ 2.25. How much does Pedro have?). Student talk in these cases was more fragmented with single words or incomplete sentences being used to convey meanings. However, given the nature of these problems, students could adequately accomplish the objectives of the groupwork task with this type of language use. A similar situation appeared in a second classroom where younger children worked in groups with a currently popular manipulative-based curriculum. In this classroom, students arranged colored objects in ways to demonstrate various partitions of numbers. These arrangements were then copied onto paper. What children said during these collaborative activities had much more to do with choosing colors and the activity of coloring than with the mathematics embedded in the task.

In fact, the children seemed to completely overlook the mathematical concepts. When they were informally interviewed about what they had learned, they were hard put to identify any mathematics in the tasks and saw no obvious relationship between the objects and learning mathematics. The task was simply something they were required to do but which gave them an opportunity to chat with their friends.

A third classroom presents a striking contrast. Mathematics was woven into the general curriculum so that what had been introduced and talked about with the teacher in a whole class setting was later encountered in projects such as the construction of puppets or the baking of cookies. Students worked together on open-ended questions that required as much control of the language of mathematics as control of calculations since not only did they have to talk among themselves but they had to talk with librarians and other teachers in order to gather additional information needed for the task. In this situation, students tended to use more complicated sentence structures such as those involving conditionals ("What if we changed this...?" or "Maybe we could...and if this didn't work, we could...."). The dialogues were more extended with students using more whole paragraphs as opposed to short, clipped sentences.

What these observations suggest is that students engage in authentic talk because they deal with authentic mathematical experiences. When the experience is rich and not isolated from the functional uses of mathematics, the language tends to be rich also. On the other hand, when the experience is reduced to abstract skills, the language is more fragmented. Likewise, it is not enough to simply have students work collaboratively on solving a mathematical sentence or an isolated word problem. The moment students begin to talk and think about what they have perceived or experienced, ideating begins. If the mathematical experience is fragmented, then children talking in this context are coming to know mathematics as isolated facts in almost the same way as they have come to know the subject in a traditional teacher-centered context with worksheets filled with number fact problems.

5. CONCLUDING REMARKS AND RECOMMENDATIONS

Talk is clearly a critical component of learning. It is the center of the social interaction in which meanings are shared, developed, and internalized (Vygotsky, 1978). Talk that occurs in an interactive context also is important for language minority students for it is the vehicle by which they develop and stretch their second language abilities (Krashen & Biber, 1988), by which they have opportunities to establish a repertoire of problem solving strategies (DeAvila, 1984), and by which they assert their own identities and begin the process of emancipation (Freire, 1970).

We have seen from the foregoing that talk for language minority children in the learning of mathematics involves much more than students simply "working" in groups. The role of language in this context concerns learning to appropriately use language (in both the primary and second language) to communicate mathematically, having an environment that accommodates the linguistic needs of second language learners so they can conceptually gain from talk, and having appropriately rich mathematical experiences that encourage students' coming to know mathematics as we wish them to know it.

For a successful rendezvous between learner and subject, teachers must carefully calculate a host of factors in engineering their classroom climate and curriculum. What then should teachers consider in order to maximize the positive functions of language in groupwork with language minority students? The following is a list of recommendations generated from the observations:

1. The teaching of mathematics vocabulary should be as important as the teaching of mathematical concepts. It should be integrated into the mathematics curriculum and it should include examples of the various ways something can be said (for example: *three fourths, three out of four, three quarters*).

2. The extent of "junky input" to second language learners should be monitored and encouragingly eliminated. What is repeatedly heard soon becomes internalized to such a degree that it is difficult to modify. Consequently, LMS need every opportunity to hear how mathematical language should be used to express mathematical concepts. The teacher, in this case, also is the most important model of appropriate language use.

3. Careful consideration should be given to the linguistic needs of LMS. Classroom conditions should be designed and planned so that chaotic noize is minimized and LMS do not have to struggle more than necessary to comprehend others' speech, thereby maximizing their understandings and development. However, this does not suggest inhibiting the naturalness of children talking.

4. There should be ample roles and opportunities in groupwork to allow LMS to participate even though they are not ready or able to produce talk. Evaluations of students' participation in groupwork should take into account not only the silent period but also a pre-production period when only single words and phrases are used in the second language. The primary language should be used to evaluate students' growth and development in mathematics.

5. Teachers can maximize educational development by providing groupwork tasks that are rich in experiential possibilities and avoiding tasks which may encourage fragmented dialogues and inappropriate language use and learning. Rich mathematical tasks however, require adopting a more holistic and inquiry-based approach to teaching mathematics which teachers may not always be able to design or recognize (Khisty, 1991).

6. Lastly, teachers can not assume that simply having students organized around a table to talk to each other accomplishes the desired learning ob-

jectives. Effective use of groupwork requires that sufficient and extensive time be given at the beginning of the school year to setting norms for how children are to work together. For example, children need to have the opportunity and guidance to develop an internalized understanding of why and how members of a group are responsible for each others' learning. Children also need to develop an understanding of roles within the group and teachers need to use these roles to assure that there is maximum status equalization among group members. In this way, students do not get omitted or overlooked because their first language is not the language of instruction.

REFERENCES

Cardenas, J., Robledo, M., & Waggoner, D. (1988). *The under-education of American youth.* San Antonio, TX: Intercultural Development Research Association.

De Avila, E. A. (1984). Motivation, intelligence, and access: A theoretical framework for the education of minority language students. In *Issues in English language development* (pp. 21-31). Rosslyn, VA: National Clearinghouse for Bilingual Education.

Freire, P. (1970). *Pedagogy of the oppressed.* New York: The Continuum Publishing Company.

Goodman, K., Smith, E., Meredith, R., & Goodman, Y. (1987) . *Language and thinking in school.* New York: Richard C. Owen Publishers.

Khisty, L. L. (1991). *Program and policy issues in the mathematics education of Hispanic bilingual students.* Manuscript submitted for publication. University of Illinois at Chicago, IL, College of Education.

Khisty, L. L., McLeod, D., & Bertilson, K. (1990). Speaking mathematically in bilingual classrooms: An exploratory study of teacher discourse. In G. Booker, P. Cobb, & T. Mendicutti (Eds.), *Proceedings of the Fourteenth International Conference for the Psychology of Mathematics Education* (Vol.3), pp. 105-112. Mexico City: CONACYT.

Krashen, S. & Biber, D. (1988). *On course bilingual education success in California.* Sacramento, CA: California Association for Bilingual Education.

Lindfors, J. W. (1990). Speaking creatures in the classroom. In S. Hynds & D. L. Rubin (Eds.), *Perspectives on talk and learning.* Urbana, IL: National Council of Teachers of English.

National Center for Education Statistics. (1981). Projections of non-English background and limited-English-proficient persons in the U.S. to the year 2000. *Forum: Bimonthly Newsletter of the National Clearinghouse for Bilingual Education, 4, 2* .

National Council of Teachers of Mathematics. (1989). *Professional Standards for Teachinq Mathematics.* Reston, VA: National Council of Teachers of Mathematics.

Pimm, D. (1987). *Speaking mathematically.* New York: Routledge & Kegan Paul.

Vygotsky, L. S. (1978). *Mind in Society: The Development of Higher Psychological Processes.* Cambridge, MA: Harvard University Press.

Wong-Fillmore, L. (1976). *The second time around: Cognitive and social strategies in second language acquisition.* Ph.D. Dissertation, Stanford University.

Lena Licon Khisty
University of Illinois at Chicago
United States of America

USE OF LANGUAGE IN ELEMENTARY GEOMETRY BY STUDENTS AND TEXTBOOKS

1. INTRODUCTION

This chapter presents some results of a study on the definitions that appear in the Spanish textbooks for Primary School (Jaime, Chapa, and Gutiérrez, 1992). Its aim is to point out the errors in the statements of definitions and inconsistent or inappropriate uses of definitions made in individual textbooks, or in series of textbooks. This study concerned geometry and, more specifically, triangles and quadrilaterals. Most of the problems that arose were strongly related to the understanding and use of language.

I have analyzed the contents of three series of textbooks for Primary Schools, both the teacher and the student version, and I have also analyzed the answers of several hundred primary and secondary students to some questions on triangles and quadrilaterals, paying attention to the ways mathematical language is used and understood by the students. In the following, I present some results from this study.

The students' answers show clearly an evolution in the way language is used by the students and how it is interpreted by them. Through the primary grades, students have to "learn" how to use mathematical language. The first steps, characterized by imprecisions, predominance of ikonic language, and insufficient use of verbal language, give way to greater verbal precision and to the use of verbal statements as the most accurate way to define concepts and to use them when proving. This is well known by researchers in mathematics education; for example, the Van Hiele model claims the existence of several kinds of language, according to students' different levels of reasoning (see for example, Fuys, Geddes, & Tischler, 1988). Furthermore, the use and interpretation of language and the inconsistencies arising from it are considered, either implicitly or explicitly, in many studies related to the process of learning mathematics. Some specific research in this field can be found in Wilson (1990), where an analysis is made of how inconsistent thinking interferes with students' abilities to reason an to use effectively definitions and examples.

2. THE STUDY

2.1 Students' uses of language

The analysis of primary and secondary students' answers to some questions on triangles and quadrilaterals shows that these answers can be grouped according to their increasingly sophisticated use of mathematical language. Next, I present the main characteristics of the various types of answers that I have found, and I illus-

248

H. Mansfield et al. (eds.), Mathematics for Tomorrow's Young Children, 248–255.

trate each one of them with examples. Although I refer to "one" student's answer, each of the examples presented was common to several students.

Type A: The language known and used by the students is visual, based on specific images. The students do not use mathematical vocabulary, that is, they do not refer to mathematical properties. Their descriptions are based on the likeness to a specific figure, on physical attributes, such as "long," "pointy," "stretched," on the position of the figure, or the students just refer to the name of the concept. In short, the students build their concept images and base their analysis of figures on specific examples that are familiar to them. The term "concept image" is taken from Vinner's theory of the formation of concepts (Vinner & Hershkowitz, 1983). According to this theory, *concept* and *concept image* are not the same. A concept is the mathematical object determined by its mathematical definition and the concept image is the concept as it is reflected in the individual mind; therefore the concept image is subjective while the concept is objective. For example a grade 1 student properly identified the squares in a set of geometrical shapes, even including *a* in Figure 1 below, *because they are squares,* and he said that figure *b* in Figure 1 was not a square *because it has something on the top that makes it look like a house.* Many students rejected *a* from Figure 1 as a square *because it is not (does not look like) a square.*

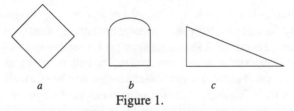

a   b   c

Figure 1.

Two grade 2 students rejected *c* from Figure 1 as a triangle, *because it is too pointy* and *because it is too long and one arm is bent and the others aren't.* When presented turned, some of the reasons given for rejecting it as a triangle were: *It looks like a set square.*

One grade 5 student had marked as squares *those shapes left over* after identifying, wrongly, other shapes asked for (circles, triangles, and rectangles). Many dissimilar shapes were incorrectly identified as squares.

One grade 6 student defined a rhombus as *what has pointy ends.*

Type B: The students use mathematical vocabulary including mathematical properties and elements, but these are not used properly. The students' reasoning is based on abstractions developed visually from specific examples. Due to the influence of their teaching, the students state mathematical properties without understanding them adequately. The students state mathematical properties and use elements in the verbal definitions of shapes; however these characteristics are not used, for example, when deciding whether or not a shape is a rectangle. The meaning of the properties is modified from a personal point of view. Also, mathematical terms can be used in a very vague manner, which does not include the usual distinctive properties. In fact, the students rely on specific known examples. The following responses are some examples, all of them from grade 6 students.

When asked if Figure 2*a* was an acute triangle, three students answered the following: (1) *Yes, because all the sides are of the same length;* (2) *Yes, because its angles measure more than 90°;* (3)*Yes, because it has two equal sides and one not equal.*

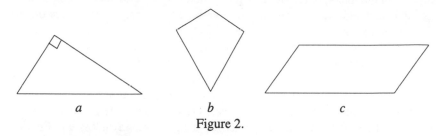

| a | b | c |

Figure 2.

One student defined a rhombus in this way: *It is a geometrical shape that has all its sides of equal length,* and identified Figure 2*b* as a rhombus.

One student identified Figure 2*c* as a rectangle *because all its sides have the same length.*

These examples show that iconic images are an essential component in the language used by the students, since their concept images rely mostly on specific ikonic representations. Therefore, it seems appropriate for textbooks to consider pictures of triangles and quadrilaterals as a powerful tool to help in the teaching of concepts.

A good selection of examples and non-examples may be an excellent way to help the students in their first steps of the use of mathematical language. The analysis of critical (necessary) and non-relevant attributes (Hershkowitz, 1990) is necessary for a proper selection of examples and non-examples. Nevertheless, I have not found this kind of presentation in any of the three series of textbooks analyzed in this study. On the contrary, very often there is a lack of non-standard shapes, or only a few of them are presented. This is not a mathematical error, but it is a serious didactic error which induces students' errors due to the visual presentation they see in textbooks.

For instance, in the lesson devoted to triangles in a grade 4 textbook, 22 out of the 23 examples presented are drawn in the standard position, that is, resting on a horizontal side (Figure 3). The grade 4 textbook in another series shows 15 triangles in the standard position and only one in a non-standard position; all the triangles are shown in the standard position in the grade 3 textbook.

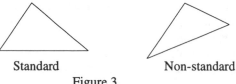

Standard   Non-standard

Figure 3.

The next two examples, from grade 2 students, show clearly the consequences of the standard presentations just mentioned.

Both of them identified shape 4*a* (Figure 4) as a rectangle, but not shape 4*b*. Their reasons for not identifying 4*b* as a rectangle were, respectively:

Although it is equal to 4a, it is in the wrong position and *It is upwards.*

One of these children identified 4*c* as a square, but not 4*d Because it is slanted and then it is not a square.*

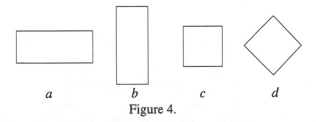

$$a \qquad\qquad b \qquad\quad c \qquad\qquad d$$

Figure 4.

Type C:Mathematical language makes sense for these students. They know that the properties stated in a concept's definition have to be considered when solving tasks related to this concept; however, the *mathematical properties stated in a definition are not understood by the students as sufficient,* because they use some other properties which spring from their mental images. That is, when a student is given a definition, he/she may add some non-relevant properties of the concept and consider them as critical. Also, when a student has to define a concept, he/she may omit some necessary properties or give a list of properties, where some of them result from others.

For example, a grade 5 student justified her correct identifications of circles and squares in a set of drawn shapes as follows: A circle is *a curved, closed line* and *the four sides of a square are equal.*

Type D: Students use mathematical language as the only vehicle for defining concepts and proving statements. These students, who give the correct kind of answers, are able to accept and use a new definition of a concept which differs from their previous definition of that concept and even change the concept itself. For example, given different definitions the students may classify a set of figures in different ways according to the definitions (Figure 5):

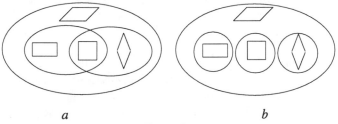

$$a \qquad\qquad\qquad\qquad\qquad\qquad b$$

Figure 5.

a) A square is a quadrilateral with 4 equal sides and 4 equal angles. Rectangle is a quadrilateral with 4 equal angles. A rhombus is a quadrilateral with 4 equal sides. A parallelogram is a quadrilateral with two pairs of parallel sides.

b) A square is a quadrilateral with 4 equal sides and 4 equal angles. A rectangle is a quadrilateral with 4 equal angles and not all sides equal. A rhombus is a quadrilateral with 4 equal sides and no right angles. A parallelogram is a quadrilateral with two pairs of parallel sides.

2.2 Ways to Use Language in Textbooks

Very often, textbooks and teachers interfere—at least in Spain—with correct progress of the students in their use of mathematical language; even more, they can be considered as inducers of wrong learning in this field, since some errors and wrong interpretations are found both in textbooks and among teachers.

I do not have numerical data of any specific research about the use and interpretation of the language used by teachers in the description and definition of triangles and quadrilaterals, but I have experience with hundreds of students at the Primary Teacher Training School. After one month of tuition on this skill and by the time they got their degree, many of these students did not have proper understanding of what a definition is and they did not appreciate (and they had also made) many of the inconsistencies which appear in the textbooks and which I will present later in this chapter.

I can also refer to the research reported in Hershkowitz and Vinner (1984), that shows that, very often, the teachers' mistaken concept images of elementary concepts remain, even after providing them with the mathematical definition.

In relation to textbooks, I now present some situations taken from texts that are mathematically incorrect. They refer to inadequate or incorrect use of language for triangles and quadrilaterals.

Type 1: Incorrect interpretation of the definition. It is possible to find incorrect interpretations stated in the textbook when it presents examples of the concept, or uses the definition to explain a classification. The reason for these misinterpretations is that the textbook uses implicit properties not stated in the text.

For instance, a student's textbook for grade 4 defines a rectangle as *the intersection of two perpendicular bands.* There is no reference to the width of the bands (that is, to the length of the sides of the rectangle), but the teacher's book explains that *the bands have different width so the sides do not have the same length.* Therefore, the meaning of the definition is different in the students' and the teacher's textbooks, because there is an implicit property in the definition used only in one of the textbooks.

Other definitions of this type are wrong. A series of textbook defines a triangle, in grade 4, as *the intersection of 3 angles* where an angle is defined as that part of the polane limited by two rays with the same origin; and, in grade 5, as *the intersection of 3 semiplanes.* Both definitions are incorrect (Figure 6) because they do not detail explicit conditions referring to the position of the angles or the semiplanes that, obviously, are used in the examples of the triangles that follow the definitions.

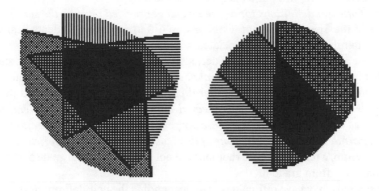

Figure 6.

Type 2: Contain two grammatical expressions usually understood with different logical meanings. In both cases the problem arises because the meaning in the ordinary (non-mathematical) context and in the logical (mathematical) context are different:

a) From the statement *polygon x has n sides with property p,* some times it is inferred that **at least n sides* have that property. This is the valid meaning in the mathematical context. The usual meaning in non-mathematical contexts is that **exactly n sides* have that property.

One series of textbooks defines, in grades 4 and 5, a trapezoid as the *quadrilateral having two parallel sides.* From the examples, it follows that the meaning is *at least two parallel sides,* since parallelograms are included in the family of trapezoids. Later, in grade 6, the student's textbook defines a trapezoid as the *quadrilateral having only two parallel sides* and the teacher's book states the same definition of the previous courses (trapezoid as the *quadrilateral having two parallel sides).* Therefore, in the teacher's book of grade 6 the expression "having two" has a different meaning from that in the books of grades 4 and 5. Similar problems arise regarding the definitions of the isosceles triangle.

b) From the statement *quadrilateral x has equal opposite sides,* some times it is inferred that **the adjacent sides may be equal.* This is the valid meaning in the mathematical context. The usual meaning in non-mathematical contexts is **the adjacent sides have to be different.*

This is to be applied also to angles. This type of problem is quite frequent with regard to the families of quadrilaterals. For instance, a grade 5 textbook defines the different families of quadrilaterals and, afterwards, explains that a square, a rectangle, a rhombus, and a parallelogram *have equal opposite sides, equal opposite angles,* In this instance the textbook is using the first meaning of the expression.

Another grade 4 students' textbook defines a rhombus as the *quadrilateral having two pairs of equal opposite angles and no right angles,* but later, in the summary of the main facts in the lesson to be remembered, it defines a rhombus as the *quadrilateral having two pairs of equal opposite angles.*

Type 3: Different definitions for a given concept are used through the series. Frequently, in the Spanish series of textbooks, in different grades, students deal with different families of polygons associated with the same name.

For instance, a series of textbooks defines, up to grade 5, the rhomboid in such a way that it is a parallelogram *with unequal sides and unequal angles.* But in grade 6, the rhomboid is defined as *the general parallelogram* and is is stated that *its properties are: equal opposite sides, equal opposite angles, and supplementary consecutive angles.* It is stated that *these properties are also true for the other three kinds of parallelograms, but each one of them also has other characteristic properties.* Therefore, a rectangle and a rhombus are not rhomboids up to grade 5, but they are rhomboids from grade 6.

The students may have difficulties in understanding the new definitions if neither the textbook nor the teacher mentions the change in the definitions from those learned in previous grades to the actual ones. Students giving answers of type C are likely to continue using their own definition and mental image, producing, as a consequence, a misunderstanding of the new definition and wrong answers. The only students able to change to the new definition without difficulties are those included in type D but, in any case, they should be alerted about the change in the definitions.

3. CONCLUSIONS

The different types of students' answers presented in the first part of this chapter show various steps in the conversion of natural language into mathematical language. Most of them may be natural, and also adequate, in certain moments during the educational process, but it is necessary that the students overcome these initial types of use of mathematical language and become more acquainted with the standard mathematical language. In this process it is also necessary to rely less and less on the mental pictures of the concept under consideration and to analyze it in terms of the properties or elements stated.

The second part of this chapter presented the problem that, quite often, textbooks (and teachers) impair the right progress in the use and interpretation of language (figures and verbal expressions) related to elementary geometrical concepts.

In my opinion, most students are not aware by themselves of the inconsistencies and ambiguities which appear in textbooks, but students who are mature enough to learn mathematical language at this level should be taught properly. Textbooks (and teachers) are considered by the students as faultless sources of knowledge. This can prevent for some time (or for ever) the right use and interpretation of mathematical language.

Some questions that I would like to raise for further discussion are:

• How does language (iconic and verbal) used in textbooks influence the formation of concepts and interpretation of mathematical language by students?

•Do inconsistencies and ambiguities in textbooks impair the student's process of learning?

•Is it possible to use these inconsistencies and ambiguities to promote learning? Wilson (1990) and Vinner (1990) have done some research on this topic.

•Do teachers actually try to make the language used in textbooks and by themselves understandable by the students?

•Are teachers aware of the errors of language in textbooks?

•Is it possible for teachers and textbooks to help the students to progress in their use of mathematical language and to apply it to problem situations?

•Are teachers aware that the process of learning mathematical language takes a long time? that students ready to advance should be encouraged to improve their language? that language used in textbooks will be understood according to the student's maturity?, that trying to make the students use mathematical language at a higher level than the level tey can understand will cause misunderstanding?

REFERENCES

Fuys, D., Geddes, D., & Tischler, R. (1988). *The van Hiele model of thinking in geometry among adolescents. Monograph No. 3.* Reston, VA: National Council of Teachers of Mathematics.

Hershkowitz, R. (1990). Psychological aspects of learning geometry. In P. Nesher & J. Kilpatrick (Eds.), *Mathematics and cognition* (pp. 70-95). Cambridge U.K.: Cambridge University Press.

Hershkowitz, R., & Vinner, S. (1984). Children's concepts in elementary geometry: A reflection of teacher's concepts? In Southwell, B. (Ed.), *Proceedings of the 8th annual conference of the International Group for th Psychology of Mathematics Education,* (pp. 63-69). Sydney, Australia: PME.

Jaime, A., Chapa, F., & Gutiérrez, A. (1992). Definiciones de triángulos y cuadriláteros; errores e inconsistencias en libros de texto de E.G.B. *Epsilon (23),* 49-62.

Vinner, S. (1990). Inconsistencies: Their causes and function in learning mathematics. *Focus on Learning Problems in Mathematics, 12*(3/4), 85-98.

Vinner, S., & Hershkowitz, R. (1983). On concept formation in geometry. *Zentralblatt für Didaktik der Mathematik , 83*(1), 20-25.

Wilson, P. S. (1990). Inconsistent ideas related to definitions and examples, *Focus on Learning Problems in Mathematics, 12*(3/4), 31-47.

Adela Jaime
Universitat de València,
Spain.

CONTRIBUTIONS TO PART SIX

Our final group of writers directed their attention towards appropriate mathematics curriculum for young children. Wright argues strongly that teachers should be familiar with research-based models of how children learn early mathematical concepts for two reasons; first, this knowledge should inform teachers' choices of activities and second, teachers should know how particular activities help children to develop appropriate problem solving strategies.

Hughes studied a group of teachers to find out what factors in fact did influence teachers' choices of activities within the context of a formal, nationally-determined curriculum. Further, teachers gave information about their role in helping children develop mathematically.

A fixed curriculum also provides the backdrop for the contribution from Yamanoshita and Matsushita which describes the expectations that are held for teachers in elementary schools, and gives examples of both particular curriculum devices employed by teachers and the strategies that children use in their development of mathematics.

The final contribution from Malaty urges teachers to abandon the "tabula rasa" that seems to be the basic assumption about the state of children's knowledge of mathematics of those who set curriculum in Finland. He goes on to describe various games and activities that build on children's prior knowledge before they enter school and on their increasing mathematical competence.

The Editors.

CONCEPT DEVELOPMENT IN EARLY CHILDHOOD MATHEMATICS:
TEACHERS' THEORIES AND RESEARCH

The first section of this chapter focuses on the results of a recently conducted investigation of teachers' theories about how children's concepts of number develop and advance. Categories of teachers' responses to an interview question about number concept development are presented and discussed. The second section overviews some recent research into children's early mathematical development. This research is in two categories: (a) research focusing on the types of strategies children use to solve mathematical problems and associations between children's age and frequencies of strategy types; and (b) research focusing on developmental paths of children's strategies. Also included in this section is a comparison of the views held by teachers and researchers of conceptual development in early childhood mathematics. The third and final section; (a) overviews concerns of some researchers about early childhood mathematics curricula, (b) outlines two current investigations into young children's number learning aimed in part at addressing these concerns; and (c) discusses the use of models of children's early arithmetical development by researchers and their potential for use by teachers.

1. TEACHERS' THEORIES ON THE FORMATION AND DEVELOPMENT OF NUMBER CONCEPTS

During the period August - October 1991, the author undertook a study which aimed to document teachers' implicit theories on the teaching of number in the first year of school. The study involved open-ended, individual interviews with teachers, and the topics addressed during the interviews included: children's beginning number knowledge and its development; approaches to group work, student collaboration, and assessment; possible commonalties in the teaching of language and mathematics; the roles of concrete materials, calculators and computers; and use of curricula and texts. What follows is an analysis of the responses of 33 teachers to one of the interview questions. This question was aimed at eliciting teachers' theories about the formation and development of number concepts in children. The interview question was stated thus:

How do children form concepts about numbers and how does their number knowledge advance and develop?

The teachers. The interviewees were selected in approximately equal numbers from each of the three eastern states of Australia and were selected by agreement of the school principal and teacher being interviewed. Each of the interviewees was currently teaching in the first year of school. Collectively the teachers had more than 480 years of teaching experience of which 190 years involved teaching the first year of school. Twenty-five of the teachers had nine or more years teaching experi-

H. Mansfield et al. (eds.), Mathematics for Tomorrow's Young Children, 258–271.
© 1996 *Kluwer Academic Publishers. Printed in the Netherlands.*

ence. Considering that participation was voluntary on the part of the school and the interviewee it seems reasonable to claim that, by and large, the typical interviewee was a confident and successful teacher.

The method of analysis. The method of data analysis was "a reductionist rather than an interpretivist one, aimed directly at producing quantitative summaries of the original interview data" (MacLeod, Rankin & Wright, 1989, p. 158). Transcripts of each of the interviews were analyzed to determine categories for the responses. The set of categories was then modified by a process which involved reconsidering the categories and relevant sections of the transcripts. The modified set of categories was then used in a final analysis of the transcripts (see also MacLeod, 1988). Table 1 shows the categories and the number of responses in each category.

Category	Number (n = 33)	%
experiences with number	18	54
role of language	9	27
prior learning	9	27
counting	8	24
materials	7	21
numbers in environment	5	15
learn from parents, others	5	15
collaboration	4	12
playing games	4	12
repetition	4	12
variety of number experiences	4	12
role of problems	2	6

Table1: Numbers and percentages of teachers mentioning the aspects of number concept formation and development.

Experiences with number. This category included reference to experiences with number, doing activities involving number, using numbers or applying numbers. Slightly more than half of the 33 teachers included a reference to this category in their response:

I think the hands-on concrete activities are ... the most important.... a lot of it at the beginning is through just mere exploration.

Through doing, through seeing, through concentrating.

Well, the activities you give them and just constant hands-on.

Just lots of different activities involving the number.

Just through experience and exposure.

Oh, lots of experience with it.

Role of language. Nine of the 33 teachers referred to language, talking or discussion:

... the more we do the more we experiment, the more we internalize, the more we then use language, the more we learn.

... they need a lot of just repetition and a lot of talk.

... and also by talking about it.

... not only that, lots of discussions.

Prior learning. Two somewhat related ideas were included in this category, viz., references to concepts beginning to develop when children are very young, and references to rote learning forming a basis for subsequent concept development. There were nine responses in this category:

Well I think from an early age. ... My two year old daughter, she's starting to count one, two. ... they develop [concepts] right from when they are a baby.

You've got to have all that rote as well because that needs to be there as a basis.

Well it forms possibly before they come to school.

... so many can do it by rote first. ... Then the concepts come later.

Counting. Nine of the 33 interviewees identified counting as important for the development of number concepts:

... making groups with numbers and you know, counting out so many things.

Things like just counting one to one.

... a lot of counting the actual things in the hand, counting things out with counters, beads—all that sort of thing.

Materials. Somewhat surprisingly, only seven of the 33 interviewees referred to the role of materials (e.g. concrete, discrete) in the development of number concepts:

Well through direct experience with discrete materials. Using materials is essential.

... in the classroom they have to really use a lot of concrete items and that type of thing.

I think probably the understanding ... comes through a lot of hands-on material—actually getting down to using materials.

Using a lot of concrete resources.

Numbers in the environment. Five responses were counted in this category which included references to ideas such as number being in children's everyday life or their environment, or responses containing specific examples of ways that children encounter number:

... they can see a lot of numbering in everyday life.

... their number knowledge is all around them.

Well I feel that they get it from their environment.

... just being aware there's a number on your house, there's a number on mum and dad's car. There are numbers on the telephone.

Learn from parents and others. Five of the interviewees included references to the role of parents, other adults or siblings:

... they've got adults talking to them and counting.

Oh, and the parent's role of course too. ... Different ages of siblings ... and if you've got older brothers and sisters.

Verbalization with mum and then carers.

Collaboration. Four of the interviewees referred to children working things out together or sharing knowledge:

... but if you've got two children they are both sort of working it out ... working out the concepts together.

... they pass that knowledge on to the other children and once they talk about it, the others are aware and they want to be part of the knowing group as well.

Playing games. Four of the interviewees referred to playing or games as contributing to the development of number concepts:

... and they are playing games with numbers. That's how my children learned.

Well they need to play around with a lot of things.

Repetition. Four of the interviewees referred to aspects such as repetition or drill and practice:

... we repeat things a lot and often times if they don't get it the first time they'll get it the fifth time.

Through a lot of practice and repetition.

Variety of number experiences. Four of the interviewees made specific reference to the importance of a range of different experiences with number. That is, as well as having experiences with number, variety in the kinds of experiences is important. This category can be likened to Dienes' perceptual variability principle, that is, "to allow as much scope as possible for individual variations in concept-formation, as well as to induce children to gather the mathematical essence of an abstraction, the same conceptual structure should be presented in the form of as many perceptual equivalents as possible" (Dienes, 1960, p. 32).

a lot of different types of number experiences in as many different ways.

through a lot of different experiences because a child might understand it through one but not through another.

Role of problems. This category included reference to problems. Somewhat surprisingly there were only two references in this category:

... solving problems that they feel [are] necessary for their lives.

... being presented with problems in life situations and having them talked about and role modeled.

Other responses. Two additional responses are listed below. The first, particularly the reference to extension, seems to refer to a need to present children with problems, questions or activities for which their current strategies are inadequate, and can be regarded as an implicit reference to Vygotsky's notion of "zone of proximal development" (1935/1978, p. 86). The second response highlights the importance of the mental processes (i.e. concentrating) that accompany doing:

I believe questioning and extension verbally into the problem solving area.

Through doing, through seeing, through concentrating. A lot of them are away with the pixies half the time.

Relating teachers' theories and curriculum emphases. Each of the three Australian states from which the interviewees were drawn has adopted a new mathematics curriculum in recent years (Mathematics K-6, 1989; Year 1 Mathematics Sourcebook, 1989; The Mathematics Framework P-10; 1988). Not surprisingly, many of the categories above can be readily identified with emphases in these new mathematics curricula and associated inservice courses focusing on developments in mathematics curricula. For example, the most popular category — the importance of experiencing, doing and using mathematics, relates to the curriculum emphases of activity-based learning (Mathematics K-6, 1989, p. 17; Year 1 Mathematics Sourcebook, 1989, p. 2) and of learning being active rather than passive (The Mathematics Framework P-10; 1988, p. 21). In all Australian states teachers are provided with advice about the use of materials, the role of language and the importance of collaboration for mathematics learning (Wright, 1991a, p. 76). Each of these three topics is readily identifiable with one of the categories of teachers' responses.

The role of problem solving. Given that problem solving is highlighted in new curricula (Mathematics K-6, 1989, p. 20-25; Year 1 Mathematics Sourcebook, 1989, pp. 3 & 12; The Mathematics Framework P-10; 1988, pp. 14 & 46-53) and inservice courses (Wright, 1991a, p. 76) it is somewhat surprising that only two of the 33 teachers made reference to the role of problems in the development of number concepts. Additionally, for both of these responses, the reference can be described more specifically. Rather than referring to the more general notion of solving or doing problems, both interviewees referred to the more specific notion of solving problems in a real-life context. The observation that only two of the interviewees referred to problem solving when responding to the interview question stated earlier in this chapter does not lead to the conclusion that most teachers are not aware of the curriculum emphasis on teaching mathematical problem solving.

Problem solving as an end rather than a means. The conclusion that can be drawn is that, by and large, teachers do not regard the activity of problem solving as being important for *developing* number concepts. These teachers regard problem solving as an end rather than a means in mathematics learning. There is a high degree of consistency between this view of the role of problem solving in mathematics and that emphasized in the new curricula in each of the three states from which the interviewees were drawn. In *Mathematics K-6,* it is asserted that "being able to analysis situations and solve real-life problems is a major reason for studying the subject" (p. 20). Very similarly, according to *The Mathematics Framework P-10,* "the value of using mathematics to solve problems is a major argument for studying mathematics at school" (p. 14), while *The Year 1 Mathematics Sourcebook* states that "developing the ability to solve problems is an ultimate, but often elusive, goal of education" (p. 3). The topic of teachers' views of problem solving is discussed further, in the next section.

2. STUDIES OF CONCEPTUAL DEVELOPMENT IN EARLY CHILDHOOD MATHEMATICS

In the area of early childhood mathematics, several researchers have documented and charted developments over time in children's mathematical strategies. Carpenter and Moser (1984), for example, conducted a three-year longitudinal study of the acquisition of addition and subtraction concepts by beginning first grade children. This study involved structured interviews with 88 children on eight occasions at approximately six-monthly intervals, and reports descriptions and categorizations of the strategies that children were observed to use when solving addition and subtraction word problems. Also reported are the percentages at each interview time of children using each category of strategy. More recently, Mulligan (1992) similarly charted developments in children's strategies for multiplication and division word problems. This longitudinal study involved interviews with 70 children on four occasions during a two-year period when the children were in the second and third years of school (6- to 8-year-olds by and large). This study resulted in the classification of five problem structures for each of multiplication and division according to differences in semantic structure. English (e.g. 1991a, 1991b) documented the strategies used by young children in solving novel problems in the combinatorial domain. One study (1991b) involved individual interviews with 50 children whose ages ranged from 4 years 6 months to 9 years 10 months. The interview tasks involved the child producing all possible combinations of two items, drawn from discrete sets. English's investigations were cross-sectional rather than longitudinal, and include an analysis of the development of more sophisticated strategies during the course of an interview (1991a). Each of the studies just described focuses on categorizing children's strategies and documenting changes in the frequencies of particular strategies as children progress through the grades.

Documenting children's conceptual advancements. Investigations of young children's conceptual development by Steffe and colleagues (e.g. Steffe, von Glasersfeld, Richards, & Cobb, 1983; Steffe & Cobb, 1988) involve detailed analyses of children's advancements as they occur in interactive teaching situations. Steffe and Cobb (1988), for example, report an intensive study of six children over a two-year period. The children were taught twice weekly for approximately eighteen weeks each year. The purpose of this study was to document the conceptual paths by which children who were classified as prenumerical and who were operating in a task oriented teaching environment, advanced to an abstract concept of number.

A common feature of the investigations described above, including those by Steffe and colleagues, is an explicit focus on describing the strategies children use to solve mathematical tasks. A distinctive feature of the methodology used by Steffe and colleagues is a focus on the mechanisms by which children make advancements in their mathematical knowledge (e.g. Cobb & Steffe, 1983; Steffe, 1991; von Glasersfeld & Steffe, 1991). The child's interactions with the teacher are considered to be crucial in these advancements and thus advancements are observed in the context of children solving problems posed by the researcher as teacher. Steffe and colleagues describe these mechanisms of advancement in terms of cognitive processes which originated in the work of Piaget, such as schemes, reflective abstractions, and accommodations (e.g. Piaget, 1970; 1980; von Glasersfeld, 1980; 1981). Prominent in the investigative methods used by Steffe and colleagues is to present children with problematic situations which are beyond the child's current ways of operating but within the child's "zone of proximal development" (Vygotsky, 1935/1978, p. 86). That is, tasks presented in the teaching sessions are designed to be just beyond the scope of the child's current strategies. In these teaching situations it is possible to observe and document qualitative advancements in the child's strategies. These observations lead to hypotheses of children's cognitive reorganizations. A primary focus of this methodology is a detailed understanding of the mechanisms of change in children's conceptions rather than merely a description of children's conceptions.

3. COMPARING TEACHERS' AND RESEARCHERS' VIEWS OF CONCEPTUAL DEVELOPMENT IN EARLY CHILDHOOD MATHEMATICS

It is equally true for teachers and researchers that what one regards as important in bringing about conceptual development in early childhood mathematics is informed by one's experience of children's learning of mathematics. Considered in this light, the teachers' theories described in the first part of this chapter arise in and are constantly reinforced during the day to day experiences of teaching mathematics in the classroom. For practitioners, any claim about what is important in the development of children's mathematical concepts must be verifiable in their classroom experience.

Documented in the work of Steffe and colleagues (e.g. 1983, 1988) is the importance of children reflecting on their own mathematical activity for the advancement of mathematical concepts, and that, in order to bring about such reflection, children should be presented with mathematical situations which are problematic for them. Principles such as these underlie more recent investigations by Cobb and colleagues (e.g. Cobb, Wood & Yackel, 1991; Cobb, Yackel & Wood, 1992; Yackel, Cobb & Wood, 1991), the origins of which include attempts to apply in classrooms, models of children's numerical development that arose in situations "in which a researcher interacts with a single child, both to investigate his or her conceptual activity and to attempt to guide the child's learning" (Yackel, Cobb & Wood, 1991, p. 391). In the first part of this chapter it was observed that teachers have a strong tendency to view problem solving as an end in mathematics learning rather than a means. This observation leads readily to a significant distinction between teachers' and researchers' theories about the role of problem solving in mathematics learning. This distinction is significant because it results in profound differences in teaching practices. A characterization of these two alternative views of problem solving and associated teaching practices follows.

Problem solving as a means. Problem solving is viewed as important to the development and advancement of mathematical concepts. Teaching practice is characterized by the use of learning activities which are problematic for children and teaching strategies designed to engage children in reflection on mathematical activity. "At the risk of over-simplification ... mathematics, including the so-called basics such as arithmetic computation, should be taught through problem solving" (Cobb, Wood & Yackel, 1992, p. 158).

Problem solving as an end. An important reason for learning mathematics is to apply mathematical knowledge to solutions of real-life problems. Teaching practice is aimed, at least in part, at teaching mathematics for its application to problem solving. Problem solving is seen as separate from and supplementary to the traditional teaching of arithmetic.

4. SOME RECENT RESEARCH INTO YOUNG CHILDREN'S NUMBER LEARNING

A recent literature review (Wright, 1992) showed that there is an urgent need for revision of early childhood mathematics curricula. Although several Australian states have produced new K-6 mathematics curricula in recent years, this has not resulted in significant change in content and teaching methods in the K-2 range (Wright, 1992). Since the late 1970s there has been a great deal of research into young children's learning of mathematics but, for the most part, this research is yet to impact on early childhood mathematics curricula in Australia. Most recently, findings by several Australian researchers have led them to question the appropriateness of early childhood mathematics curricula. English (1990), for example, argued against the "underlying assumption that it is futile to engage children in activities that are beyond their (assumed) current stages of development" (p. 37), and called for "greater recognition of young children's cognitive competence" (p. 41). Young-Loveridge (1988), a New Zealand researcher, criticized the view that young children should be given greater autonomy in their learning of number concepts:

What is essential is that every child is given the opportunity to participate in experiences involving numbers, and counting particularly. However, this does require intervention on the part of the teacher. Children's number skills are unlikely to develop appreciably if we sit back and wait for the process to occur naturally (p. 39).

In 1990, Wright (1991c; in press-a) interviewed 15 children from each of two classes beginning the first year of school, to assess their number knowledge. One conclusion of this study was that the typical mathematics program at this level is not well suited to the average and more advanced children (1991c). A similar conclusion was reached by Young-Loveridge (1989) in New Zealand, when she studied the gains in number knowledge by 81 children, during the first year of school: "high scorers made smaller gains than ... middle or low scorers" (p. 59). She concluded that "the relationship was due in part to the match between the school mathematics programme and the existing skills of less knowledgeable children being better than that for children who came to school already knowing a great deal about numbers" (p. 60). At the beginning of the first year of school, many children are ready to develop further their early notions of addition and subtraction, and a highly appropriate way to do this is to engage these children in problem-centered learning tasks. Yet, as confirmed in state curricula and prominent texts, the classroom mathematics for many of these children focuses on sorting, matching, classifying and sequencing, and ordinal and cardinal number up to ten—activities which they do not find challenging because, in the range from one to ten at least, these children are facile with the number word sequence and additionally, use counting in relatively powerful ways (Wright, 1991c). Further, even for the less advanced, the topics typical of texts and curricula are not necessarily the most appropriate. A strong case exists (Wright, 1991b; 1992) for at least partially replacing these with topics such as experiences with spatial and auditory patterns, number word sequence activities, and counting in problematic situations (e.g. Steffe et al., 1983, 1988; Wright, 1989; 1991a; 1991b).

5. CURRENT INVESTIGATION

In April 1992, the author began an interventionist teaching experiment (Cobb, 1985, p. 144) involving the application of theoretical models of young children's arithmetical development (e.g. Steffe et al., 1983; Steffe & Cobb, 1988; Wright, in press-a) in a classroom at the Kindergarten year level (5- and 6-year-olds). The study aims to document the psychological and social processes underlying problem-centered mathematics at this level and involves a research methodology adapted from the work of Cobb and colleagues (e.g. Cobb, Wood & Yackel, 1991; Cobb, Yackel & Wood, 1992; Yackel, Cobb & Wood, 1991). This involves a research team working in collaboration with the class teacher to design learning activities and associated teaching strategies which are informed by the theoretical models referred to above. The instructional approach includes whole class teaching, small group problem solving and teacher led discussion of solutions. Additionally, the theoretical models were applied in documenting the arithmetical development of each child in the class via interviews at the beginning middle and end of the teaching experiment which continued for twenty weeks of the school year.

In the course of this investigation several key questions have arisen:
(a) How can mathematics in the first year of school be made more challenging?
(b) What kinds of learning activities and teaching strategies are most likely to result in children reflecting on their mathematical activity and cognitive reorganizations?
(c) How can mathematical discourse be fostered at this level?
(d) How can specific learning activities developed in the one-to-one context of constructivist teaching experiments be adapted for use in whole class teaching situations or small group work?
(e) Is an enquiry or problem-centered approach feasible or desirable at the Kindergarten year level?

6. ASSESSING YOUNG CHILDREN'S ARITHMETICAL KNOWLEDGE

Assessing young children's arithmetical knowledge is a fundamental aspect of research into young children's arithmetical development undertaken by the author in recent years. As indicated above, in the teaching experiment currently being conducted, children's arithmetical knowledge is documented at the beginning, middle and end of the teaching cycle. In a similar vein, the study conducted during 1990 (Wright, 1991c, in press-a) involved documenting children's arithmetical knowledge at the beginning, middle and end of a school year. Detailed descriptions of the author's approach to assessing young children's arithmetical knowledge are beyond the scope of this chapter and can be found in Wright (in press-a; in press-b). In brief, this includes determining a stage of early arithmetical learning (Table 2), and levels of facility with forward number word sequences (FNWSs) (Table 3) and backward number word sequences (BNWSs) (Table 4). The model of stages of early arithmetical learning has its origins in the work of Steffe and colleagues (1983; 1988) and related work by Wright (e.g. 1989), and the number word sequence models draw on the work of Fuson (1988) and Wright (1989; in press-a). Also assessed are ability to identify numerals, order numbers, and subitize (e.g. Kaufman, 1949; von Glasersfeld, 1982). For more advanced children, concepts of tens and ones are also assessed. This is done using a method adopted from Cobb and Wheatley (1988).

Stage	Label	Description
0	Preperceptual	Cannot count the items of visible collections (e.g. a collection of 15 counters).
1	Perceptual counting	Can count the items of visible collections but cannot use counting to solve additive tasks involving screened collections.
2	Figurative counting	Can count to solve additive tasks involving screened collections but counts from "one" rather than count-on.
3	Sequential integrations	Can count-on to solve additive and missing addend tasks involving screened collections. May also count-off-from to solve subtractive tasks. Also referred to as the stage of the Initial Number Sequence.
4	Progressive integrations	Can count-down-to to solve subtractive tasks and can choose the more efficient of counting-down-from and counting-down-to. This is also referred to as the stage of Implicitly-nested Number Sequences.
5	Part/Whole operations	Uses a range of strategies other than counting-by-ones to solve additive and subtractive tasks. This is also referred to as the stage of Explicitly-nested Number Sequences.

Table2: Stages of early arithmetical learning

Level	Label	Description
0	Cannot produce FNWSs (e.g., from "one" to "twenty")	
1	FNWS from "one" as an unbreakable string.	If one or two errors such as omissions are ignored, the child can produce the number word sequence from "one" to around "twenty". The child cannot produce the number word immediately after a given number word. Dropping back to "one" does not appear at this level.
2	FNWS from "one" to "ten" as an unbreakable string.	The child can produce the number word immediately after a given number word in the range "one" to "ten" but drops back to "one" when doing so.
3	FNWSs as chains in the range "one" to "ten."	Can produce the number word immediately after a given number word in the range "one" to "ten" without dropping back, but has difficulty producing the number word immediately after a given word, for numbers beyond "ten".
4	FNWSs as chains in the range "one" to "thirty."	Can produce the number word immediately after given number words in the range "one" to "thirty" without dropping back.
5	FNWSs as breakable chains in the range "one" to "one hundred."	Can produce the number word immediately after a given number word in the range "one" to "one hundred" without dropping back.

Table 3: Levels of facility with FNWSs in the range "One" to "One hundred".

Level	Label	Description
0	Cannot produce BNWSs (e.g., from "one" to "twenty")	
1	BNWS from "one" as an unbreakable string.	Can produce the BNWS from "ten" to "one" and can produce BNWSs from number words less than "ten".
2	BNWS from "one" to "ten" as an unbreakable string.	The child can produce the number word immediately before a given number word in the range "one" to "ten" but drops back to "one" when doing so.
3	BNWSs as chains in the range "one" to "ten."	Can produce the number word immediately before a given number word in the range "one" to "ten" without dropping back, but has difficulty producing the number word immediately before a given word, for numbers beyond ten.
4	BNWSs as chains in the range "one" to :"thirty."	Can produce the number word immediately before given words in the range "one" to "thirty" without dropping back.
5	BNWSs as breakable chains in the range "one" to "one hundred."	Can produce the number word immediately before a given number word in the range "one" to "one hundred" without dropping back.

Table 4: Levels of facility with BNWSs in the range "One" to "One hundred".

7. USEFULNESS OF THE MODELS

Most relevant to the focus of this chapter is the question of the extent to which the theoretical models referred to above are of use to teachers. That is, could these models form the basis of an approach to assessing children's early arithmetical knowledge and teaching children that could be used widely by teachers as well as researchers? A four-year (1992-5) research project being undertaken by the author will directly address this question. The aim of this project is to apply the theories of children's construction of arithmetical knowledge referred to here in the development of a program of intervention in the number learning of "at risk" (e.g. Levin, 1989; Slavin & Madden, 1989) first-grade students (i.e. 6- and 7-year-olds). Additionally, the intervention program will become the basis of a course of study for specialist teachers.

The approach which has been adopted for the intervention program involves (a) identification of "at risk" first-grade students through interview-based assessment, and (b) withdrawal of selected students for daily individualized teaching sessions of 30 minutes' duration, for an extended period, for example up to six months. In 1992, this project involved a teacher in each of six schools and in 1993, a teacher in each of ten schools. By the end of 1994 at least 30 schools had participated in the project.

Reading Recovery and Maths Recovery. In organizational terms the proposed program of intervention and associated specialist teacher professional development is similar to the Reading Recovery program (e.g. Clay, 1979; 1987; 1990) which originated in New Zealand, has been adopted in several Australian states and has also been widely adopted in North America (e.g. DeFord, Lyons & Pinnell, 1991; Pinnell, 1989; Pinnell, G. S., Fried, & Estice, 1990; Pinnell et al., 1991). For example, Reading Recovery operates with first-grade students who are least advanced in reading, involves a year-long teacher development program and involves individualized teaching of students over an extended part of the school year. Beyond this, there is significant common ground in the theoretical underpinnings of Reading Recovery (e.g. Clay, 1979; Pinnell, 1989; Deford et al., 1991) and constructivist theories of young children's early arithmetical learning described earlier in this chapter (Steffe et al., 1983; 1988). Thus, important in the work of both Clay and Steffe, is an emphasis on understanding children's meanings and strategies, and the explicit rejection of approaches which focus on "teaching skills in isolation" (Pinnell, 1989, p. 180). Together, the work of Clay and Steffe signals a shift from generalist theories of success or failure in learning, to more powerful, subject-specific theories. As expressed by Cambourne (1990), "it is theoretically inconsistent to have one theory which explains successful learning and quite a different theory to explain unsuccessful learning" (p. 290).

REFERENCES

Cambourne, B. (1990). Beyond the deficit theory: A 1990s perspective on literacy failure. *Australian Journal of Reading, 13,* 289-299.
Carpenter, T. P., & Moser, J. M. (1984). The acquisition of addition and subtraction concepts in grades one through three. *Journal for Research in Mathematics Education, 15,* 179-202.
Clay, M. (1979). *The early detection of reading difficulties.* Auckland, New Zealand: Heinemann.
Clay, M. (1987). Implementing Reading Recovery: Systemic adaptations to an educational innovation. *New Zealand Journal of Educational Studies, 22*(1), 55-58.
Clay, M. M. (1990). The Reading Recovery programme, 1984-88: Coverage, outcomes and Education Board district figures. *New Zealand Journal of Educational Studies, 25*(1), 61-70.
Cobb, P. (1985). A reaction to three early number papers. *Journal for Research in Mathematics Education, 16,* 141-145.

Cobb, P., & Steffe, L. P. (1983). The constructivist researcher as teacher and model builder. *Journal for Research in Mathematics Education, 14,* 83-94.

Cobb, P., & Wheatley, G. (1988). Children's initial understandings of ten. *Focus on Learning Problems in Mathematics, 10*(3), 1-26.

Cobb, P., Wood, T., & Yackel, E. (1991). A constructivist approach to second grade mathematics. In E. von Glasersfeld (Ed.), *Radical constructivism in mathematics education* (pp. 157-176). Dordrecht, The Netherlands: Kluwer.

Cobb, P., Yackel, E., & Wood, T. (1992). Interaction and learning in mathematics classroom situations. *Educational Studies in Mathematics, 23*(1), 99-122.

DeFord, D. E., Lyons, C. A., & Pinnell, G. S. (Eds.). (1991). *Bridges to literacy: Learning from Reading Recovery.* Portsmouth, NH: Heinemann.

Dienes, Z. P. (1960). *Building up mathematics.* London: Hutchinson.

English, L. (1990). Mathematical power in early childhood. *Australian Journal of Early Childhood, 15*(1), 37-42.

English, L. (1991a). Young children as independent learners. In G. Evans (Ed.), *Learning and teaching cognitive skills* (pp. 72-88). Melbourne: ACER.

English, L. (1991b). Young children's combinatoric strategies. *Educational Studies in Mathematics, 22,* 451-474.

Kaufman, E. L., Lord, M. W., Reese, T. W., & Volkmann, J. (1949). The discrimination of visual number. *American Journal of Psychology, 62, 498-525.*

Levin, H. M. (1989). Financing the education of at-risk students. *Educational Evaluation and Policy Analysis, 11*(1), 47-60.

MacLeod, G. R. (1988). Teacher self-evaluation: An analysis of criteria, indicators and processes used by teachers in judging their success. *International Journal for Educational Research, 12,* 395-408.

MacLeod, G. R., Rankin, M., & Wright, R. J. (1989). An analysis of experienced and student teachers' definitions of the concept of intelligence. *Unicorn, 15,* 157-162.

Mathematics K-6. (1989). Sydney: N.S.W. Department of Education.

Mulligan, J. T. (1992). Children's solutions to multiplication and division word problems: A longitudinal study. *The Mathematics Education Research Journal, 4*(1), 24-41.

Piaget, J. (1970). *Genetic epistemology,* [E. Duckworth trans.]. New York, NY: Columbia University Press, 1970. (Originally a Woodbridge Lecture delivered at Columbia University, 1968.)

Piaget, J. (1980). *Adaptation and intelligence: Organic selection and phenocopy.* Chicago: University of Chicago Press. (Originally published 1974.)

Pinnell, G. S. (1989). A systematic approach to reducing the risk of reading failure. In J. B. Allen & J. M. Mason (Eds.), *Risk makers, risk takers, risk breakers: Reducing the risks for young literacy learners (pp. 178-197).* Portsmouth, NJ: Heinemann.

Pinnell, G. S., Fried, M. D. & Estice, R. E. (1990). Reading Recovery: Learning how to make a difference. *The Reading Teacher, 43*(4), 282-95.

Pinnell, G. S., Lyons, C. A., DeFord, D. E., Bryk, A. S., & Seltzer, M. (1991). *Studying the effectiveness of early intervention approaches for first grade children having difficulty in reading.* Columbus, OH: Educational Report # 16, Ohio State University. (43 pp.)

Slavin, R. E., & Madden, N. A. (1989). What works for students at risk: A research synthesis. *Educational Leadership, 47*(5), 4-13.

Steffe, L. P. (1991). The constructivist teaching experiment: Illustrations and implications. In E. von Glasersfeld (Ed.), *Radical constructivism in mathematics education* (pp. 177-194). Dordrecht, The Netherlands: Kluwer.

Steffe, L. P., & Cobb, P. (1988). *Construction of arithmetic meanings and strategies.* New York, NY: Springer-Verlag.

Steffe, L. P., von Glasersfeld, E., Richards, J., & Cobb, P. (1983). *Children's counting types: Philosophy, theory, and application.* New York, NY: Praeger.

The Mathematics Framework P-10. 1988. Melbourne, Australia: Victorian Ministry of Education.

von Glasersfeld, E. (1980). The concept of equilibration in a constructivist theory of knowledge. In F. Benseler, P. M. Hejl, & W. K. Kock (Eds.), *Autopoiesis, communication, and society* (pp. 75-85). New York, NY: Campus-Verlag.

von Glasersfeld, E. (1981). An introduction to radical constructivism. In P. Watzlawick (Ed.), *Die Erfindung der Wirklichkeit.* Munich, Germany: Piper.

von Glasersfeld, E. (1982). Subitizing: The role of figural patterns in the development of numerical concepts. *Archives de Psychologie, 50,* 191-218.

von Glasersfeld, E., & Steffe, L. P. (1991). Conceptual models in educational practice. *The Journal of Educational Thought, 25,* 91-103.

Vygotsky, L. (1978). Educational implications: Interaction between learning and development. In M. Cole, V. John-Steiner, S. Scriber, & E. Souberman (Eds.), *Mind in society: The development of higher psychological processes* (pp. 79-91). Cambridge, MA: Harvard University Press. (Translator M. Lopez-Morillas, original work published 1935.)

Wright, R. J. (1989). *Numerical development in the kindergarten year: A teaching experiment.* Doctoral Dissertation, University of Georgia.

Wright, R. J. (1991a). An application of the epistemology of radical constructivism to the study of learning. *The Australian Educational Researcher, 18*(1), 75-95.

Wright, R. J. (1991b). The role of counting in children's numerical development. *The Australian Journal of Early Childhood, 16*(2), 43-48.

Wright, R. J. (1991c). What number knowledge is possessed by children entering the kindergarten year of school? *The Mathematics Education Research Journal, 3*(1), 1-16.

Wright, R. J. (1992). Number topics in early childhood mathematics curricula: Historical background, dilemmas, and possible solutions. *The Australian Journal of Education, 36,* 125-142.

Wright, R. J. (in press-a). A study of the numerical development of 5-year-olds and 6-year-olds. *Educational Studies in Mathematics.*

Wright, R. J. (in press-b). *Interview-based assessment of young children's arithmetical knowledge.* In B. Doig & J. Izzard (Eds.), Assessment in the mathematical sciences. Melbourne, Australia: ACER.

Yackel, E., Cobb, P., & Wood, T. (1991). Small-group interactions as a source of learning opportunities in second-grade mathematics. *Journal for Research in Mathematics Education, 22,* 390-408.

Year 1 mathematics sourcebook, (1989). Brisbane, Australia: Queensland Department of Education.

Young-Loveridge, J. M. (1988). Is greater autonomy always in the best interests of children's mathematics learning? *Australian Journal of Early Childhood, 13*(3), 37-40.

Young-Loveridge, J. M. (1989). The development of children's number concepts: the first year of school. *New Zealand Journal of Educational Studies, 24*(1), 47-64.

Robert Wright
Southern Cross University
Australia

TEACHERS' BELIEFS ABOUT CONCEPT FORMATION AND CURRICU-LUM DECISION-MAKING IN EARLY MATHEMATICS

1. INTRODUCTION

Our invitation to contribute to the program of Working Group 1 asked us to address the third theme of the Group–namely, the mathematics curriculum for young children. In particular, we were asked to address the following questions:
How are decisions made about what the content should be in a classroom for young children, and how do these decisions reflect the teacher's (or curriculum writer's) beliefs about how concepts are formed by young children?
Although each of us had published previously in the area of early mathematics (eg Hughes, 1986; Desforges & Cockburn, 1987; Mitchell, 1991), none of us felt that we had addressed these questions in our earlier work in a direct way. We therefore decided to carry out a small-scale study of teachers' beliefs and content choices in order to provide some data with which to address the questions. The findings of this study form the basis of our chapter.

The chapter is divided into three main sections. First, we briefly describe the context in which the study was carried out, and specifically the National Curriculum which was recently introduced in England and Wales. We then describe how the study was carried out and present some of its main findings. Finally, we draw some conclusions and possible implications for the agenda of the Working Group.

2. THE NATIONAL CURRICULUM

Many readers will be aware that a National Curriculum was introduced in England and Wales as part of the 1988 Education Reform Act. Essentially, the National Curriculum specifies what is to be taught in ten foundation subjects between the ages of 5 and 16 years. Four of the ten subjects–English, Maths, Science and Technology–have special priority and are known as the core subjects. Each subject is divided into a number of areas, or attainment targets, and the National Curriculum documents set out specific targets which are to be achieved at each of 10 levels within each attainment target.

In mathematics there are currently five attainment targets: using and applying mathematics; number; algebra; shape and space; and handling data. Attainment target 4 (shape and space), for example, states that pupils should ultimately be able to "recognise and use the properties of two and three dimensional shapes and use measurement, location and transformation in the study of space" (Mathematics in the National Curriculum, Department of Education and Science, 1991, p.13). Level 2 on each target describes the expected achievement of the average child at the end of Key Stage One (aged 7). Level 2 on attainment target 4, for example, stipulates that children should (a) use mathematical terms to describe common 2D and 3D

272

H. Mansfield et al. (eds.), Mathematics for Tomorrow's Young Children, 272–284.
© 1996 *Kluwer Academic Publishers. Printed in the Netherlands.*

objects; and (b) recognise different types of movement. Level 2 on attainment target 2 (number) requires that the child should be able to (a) demonstrate that they know and can use number facts, including addition and subtraction; (b) solve whole number problems involving addition and subtraction; (c) identify halves and quarters; and (d) recognise the need for standard units of measurement.

In order to achieve these levels of attainment legally binding "programmes of study" have been laid down. Programmes of study stipulate, in broad terms, the curriculum content which must be followed by all children. For attainment target 4 (shape and space) for example, the programme of study requires that at level 2 children should work on, amongst other things, "rrecognising squares, rectangles, circles, triangles, hexagons, pentagons, cubes, rectangular boxes, cylinders and spheres; they should work on describing the properties of these shapes, on recognising right angles, types of movement (including translation and rotation)." At this level of generality, curriculum content is statutorily defined: teachers have no choice. They do have choice however, in the specific examples they select, in the order and manner of presentation and in the method of teaching. In advising teachers' planning, the Department for Education has issued "non-statutory guidance" (DES, 1991). The purpose of the non-statutory guidance is to help teachers in their interpretation and implementation of the National Curriculum. Advice is given in very general terms in regard to teaching methods, classroom organisation, lesson planning and evaluation. The advice is eclectic in nature and draws on well known documents in mathematics education such as the Cockcroft Report (1982). Like the National Curriculum, non-statutory guidance leaves teachers with a great deal of choice in defining the curriculum experience of pupils.

An integral part of the National Curriculum is that all children are to take part in standardised national assessments at the ages of 7, 11, 14 and 16. These assessments were first introduced for 7-year-olds in 1991, and will be gradually introduced at other ages over the next few years. The precise nature of the assessments is still evolving, but for the 7-year-olds it is currently based on a mixture of teacher assessment and standardised assessment tasks (SATs). The assessment results of each school will be made public, as part of a wider attempt to raise educational standards through increased parental choice and the operation of market forces.

When the National Curriculum was first proposed, there was some concern within the mathematics education community that it would herald the return to a narrower curriculum and to more traditional teaching methods. In practice, these concerns do not seem to have materialised. This is partly because the National Curriculum itself—at least in the area of mathematics—is not in fact very different from what might currently be considered "good practice" in British primary schools (see Stoessiger and Ernest, 1992, for further discussion of this point). However it is also because, as we have just seen, the National Curriculum and non-statutory guidance still allow primary teachers in England and Wales to have considerable autonomy over teaching methods. These comments, it should be noted, apply only to the effects of the National Curriculum by itself; the possible narrowing effect that assessment might have on the curriculum is another matter, on which it is too early to draw any conclusions.

3. OUR STUDY

In order to throw light on the questions posed at the start of the chapter, we carried out a series of interviews with 12 teachers of young children in the South West of England. Eight of the teachers taught children in the first two years of compulsory schooling (ie between the ages of 5 and 7 years), while four teachers taught in nursery schools for children aged between 3 and 5 years (for whom the National Curriculum does not apply). The sample was recruited through personal contact with particular schools, and the schools varied on a number of dimensions (such as rural/urban and small/large). The teachers had taught in these schools for varying lengths of time, ranging from one term to ten years. Collectively they possessed a wide range of previous experience, including posts as headteacher, primary support teacher and junior teacher (7-11 year range), as well as one teacher who was in her first post. In one case 'the teacher' was in fact a husband and wife team who shared the job on an equal basis–they were interviewed together, and in view of the similarity of their replies, were treated as a single teacher in our analysis. The interviews took place either in the teachers' classrooms after school had finished or in their homes during the holidays.

At the start of interview, the teachers were asked if they had a particular interest in mathematics and whether they felt as confident with mathematics as with other areas of the curriculum. Seven of the 12 teachers said they had no particular interest in mathematics; 3 teachers expressed an interest (in two cases they had a mathematics coordinating role in the school), while the remaining 2 teachers admitted a particular weakness in the area. Only 2 teachers expressed a lack of confidence in teaching mathematics—one because of her own experiences at school, while the other was in her first teaching job. These responses supported our impressions that the teachers were not in any significant way atypical of the great majority of teachers working with young children in British schools today.

Each interview then proceeded in the following way. First, we asked in general terms how decisions were made about the mathematical activities which took place in the classroom, what use was made of published schemes and National Curriculum documents, and how far these decisions reflected the teacher's own beliefs about how children learn maths. Then we focussed in on two specific areas of the curriculum–cardinal number and shape. These topics were chosen because they form two out of the five attainment targets in the National Curriculum and are salient parts of the traditional curriculum for this age range. They thus have an established history and future and we could expect teachers to be familiar with them. We asked what the teachers did in their classroom in each of these areas, how they thought children learnt from these activities, and what their role as teachers was. We also asked them how they would approach each area if the children were younger or older. All the interviews were tape-recorded and the main points transcribed for more detailed analysis.

3.1 How are decisions made about classroom activities?

All but one of the teachers said that they had a central role in deciding which mathematical activities took place in their classrooms. The exception was a teacher of an overflow class whose curriculum was largely determined by filling gaps which other teachers had left. The remaining 11 teachers made it clear that they had the major responsibility for decisions on content at the level of detail. At the same time, they pointed out that the process was essentially a collaborative one involving other staff in the school; the infant teachers consulted colleagues within the same year group, while the nursery teachers consulted their nursery assistants or nursery nurses.

While the precise nature of the decision-making process varied from school to school, there was sufficient similarity to allow a general picture to be drawn. Typically, the infant teachers would get together with immediate colleagues and choose general topics or areas which they hoped to cover during the planning period; these topics were frequently cross-curricular. The teachers would then generate specific mathematical activities from these topics which were appropriate for their classes. Several teachers said that they consulted National Curriculum documents at this point to check that they had covered the maths curriculum: at the same time they might draw on published schemes of work (the most common being Scottish Primary Maths Group or Nuffield Maths) to generate further ideas. Decisions also had to be made on a daily basis about what activities were to be provided for particular groups of children. Here the teachers mentioned the importance of matching activities to children's age, interests and abilities. For the nursery teachers the process was similar to that described above, but simpler, in that much less account was taken of National Curriculum documents or published schemes.

The relatively subordinate role accorded to National Curriculum documents in the above account was reinforced by the teachers' responses to a further question, on the extent to which the National Curriculum had changed their practice. Most teachers said there had been little, if any, change. Those who did indicate a change suggested it had been positive, in that it gave them a framework to operate within, or that it had made them aware of other aspects of maths, or that it had made them think more systematically about what they were providing for the children. One teacher suggested that any difference was purely terminological:

Well, we do the things we always did do, but we do it and say 'oh yes that's data collection' as opposed to "this is sets."

None of the teachers said that the curriculum had been made narrower, or complained that their autonomy had been seriously reduced as a result of the National Curriculum. However, one teacher did point out that the SATs had had more effect on her practice than the National Curriculum itself.

3.2 How do these decisions reflect teachers' beliefs?

Having established with the teachers how decisions were made about classroom activities, we asked them how far these decisions reflected their beliefs about how children learn maths. We also asked them to expand on what these beliefs were. In addition, at several points in the interview we asked them to explain the rationale behind certain activities, or to say in what ways children learned from doing them.

These questions proved to be surprisingly difficult for the teachers to answer. While most of them found it relatively straightforward to describe the decision-making process, they found it much harder to reflect on and talk about their views of learning. Typical comments were:

This is a new thing for me, really, I'm thinking out loud.

When you've been teaching a few years you tend to do everything instinctively. It just all naturally flows on.

You think 'that's what they need', you just do it as a matter of course after a while.

It's difficult to verbalise and analyse what I do, I just get on and do it without really thinking.

I've never thought about why, there's so much going on there's no time to think about it all.

It's very difficult isn't it to get your mind to thinking what you really think–you know why you are doing it but sometimes it's difficult to explain why; I find it very difficult to put what I believe into words, because you just do it, you just go and do it.

You've asked me why and I'm going to say I don't know (laughs). It's terrible isn't it, it's just all so automatic.

In these ways the teachers indicated that their knowledge was implicit and automatic. This is consistent with findings on expertise in other fields–expert mathematicians, chess players, economic analysts and car drivers all make the same sort of claims to automatic thinking. Interestingly, the teachers in our sample were defensive about this feature of their thinking. Yet, despite this defensiveness, and their own hesitancy, we were still able to put together a picture of the teachers' beliefs about teaching and learning. The main elements of these beliefs are given in the following section.

3.4 Teachers' beliefs about teaching and learning

There appeared to be a common view amongst the teachers that practical, sensory experience is crucial for learning. This view can best be summed up by the phrase "learning by doing." Six of the 12 teachers actually used that particular phrase, 3 of the other teachers talked about "practical work," while 2 others talked about "learning through experience." Thus it would seem that learning through sensory experience is a common and salient belief amongst these teachers.

There was an interesting age-related difference in what the teachers thought should accompany "learning through experience." For the nursery teachers, experience and learning seemed equivalent: experience is learning, and learning is experience. For the teachers of older children, however, there were indications that something deliberate and mindful must be done to or with experience. Experience must be organized or interrogated, and words like "investigation," "exploration," "plannning" and "modelling" all got a mention. There was less consensus among the teachers in articulating precisely how this experience led on to learning. Some teachers emphasised practice and repetition of the same activity, while others emphasised a variety of experiences. Several teachers explicitly said that they did not know how the activities led on to learning:

What I don't understand–and I don't know that anyone does–is how they acquire those concepts.

I think that a lot of the time as a teacher you are not aware of how they are learning.

You're not exactly sure what is going on but you try and give them as many different opportunities as you can.

Many of the teachers also pointed out that learning was more likely to take place if activities were related to children's interests, or if the activities "made sense" to them, or if they were "fun." For some teachers it was important that the underlying concept should sometimes be "disguised." so that the children were not aware of what they were supposed to be learning: "You make it fun for them so they don't realise it's maths." Criticisms were also made of what children learnt through "paper and pencil" activities, such as completing pages of sums in a workbook. It was thought that these activities only led to a partial understanding of the concept; full understanding would not come without practical experience. There was however some conflict here with the earlier mention of learning being "fun," in that more than one teacher admitted that her children actually enjoyed completing pages of sums.

We also noted comments the teachers made about their own role in the learning process. Here, their responses were more disparate, although there were still some common threads. For example, 9 of the 12 teachers explicitly mentioned assessment as a crucial component of teaching, 8 teachers mentioned providing a range of activities, while 6 teachers mentioned the capacity to respond to occasions as they arose. The essence of teaching, according to these teachers, is the capacity to assess children, to know where they are in conceptual development and then to provide an environment rich in opportunities for meeting the concept in question. The teacher must also be alert to opportunities for drawing attention to the concept in the everyday lives of children.

The teachers' role beyond that was described in a range of different metaphors, such as "guide," "facilitator," "leader," "supporter," "catalyst" and "enabler." The correspondence between these terms can perhaps be seen more in what is not said than in what is said. Few teachers, for example, said that their role was to 'teach' or 'instruct' children, and indeed there were some who explicitly said that this was not their role. The following teacher, for example, gave a clear account of how she saw the relationship between her role and children's learning:

I think my role is more the language side of it. I think the children will grasp the concepts themselves. It's very difficult to actually teach a concept because if they don't get it how do you make them get it? You just have to provide the material, provide the language, and it's going to click one day, and when it does they've got it and they're going to understand.

At the heart of this assertion is a sympathy with, if not an explicit definition of, the "learning paradox" first defined by Plato in the Meno and discussed most recently by Bereiter (1985, 1990). The modern variant of the problem has been put most succinctly by Fodor (1980):

There literally isn't such a thing as the notion of learning a conceptual system richer than the one that one already has: we simply have no idea of what it would be like to get from a conceptually impoverished to a conceptually richer system by anything like a process of learning (p.149).

The teachers' general beliefs about learning were entirely consistent with what they said about the two specific areas of the curriculum, cardinal number and shape. We will briefly consider what they said about each of these areas in turn.

Cardinal number. The teachers were asked what they did in their classroom in relation to cardinal number. This question generated a large list of activities, of which the main ones were sorting, matching, ordering, counting, one-to-one correspondence, recognition of numerals, matching sets to numerals, writing numerals, addition and subtraction. For the most part these activities were embedded in specific concrete situations, such as sorting sets of beads, blocks or pegs; matching cups, saucers and plates; or counting the numbers on ladybirds or dice. Songs, rhymes, stories, games and computer software were frequently mentioned as vehicles by which particular concepts were put across or reinforced. Several teachers described how they used the children themselves in such activities; one teacher used registration as a time for discussing how many children were absent, how many were having packed lunches, and so on; another described how she would get the children to sort themselves into sets, such as "three boys with brown hair"; while a third talked about "matching boys to girl partners." Others described how they attempted to link the activities to the children's own interests, or used cross-curricular topics as a basis for number activities.

While the teachers found it relatively easy to say what activities they provided for the children, they found it much harder to explain why these activities were used, or how carrying out these activities led to children learning particular concepts. Instead, they tended to fall back on general principles, such as emphasising the importance of learning through experience, or the value of making activities meaningful or enjoyable. Some teachers went further, however, and explicitly justified the provision of a wide range of activities, or of repetition:

The more practice they have the more they come to see 5 in lots of different situations and understand what 5 is.

It's the actual doing the physical exercise of putting out the same number of things over and over again, that's how they learn. For example, if 3 children need 3 cups, 3 saucers and 3 plates by the time they get to plates they have the idea.

However, some of the teachers admitted their uncertainties here. One teacher, for example, when asked why she did a lot of sorting, replied:

It's concept forming, that's how I think they learn their concepts, but I don't really know.

Again, the teachers saw their own role primarily as providers and coordinators of these activities. One saw herself as "a guide, I'm there to help them find their way through the maze." Others stressed the importance of stimulating children with particular activities, or questioning them about what they were doing. Some mentioned they had a more formal role here, for example in telling the children the names of numbers or demonstrating to them how they counted:

I think you have to tell them "that number says one and that's two" because they'll never recognise that themselves. Well maybe they would eventually but it would take a lot longer.

The teachers were also asked how they would approach the area of cardinal number if the children were younger or older. For the most part they stressed that the same general principles would obtain. However, there was a general consensus that with younger children there would be less written work and more practical work, whereas for the older children it would be the reverse.

Shape. The teachers were also asked what they did in their classroom in relation to shape. As with cardinal number, they responded to this question by describing a rich range of activities. These included sorting, matching, modelling, making plans and patterns, drawing, playing shape games and using computer software. The materials used included both specialist equipment such as Logiblocks and everyday objects such as cardboard boxes and packets of Toblerone™. Several teachers described how they used cross-curricular topics to introduce ideas about shape—for example, a topic on houses led to dicussion of the shapes of windows, doors, roofs and arches.

From the point of view of children's learning, the purpose of these activities was to provide experiences of different shapes so that children would understand their properties. Several teachers pointed out that children's learning would be severely limited if these sensory experiences were not provided:

They've got to handle shapes in order to know a shape's feel and what a shape means. [It's no use] saying to a child"'this is a triangle" without touching and feeling it or never actually walking around a triangle shape or making themselves into a triangle or making triangles with their fingers...I don't think the child can think abstractly, they need concrete examples all the time.

At the same time, it was considered important for children to learn the "right language" or "standard language" for shape. This included terms like "triangle," "square" and "circle" for 2D shapes, "cube," "cylinder," "sphere" and "prism" for 3D shapes, as well as the appropriate use of words like "side," "edge" and "face," and terms like "symmetry" and "tessellate."

Our interviews uncovered an unexpected division amongst the teachers in whether 2D shape should be covered before, after, or at the same time as 3D shape. Those who argued for the priority of 2D shape did so on the grounds that the terminology was closer to the language with which children were already familiar. Those who argued for 3D first usually pointed out that children were more familiar with 3D objects, such as boxes or balls, or that they were easier to handle ("more tactile") than 2D shapes. Clearly, what united both sets of teachers was the principle that children should move from the more familiar to the less familiar; what divided them was whether the familiarity criterion should apply to the language being introduced or to the shapes themselves.

As with cardinal number, the teachers saw their role primarily as one of providing experiences, of enabling or facilitating learning, and of stimulating children's interest or "opening doors" for them. At the same time, they also saw their role as introducing the appropriate terminology, and telling children explicitly about the properties and names of particular shapes. While most teachers preferred to do this informally ("grasping the situation as it arises"), some recognised that it 'often has to be quite a formal situation':

I do a lot of group activities on the carpet talking about shape–"find me a triangle," "find me a circle," "what can you tell me about the shape?"—introducing and extending language.

A closer analysis of what the teachers were saying revealed an interesting correspondence with the scheme for spatial awareness described by van Hiele and van Hiele (1959). The van Hieles proposed that children develop mathematical conceptions of space in three phases, moving from "holistic awareness" through "parts awareness" to "property awareness." Holistic awareness involves having a sense of shapes as wholes but with no evidence of awareness of details. Parts awareness involves a capacity to see shapes in shapes and having some sense of the parts which go to make up a shape. Having a sense of connections among parts leads to "property awareness," that is, the sense that shapes have general properties (for example, appreciating that rectangles are special cases of parallelograms). Holistic awareness involves discriminating one shape from others, naming and focusing on outline. Parts awareness involves looking for similarities and differences, and for shapes within shapes. Property awareness involves finer identification of properties.

The following quotations from teachers in regard to their activities and objectives as children move from starting points to more advanced activities seem to us to hold a strong correspondence to this scheme.

Holistic Awareness

They usually know the names of the shapes before they come to me, if not they soon learn, they get to know them with these little games.

Opening their eyes to these things, they might never have thought about it before...never thought about what shape it was before.

Parts Awareness

Things like the faces on the solid shapes eg circle on the end of a cylinder...looking at things with more discrimination.

I talk about sides and faces quite early on.

Properties Awareness

As long as they're learning the properties of the shape, that's the most important as they are discovering for themselves, what that shape is, what it will do, how it will fit together, what you can do with it, then they learn what it is called.

Increasing awareness of the properties of solid shapes, recounting their awareness, e.g., which things roll, which things slide.

Of course this perceived correspondence between the teachers' views and the van Hiele scheme on the development of shape is very much in the eye of the beholder. The van Hieles' work was research-based. The teachers' views might be experience based. Or they might have been imposed by mathematics schemes or acquired on training courses. Our evidence allows us no further comment except to say that the activities provided by the teachers were entirely consistent with their expressed beliefs about progress in this concept domain.

4. SUMMARY AND CONCLUSIONS

We can now return to the questions posed at the start of the chapter, and consider what answers our study has provided. The questions, it will be recalled, were as follows:

How are decisions made about what the content should be in a classroom for young children, and how do these decisions reflect the teacher's (or curriculum writer's) beliefs about how concepts are formed by young children?

The teachers in this study were centrally involved in making decisions about content in their classrooms. Typically, they would draw on a number of sources–including their colleagues, National Curriculum documents, published schemes and their own previous experience–to generate a wide range of mathematical activities. A large amount of energy and and ingenuity was clearly being spent on devising activities which were both interesting for the children and appropriate for their age and ability, while at the same time meeting the demands of the National Curriculum. Moreover, the teachers found little difficulty in describing to us the decision-making process and the activities which it generated.

In contrast, the teachers found it much harder to answer our questions on the extent to which these decisions reflected their beliefs about concept formation. Several teachers remarked that they were not used to articulating the rationale behind their practice—they simply got on with it. Others said they had little idea of how concepts were actually formed, or suggested that the process was essentially mysterious: they just "clicked into place." Nevertheless, we were still able to extract from the interviews some common beliefs about children's learning and their own role as teachers.

What seemed to be widely held was the belief that children learn through practical activities, particularly those which are in some way meaningful to them. Learning without some kind of sensory experience will lead only to partial understanding. Practice, repetition, and a wide range of experiences are also important, although there was less consensus here. The teachers' role was seen primarily as an enabling one, providing the activities and ensuring that children get the most benefit from them. There is little value in direct teaching or instruction, although in some areas—most notably that of shape—the teachers must supply appropriate vocabulary at appropriate moments.

Despite probing, the teachers gave us no account of the basis of their beliefs. They did not quote theorists, theory, or common sense. Rather, their views appeared to be taken for granted.

At one level, then, there is some correspondence between our account of teachers' beliefs and their account of the decision-taking process. Both accounts, for example, place considerable emphasis on the need to provide a wide range of practical activities to promote particular kinds of learning. However, we are cautious about drawing the conclusion that teachers' beliefs about concept formation play a prominent role in the decision-making process. For this would imply, first, that the teachers had clearly articulated beliefs about children's concept formation, and secondly, that these beliefs were actually influential in the decision making process. We are even more cautious about whether this is a productive formulation for understanding classroom life or promoting mathematics education.

Taken at face value the question we were posed "how do teachers' beliefs about concept formation influence decisions about curriculum content?" implies that teachers have clearly articulated beliefs about concept formation and that these beliefs are influential in some way in the decision making process. Taken at face value there is nothing in our data to support either of these premises. Teachers beliefs about "concept formation" might be seen as shadowy and to play little conscious part in their decisions about content.

But to take this apparently self evident line is, implicitly, to adopt the view that there are abstract, decontextualised formal concepts independent of practice, available for inspection and mobile from setting to setting. Such a view of knowledge has recently been challenged by sociologists and cognitive anthropologists. Brown, Collins and Duguid (1989), for example, argue that traditional schooling is based on a view of knowledge as a "self sufficient substance ... independent of the situations in which it is learned." The aim of schooling often seems to be the transfer of this "substance" into the minds of children.

The activity and context in which learning takes place are thus ... merely ancillary to learning—useful but fundamentally distinct and even neutral to what is learned (p. 32).

It is this view of knowledge which generated our research question.

Brown, Collins and Duguid argue that such a view of knowledge is no longer tenable. They suggest that recent research in developmental and social psychology and in anthropology indicate that knowledge is not seperable from the activities and situations in which it is deployed. In this view knowledge is an inseparable part of the activity and culture in which it is produced and used. To ask questions about concepts is to ask questions about cultural practices.

Settings may be said to coproduce knowledge through activity. Learning and cognition ... are fundamentally situated (p.32).

From this perspective, when teachers talk about "activities" but question their relationship to "concepts" they are perpetrating (and perhaps being encouraged in this by our interviews) a category error. From an anthropological view, teachers' beliefs about activities are their beliefs about concept formation. Their position in chosing these activities is their position on concept formation. Activities should arrest attention ("interest," "fun," "relevance," "meaning"), promote practice ("repetition") and procure meaning through language ("labelling," "naming" "discussing"). The teachers are embedded in particular cultural practices at a particular point in history. The particularities gain their significance from the social setting.

If we have learned anything from this study it is perhaps that it will prove less fruitful to explore the mentalistic links between beliefs' and "decisions" in promoting teaching and learning than to explore the social links between activities and immediate purposes. Here, the teachers in our sample had not shadowy but very definite views on activities and the immediate purposes they would fulfill. Their clarity poses the questions: what is the relationship between these activities and a mathematics education and/or how can an (idealized) mathematics education be realized within the cultural practice of the classroom?

REFERENCES

Bereiter, C. (1985). Toward a solution of the learning paradox. *Review of Educational Research, 55*(2), 201-226.

Bereiter, C. (1990). Aspects of an educational learning theory. *Review of Educational Research, 60*(4), 603-624.

Brown, J. S., Collins, A., & Duguid, P. (1989). Situated cognition and the culture of learning *Educational Researcher, 18*, 32-42.

Cockcroft, W. H. (1982). *Mathematics counts.* London, UK: Her Majesty's Stationery Office.

Desforges, C., & Cockburn, A. (1987). *Understanding the Mathematics Teacher: A Study of practice in first schools.* Lewes, UK: Falmer Press.

Fodor, J. A. (1980). Fixation of belief and concept acquisition. In M. Piattelli-Palmerini (Ed.), *Language and learning: the debate between Piaget and Chomsky.* Cambridge, MA: Harvard.

Hughes, M. (1986). *Children and number: Difficulties in learning mathematics.* Oxford, UK: Basil Blackwell.

Mitchell, C. (1991). *Exploring mathematics with younger children.* Derby, UK: Association of Teachers of Mathematics.

Stoessiger, R., & Ernest, P., (1992). Mathematics and the National Curriculum: Primary teachers attitudes. *International Journal of Mathematics Education in Science and Technology. 23*(1), 65-74.

van Hiele, P. M. (1959/1984). A child's thought and geometry. In D. Fuys, D. Geddes, & R. Tischler (Eds.), *English translation of selected writings of Dina van Hiele-Geldof and P. M. van Hiele.* Brooklyn: Brooklyn College.

Acknowledgements: We are very grateful to the School of Education Research Fund and to the Nuffield Foundation for their financial support in the preparation and presentation of this chapter. We are also very grateful to Tricia Nash and Felicity Wikeley for their help in carrying out the interviews described here.

Martin Hughes
Charles Desforges
Christine Mitchell

University of Exeter
United Kingdom.

T. YAMANOSHITA & K. MATSUSHITA

CLASSROOM MODELS FOR YOUNG CHILDREN'S MATHEMATICAL IDEAS

1. FORMATION OF MATHEMATICAL IDEAS

There are a lot of children at the primary level who have trouble with the formation of mathematical ideas. For example, they sometimes write "201" to express twenty-one for the reason that twenty is "20" and one is "1." They cannot add single-digit numbers with carrying, and often make mistakes in subtraction with borrowing. Some children have difficulty in adding and subtracting three (or more)-digit numbers, and others are unable to imagine the magnitude of one hundred million (one *oku* in Japanese notation). Also, there are many children who do not understand the meaning of multiplication and division, not to speak of the concept of fractions.

There is something in common among the children who have these difficulties. They regard numbers as signs with no meanings, and have no images of numbers and calculations. Therefore once they forget computational algorithms, they can never reinvent the processes of calculation.

How can we help children form mathematical ideas meaningfully? The teaching methods we will introduce here are those developed by the Association of Mathematical Instruction (AMI) (see Ginbayashi, 1984; Kobayashi, 1988) to which we belong. In Japan, the *Course-of-study* made by the Ministry of Education prescribes what children should learn in each grade, and teachers must use textbooks which are authorized by the Ministry of Education. Generally speaking, both parents and children believe that children in the same grade should be equally taught the same mathematical content at school, although this it not the case with learning at Juku (Yuki, Sato, & Hashisako, 1988). Thus school teachers are expected to teach 30 to 40 children of different abilities in a class the same subject matter, which includes too much content. AMI's teaching methods have been developed under these circumstances, and are now influencing the textbooks.

We can sketch out AMI's methods from the viewpoints of mathematical content and modeling activities. Turning first to mathematical content, AMI's instruction in numbers and calculations builds on two theories: the *theory of quantities* and the *water supply method*. The theory of quantities claims that number concepts and operations should be derived from different kinds of quantity and its operations. The most general framework of the theory is shown below.

	Extensive	*Intensive*
Discrete	Discrete & extensive (e.g. 3 apples)	Discrete & intensive (e.g. 3 apples per dish)
Continuous	Continuous and extensive (e.g. 3 km)	Continuous and intensive (e.g. 3 km/hr)

Table 1: Classification of quantities based upon the theory of quantities.

H. Mansfield et al. (eds.), Mathematics for Tomorrow's Young Children, 285–301.

Discrete quantity has a minimum unit which can not be divided any more, while *continuous quantity* has no natural minimum unit without being measured by a naturally-constructed unit. Thus natural numbers are derived from discrete quantity, while decimals and fractions are derived from continuous quantity. The classification principle of extensive and intensive quantity is different from this. *Extensive quantity* expresses breadth or magnitude (e.g., volume, length, weight), and has additivity. On the other hand, *intensive quantity* expresses intensity or property (e.g., velocity, density), and is represented by the quotient of two extensive quantities. Therefore extensive quantity is related to addition and subtraction, while intensive quantity is related to multiplication and division. One may notice this theory of quantities has much in common with the theory propounded by Schwartz (1988). However, AMI's theory was developed earlier and in more detail (see Toyama & Nagatsuma, 1962). It has been embodied in many teaching practices.

The *water supply method* is a kind of calculation system. It analyzes calculation problems and arranges them from the more typical (e.g., 222 + 222) to the more specific including 0s and carrying or borrowing, just as water is supplied from a reservoir to each house.

Concerning the second point, we think mathematics learning should involve various types of modeling activities with representations so that children can form mathematical ideas meaningfully (see Figure 1).

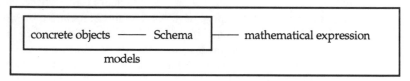

Figure 1: Representations seen in modeling activities.

Concrete objects are some selected real-world settings which correspond to one mathematical idea. A *Schema* is a half concrete and half abstract model which represents the interpretation and structure of a mathematical expression constructed by the theories mentioned above. "Schema" is derived from German and used in a unique sense in AMI. A typical example is what AMI calls a "tile." A more complete explanation of this will be presented in the following sections. According to the stage or level of learning, a Schema takes several modes of external representation: a manipulative physical object, a drawing of it, and a diagram. In addition, it is expected to be internalized and become a mental model. AMI teachers suppose that children can treat a mathematical expression meaningfully by operating a Schema as a mental model even in the absence of external models. Thus concrete objects and a Schema function as different types of models of a mathematical expression. In particular, an effective Schema has been regarded as a key to successful mathematics learning. To put it briefly, children shift from concrete objects to mathematical expressions through the medium of a Schema, as their learning proceeds. Still, this process is thought to be not one-way but reversible. For instance, when a child has difficulty with a mathematical expression, he/she is encouraged to go back to a manipulative object or a drawing of it.

The theory of quantities, the water supply method, and many Schemas were created mainly by two researchers, Toyama and Ginbayashi, who were originally mathematicians and introduced Piaget's studies of mathematical cognitive development into Japanese mathematics education. However, the teaching methods have been revised and expanded through testing by a lot of teachers in classrooms from elementary to senior high school for more than forty years.

Important questions now arise. AMI teachers provide all the children with the same Schema in variousways and promote them to use it. How can each child convert such a Schema into his or her own model? How can children of different abilities in a class learn mathematics meaningfully with the same Schema?

In the following sections we will answer these questions by illustrating how a Schema functions in AMI's teaching practices at the primary level. They are used by many AMI teachers, but some of the teaching strategies in putting them into practice wereuniquely devised by Yamanoshita.

2. NUMBER CONCEPTS, ADDITION AND SUBTRACTION

2.1 Number concepts

Natural numbers. Our practices at the primary level begin with teaching the cardinal aspect of natural numbers. First, children classify different concrete objects in the classroom and the resource room into the same kind, for example, 'bags," "caps," "notebooks," and so on. Then children do one-to-one correspondence between the set of concrete things and actual tiles (made of paper). At this step they pay attention to the size or magnitude of the set by disregarding the other differences (e.g., color, shape). Next, through the medium of tiles, children abstract number (cardinal number) from different kinds of quantity (discrete quantity). Thus tiles, whether actual or drawn, function as a Schema of number.

It is difficult to recognize more than five objects without counting. Hence we teach children to regard 6 to 9 as *five and some*. Five tiles are "canned" into a FIVE tile, and ten tiles are two FIVE tiles (see Figure 2). We call this base system "5-2 system." We use the word "canned" because the children wrap each group of five tiles with foil, which is likened to canning fruit.

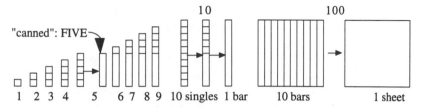

Figure 2: Tiles representing natural numbers based upon the 5-2 system.

Again, two FIVE tiles are canned into one bar (ten), ten bars are canned into one sheet (one hundred). Using the system, children easily understand the principle of place value. Four (or more)-digit numbers are also expressed through the use of tiles. We usually make one *oku* (one hundred million) tile by putting 1 mm x 1 mm tiles together with graph paper. One *oku* tile is such a huge square (10 m x 10 m) that children are very surprised at the size of it. Through this model children can realize the magnitude of one hundred million. (Three-digit numbers and four (or more)-digit numbers are supposed to be taught in the second and the third grade respectively. In Japan, the first grader is six or seven years old.)

We know that in the United States and some other countries Dienes blocks are often used to teach the principle of place value and algorithms of addition and subtraction (Dienes, 1960; Resnick, 1982). Dienes blocks and tiles are similar except that the blocks are three-dimensional and the tiles are two-dimensional. However, we think that the tiles are more effective than the blocks for several reasons. First, tiles are more readily allow children to recognize the magnitude of large numbers, such as in case of one oku. Secondly, and more importantly, tiles are more widely applicable, based on the theories of quantities and calculations. In fact, we use tiles to teach the concepts of decimals and fractions as well as natural numbers, the principle of place value, and the number operations of multiplication and division as well as addition and subtraction, based upon the theories of quantities and calculations. We shall look at instances of this below.

Decimals. The concept and the principle of place value of decimals are learned through the use of tiles as follows. We can divide a single tile into ten 0.1 tiles, 0.1 tiles into ten 0.01 tiles and so on. Actually children cut a single tile (10 cm x 10 cm) into ten 0.1 tiles or a hundred 0.01 tiles. This is a Schema of decimals. Thereby children can come to construct images of not only natural numbers but also decimals. (Decimals are supposed to be taught in the third and the fourth grade.)

2.2 Addition and subtraction

Every addition and subtraction of multi-digit numbers can be decomposed into some additions and subtractions of single-digit numbers. In the water supply method, single-digit addition and subtraction are called "elementary processes," while the multi-digit addition and subtraction are called "compound process." Compound processes are thought to be a synthesis of the elementary processes and the principle of place value.

Addition and subtraction of single-digit numbers are thus fundamental. Let us start with addition. Addition with no carrying (e.g., 3 + 6) is easy. But in the case of addition with carrying (e.g., 7 + 6) the procedure is so complicated that many children have difficulties with it. Using the 5-2 system, the procedure for 7 + 6 is decomposed into the following steps: First, 7 is expressed as one FIVE and two ONEs, and 6 as one FIVE and one ONE respectively; next, two FIVEs make one TEN, and two ONEs and one ONE make three ONEs (see Figure 3).

Children have more trouble in visualizing the whole process of calculation in subtraction than in addition. The most fundamental meaning of subtraction is taking away. But, in this case, the minuend is decomposed and does not keep its initial state after the tile operation. This is thought to be the main cause of children's difficulty in understanding subtraction as taking away.

To lessen the difficulty, Yamanoshita designed and used "two-colored tiles." One face is yellow and the other is red. First, children represent the minuend by yellow

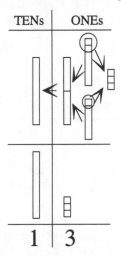

Figure 3: Tile operation in addition with carrying.

tiles; then they turn over as many tiles as the subtrahend is worth; after the tile operation, the answer is represented by yellow tiles, the subtrahend by red, and the initial state (minuend) by all the tiles regardless of color. The understanding of subtraction is more easily gained through the use of two-colored tiles.

Using two-colored tiles in subtraction with borrowing, the children in her class invented two ways of calculation (see Figure 4). In the first method, (A), first a TEN was decomposed into two FIVEs; then one FIVE and two ONEs were taken away respectively (actually, turned over to become red); and finally one FIVE and one ONE left (still yellow) were joined. On the other hand, in the second method, (B), a TEN was decomposed into one FIVE and five ONEs; then the one FIVE and two ONEs were taken away simultaneously; and finally three ONEs and three ONEs were joined. The first method is based on the 5-2 system, while the second is based on the ordinary decimal system.

Twenty-seven out of thirty-four children used the first method. The rest, who were rather accustomed to manipulating mathematical symbols, adopted the second method. They went on to learn subtraction with borrowing in two groups. The methods gradually converged into the second method (B) when they came to solve various types of problems, as many of those using AMI teaching practices have reported.

In what ways are the 5-2 system and the use of tiles based upon it helpful for children? To use an ordinary decimal system, children have to remember composition and decomposition of ten and one-digit numbers before they learn addition and subtraction of multi-digit numbers. This is rather difficult for children, especially those of lower cognitive ability. The 5-2 system reduces the number of possibilities. For example, though the number 10 can be decomposed into 9+1, 8+2, 7+3, 6+4, 5+5, it is decomposed only into 5+5 in the 5-2 system. In short, the 5-2 system helps children's learning by reducing cognitive effort. What has to be noticed here

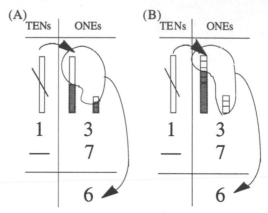

Figure 4: Two ways of calculation of subtraction with
borrowing using two-colored tiles.

is that tiles permit children to use an ordinary decimal system as well as the 5-2 system. In this way, it is possible that children of different abilities in a class learn mathematics meaningfully using the same Schema. This brings us to the other question raised in the beginning. One AMI teacher reports that the children who invented the 5-2 system method of calculation with tiles said, "Tiles move in my head!" These words seem to suggest that the children have converted the given Schema into their own mental model.

In Yamanoshita's class, the process of the conversion was observed as follows. At first the children solved the problems manipulating actual tiles. Then they proceeded to draw tiles while looking at actual ones; and gradually they came to draw tiles, without actual tiles being present, but still according to the procedure of tile operation, as if they were operating tiles mentally. This shift may have been prompted by the teacher's instruction, "Let's project tiles onto the TV in the brain." We think that children begin to operate the Schema as their mental model from this stage of learning. Finally they solved the problem by calculating only with the help of auxiliary signs.

There is another aspect to be described. The children named the first method described above (A) as "Poy-Poy-Gachan", and the second method (B) as "Poy-Gachan" to express the steps of calculation they had invented. "Poy" and "Gachan" represent the sound of separating and joining tiles. We think that the association between each step of calculation and sound made it easier for the children to articulate the whole process of calculation, to become aware of each step, and then to make a mental simulation of it (see Matsushita, in press, for more detailed analysis of the 5-2 system). Thus, it seems reasonable to suppose that children can convert the teacher-given Schema into their models. (These additions and subtractions are supposed to be taught in the first grade.)

2.3 Multiplication

The multiplication table in Japanese, which is called *kuku*, is easy to recite rhythmically, and thereby many Japanese children can memorize it. But they do not understand it in connection with real situations of multiplication.

According to the theory of quantities, multiplication has three meanings:

A. Intensive Quantity x Extensive Quantity1 (Basis) = Extensive Quantity2 (Distributed Quantity)
   For example 3 apples per dish x 4 dishes = 12 apples, or 3 m/s x 4 s = 12 m.
B. Multiplying Factor   For example 3 lots of 4 = 12.
C. Cartesian Product   Extensive Quantity x Extensive Quantity = Extensive Quantity
   For example 3 cm x 4 cm = 12 cm².

As for the idea of repeated addition, AMI regards it as a way to calculate multiplication, not a meaning of it. We think that Type A is the most fundamental for the following reasons. For one thing, it applies not only to the multiplication of natural numbers but also to that of decimals or fractions, and 0s or negative numbers, unlike repeated addition. What is more, in Type A these multiplications can be easily abstracted from real situations. Some Japanese textbooks introduce multiplication with Type B, but it is difficult for the students in the second grade, where we are expected to start teaching multiplication, to understand Type B, because it represents a function or relation which is invisible. One final point is that Type A is helpful as leading to the meanings of proportion and calculus. Thus Type A is used in introducing multiplication; Type B and C are also learned after children have attained proficiency in Type A.

We will give an example to illustrate how the children in Yamanoshita's class learned the meaning and calculation of multiplication. They began it by finding some kinds of intensive quantities in familiar animals and plants as follows.

Teacher: (Pointing to the picture shown in Figure 5.) Some rabbits are playing in the field. Oh, there is
            something strange about them.
Children: They have no ears!
Teacher: Let's put ears on them.

Figure 5: Rabbits without ears.

Then the teacher told the class to draw the ears of the rabbits. The children drew two long ears on the head of each rabbit, while with a serious look the teacher drew five ears on one head, ten ears on another and the like.

Children: They are strange!! Every rabbit has to have two ears.

The children and the teacher discussed and decided to express the sentence "Every rabbit has to have two ears" as: "2 ears per rabbit" and to write it as 2 ears/rabbit . To represent "2 ears per rabbit' children placed two-colored tiles as shown in Figure 6. One red tile represents a rabbit, and two yellow ones its ears. As illustrated in the picture of a tile Schema, a new type of quantity (that is, intensive quantity) is composed of two quantities. Thus, to use the term in Schwartz (1988), multiplication and division are "referent transforming composition,"while addition and subtraction are "referent preserving."

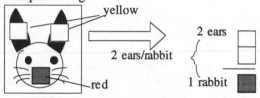

Figure 6: Making a tile Schema of intensive quantity from the concrete object.

Then the children noticed that various kinds of intensive quantity are included in natural things, for instance, "6 legs per beetle," "3 leaves per clover," "0 navels per frog" and the like, and then expressed their findings by a tile Schema. Similarly, they found out some intensive quantities in artificial things such as "12 caramels per box" and "8 oranges per bag."

Having acquired the concept of intensive quantity, the children went ahead to study the meaning of multiplication with a problem like this. "Mother is going to serve three cakes on each dish. She has four dishes for guests. How many cakes shall she buy? Let's help Mother!" They represented this concrete situation with a tile Schema of multiplication, first by putting actual tiles and next by drawing them with graph paper. After that, they expressed the meaning they constructed as a mathematical expression. In the case of six dishes, they placed tiles as shown in Figure 7, and noticed that using a canned FIVE made it easier to find the answer.

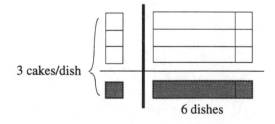

Figure 7: Making a tile Schema of multiplication.

While trying to solve the problem "There are 6 caramels in each box. How many caramels are there in 7 boxes?", the teacher suggested to the class that they should make a "canned TWENTY-FIVE" by uniting five canned FIVEs to find the answer more easily (see Figure 8). It may safely be assumed that using a larger unit such as a canned FIVE and a canned TWENTY-FIVE not only helps children find the answer more easily, but also helps them to convert a tile Schema into a mental model, because the number of objects to be operated on mentally is lessened by changing some smaller units into a larger one.

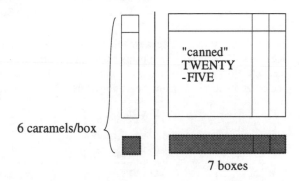

Figure 8: Tile Schema of multiplication including "canned" TWENTY-FIVE.

After the children had gained a good understanding of the meaning of multiplication with some examples, the teacher invited them to make the whole multiplication table (*Kuku*, in Japanese) for themselves. They made it in the following order: 2 x n, 5 x n, 7 x n, 3 x n, 8 x n, 1 x n, 6 x n, 4 x n, 9 x n, 0 x n. This order is arranged according to the ease of making a multiplication table with a tile Schema in the 5-2 system. For instance, it is because 8 is 3 + 5 that 8 x n follows 3 x n. Finally, each child made his or her own booklet of multiplication tables, by relating concrete situations (in the form of pictures or word problems) to mathematical symbols (in the form of mathematical expressions and answers) through the medium of the tile Schema. (See Figure 9 next page.)

Let us consider the two questions posed in the beginning here again. There was a child who was regarded as intellectually handicapped. All the concrete situations he related with the multiplication 2 x n were the type which asked how many ears n rabbits had. And the situations for the other multiplications were made up of cakes or oranges or n boxes. This seems to show that the kind of quantity at his disposal is very limited. Still, he completed his booklet by himself, using actual tiles at times when he could not fill in the kuku. One can safely state that he understood multiplication in his own way through those quantities. There were some other children as well as him who had difficulties in learning a multiplication table. They did not lose confidence in their ability to learn multiplication nor dislike learning it. It is because they knew they were able to reinvent a multiplication table and find the answer by drawing a tile Schema. A canned FIVE and a canned TWENTY-FIVE helped them do this.

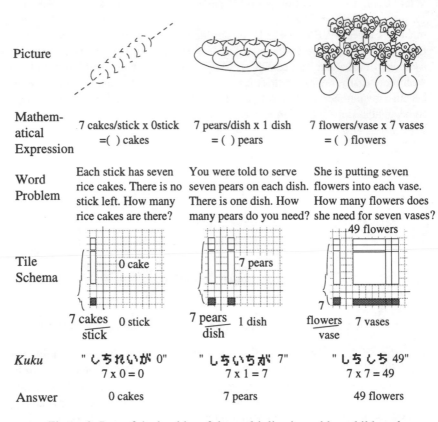

Picture			
Mathematical Expression	7 cakes/stick x 0stick = ( ) cakes	7 pears/dish x 1 dish = ( ) pears	7 flowers/vase x 7 vases = ( ) flowers
Word Problem	Each stick has seven rice cakes. There is no stick left. How many rice cakes are there?	You were told to serve seven pears on each dish. There is one dish. How many pears do you need?	She is putting seven flowers into each vase. How many flowers does she need for seven vases?
Tile Schema	0 cake	7 pears	49 flowers
	7 cakes / stick 0 stick	7 pears / dish 1 dish	flowers / vase 7 vases
Kuku	" しちれいが 0" 7 x 0 = 0	" しちいちが 7" 7 x 1 = 7	" しちしち 49" 7 x 7 = 49
Answer	0 cakes	7 pears	49 flowers

Figure 9: Part of the booklet of the multiplication table a child made.

What we have tried to show here is that a tile Schema of multiplication in some modes of representation can be a useful model for each child in different ways. To some children who have learned a multiplication table, it is a mental model which gives meaning to mathematical symbols; to others who are uncertain about it, a drawing of the Schema is a tool of reinventing it. In addition, to the children who have less cognitive ability, it is a manipulative tool for solving a problem in some concrete multiplicative situations familiar to them.

The tile Schema gives an interpretation not only to multiplication but also to division. In fact it clarifies the difference between two meanings of division, sharing (such as "There are 12 cakes. If you divide them among 4 children equally, how many cakes does each child have?") and grouping (such as "There are 12 cakes. If each child can have 3 cakes, how many children can get 3 cakes?"). What is to be answered is intensive quantity in the sharing problem, while it is extensive quantity (basis) in the grouping problem. Thus a tile Schema mentioned earlier becomes an analog of multiplicative structure which relates multiplication and division. (Division is supposed to be taught in the third grade.)

2.4 Fractions

There are various concepts of fractions as follows: partition, quantity (continuous quantity), ratio, a result of the division of two numbers and so on. AMI teachers believe that the quantitative concept is the most essential in the introduction of fractions. Why? Addition, subtraction, multiplication, and division of fractions can be explained by the quantitative concept in the same way as those of natural numbers and decimals. On the contrary, the other concepts cannot give a good account for all the operations. For example, fractions as partition apply only to addition and subtraction, and fractions as ratio only to multiplication and division.

However, we have found some difficulty in teaching fractions as a quantity. In Europe and some other countries fractions are used in everyday life to express quantities which cannot be expressed as natural numbers, whereas in Japan decimals, instead of fractions, are used for this purpose. Therefore the concept and calculation of fractions as quantity are not easy for Japanese children to understand. For instance, when we ask "How long is one-third of two metre ?" most children answer at once, incorrectly, "It's one-third metre." The fact that children confound fractions as quantity with fractions as ratios causes mistakes like this.

To help children understand fractions as quantity, we invented the following method in cooperation with other members of Hokuriku-district Study Group of AMI (Fuse, Takekuma & Yamanoshita, 1988).

First, the teacher pours a little more than 2 liters of colored liquid such as pineapple juice into a 10 cm x 10 cm x 40 (or so) cm vessel. Then she asks the class how much juice there is in the vessel. Because children know that a liter measure is 10 cm x 10 cm x 10 cm, they can find that a 10 cm height on the vessel indicates 1 liter and guess that the amount of juice is 2 liters and a little. But they cannot tell the precise amount. Next, the teacher suggests to the class that they should use a piece of yellow paper instead of real pineapple juice to confirm the amount of it (see Figure 10).

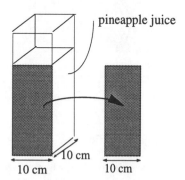

Figure 10: Tracing the quantity on paper.

Folding the paper as shown in Figure 11-1, children find 3 fragments equal 1. Thereby they can conclude the amount of juice is 21/3 liters. Similarly, children try to confirm the amount of liquid which is represented by various rectangles.

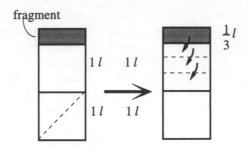

Figure 11-1: Origami fraction (including one kind of fragment).

In the case of the rectangle shown in Figure 11-2, they fold it in the same way but get a new fragment. In such cases, children refold to find how many new fragments are equal to the old fragment and find 2. So they get 1 2/5 liters.

Sometimes it is difficult to measure the amount of real things. But once we represent the amount by rectangles of paper, we can find it by folding the paper. In this way we help children form the concept of fractions by operating a tile-like Schema. We call this method "origami fraction" after the Japanese art of folding paper.

When children come to learn the addition and subtraction of fractions, they can invent rules of calculation for themselves using the method of origami fraction.

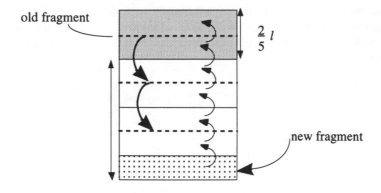

Figure 11-2: Origami fraction (including two kinds of fragment).

For example, they try to add mixed numbers such as 1 2/5 + 21/5 and find that whole numbers and proper fractions should be added separately (see Figure 12-1).

When cancellation is needed as in 5/8 +7/8, they find that cancellation means changing smaller fragments into bigger ones (Figure 12-2).

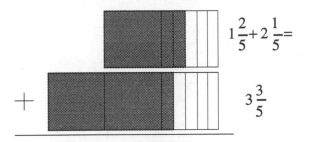

$$1\frac{2}{5}+2\frac{1}{5}=$$

$$3\frac{3}{5}$$

Figure 12-1: Addition of fractions using origami (the case of mixed numbers).

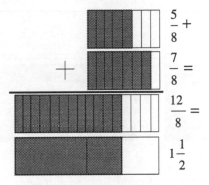

$$\frac{5}{8}+$$

$$\frac{7}{8}=$$

$$\frac{12}{8}=$$

$$1\frac{1}{2}$$

Figure 12-2: Addition of fractions using origami (including cancellation).

In a similar way, children can learn the addition of fractions with different denominators, as well as subtraction, multiplication and division with the help of origami fractions. (Fractions are introduced in the third grade; their addition and subtraction are supposed to be taught in the fourth and fifth grade and their multiplication and division in the sixth grade.)

Take the learning of multiplication for example. In Yamanoshita's class, the children started work on it from the following problem. "Father is going to spread fertilizer on land of area 2 1/5 m². He uses 1 3/4 liters of fertilizer for 1 m² of land. How much fertilizer is he going to use for 2 1/5 m² ?" At first they wondered if multiplication of fractions was the correct operation, although they rather easily made a mathematical expression, 1 3/4 (L/m²) x 2 1/5 (m²) = ? (L) Some children commented on it. "Fractions can be expressed as decimals, and we learned multiplication of decimals before. So I think multiplication of fractions is also possible." "Whole numbers are expressed as fractions too. For example, 2 equals 4/2. So we can multiply fractions."

They went ahead to learn how they should calculate. First, they arranged some pieces of paper in the form of a tile Schema of multiplication of natural numbers. Looking at the arranged paper, they started to discuss how to find the value of "?." Soon they noticed that they had to find how much the smallest rectangle represents.

"It is 1/20 because we folded a square piece of paper lengthwise into four and crosswise into five."

As a result, they found the value of "?" by calculating as follows.

$$2+1\frac{2}{4}+\frac{1}{5}+\frac{3}{20}=2+1\frac{10}{20}+\frac{4}{20}+\frac{3}{20}=3\frac{17}{20}$$

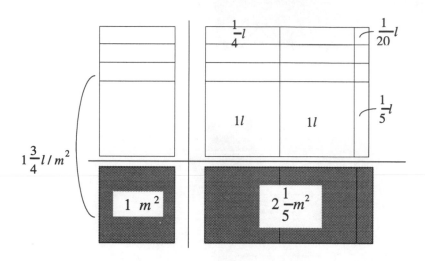

Figure 13-1: Tile-like Schema of multiplication of fractions using origami (including some kinds of rectangle).

Still, they were disappointed, thinking multiplication of fractions needed the addition of fractions with different denominators which they found troublesome. Here the teacher asked the class, "Is there any easier way to find the answer?" While discussing it, one boy said, "A rectangle for one-fifth equals 4 small rectangles for one-twentieth." Another boy sitting next to him added, "Can't we fold the whole paper by this smallest rectangle?" The children folded as shown in Figure 13-2, and drew lines along the folds. "There are 7 rectangles in length and 11 in width, so 77 rectangles in all." "Well, that's seventyseven-twentieths !" "It's three and seventeen twentieths ! The same answer as we found before!" They were very pleased. "But where have 7 and 11 come from?" "Ah hah! Folding paper is like changing a mixed fraction into an improper fraction." "Yeah, 21/5 is 11 fifths and 1 3/4 is 7 fourths . Seven and 11 have come from 7 in 7 fourths and 11 in 11 fifths ." Summing up what was discussed, they made the following mathematical expressions.

$$1\frac{3}{4}\times2\frac{1}{5}=\frac{7}{4}\times\frac{11}{5}=\frac{7\times11}{4\times5}=\frac{77}{20}=3\frac{17}{20}$$

In this way, the children discovered the rule for multiplying fractions;

$$\frac{b}{a}\times\frac{d}{c}=\frac{b\times d}{a\times c}$$

by devising a tile-like Schema of multiplication of fractions.

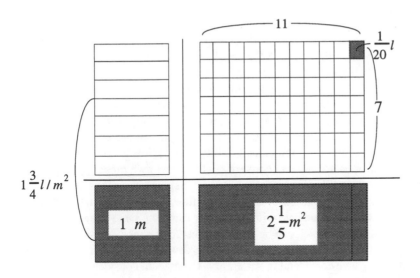

Figure 13-2: Tile-like Schema of multiplication of fractions using origami (including only one kind of rectangle).

In the teaching practice described above, what role did a Schema made of origami play? One of the features of an origami fraction is that it is made through the children's work with folding. Following that, they convert it into their own models by recognizing its usefulness. At the first stage of learning, the Schema was just a tool for finding an answer. But once the children found it, they focused their attention on how they did it. It hence became a tool of thinking about a rule for calculations at the next stage.

Here again it seems that it depends upon the child's ability how a Schema actually functions. At the same time, a Schema is a tool of communication between children of different abilities. For example, one boy, who had difficulty in manipulating mathematical symbols, wrote about the process of discovering the rule for calculations in the class by reflecting upon it for himself. Without the help concrete models like origami fraction, he could not have shared the process nor, as a result, learned the operations of fractions meaningfully. Another boy, who had already learned the rule at *juku* wrote, "I felt I realized why the rule works well. Origami fraction is great!" Generally, a child cannot explain a mathematical rule to the other children in a class if he/she just learns it without understanding. It seems that the Schema, to the boy, was a tool of understanding and explanation. In this way, the same Schema has different significance or usefulness for children of different abilities. Still, it is a common referent which supports communication between them. Through such a communication, they understand mathematics more deeply.

3. FINAL COMMENTS

We have discussed AMI's methods of teaching number concepts and calculations at the primary level around our classroom models and children's activities with the models. As mentioned above, different versions of tile Schema play a crucial role in children's understanding them. A Schema is a key to relating children's modeling activities with theoretical mathematical content.

We posed two questions in the beginning of this paper. We believe we have already given answers to them by looking into the teaching practices of subtraction with borrowing, multiplication of natural numbers, and multiplication of fractions. The point is as follows: the same Schema, in some modes of representation, functions differently according to the child's ability. Although it is more or less provided by a teacher, cach child can convert it into his/her own model to help learn mathematics meaningfully. This is not to say that a Schema is a means of individualized learning. Rather, children of different abilities can enhance the quality of learning while they communicate with each other using the same Schema.

There is an objection which can be raised against AMI's methods. Some people may think a Schematic representation should be devised by children themselves and then it would have considerable variability. They would consider AMI's methods too teacher-initiated and too standardized. This objection is seemingly reasonable. However, one must not forget that the number of powerful Schematic representations is limited, and that it is difficult for children to create them from the beginning. Though we provide the Schematic representation for the children, they begin to use it as their own thinking tool once they get proficient at its operation and the meanings it produces. In fact, they can find out some mathematical rules for themselves through the help of a tile Schema, as we have seen in the learning of subtraction with borrowing and multiplication of fractions. In short, providing a Schema for children does not necessarily imply that mathematics learning is teacher-initiated throughout. Also, one has to recall that the same Schema functions in variable ways according to the child's ability, and that it permits children to think in variable ways. From this viewpoint, we may say that a Schema does have psychological variability although it lacks perceptual variability.

We should mention the difficulties in implementing AMI's methods. As we have seen, one of the advantages of AMI's Schemas is that they are highly systematized and coherent. Being highly coherent, however, means that later learning strategy depends strongly on earlier learning. For example, the learning of multiplication of fractions using a tile-like Schema with origami requires both the learning of multiplication using a tile Schema and the learning of the concept of fractions with origami. A problem arises here. In Japan, the teacher in charge of a class is changed once every year or two; accordingly, a child is taught mathematics by three to six different teachers at elementary school. It is very probable that some of them adopt different methods from AMI's. In this case, the advantage mentioned above will be lost. It is still possible that teachers use AMI's methods, however. When children have not learned what is required for the present material, a teacher may design a teaching program which includes children's re-learning. We believe that the Schemas are worth teaching and learning in such a way.

REFERENCES

Dienes, Z. P. (1960). *Building up mathematics*. London: Huchinson Educational.
Fuse, M., Takekuma, T., & Yamanoshita, T. (1988). *Origami fraction*. Tokyo: Kokudo-sya. [in Japanese]
Ginbayashi, K. (1984). *Principles of mathematics education: Achievements of AMI*. Tokyo: AMI. [in Japanese]
Kobayashi, M. (1988). *New ideas of teaching mathematics in Japan*. Tokyo: Chuo University Press.
Matsushita, K. (in press). Helping children acquire mathematical knowledge through semantic and pragmatic problem solving: An analysis of "teaching experiments." In AMI, *Human Development*.
Resnick, L. B. (1982). Syntax and semantics in learning to subtract. In T. P. Carpenter, J. M. Moser, & T. A. Romberg (Eds.), *Addition and subtraction: A cognitive perspective*. Hillsdale, NJ: Erlbaum.
Schwartz, J. L. (1988). Intensive quantity and referent transforming arithmetic operations. In J. Hiebert & M. Behr (Eds.), *Number concepts and operations in the middle grades*. Reston, VA: NCTM; Hillsdale, NJ: Erlbaum.
Toyama, H., & Nagatsuma, Y. (1962). *The theory of quantities*. Tokyo: Meiji-Tosyo. [in Japanese]
Yuki, T., Sato, Z., & Hashisako, K. (1988). *Juku: How it is viewed by children, parents, and teachers*. Tokyo: Gyosei. [in Japanese]

Acknowledgments. We would like to thank Hiroyuki Ito for his assistance in making the figures and table.

Toyoko Yamanoshita
Chisaka Elementary School

Kayo Matsushita
Kanazawa University

Japan

JOENSUU AND MATHEMATICAL THINKING

Joensuu is a Finnish town in the most eastern part of Finland. It is about 125 years old, with 50 000 inhabitants. The University of Joensuu is 25 years old. The Faculty of Education has a Teacher Training College, the roots of which go back more than 100 years. By tradition, each Teacher Training College in Finland has a Normal School. So Joensuu, at the moment, has a normal school for all the grades.

School mathematics in Finland, like almost everywhere in the world, has seen different changes since the end of the 60s. In the 80s the "Back-to-Basics" movement brought arithmetic back to primary school as the main content of the mathematics syllabus. In reaction to the "New Math" formality, education in primary school has put emphasis on arithmetic skills. These are facts, which can be easily seen from primary school textbooks, but the situation in the classroom is more clear.

This I came to learn from my daily observations of mathematical lessons in Joensuu's normal school since 1986. Before this time, and for 20 years, I was mainly interested in secondary school education, but my work in the primary school teacher training department has shown me that any improvement of mathematical education has to begin from primary school and kindergarten.

1. SCHOOL CURRICULUM OR CHILD CURRICULUM?

Despite the fact that our children do not get any mathematical formal education before primary school, they attend the first grade at age seven with rich mathematical experiences. Numbers, numerals and arithmetical operations are not new to them, even the operation of division to some of them. Some of these children show understanding of fractions, decimals, per cents and even negative numbers. On the other hand, the primary school curriculum seems to be based on a postulate, according to which *students know nothing about mathematics*. They have to stay more than two weeks till they get the chance to write the numeral "1" in their books and for more than two months they learn to add and subtract with only five numbers: 1,2,3,4 and 5.

This slow teaching process does not give motivation to most of the students either to take part in classroom activities, or to do exercises. The students' motivation increases when the teacher by mistake asks them to add or to subtract with larger numbers than those they have formally studied. This motivation decreases when the teacher asks them to forget about his question, mentioning that these numbers have not been studied yet. From the first experiences with formal mathematical education, first grade students feel that we do not appreciate their pre-school mathematical experiences. They feel some kind of frustration when the teacher shows an exercise page like "35", when they have already found it. They do not understand why the teacher can not trust their abilities to find such a page. To make a

H. Mansfield et al. (eds.), Mathematics for Tomorrow's Young Children, 302–316.

protest, they usually look to the opposite side of the teacher's book, that is the offering model.

These examples show that the school curriculum has to take care about children's experiences and moreover individually. Thus, we can have in the same class different curricula for different children. Otherwise we can lose even children of high mathematical abilities if we do not offer to them a challenging curriculum. When such children lose interest in mathematics they sometimes turn into what is called troublemakers. Some of these students can later become interested in mathematics, but also others can lose this interest for ever. We then are responsible for offering each child a special curriculum: the child's curriculum.

2. GENERAL OBSERVATIONS

The next observations I got from daily observations of classroom activities in Joensuu's normal school. I call it "general" for two reasons. First is that each reader can find in it something with which he or she is familiar. The second reason is that they are not dealing with specific school mathematical topics.

Teaching in primary school is clearly putting emphasis on mastering arithmetical skills. The main aim is clear: accuracy in calculating. The lesson normally has the following structure; mental arithmetic for about 5 -15 minutes, giving new rule for about 5 -10 minutes and different exercises for the rest of the 45 minutes lesson. Moreover, one third of the lessons are only exercise lessons. Rule giving takes even less than 5 minutes to allow longer time for making exercises.

As a result the students show a high level of mechanical performance. This can be shown in test results, where it is common for students to gain full marks. This happens even in cases when nobody was able to solve the word-problem offered at the end of the test. Teachers became of the opinion that word-problems are too difficult for children to be the criterion of their achievement. On the other hand, in each lesson the students do not find any difficulty in solving most of the word-problems. The reason is that these so called problems can be solved using only one operation, the operation discussed in the lesson. So, the solution of such word-problems is not based on understanding of mathematical concepts. They are just additional drills.

3. SPECIFIC OBSERVATIONS AND INVESTIGATIONS

Nothing has affected me, to decide content and develop classroom strategies for optimal formation of mathematical concepts in young children, like daily observations of classroom activities in Joensuu's normal school.

During the teaching practice of my students, beside observations, I was able to make different kinds of investigations. One of them was the use of strategies to improve word-problem solving ability, based on understanding of mathematical concepts. But this may need a special article. The next examples give some evidence about the need of understanding mathematical concepts to solve also non word-problems.

In the topic "Decimals" for grade 4 (age 10), the children were able to do all the textbook exercises without mistakes. At the end I asked my student to give the children new kinds of exercises. Let us examine two of them as a model:

Can you write this decimal as a common fraction: 1.7 =
Complete   1 = ____ x 0.1

The most common solution to the first problem was one-seventh and the most common solution to the second problem was zero. These mistakes show clearly not only the misunderstanding of the decimal concept, but also the misunderstanding of the fraction concept and multiplication operation. Moreover these mistakes show how the students behave in facing mathematical problems. It is just a response without thinking; because, how can a number greater than one, 1.7, be equal to a number less than one, namely one-seventh? The answer to multiply by zero in the second problem is something unbelievable. The pattern of thinking here is the following; multiplying by zero brings zero to the right side of the digit "1" and thus the digit one moves to the left of the decimal point. This is related to the mechanical rule they use in multiplying by 10, 100, 1000, and so on.

This situation is not connected solely with the fourth grade or with decimals. This situation is not related only to those cases where the children can not find the correct final result. Next we asked the third grade students (age 9) to calculate 479+367-478. Most of the students got the correct final result "368", but only after a long time and much hard work. The same problem we proposed to higher classes the result was the same, even in the case of the sixth grade.

Students first sum the first two numbers, then they subtract the third number from the sum they got before. They write carefully the corresponding digits in a vertical column, they make special learned marks of carrying and changing. Students used to have squared papers for mathematics. This is the case in both exercise books and also textbooks, which tend to encourage the students to be accurate.

Why did they solve the mentioned problem in such a mechanical way? The answer is not difficult to find. Since the third grade they have learned what is called "The rule for the order of operations", according to which calculating proceeds always from left to right. To assure the students that the rule is absolute, one of the textbooks gives a drawing of a brownie reading a newspaper, under which is written "You read from left to write, so you do the same in calculation". Since the third grade, students had learned to make posters of such a statement and put it in front of them over the board. They also have practiced too much to remember such rule.

For this reason we proposed the same problem to second grade (age 8) students, who had not yet learned the rule for the order of operations. The result was much better.

4. MATHEMATICAL THINKING AND MECHANICAL TRAINING

Understanding or memorizing? Thinking or performing? Which one has to be emphasized at primary school? These kinds of questions have always been some of the most argued questions in teaching mathematics for young children. In several cases, the answer was that we have to accept memorizing and performance in primary school to reach the full understanding later, when the children get more ability to think. Moreover, in some discussions, primary school mathematics was accepted to be arithmetic, where the junior secondary school is the phase of transition into mathematics.

Where the above arguments can be based on psychological theories, my daily observations are quite different. Most of the children come to school with readiness to think mathematically, they have a great curiosity to learn, especially the curiosity to understand, but the formal mathematical education asked them to be mainly as accurate and as systematic as a machine in calculation.

After primary school education, children become able to make the calculation even of the area of a figure which does not exist. This happens when a textbook of the seventh grade asks the students to calculate a right triangle's area, when the hypotenuse's length is 8 cm and the opposite height's length is 5 cm.

When the children come to school they often start their questions with the word "Why", but after some time they change their questions to start with the word "What." So, at the beginning they are sure in their thinking abilities to understand, but after some time they become sure in the teacher's knowledge to give advice "What to do?"

Always we have some students with poor academic abilities. This doesn't mean that we have the right to forget about the majority and use 6 years of primary education to give the students the ability to imitate machines' accuracy in calculation, through mechanical training. This can not be correct in a time we see machines everywhere. Machines can be more accurate than a person, but we need to have a person who is able to make more accurate machines. Therefore, from the beginning, we have to decide a real mathematical content, through which the understanding of mathematical concepts is a major objective. To reach this objective, mathcmatical educators have to work for developing classroom strategies.

That mathematics promotes the mind is not an absolute fact. It depends on the teaching/learning process we provide. Strategies, which can make the students active thinkers, are those which can promote the mind. We do not serve even children of poor academic abilities when we just train them to perform, but we do serve them and others, when we can give all the chance to think. Thinking ability is different from one to another, but we have to try all our best to develop this ability in each child. Finally, thinking and not performing is the sign of humanity. It leads to understanding and understanding offers pleasure. This pleasure is needed, among others, to ensure human culture's need for mathematicians.

5. FROM OBSERVATIONS, INVESTIGATIONS AND PHILOSOPHY TO ACTING

Observations showed that in primary school we mainly train the children to master arithmetical skills. This is neither enough, to make them able to solve a real mathematical problem, nor the way to affect their intellectual development, at this long and vital time of their growth. The first need to solve mathematical problems is the need to understand the mathematical concepts. How to make students understand mathematical concepts? This is the main question, which we are going to discuss in this paper.

The observations and investigations I began in 1986 affected me to act to change the teaching of mathematics in primary school, from putting emphasis on training to putting emphasis on thinking. To reach this objective, it was necessary to design and examine strategies to develop the mathematical thinking of primary school students. These strategies include strategies for the discovery of mathematical concepts.

First attempts to change mathematics teaching in Joensuu took place in the first two years 1986-1988, within the teaching practice of my students. In 1988 I established two mathematical clubs for the first two grades in Joensuu's normal school and now these clubs serve all of the six grades of primary school. In 1990 with the help of 60 hours of in-service education for about 40 teachers, mathematical clubs spread to most of the primary schools of Joensuu. In 1991 similar in-service education was organized for the teachers of another town, Savonlinna. Also, other shorter in-service education was provided in other places of the country. To answer the request of the teachers, a part of the mathematical clubs' materials has been published in two books and also a related didactics book has been published.

6. THE SITUATION TODAY

At the moment, different teachers use mainly mathematical clubs' materials in their normal classes, especially in Joensuu.

They ensure that the use of these materials has developed a teaching/learning process where nothing is given ready as a rule. They say that the strategies used have obviously raised students' interest in mathematics, and even students' marks in tests. They explain the reason. In mathematical lessons, students feel the joy of being in a discovering journey, in which they have to think to find out and understand. Teachers ensure that the clubs' strategies have been of value not only for gifted students but also to others; even weak students have got an opportunity to understand.

The final result is that in teaching mathematics Joensuu's teachers, and not only of primary school, are now interested in putting emphasis on thinking more than training. Some parents and some teachers from neighboring places send their children of mathematical interest to Joensuu, to attend mathematical clubs.

On the other hand, the work we started in 1986 seems to be endless. Each new activity leads to another. In autumn 1992, I got the chance to develop and test my strategies in teaching mathematics in two kindergartens of Joensuu. This was the first attempt to teach mathematics in kindergartens in Finland. Our strategies enabled us to offer 6 year-old children much more than the first grade of primary school does. For instance, students were able to solve equations and inequalities. We took care of all students as individuals to meet with their needs and to develop their abilities. The content reached by some students was even more than what the primary school offers in the first two grades. These results open the door to investigate two effects of our strategies. First is how far some students can learn mathematics, and the second is how early we can start teaching mathematics. This is one of our main concerns this year. Teaching mathematics in kindergartens is now appreciated. The success we got has encouraged all other kindergartens of the town to join us this year. So, we have beside the qualitative aspects in our activities quantitative ones.

In autumn 1992 and in spring 1993 a 37 hour in-service education was organized by the University of Helsinki to make more teachers from any province of the country able to use Joensuu's strategies. Similar in-service education has taken place in other universities and to different school teachers; from kindergarten teachers to tertiary education teachers. This kind of in-service education is needed, for different reasons. One is the acceptance of teaching as an art. How teachers use their voices, hands and so on is a component of this art.

7. THE AIMS AND NATURE OF JOENSUU'S STRATEGIES

Among others, we aim at an intensive education of mathematics. Sometimes, in minutes the children can learn what they learn normally in months, and even content divided into parts for several grades. This is done through strategies in which the learning is a result of children's activity. So, these are discovery strategies.

In learning a concept, the child has to do and to think, to discover the concept. Doing and thinking can happen simultaneously, or in order one precedes the other, or in a sequence of both. Also, there are successful attempts to finally discover the term used and even the symbol used, in the case of having such a symbol.

Doing and thinking, and thinking and doing processes are guided by heuristic questions, which have been constructed and developed, especially through several trials. These questions are used in an oral or written way, or both. In discovering a concept, its name, and its symbol the history of mathematics, normal language and etymology have special places in our strategies. These strategies are also used to give students opportunities, to go more deeply to the insight of a concept learned before.

The main principle in these strategies is to encourage children's curiosity, to find out the reason of everything they learn, as much as possible and as deeply as they can. Because of the nature of mathematics and its culture, causal thinking is not only regarded as a tool for understanding, but also as one of the main objects in teaching mathematics. Thinking about the cause makes mathematics learning more meaningful and gives pleasure. It is just a game, a mental one. For our young children, doing and investigating concrete materials are necessary to use and develop this thinking.

Now it is time to give a concrete example of these strategies.

8. HOW TO DISCOVER THE DECIMAL SYSTEM?

"Decimal system" is indeed a term used even with young children, but the most important is to understand it. We offer the next activities to our students to discover it. The process used enables us to assist children's minds to form this concept.

We start this activity by asking students to put their "Unifix" box on their desks. After that we ask them to put away all the long colored rods inside their desks, except one. Now we ask them an important question: **Does this rod fit well inside the box?** (They say "Yes.") Then we ask them to break the rod apart into its individual "block,", and spread them on their desks.

What do we have to do with the empty box? We ask the students to put ready the cover to the right side and the other part to the left, and be ready to use it. After that each student gets a paper with the following figures on it: to record the results of their actions.

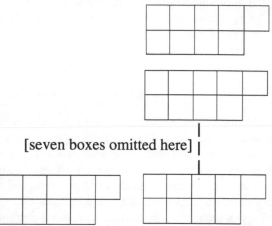

[seven boxes omitted here]

Today we shall use this paper and the blocks to discover something new in mathematics. OK? They say "Yes".
So, now we shall begin. Are you ready? They say "Yes".
Put one block inside the cover of unifix-box. Have you all done it? They answer "Yes". GOOD.
1) **How many blocks do you have inside the cover?** (They say "One.") So, we use the first figure, in the paper and make a cross inside it. **How many squares do we need?** (They say "One.")

(For this kind of demonstration the teacher uses a transparency and overhead projector, or the board.)
2) **Which digit do we have to write on the line under the figure?** (They say "1")
3) **Here?** (They say "Yes.")

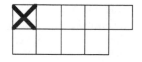

1

4) **Can you do the same?** (They say "Yes.")
    Now go ahead to the next figure. First; put one block more inside the cover.
5) **How many blocks have you got inside the cover?**
6) How many crosses do you have to make inside the figure?
7) **Which digit do you have to write on the line under the figure?**
    Continue by doing the same.

8)   **How many blocks do you have to add each time?** (They say "One.")
     Right. Do so please.

Students keep working, till they meet the next problem:

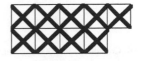

9

They have 9 blocks on the cover and one block still outside, on the desk. All the squares have been used. (Below the figure, the digit 9 is written.)

The students explain the problem and then they ask: **What to do?** (Some of the children find the solution for the whole problem at that stage, without any guidance. For others we continue.)

9)   **Can you collect all the blocks in one?** (They say "Yes.") Collect it please, and keep it in your hand.
10) **How many rods do you have in your hand?** (They say "One.") So, small pieces, the "blocks," we put before inside the cover, to the right.
11) **Where do we have to put this rod?** (They say "Inside the box itself.") Wonderful.

Now look at the last figures in your paper.

If we have to put this rod inside the box, to the left;
12) **Where do we have to make a cross to represent it?** (They say "In the left figure.")
     So please, do it.
13) **What do we have to write under this figure?** (Which digit do we have to write under this figure?)
     (They say "1".) This is great. Do it please.

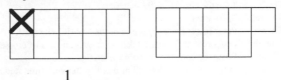

1

So, the blocks were just ones. The rod consists from nine ones and one additional one. This new unit is not of ones.
14) **What is it?** (Students say "Ten.") So, the digit you wrote last, is not of ones.
15) **Of what is it?** (Students say "Of tens.") RIGHT. Now, look at the unifix-box's cover.
16) **How many blocks are there?** (They say "None.")
17) **How many crosses do we have to make in it?** (They say "Nothing.")
This is a great discovery for today.
So, tell me please:
18) **What do we have to write below the right-hand figure to mean "nothing"?** (Students say "Zero.")
Yes. So, you have this idea. Great.

19) **How do we write this zero? Who can come and write it?** (A student does it as below.)

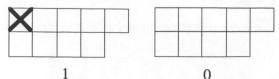

                  1   0

Yes. Correct. About 2000 years ago, the Hindus invented this symbol. It was more rounded as a circle, to
   be noticed that we have nothing.

Now I ask a question and please be careful.

20) **Is the next statement true?** (The teacher writes) **1 = 10 ?** (Students say "No.")

21) **Why?** (Students say "First is one and the second is ten.")

RIGHT; Now, all of you, BE READY.

We shall play a game. First take the rod from the box and put it on the desk.

22) **Have you all done it?** (After they all have done it, we continue.)

Now take all of unifix materials from your desk and put them on the desk beside the rod we have now.
   Go on. Have you done it? (They say "Yes.")

**I'll say a name of a number and you have pick up in your hand the corresponding unifix materials
   and hold them up. OK.**

Teacher: Twenty (In Finnish language it is just "TWO TENS.")

Teacher: Right.

Now you have to put them in one of the box's parts.

23) **In which part do you have to put? In the left part or the right part?** (Students say "The left
   part.")

24) **Why?** (Students say "Because these are tens.")

RIGHT. Please do it.

**Now I'll give you a similar paper to the one we have used. In each row there are two figures of 9
   squares (Those are familiar figures).** (After distributing the papers the teacher continues). Look
   at unifix-box's parts. Use the first row of figures to make the correct number of crosses in the
   correct figure.

25) **Have you done it?** (They say "Yes.")

Now you have to write on the line under each figure the correct digit. Go ahead.

26) **Have you done it?** (They say "Yes.") Please, raise your paper up.

THIS IS GREAT. Now, let us continue the game. I'll say the names of other numbers and you have to do
   each time the same as you see on the screen. (Should students be able to read, otherwise it has to be
   given orally).

First: Take the correct unifix material.

Second: Raise it up.

Third: Put it inside the correct part of the box (left or right).

Fourth: Use a row of figures. Make the correct number of crosses in the correct figure.

Fifth: Write the correct digit below each figure.

In the beginning the teacher does all of it orally, but with time students learn most of it independently.
The teacher then has to say only the number's name.

The numbers we say to the students are 30, 50, 80 and 90.

Later, we play a similar game with numbers; 34, 56, 78, 87, 95.

This time, and also in the case of large numbers "80" and "90" before, we have to cancel the second step
"Raise it up".

Between these two games, we check students' ability to make summation of tens.
This proceeds as follows:

27) **What is the new unit we learn today?** (The students say "Ten.")

28) **Can you add by tens?** (They say "Yes.")

Now, be ready to write and compute correctly.

Teacher: (Orally) 20 plus 30 equals.
29) What did you find? (They say "Fifty.")
LET US CHECK.
30) Who would like to come to write the whole statement on the board?
A student comes and writes: 20 + 30 = 50
31) How to read it? (Students say "Twenty plus thirty equals fifty.")
(Fortunately in Finnish it is just : "TWO TENS PLUS THREE TENS EQUALS FIVE TENS.")
Yes. Write over the correct digit the letter T to denote "TEN". Please, everybody raise your book up. All are correct; all have put it correctly like now on the board:

$$\begin{matrix} T & T & & T \\ 2\,0 & + & 3\,0 & = & 5\,0 \end{matrix}$$

One more; I give it orally as before. "Forty plus fifty."

After checking this, it is ttime to play the game of the numbers 34, 56, 78, 87, and 95 mentioned above.

Next the teacher has to place on the board a new poster :

NEW ADDITION AND NEW GAME

Let us start first with the addition. Are you ready to write? ("Yes.") The teacher says "Sixty five plus thirty two".

$$\mathbf{T\,O}$$

Teacher: So, you wrote (writes, including the "T" and the "O" above) 65 + 32 =
Of course you have noticed my writing of the letters "O" and "T".
(The students say "Yes.") . (In Finland I usually use blue in writing the tens' digits and green in writing the hundreds. This is due to the color of bank notes of ten and a hundred marks.)
32) What are they denoting? (Students say "Ones and tens.")Yes, indeed, they are.
33) How many ones do you have? (They say "Seven.")
34) How did you get that? (Students say "The sum of 5 and 2 is seven.")
35) Who would like to come to write it in the correct place? (A student writes "7" on the board under the letter "O.")
36) And how many tens have you got? (They say "Nine.")
37) Who would like to come to write it in the correct place? (A student writes "9" on the board under the letter "T.")
Teacher: That's correct. After that the teacher replaces the poster with the next one:

THE LESSON'S GAME

The teacher distributes a paper of the familiar rows of figures.

Please be ready. Through this game we shall discover the secret of our numeration system.

The beginning is familiar to you.

38) Use the unifix-box's two parts and the unifix materials to illustrate the number 97.
39) Are you ready? (The teacher goes through students to make a check.)
All right. Please, use a row of figures and make corresponding crosses to the number 97, and then write the correct digit below each figure.
40) Have you done it? (Students say "Yes.")
Teacher: Now you have to continue the game as you have done before.
41) How many blocks do you have to add each time? (Students say "One.")
42) Where you will put it? (Students say "Of course inside the cover, to the right.")
43) What do you have to do after that? (Students say "Making the crosses in the figures of the row below.")
44) What do we finally have to do? (Students say "We have to write the correct digit below each figure")

Teacher: You know what to do. So, let us start.

Students keep working, till they meet the next problem:

 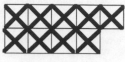

9   9

They have 9 rods inside the unifix box and 9 blocks inside its cover. They have
crossed all the squares. Under each figure is written the digit 9.

Students still have one block outside the two parts of the box. Solving the problem
is easier than before. The idea is not really new. They have used it before in discovering "Ten." Usually students solve independently the problem by using the last
box on the left, illustrated below.

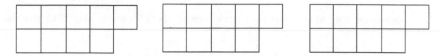

It is easy also because the colored rods in the box show that there is still a place in
the box for only one rod of ten. Students collect the last 10 blocks in one rod and put
it inside the box. They in fact discover the next greatest unit to ten. They make only
one cross in the last figure from the right and write below the digit "1". Under other
figures they write "0".

The teacher has to ask students to close the box and raise it up to be seen.

45)   How many boxes do you have in your hand? (They say "One.")
So, small pieces, the "blocks", were ones. The rods were tens.
46)   What is the new unit you have in your hands? (Students say "Hundred.")
So, you have the idea.
47)   How many rods are there inside the box? (Students answer "Ten.")
Then:
48)   How many tens are in a hundred? (Students say "Ten.") So, when we look at a numeral from
right to left first we have ones.
49)   What is the next digit representing? (Students say "Tens.")
50)   And, what is the next digit representing? (Students say "Hundreds.")
Now look at the next numeral;   1 4 3
51)   What is the digit 3 representing? (Students say "Ones.")
RIGHT.
52)   Which letter do I have to write over 3? (Students say "O.")
                                                                O
Right.   1   4   3
53)   What is the digit 4 representing? (Students say "Tens.")
Right.
54)   What letter do I have to write over 4? (Students say "T.")
                                                      T   O
Yes, like that.   1   4   3
55)   What does the digit 1 represent? (Students say "Hundreds.")
56)   What letter do I have to write over 1? (Students say "H.")

	H	T	O
Yes; I'll do it:	1	4	3

So, let us read it starting from left; "One..."
It is easier in the Finnish language; "Hundred, four tens, three."
Let us say it again. Now be ready for the next game. Each two of you have to use your unifix materials together to illustrate the number on the board: 143.

The teacher has to continue this game. Also *different groups of students* can work together to have enough unifix materials to illustrate numbers of only hundreds like; **200, 300, 400, 500.** It is important to offer numerals like 206, where there is no digit on the place of ten (in our opinion zero is not a real digit, it is just a place holder).

These kinds of problems we normally offer on the overhead projector, where the next numeral is still unseen, till all students finish their work.

Besides checking and discussing with each group, doing exercises in groups gives opportunity to students to discuss with each other the problem solving idea.

We also give the contrary type of these kinds of problems. We illustrate by unifix materials a number, and students have to write in their books the corresponding numeral.

It is also important to give students the opportunity to construct their own problems, solve them, change problems with other students and check their solutions. This part of our strategies is important, for different reasons. Among others it shows us, "Are our proposed problems sufficient for special group? And are they sufficient for special student?" One other important reason is that there are some kinds of problems, like the last mentioned by us, the objectives of which are difficult to achieve completely in a large group.

For the last reason and moreover to raise the students' level of abstraction, we use iconic illustrations of unifix materials in a different form for both kinds of problems. First we give an iconic illustration of number and after that students have to write the corresponding numeral, and also we use the opposite case; first we give a numeral and students have to draw the corresponding illustration figure. We have to encourage them to make it more and more simple. The next is our favorite, we often use it later.

This form in many cases is sufficient to illustrate the number 126 in the teaching/learning process of different topics.

After using unifix materials and iconic illustrations, and to be sure that the relation between the units of ones, tens and hundreds through concrete materials and iconic illustration is clear we give the next two exercises.

The teacher gives the next numbers in the next order orally and asks students to write it in different lines in their books; 5, 10, 47, 100, 200, 639 and 12. After that the teacher checks students writing through discussion. Also the use of a transparency to make a quick check is quite good.

After discussing any errors, the teacher gives the next problem. The teacher reads; "2 + 3 is equal to ...", then he or she asks the students how to complete the statement, and finally the students are asked to write the whole statement. The teacher does the same with the next cases; 100 + 300, 10 + 20, 5 -2, 300 - 100 , 30 - 10, 15 + 2, 15 - 2, 12 + 13, 10 - 3, 20 - 3 and 27 -12. Finally the teacher has to check students' writings as mentioned before.

The success of students in the last two exercises means that number names and their notation are understood, and the last one shows the ability to apply the understanding of place value.

On the other hand we offer more difficult problems, which show how far children can apply their understanding of the decimal system and especially the place value idea. Among other activities we ask them to change one or two numbers in a false statement to turn it into a true one. The following are two of the statements provided: 12 + 205 = 307 and 490 - 19 = 300.

Other problems allow the children to discover by themselves new topics. As an example we give them the next problem 34 - 9 and let them use unifix materials to discover what is called borrowing.

9. REFLECTIONS ON DECIMAL SYSTEM DISCOVERY STRATEGY

The use of 9-square figures has given us the chance to make the students understand deeply the decimal numeration system. This model is isomorphic to our Hindu-Arabic decimal system. On the other hand the use of a unifix rod has made the discovery of the new unit "ten" easy. By analogy, the use of the unifix box has made the discovery of the new unit "hundred" easy. Unifix materials have made us able to give the students to have in hand something concrete to represent abstracts; the unit ten and the unit hundred.

This forming process of these abstract concepts, using unifix concrete materials and 9-square iconic figures, makes us optimistic that this understanding will stay for ever. It is discovered through activities including problem solving.

In the Finnish language we can say that tens and hundreds are units. This also enables the writer to plan strategies for effective teaching/learning of other topics among others fractions. In this last case, similar fractions are fractions of the same unit. For instance adding of 2 eighths to 3 eighths, is the same as adding, 2 to 3. The reason is that they are of the same unit "eighths," which have to be remembered at the end. This enables us to teach addition and subtraction of similar fractions, and also multiplying by a whole number at the same time in one lesson.

In most cases the teaching/learning strategies we use are in need of both special materials and heuristic questions. For this reason, the demonstration of more than one example in the space of this chapter is difficult.

We chose this example not because it is the best example we have to illustrate our strategies, but because it deals with the essential part of the primary school curriculum, the decimal numeration system including the great human invention of place value.

The reader can think about other activities and games, which can raise the level of understanding of these concepts and facilitate the application of this understanding in solving problems. We cannot in this space demonstrate in detail other activities and games. As an example of using other materials we mention the replacing of unifix blocks, rods and boxes, with coins of marks, and banknotes of tens and hundreds of marks to illustrate given numerals and the opposite, offering first money and then asking children to write the corresponding numeral. Instead of unifix materials we also use figures of points (in other cases figures of segments) and ask children to ring each ten points or segments to get a new unit "ten" and using another color to ring each ten of tens to get a new unit "hundred" and finally write the corresponding numeral.

These kinds of activities enlarge the space of the decimal system concept, but they are not alternatives to using unifix materials. Changing 10 coins into a banknote of 10 marks is more complicated than collecting 10 blocks to form a rod. We cannot fix 10 coins together to get a banknote, but we can fix 10 blocks together to get a rod. Moreover the shape of this rod is close to the shape of the digit "1" needed in writing the numeral ten. This we cannot also achieve by ringing ten points or segments. Using points, segments and other figures gives us a chance to develop students' matching of number and space and develop space perception abilities. On the other hand the display of these figures in different forms offers students experiences needed in learning arithmetical operations, especially visually different decompositions of a number.

10. STRATEGIES FOR EFFECTIVE EDUCATION OF MATHEMATICS

Mathematics was discovered by humans and human children can rediscover it. The logic of mathematics is a human logic, so the natural way to teach mathematics is to make use of its logic. Discovery has given pleasure to mathematicians, so the process of learning, which is a process of discovering, has to give pleasure to young children. Young children, and not only young, cannot live long enough to repeat the history of the mathematical discoveries of many generations of human beings working for thousand of years, so the mathematical work done must be introduced to children in the most effective way. This is the theoretical base on which our strategies are built.

The decimal system example shows how our strategies can offer effective education. Addition and subtraction with 3-digit numerals is the main target of the first two primary school years in many different countries. This target was easy to achieve in primary schools and kindergartens in about 3-4 weeks. At schools we mainly dealt with the group as a whole whereas in kindergartens we mainly dealt with individuals and small groups. It is remarkable that even in kindergartens within two weeks some children were able to write two 3-digit numerals and find their sum and their difference with a high level of reasoning.

Effective education is not related to only the quantitative aspect of education, but even the quantitative aspect is a result of the qualitative aspect.

The understanding of the decimal system in our example enabled our children to deal with hundreds as well as with ones. Adding 200 to 300 is not different from adding 2 to 3. Children cannot see this analogy of they learn the numbers in a sequence, …10, 11, 12, …. This mechanical partition of the subject and slow teaching cannot help students understand the decimal system as a whole. Learning numerals in a sequence does not help the students understand the place value idea. Learning numbers, …9, 10, 11, … in a sequence by adding one each time leads to a misunderstanding of the number notation system.

The decimal numeration system was invented through different generations attempts in different cultures. Single discrimination of numerals does not make the general idea of place value understandable. Students then see each numeral as isolated from the others. For instance 10, 11, 12, are just new numerals coming after 9. This is one of the reasons why children completed the sentence "1 = _ x 0.1" with "0" as mentioned earlier.

In our work, begun in Joensuu, the main objectives have been the understanding of mathematics and developing students' mathematical thinking. To achieve these objectives, we developed heuristic teaching/learning strategies. These strategies are based on the nature and structure of mathematics. On the other hand, these strategies offer students enjoyable activities involving doing, thinking, and communicating. In building a mathematical curriculum, the question to us is not only organizing content and then finding convenient strategies, but it is to look within convenient strategies to organize and consequently choose, suitable mathematical content. Within our strategies we develop the national curriculum and turn it into a child's curriculum. Students have the right to learn as much and as deeply as they can. Age/grade are not the only criteria by which curriculum should be chosen; within our work we see that student ability and teaching strategies are also important criteria. Effective education for all is needed, not only to develop mathematics and its use, but to develop the mathematical thinking of everybody.

REFERENCES

Malaty, G. (1982). Understanding of mathematical concepts: classification, evaluation, results. *International Journal of Mathematical Education in Science and Technology*, *13*(3), 347-354.
Malaty, G. (1988). What is wrong with the 'back-to-basics' movement, and what was wrong with the 'new-math' movement. *International Journal of Mathematical Education in Science and Technology*, *19*(1), 57-65.

George Malaty,
University of Joensuu
Finland

N. A. PATEMAN

FUTURE RESEARCH DIRECTIONS IN YOUNG CHILDREN'S EARLY LEARNING OF MATHEMATICS

1. LOOKING BACK

1.1 A brief recent history of early mathematics learning

Let us define the modern era of schooling as dating from the industrial revolution. Mass education became a practical necessity at about that time in order that a satisfactorily-trained work force would become available to meet the demands of the rapidly changing commercial world. No longer could the traditional apprenticeship system, based on a one-to-one relationship between artisan and novice, produce sufficient numbers of semiskilled workers; nor were newly-needed skills able to be acquired under the old system. Workers were now needed who were to some degree dogmatized and socialized into acceptance of new roles whose facets were dependent on an entirely new conception of industry. The modern school was thus begun to teach rudiments of reading, writing, and numbering to the masses in order that many of their number would be employable in the factories that were rapidly emerging. As the associated expansion of the marketplace occurred, the need for clerks (and secretaries) grew very rapidly; these classes of worker needed bookkeeping (and secretarial skills) to take on the work of calculating accurately and transposing the results in a good hand into the increasingly-important ledgers of companies (and to draft business and legal correspondence). Here we see the sources of school curricula that emphasized quick, accurate acquisition of number facts (and legible handwriting) in the elementary school; have those emphases been reduced in schools to match the rate of invention of machinery to carry out the tasks of calculating, bookkeeping and writing?

Society now demanded that large numbers of its members be educated, and educated very differently from before. Thus a need arose to find effective ways to choose content appropriate to these changing demands, and to teach that content successfully to a segment of the population heretofore quite unaccustomed to the academic pursuit of knowledge. The tasks of choice of content and methodology were clearly now entirely different from the days of classical education. A field of study, research in education, began to emerge. Curriculum and methodology in education in general, and mathematics education in particular, became worthy of study in their own right. The preparation of teachers in large numbers also became necessary, creating another field of study: teaching and how best to do it. But as Kilpatrick (1992) reports, the emergence of education as a legitimate study in the academy lagged well behind the provision of mass education. Although the arguments supporting the need for mass education may now be different, it remains an imperative for current society, and so the study of teaching and learning goes on.

H. Mansfield et al. (eds.), Mathematics for Tomorrow's Young Children, 317–327.
© 1996 *Kluwer Academic Publishers. Printed in the Netherlands.*

Smith (1908) made many observations in his classic text, *The Teaching of Elementary Mathematics* that sound startlingly modern to present-day readers. His historical analysis makes clear that there had been a powerful European influence on practice from the beginnings of mass education as we know it, and that this was still the case at the turn of this century. That influence still persists to this time. Smith's editor made a criticism that would be echoed by many today when, in the preface to the 1908 edition, he lamented that:

Arithmetic is universally taught in schools, but almost invariably as the art of mechanical computation only. The true significance of the processes employed are concealed from pupil and teacher alike (p. ix).

Smith, writing over 90 years ago remember, blamed the departure from what he calls the "object method," by which he meant the use of manipulatives as the basis for understanding number relationships, on the adoption of Hindu numerals in the 1500s. By inference then, teachers made use of objects in their mathematics teaching (of course, not to the masses) several centuries ago. Teaching after the import of Hindu numerals changed for the poorer in Smith's opinion and focused much more on acquisition of procedures involving the use of these new numerals, while teachers discarded their abaci and counting frames. Three hundred years later, Pestalozzi revived the use of objects and returned to emphasizing the development of understanding. However in New York, at least in the last quarter of the nineteenth century, arithmetic instruction was dominated by a rhyming rules approach; there were many rules, people are able to remember rhymes, hence the approach. In describing a different method of instruction, Smith (1900) said of Pestalozzi that he:

led the child to consider all objects which were of interest to him, nor did he fear (O modern teacher!) to let him use the most natural calculating device of all—the fingers (p. 81).

The Pestalozzian progression began with concepts, then considered operations, and finally what Smith describes as "shorthand characters." Kranckes, circa 1819, recommended to teachers the "Method of Discovery" (Smith, p. 88) with rules generated from exercises and observations. However Smith observed that Kranckes improved on Pestalozzi by rejecting abstract problems, preferring rather that the problems should "touch the daily life of the child (Smith, p. 88)."

Smith (1900) also made the observation that although children have some acquaintance with the numbers one to five before coming to school, "... the ability to count must not be interpreted to mean that the child has necessarily any clear notion of number." (p. 91). An indication that some concerns seem to be ageless is given by his comments to the effect that:

It is hardly necessary to say that the old expressions, "borrow" and "carry," in subtraction and addition are rapidly going out of use; they were necessary in the old days of arbitrary rules, but they have no advocates of any prominence today (Smith, 1900, p. 122).

One of the earlier writers on teaching mathematics much admired by Smith was a Frenchman, Laisant. Smith recorded the following rules of action, as they were outlined by Laisant:

Follow a rigorously experimental method and do not depart from it; leave the child in the presence of concrete realities which he sees and handles to make his own abstractions; never attempt to demonstrate anything to him; merely furnish to him such explanations as he is himself led to ask for; and, finally, give and preserve to this teaching an appearance of pleasure rather than of a task which is imposed (Smith, 1900, pp. 140-141).

Looking beyond the use of solely masculine pronouns, the ideas outlined above seem remarkably modern and quite constructivist, although some further clarification from Laisant on the role of explanation might be very enlightening.

In summary, many of the ideas contained in the quotes used above in this chapter are easily interpretable in modern terms as ideas that many current educators often think of positively as recent developments in education; concern for the child as a learner over and above the demands of the discipline of mathematics, recognition of the importance of active engagement in the learning process, the understanding of the limited value of memorizing arbitrary rules as sufficient basis for mathematics learning, and the importance of connecting mathematics with the life of the child. These ideas, encompassing much that mathematics educators today consider exemplary practice, were being advocated around the turn of this century. Once again we see very similar ideas enjoying prominence a few scant years from the turn of the millennium.

1.2 Changing conceptions of research in mathematics education

Psychology dominated the field of mathematics learning from the early days of mathematics education (Kilpatrick, 1992). This can be seen from the tenor of many of the quotes provided in the preceding section; already we see expressed concerns related to issues of how learning takes place in the mind. Newer branches of psychology, cognitive science and information processing, made their claims to theoretical and practical importance in mathematics education based in part on this long association of the parent field with mathematics learning. In more recent times, younger sciences, sociology for example, are making their claims to consideration in the field. The words of Smith (1900) clearly indicate that mathematics educationists were already psychologically oriented and thinking, in some cases, along remarkably constructivist lines. The striking distinction from modern perspectives is the lack of any consideration given by writers at the turn of this century or earlier to social processes, and the role these play in the learning of mathematics. If there is anything that we now recognize as critically important that our earlier counterparts paid scant attention to, it is this area of human interaction, and the parallel acceptance of the classroom as, above all other things, a social place.

Now and for the future, it is clear from reading the Cobb et al, Renshaw, and Steffé chapters, that, as with all human endeavors, social and political aspects of mathematics teaching and learning must also be considered as important. The most difficult question for the future will be precisely how does the teacher of mathematics learn about these social aspects and then use the knowledge to positive effect in creating a classroom in which children learn mathematics?

Cobb et al's chapter makes it vividly clear that the role of ideology in curriculum and research in mathematics education is not yet well understood. Psychology has dominated the theories available to teachers and researchers in mathematics education since the beginning of theoretical approaches to studying the areas of teaching and learning. But psychology, in its application to education, is not an entirely objectified field free from the constraints of ideologies. At the point where a teacher makes curriculum decisions about what to teach and how to teach, a strictly psychological theory can only partially inform the teacher's actions. Teachers' beliefs and attitudes also must inform practice—personal convictions about why they are teaching, knowledge about their students and the capacities of those students, estimations of the importance of mathematics for students; these are legitimate concerns that help shape each teacher's approach to teaching. This is an area almost untouched in the field. Strongly supported by the National Council of Teachers of Mathematics (NCTM) publications, *Curriculum and Evaluation Standards for School Mathematics*, and *Professional Standards for Teaching Mathematics*, the mathematics education community in the United States, and to some extent internationally, is urging teachers at all levels to teach differently. It appears that NCTM and other bodies are giving tacit approval to approaches to teaching mathematics that are informed by constructivist philosophies about learning. Notice that I do not say "constructivist approaches to teaching!" I remain unconvinced that there are clear-cut approaches to teaching that can be so labeled.

1.3 Research and our authors

Even though the research paradigms embodied in our chapters do not range broadly, there is a variety of approaches described. Two distinct functions of research are typified, to advance theory and to describe innovative classroom practice. Some of our chapters are almost entirely theoretical (much of Cobb et al; Steffé; Renshaw; Fischbein; Brun) and were developed in some cases almost independently from classrooms, but with strong suggestions for the practice of teachers. Others are essentially practical (Yamanoshita & Matsushita; Gelfman et al; Masanja; Malaty) and give us very direct discussions of classroom practice, but such descriptions of practice cannot help but inform the reader's theoretical perspectives.

A third class of studies (parts of both Cobb et al and Steffé; Wright; Reynolds & Wheatley; Bednarz; Khisty; Poirier & Bacon; Nunes; Irwin; Hughes et al) was classroom-based, with the researchers involved in the classrooms to different degrees and with the results impacting both theories of learning and teaching, and the practice of teaching mathematics.

The most common forms of research used were variations of the teaching experiment, classroom observations (with varying degrees of intervention by the researcher), and teacher surveys based on observed practice. Some studies concentrated on the teacher's role, some on the curriculum employed, while still others looked more closely at the children's learning. A common feature of almost all the chapters written by people working directly with teachers is that there was a significant time commitment on the part of the researcher or researchers.

2. WHERE DO WE GO FROM HERE?

This is a difficult question to answer! Asking it presupposes that where we are in mathematics education is clearly understood and the mechanisms for moving forward are also known in sufficient detail for progress to be made. Society will continue to expect that its children will be educated, and that an important part of that education will include an introduction to mathematics. The difficulties begin almost immediately! What does it mean to be educated? What aspects of mathematics are appropriate? Reading the popular press it becomes rapidly apparent that the word mathematics means very different things to different segments of the population! So one of our issues becomes "whose view of mathematics" should hold sway in our schools? At what age should a particular child be inducted into any particular aspect? How is a particular aspect best introduced? Is there a preferred order of aspects of mathematics? How could such an order be determined? What is the source of this order? Attempts to answer these fundamental questions are at the heart of the fields of educational research and mathematics education.

The history of education clearly demonstrates that we do not have the detailed knowledge that will allow us to make changes so easily, nor do we as teachers and mathematics educators have the political capacity to engender change by ourselves. Does anyone know of any other field where the neophytes who are just beginning their careers are supposed to be the change agents, and in locations traditionally hostile to change? Keeping these cautions in mind, I will make some suggestions encompassing several areas: research into mathematical content; into the connection between teaching and learning of mathematics; and into the social dimensions of learning mathematics.

My basic premise will be that the purpose for doing research into mathematics education is to facilitate changes in the way mathematics is chosen and taught in our schools, not change for change's sake, but change perceived as necessary to allow today's young children to cope with the demands of the society they will be expected to help shape in the near future. Another premise that influences what follows is that "pure" research supposedly carried out for the sake of adding objective knowledge to the field will not prove to be useful, because it will ignore the critical social aspects of the learning-teaching situation. I strongly believe that the chapters in this book in the main support me in the contention that we will need studies of sufficient complexity to expect that the recommendations arising from the studies spring from a strongly-grounded grasp of the reality of schooling. Cobb et al (this volume) point out that it is unlikely that change will be possible for so long as the microsociological and macrosociological realms are kept unrelated.

2.1 Researchable elements: The complexity of the classroom

For the immediate future it is most likely that we will continue to see education provided essentially by one person in a classroom with responsibility for as many as thirty students in arrangements that have changed very little for many years. This provides us with a familiar set of participants and a well-known set of contextual constraints. A deceptively simple set of elements will continue to be the focus of research: the teacher, the students, the content, and the classroom. So now we are led to an important research issue for the future: What then are the possible dimensions of research in the mathematical education of young children and how can information about social aspects of classroom interaction influence these dimensions? Traditionally in relation to the content and teaching of mathematics, we have given the weight of our consideration to those studies that look at either what children could and could not do in terms of mathematics content, or with the behavior of the teacher in implementing methodology. Such studies have always been concerned with what mathematics content is appropriate at each class level, or with determining better teaching methods. They reflected a view of knowledge that was simply-structured and quite independent of the learner–either students "knew" the mathematics or they didn't; either the methodology was or was not responsible for the learning. The view of mathematics discernible in such studies was as a strictly hierarchical discipline; both the researcher's and the teacher's views of how learning occurred were not open to examination—if the correct material were chosen and the students had the correct background for that material, then they would of course learn the new material, if the methodology were effective. More often than not in many early studies, "knowing" was difficult to distinguish from "remembering."

Much of the research done in the field of mathematics education in general and early childhood mathematics learning in particular is claimed by teachers to have been of little use to them; too often the results of the research were equivocal, with little in the way of clear-cut prescription, either because no significant differences were found to advocate one method over another, or because the research was carried out in circumstances very different from those pertaining in the classroom. This holds for choice of content, choice of methodology, in fact every aspect of teaching mathematics to children. I would claim that the reasons for this are more to do with the nature of the research undertaken and the directions it has taken until very recently. Research based on quantitative paradigms has produced little in the way of advice for teachers as to how to conduct their classrooms in the struggle to teach mathematics.

Thus it is heartening to acknowledge the rapidly growing body of work based on qualitative paradigms that accepts that classrooms are complex places and understands that reducing the description of those classrooms to a few operationalized variables renders them unrecognizable and severely limits the usefulness of the results of the research.

Qualitative approaches allow one to ask *how* do children learn mathematics under the influences of the social interactions they engage in daily, instead of what mathematics do children know or should know. Questions like this have been engaging more and more researchers in the last several decades.

Our immediate concern then should be to continue to mount studies that take as their starting point the premise that teaching and learning are *not* simply-related. Accepting the classroom as a place of social complexity, and acknowledging the need for the researcher to, in an important sense, fit into the environment as a participant, means that the study designers should expect a long-term involvement from the participants in the study. Data must be collected from many sources; ideally, it should be analyzed formatively, to allow the information gained to help shape the direction of the study, and to take advantage of understandings as they are made.

Perhaps though it is time to reflect on what mathematics has now become—taking seriously the position that mathematics is a social activity, that it is the product of humans working together and reaching agreements about its nature—should we not subject the very mathematics we expect children to learn to serious scrutiny? An obvious direction to investigate is the influence that the computer will have on what children (and people in general) perceive mathematics to be. We now have symbolic manipulators, calculators that perform fraction operations; children of all ages have ready access, by and large, to calculators. Do they now see mathematics differently? How should this affect school mathematics?

2.2 Researching teaching and learning

Possible directions for future research into the teacher's role are provided for us by Koehler and Grouws (1992) who outline four levels of recent research into mathematics education generally. Each level incorporates those preceding it; complexity increases as we move from trying to directly link student outcomes to teacher characteristics (Level 1) to incorporating the behavior of teachers. At the next level, augmentation consists of including variables descriptive of classroom processes. Now interactions between students and teachers are considered. Level 3 adds pupil characteristics and splits outcomes into achievement and attitude. Add in teacher knowledge of content, pedagogy, theories of learning, teachers' beliefs about teaching and about mathematics; and student attitudes in different dimensions, and separate student outcomes into cognitive and affective, mediated by race and gender, and we have Level 4 in all its complexity.

In relation to the question of how children learn mathematics we will in the future look for answers in different places and in different ways from those of the past. It is clear that we have already moved away from a strictly behaviorist conception of learning in general and learning mathematics in particular. The Level 4 focus mentioned above on research into the teaching-learning interaction indicates how complex the research must become. Studies wishing to make a significant contribution to the field can no longer afford to be unidimensional and examine one aspect with little or no consideration of the other aspects. In essence researchers will need to problematize each aspect within any one study—the mathematical content itself must not be taken for granted, the classroom environment must be treated as a social system, with one only one aspect of that environment being constituted by the teacher-student and student-student interactions. The social system in a single classroom is of course embedded in a larger system, namely the school, which in turn is located within a still larger community; these realities must bring other aspects into the research. The methodologies chosen must be sufficiently sophisticated to deal with the complex data; similar complexity is already dealt with in anthropology and sociology. We must continue the emerging trend of learning methodological techniques from those fields.

2.3 Researching the influence of technology

An example that illustrates the complexity underlying research in this direction may be provided by considering the problems embedded in attempting to answer the two related questions of how influential *can* the computer be in the mathematical education of young children, and how influential *should* the computer be permitted to become? These are two very different questions; the effects of the early introduction of children to a technology other than that relying on paper-based printed text cannot yet be known, because that technology is necessarily in its infancy—the information society, based on the ready availability to people *en masse* of extraordinary computing power to manipulate vast amounts of data, is only just pushing aside the industrial society, or rather transforming it.

Many early studies into the first of these questions took a relatively simplistic approach and considered the effects of one student sitting at one computer engaging with material presented in an already predetermined sequence. Seymour Papert regarded this approach as allowing the computer to program the child, and advocated approaches that led to the child programing the computer, or at least controlling its use. Later studies looked at students controlling the computer—the prevalence of studies into the effects of using various forms of Logo come readily to mind. Some of these latter studies indicated clearly that the mathematics learned by students in interaction with the computer was subtly changed from that learned in regular classrooms. Perhaps a fruitful approach will be to take a closer look at these changes, and to examine more closely the interactions between students as they work at computers in groups and singly. We need to know if the mathematics changes and if it does whether those changes will help students fit into the world as it changes or not! We even need evidence that may allow us to make decisions about the possibilities for changing computers, or for deciding how much interaction children should have with them. Recommendations for change are value-laden judgments; we need research to allow us to make informed judgments.

And this means that we need research techniques that can allow us to recognize the complexity of the relationship between *can* and *should* questions: in this case, that relationship is typified in the recognition that "use of computers" is not a dichotomous variable introduced into an existing set of immutable elements, including mathematics of a particular nature and teaching of a particular kind. The reality is that using computers in mathematics teaching (and in other subjects too) has profound effects on the *kind of mathematics that is learned,* and further, on *how that mathematics is learned.* Only studies designed to deal with the complexity of this and similar situations, say studies at Grouws & Koehler's (1992) Level 4 (see above), will provide really useful information for teachers wishing to change their approach to teaching mathematics.

2.4 Research and the role of the teacher

Everything said in the preceding chapters of this book has some message for the practice of teachers. Many of the studies speak from classrooms directly to teachers of mathematics in elementary schools. A really difficult question is how do teachers first of all seriously take hold of the ideas in these chapters, how do they then fit them within their own conceptual frame of their work as teachers, and finally how do they bring this reorganized frame of reference into the lives of their students? I advocate continuing development of the idea that teachers can be and must be researchers of their own classrooms; but this will take some doing—we need collaboration among teachers and mathematics educators, that collaboration may prove most fruitful if it is located not in college classrooms, or professors' offices, but in teachers' classrooms with the full support and encouragement of school administrators.

It is possible to frame future work with teachers in terms of how that work relates to the teachers' curriculum, given the definition adopted in the introduction to this book. Context partly determines curriculum; social interaction partly determines curriculum; but I would speculate that curriculum may only be fully captured historically. How do we capture the essence of classroom life? How do teachers learn to write or remember the events of each day, and to give each event sufficient coherent meaning to use the information in planning for the next day? So we need research into the possibilities of teachers taking themselves seriously as curriculum developers; Cobb et al's account of teachers taking control of the curriculum they taught provides us with an interesting example, all the more so for the political dimensions it touches upon.

I think writing "immediate histories" will continue to be an exciting avenue for research, especially in those collaborations which attempt to include accounts of the consequences of the growing multipluralism of classroom cultures. This area of research in mathematics education, delving into the notion of classroom culture and the role that culture plays in mathematics teaching and learning, is another area that remains relatively untouched. The concept of culture as something static and unchanging is no longer prevalent—rather it is seen as a powerful force that teachers must learn to work with and incorporate into their teaching. The single most important element of research directed to this area may be the commitment of time; without this commitment there can be no development of the relationship of trust among participants that should ideally be in place before cultures of classrooms can be investigated meaningfully.

2.5 Living with uncertainty

In teaching mathematics there may be no easily determined path to success for any one individual child, let alone for a whole class treated as a unit. Perhaps the hardest lesson for teachers to learn will be how to deal with the uncertainty of the effects of their practice. This is one of the areas where we need serious investigation. Scientistic precepts based on simplistic notions of cause and effect can have no place in the real world of interacting with children and attempting to teach them mathematics. Inevitably language assumes importance. We know that communication through language is a critical aspect of mathematics education—but whose language should hold sway in the classroom? Bednarz (this volume) makes some interesting observations about how well children interpret adult language. Much more work is needed in this direction.

Thus issues of how language and communication impact on mathematics learning, and of how mathematics fits into other realms of human interests, need to be investigated, preferably in classrooms in order that teachers may be helped to begin to understand the sources of uncertainty. Humans are essentially complex beings; living with that complexity, however perplexing it may be, is essential for all of us, and no less so for those individuals who wish to make a career of educating small children.

3. FINAL REMARKS

Mathematics is learned in a complex social environment; the connection between teaching and learning and this environment is similarly complex; our understanding of the nature of mathematics as a social activity is changing; we are only now beginning to understand the role of language and the importance of children's personal activity in learning mathematics. Finally, we live in an age of unprecedented technological developments that have already changed our world in unexamined and unquestioned ways. For a variety of reasons, schools to this point have not managed to incorporate very many of this multitude of recent developments, either by the adoption of hardware on a large scale, or by acceptance at the level of school curriculum of recent intellectual changes in how the very nature of subjects like mathematics and the sciences are now seen by mathematicians and scientists.

The nature of our educational establishment makes its response to societal change by necessity mostly reactive and rarely proactive. But we are at a point in time when schools can no longer afford to lag way behind and thus become increasingly irrelevant; our curriculum and our teaching must respond to societal needs and that response must be swift. Mathematics educators have a broad range of areas to choose from if they wish to be part of the ongoing push for change in how mathematics will be taught in schools. Their endeavors will only succeed if they are willing to commit time and energy to schools and teachers, to adopt methodologies that acknowledge the social complexity of the classroom, to call into question the appropriateness of content choices in mathematics, to bring sophisticated approaches to the use of technology in classrooms, while at the same time dealing sympathetically with children and teachers as they grow in their knowledge of mathematics and their awareness of its place in their lives. No group is more worthy of our energy and commitment to change than the children in our elementary mathematics classrooms.

REFERENCES

Kilpatrick, J. (1992). A history of research in mathematics education. In D. A. Grouws (Ed.), *Handbook of research on mathematics teaching and learning* (pp. 3-38). New York, NY: Macmillan.

Koehler, M., & Grouws, D. A. (1992). Mathematics teaching practices and their effects. In D. A. Grouws, (Ed.), *Handbook of research on mathematics teaching and learning* (pp. 115-126). New York, NY: Macmillan.

National Council of Teachers of Mathematics. (1989). *Curriculum and evaluation standards for school mathematics.* Reston, VA: The National Council of Teachers of Mathematics.

National Council of Teachers of Mathematics. (1991). *Professional standards for teaching mathematics.* Reston, VA: The National Council of Teachers of Mathematics.

Smith, D. E. (1900). *The teaching of elementary mathematics.* New York, NY: The Macmillan Co.

Neil A. Pateman
University of Hawaii
United States of America

Mathematics Education Library

Managing Editor: A.J. Bishop, Melbourne, Australia

KLUWER ACADEMIC PUBLISHERS – DORDRECHT / BOSTON / LONDON